COMPUTER USE
IN PSYCHOLOGY

(THIRD EDITION)

EDITORS:
MICHAEL L. STOLOFF
AND
JAMES V. COUCH

AMERICAN PSYCHOLOGICAL ASSOCIATION, WASHINGTON, DC

The editors of *Computer Use in Psychology: A Directory of Software, Third Edition* have not reviewed or tested the software listed in this directory, and listing of products in this directory does not constitute an endorsement of the product by the editors or by the American Psychological Association. It is the recommendation of the editors that no software be purchased soley upon the basis of the information listed in this directory. This directory should be used to identify software that may be of interest. Following identification of the software, it is prudent for the psychologist to contact the publisher or software author and further explore the uses of the software package. Most of the entries in this directory list product reviews and user site references that may be contacted for more information on the product. In addition, many publishers and software authors have demonstration programs, which are either free or very low cost, that provide a trial run using the software.

Published by the
American Psychological Association, Inc.
750 First Street, NE
Washington, DC 20002

Copies may be ordered from:
Order Department
P.O. Box 2710
Hyattsville, MD 20784
(800) 374-2721

Cover design by Michael David Brown
Printed by Kirby Lithographic Company, Inc.
Technical editing and production by Linda J. Beverly

Printed in the United States of America

ISBN 1-55798-173-6

Third edition, first printing

Contents

Introduction v

Program Listings

    Academic Software 1

    Clinical and Applied Software 71

    Testing Software.. 117

    Statistics and Research Aids 251

Indexes

    Title Index.. 329

    Course Index.. 341

    Clinical and Applied Software Index... 345

    Testing Software Index 347

    Statistics and Research Aid Index.. 353

    Author Index.. 357

New Software Submission Form.. 365

Introduction

Computer Use in Psychology: A Directory of Software, Third Edition, is a compilation of computer programs and databases useful to psychologists working in clinical practice or academia. Listings are designed to provide sufficient information about program content, equipment requirements, and price to allow the reader to identify products that may be suitable for their use. Readers may then use publisher or author contact information, published program reviews, and user site references to gather additional information before committing to a purchase. This volume can be used to overcome the first difficult step in the software selection process–identification of programs that may be suitable for specific needs.

The *Directory* lists software that falls into four major categories: academic software (classroom or laboratory use), clinical software (useful for client treatment), statistics and research aids, and psychological testing programs. Software used for automation of the mental health professional's business office (billing, scheduling, record keeping, accounting, etc.) has been excluded from this volume because listing of these programs recently appeared in another publication of the American Psychological Association, *Hardware, Software, and the Mental Health Professional* (Stoloff, Brewster, & Couch, 1991). General purpose programs such as word processors, spreadsheets, databases, and utility software have also been excluded from this book. This directory focuses on specific purpose software

designed for psychologists that is not typically available at retail computer outlets.

The process of listing software began by asking the publishers or authors of the 883 programs listed in the second edition of the *Directory* (Stoloff & Couch, 1988) to update their listings, deleting programs no longer available and adding new programs. Additional information request forms were sent to publishers or authors who had programs described in the *APA Monitor; Teaching of Psychology; Behavior, Research Methods, Instrumentation, and Computers;* or *Social Science Microcomputer Review*. These four journals were systematically scanned from 1988 through 1991. Software was also gleaned from an examination of the *Counseling Software Guide* (Walz, Bleuer, & Maze, 1989) and two volumes of *Tools for Learning: Courseware Catalog* (IBM Academic Information Systems, 1989, 1990). Several publishers or authors returned the new software submission form that appeared in the second edition of the *Directory*, and unsolicited direct mail advertisements were also used to identify software.

As a result of this process, approximately 1,700 potentially listable programs were identified. For each program, our staff completed a 4-page information request form and mailed the form to publishers for verification and additional data. At least one follow-up letter was sent to each publisher or author who did not respond to our initial request. In addition, at least one follow-up phone call was placed to publishers who failed to respond to our mail queries but were believed to have five or more relevant programs. The descriptions of all of the programs listed in this directory were submitted or verified by the program's publisher or author. Programs were listed in this directory only if the publisher or author returned a written response to our inquiry.

Directory Contents

The *Directory* lists 869 programs. Updated listings of software that appeared in the second edition (Stoloff & Couch, 1988) account for 37% of the listings. The majority of listings (63%) are completely new. The software listed in this directory is compatible with a variety of machines, however, most of the programs (719) are available in IBM-compatible formats. Many programs are available in Apple II (301) or Macintosh (78) compatible versions.

The academic software section lists 180 programs useful for teaching experimental psychology, statistics, sensation and perception, cognitive psychology, general psychology, social psychology, learning, abnormal psychology, and many other courses. Many of the programs would be appropriate for laboratory sections of psychology courses.

The clinical software section describes 118 programs. The largest group of these programs are designed for cognitive rehabilitation of the brain-damaged patient. Programs for career counseling comprises the second largest group. Many other therapeutic aids and aids to the counselor are included in this section.

The testing software section is by far the largest in the *Directory*, containing 363

listings. Numerous history, health, and symptom checklists, and other diagnostic aids are listed for children, adolescents, and adults. Tests that assess personality, neuropsychological functioning, intelligence, and academic or vocational potential are included. A variety of programs are listed that administer and/or interpret popular psychological tests such as the Minnesota Multiphasic Personality Inventory (MMPI), Sixteen Personality Factor Questionnaire (16PF), Wechsler Intelligence Scale for Children (WISC), Wechsler Adult Intelligence Scale (WAIS), and Rorschach.

The statistics and research section contains 208 listings that include comprehensive statistical analysis packages and special purpose tests (such as ANOVA, nonparametric tests, correlation and regression, and many others). There are programs for test development, survey administration, survey analysis, and data management. This section also includes a variety of useful programs including some that control laboratory equipment, others that create graphics, and several CD-ROM databases.

Program Listings

The software described in the directory contains information provided by program publishers or authors. This information has been corrected by the *Directory* editors for style and consistency, and to eliminate obvious advertising hype. However, the accuracy of program listings was the responsibility of the submittors, and could not be verified by the *Directory* editors.

Each program listing begins with the program title; authors; and publisher's name, address, and phone numbers. A brief program description follows.

Program descriptions conclude with statements that indicate whether printed program manuals or booklets, on-line help, or a tutorial program is included with the software. When provided by the publisher, the date of last update of the program is also indicated.

Each program was assigned a single type or course code. This code was used to create the program type and course indexes. Software was classified into the most precise category, so that a program that interprets the MMPI would be classified "MMPI" rather than "personality testing." Similarly, an academic program that simulated classical conditioning would be classified for a course in learning, even though the program may also be appropriate for courses in experimental or general psychology. Some programs were difficult to classify, and readers interested in particular types of programs may have to check several categories to identify relevant programs. For example, software in the clinical chapter classified as career counseling is often similar to vocational testing software that appears in the testing software chapter. Similarly, many programs listed in the statistics and research aids chapter may be useful in academic settings for teaching statistics and experimental psychology courses.

The next section of each listing contains a description of the minimum equipment requirements for up to three versions of each program. Descriptions are written in a standardized format and contain the following information when provided by the publisher or author: (a) computer make and models; (b) minimum random access memory (RAM) required; (c) hard disk drive required, optional, or incompatible and minimum size requirements; (d)

number and size of diskette drives required; (e) display requirements; (f) printer requirements including laser printer compatibility; (g) modem, mouse, and other special equipment requirements; (h) operating system software requirements; and (i) price for a single user system, network, site license, lab pack, and other cost considerations.

Citations for published software reviews provided by the publisher or author or used by the *Directory* editors to identify programs for inclusion in this book are listed. Each program listing concludes with publisher or author provided user site references, the name, address, and phone number of individuals who are using the program and may be contacted for comments about the usefulness of the software.

Selecting Software

This directory has been designed to serve as an aid in the selection of software. There are three major issues to be addressed when software is selected, and the directory helps you begin to consider all three: functionality, compatibility, and price.

Functionality

The issue of software functionality is really the question of whether a program will do something useful for you. Users of this directory will include college professors, neuropsychologists, therapists, career counselors, and others–each with a unique set of automation needs. To identify programs of potential value, start by using the software type or course indexes, or scan the titles of programs to find listings of potential interest. Read the descriptions of potentially useful programs, and phone, fax, or write to the publisher or author to obtain additional information. With a trip to the library, a copy of a published review may be obtained. Finally, after you are somewhat confident that a program is going to be useful to you, you might contact a user site reference to get some candid feedback or ask some questions. (The *Directory* editors ask that you contact user site references sparingly so that these individuals are not unduly harassed.)

Compatibility

Compatibility is the question of whether a piece of software will operate on a particular computer. Computers are built in a modular fashion, and there are many variations. Generally if your computer has the minimum requirements or a higher level then is given in a directory listing, then the software will operate. Some compatibility tips follow.

Software compatibility for IBM compatible computers has not been a major problem for the past 2-3 years. Before then, some brands of clones were unable to run all IBM-compatible software. In recent years, however, equipment has become more standardized, virtually eliminating brand consideration when checking for compatibility. This has not been the case for Macintosh computers. Later models of the Macintosh computer are not necessarily compatible with software released for earlier versions of the machine. Before purchasing Mac software, verify with the publisher or author that the program has been tested and operates properly on the model of Macintosh computer you will be using.

IBM compatible display systems have excellent "backward compatibility." This means that if you have a later version of the IBM-compatible display, you will be able to run software written for earlier display types. In order, starting with the earliest type, the most common IBM-compatible display types are: monochrome text, monochrome graphics (Hercules), CGA, EGA, VGA, and SuperVGA. Thus, if you have a VGA display, you can run any program except those that require SuperVGA. On the other hand, if you have a CGA display, you will be able to run software written for monochrome text or graphics or CGA, but you cannot run programs that require EGA, VGA, or SuperVGA.

The software that runs a computer is called the operating system. Each operating system is usually described with a word and a number that indicates its version. For IBM-compatible computers, the primary operating system is called DOS (although other operating systems can be used on these machines such as OS/2 and UNIX). At the time this book was published, the current version of DOS was 5.0. DOS has excellent backward compatibility. As described above for displays, backward compatibility means that later versions of this operating system do not have any difficulty running programs designed for earlier versions. For example, if you have a computer that is running DOS 4.0, you will be able to run programs designed for DOS 3.3, 3.1, or 2.1, but you will not be able to run a program that requires a later version of DOS, such as 5.0.

The operating program for Macintosh computers is called the System. At the time of publication of this book, System 7 was the most recent version. Macintosh operating systems often are not backwards compatible. Frequently, if a program is written for a particular system, it will not operate on any other system. With Macintosh, you may need to have the exact system specified by the program developer to run the program. Before purchasing Mac software, verify with the publisher or author that the program has been tested and operates properly on the Macintosh System you will be using.

Another compatibility issue involves use of computer networks. The editors of this directory asked publishers and authors to indicate whether their programs are compatible with networks, but the answers often depended upon network hardware and operating software. Because of this, the data were believed to be unreliable and were omitted from this directory. There are three levels of compatibility with networks. A true networking program will allow several users to simultaneously access a single copy of a program stored on the server hard disk drive of a network of linked computers. Other programs may only allow one user to access a program a time, but can be installed on a network so that different users can take turns using a single copy of the software. Finally, some programs are incompatible with networks and cannot be installed on one. The problem of network compatibility is compounded by the fact that there are many different network hardware and software schemes, and programs may be compatible with some schemes, but may be incompatible (or untested) in others. If you are interested in networking, contact the publisher or author of the program you are interested in using, to determine whether the software is compatible with your network.

Price

Software varies tremendously in price. Some cost thousands of dollars, and many programs listed in this directory are free. Some programs have different prices for different versions, so some definitions are needed. The single user price is the cost for a license for use of software by one person, or one person a time, or installation of the software on a single computer. The multiuser price is the cost for installation of the software on a computer network that would allow multiple simultaneous users. (Often the number of users is limited, or the cost depends upon the number of users or computers attached to the network.) A site license is a license to duplicate the software for use on several machines, by several simultaneous users. Site licenses often limit the number of users or adjust the price for the number of users. A lab pack is a set of duplicate program disks–it is like purchasing multiple copies of the program. Per administration fees are fairly common with psychological testing software. In this case, the user is charged for each utilization of the software (each administration of the test, or interpretive report generated).

References

IBM Academic Information Systems. (1989). *Tools for Learning: Courseware Catalog*. Milford, CT: International Business Machines Corporation.

IBM Academic Information Systems. (1990). *Tools for Learning: Courseware Catalog*. Milford, CT: International Business Machines Corporation.

Stoloff, M. L., Brewster, J., & Couch, J. V. (1991). *Hardware, Software, and the Mental Health Professional: The Complete Guide to Office Computerization.* Washington, DC: American Psychological Association.

Stoloff, M. L. & Couch, J. V. (1988). *Computer Use in Psychology: A Directory of Software, Second Edition.* Washington, DC: American Psychological Association.

Walz, G. R., Bleuer, J. C. & Maze, M. (1989). *Counseling Software Guide.* Alexandria, VA: American Association for Counseling and Development.

ACADEMIC
SOFTWARE

ABI-1

Gene D. Steinhauer

AB i
2124 Kittendge, Suite 215
Berkeley, CA 94704
(510) 582-6343

Animated simulations of psychological experiments. Includes Faces, Rat Race, Rat 1–Pigeon 1, Rat 2, and Rat's Alley. Detailed manual included.

Classification: Experimental Psychology

Hardware Requirements and Price
Apple II+, IIe, IIc; 1 disk drive (5-1/4). *Single User Price: $50.00 Site License: $300.00*

IBM PC, XT, AT, PS/2, & compatibles; 64 K; hard disk optional; 1 disk drive. CGA, EGA, or VGA display. *Single User Price: $50.00 Site License: $300.00*

Macintosh, 1 Mb, hard disk optional, 1 disk drive. *Single User Price: $50.00 Site License: $300.00*

ABI-2

Gene D. Steinhauer

AB i
2124 Kittendge, Suite 215
Berkeley, CA 94704
(510) 582-6343

Animated simulations of psychological experiments. Includes Journals, Memorize, Eye Blink, Interact, Stability, and Pearson r. Detailed manual included.

Classification: Experimental Psychology

Hardware Requirements and Price
Apple II+, IIe, IIc; 1 disk drive. *Single User Price: $50.00 Site License: $300.00*

IBM PC, XT, AT, PS/2, & compatibles; 64 K; hard disk optional; 1 disk drive. CGA, EGA, or VGA display. *Single User Price: $50.00 Site License: $300.00*

Macintosh, 1 Mb, hard disk optional. *Single User Price: $50.00 Site License: $300.00*

ABI-3

Gene D. Steinhauer

AB i
2124 Kittendge, Suite 215
Berkeley, CA 94704
(510) 582-6343

Animated simulations of psychological experiments. Includes Widgies and Inforat. Detailed manual included.

Classification: Experimental Psychology

Hardware Requirements and Price
Apple II+, IIe, IIc; hard disk optional; 1 disk drive. *Single User Price: $50.00 Site License: $300.00*

IBM PC, XT, AT, PS/2, & compatibles; 64 K; hard disk optional; 1 disk drive. CGA, EGA, or VGA display. *Single User Price: $50.00 Site License: $300.00*

Macintosh, 1 Mb, hard disk optional, 1 disk drive. *Single User Price: $50.00 Site License: $300.00*

ABstat
Edwin R. Anderson

Anderson-Bell
Department 458
P.O. Box 5160
Arvada, CO 80005
(303) 940-0595
(800) 745-9751

Menu- and/or command-driven program to be used at college, graduate, and professional levels to teach basic statistics and analyze research data. Analyses include: Descriptive, regression, correlation, *t*-tests, ANOVA, crosstabs, categorical, and nonparametric statistics. File compatibility with Lotus, dBase, and ASCII. Data management, analysis, and graphics in one package. Student version also available. Educational and quantity discounts available. Detailed manual and tutorial program included. On-line help available. Latest release September 9, 1991.

Classification: Statistics

Hardware Requirements and Price
IBM PC, XT, AT, PS/2, & compatibles; 320 K; hard disk optional; 2 disk drives. Graphic display required. Laser printer optional. Requires DOS 2.1. *Single User Price: $395.00*

Reviews
Datapro. (June, 1991). P1M11-310-10i.
Ophthalmology Times. (May 15, 1991). 31.
Software for Compensation Professionals. (1990). 4-5.

Accuracy and Precision
Hiroshi Ono
Mark Wagner
Kenneth Ono

Conduit
University of Iowa-Oakdale Campus
Iowa City, IA 52242
(319) 335-4100
(800) 365-9774

Designed to demonstrate two important psychophysical concepts that are commonly confused–accuracy and precision. The two procedures in this package show how these concepts are distinct. Students can control standard stimulus length, location of the standard, horizontal and vertical separation of the standard and comparison, the number of experimental trials, and the presentation order of the trials. Accuracy and Precision provides an analysis of the collected experimental data. Detailed manual included.

Classification: Experimental Psychology

Hardware Requirements and Price
Apple II+, IIe, IIc, IIgs; 64 K; 1 disk drive. Color display recommended. *Single User Price: $80.00*

IBM PC, XT, AT, PS/2, & compatibles; 256 K; 1 Mb hard disk optional; 1 disk drive. CGA, EGA, or VGA display. *Single User Price: $80.00 Network Price: $480.00*

Acquire Knowledge Acquisition System and Expert System Shell
B. A. Schaeffr
I. R. Morrison
B. J. Smith

Acquired Intelligence Inc.
205-1095 McKenzie Avenue
Victoria, BC V8P 2L5 Canada
(604) 479-8646
Fax: (604) 479-0764

Acquire is an automated knowledge acquisition system, complete with machine learning capabilities and an expert system shell for developing knowledge-based applications. It guides the user through the knowledge acquisition process, capitalizing on natural pattern-recognition skills that facilitate the process. Program is suitable for the development of knowledge-based applications. Detailed manual included. On-line help available. Latest release September, 1991.

Classification: Cognitive Psychology

Hardware Requirements and Price
IBM PC, XT, AT, PS/2, & compatibles; 1.5 Mb, 6.5 Mb hard disk required; 1 disk drive. Laser printer optional. Requires DOS 3.0. *Single User Price: $995.00 Educational Discount Price: $495.00*

User Site References
M. Joshko, Queen Alexandra Hospital for Children, 2400 Arbutus Road, Victoria, BC, V8N 1V7, Canada, (604) 477-1826

J. MacGregor, School of Public Administration, University of Victoria, P.O. Box 1700, Victoria, BC, V8W 272, Canada, (604) 721-8082

D. L. Russell, 2223 Fern Road, Nanaimo, BC, V9S 2W8, Canada, (604) 758-1003

Alley.Rat Pack
Mark Cunningham

Crofter Publishing
4310 South Semoran, #690
Orlando, FL 32822

A simulation of a rat running a straight alley, obeying the principles of behavior found by Clark Hull. Students decide how many trials to run each day, and how many days to run each session. They decide whether they want to watch the rat run (animation) or see a plot of run-speed developed trial-by-trial. Students also set hours of deprivation, reinforcement amount, and inter-trial interval. Rats can be saved in a colony, and brought back for additional study. Detailed manual included.

Classification: Learning

Hardware Requirements and Price
Apple II+, IIe, IIc, IIgs; 64 K; hard disk optional; 1 disk drive. Requires ProDOS. *Single User Price: $90.00*

IBM PC, XT, AT, PS/2, & compatibles; 256 K; hard disk optional; 1 disk drive (5-1/4). CGA display required. Requires DOS 2.1. *Single User Price: $90.00*

Animal Behavior Data Simulation

Oakleaf Systems
P.O. Box 472
Decorah, IA 52101
(319) 382-4320

Software simulates 25 animal behavior experiments. Students can use program to obtain data to test hypotheses of their own or those suggested by the instructor. Students vary the value of independent variables and specify the number of replicate values to be simulated. Data can be analyzed without leaving program. Latest release January, 1990.

Classification: Animal Behavior

Hardware Requirements and Price
Apple II, 64 K, hard disk optional, 1 disk drive. Lower case chip. *Single User Price: $69.95*

IBM PC, XT, AT, PS/2, & compatibles; hard disk optional; 1 disk drive. *Single User Price: $69.95*

Macintosh, hard disk optional, 1 disk drive. *Single User Price: $69.95*

ANOVA/TT

Max Vercruyssen
James C. Edwards

Psy-Med Associates
1386 Frank Street
Honolulu, HI 96816
(808) 734-2578

Analysis of variance teaching template for Lotus 1-2-3. Instruction booklet included. Latest release 1990.

Classification: Statistics

Hardware Requirements and Price
IBM PC, XT, AT, PS/2, & compatibles; 256 K; hard disk optional. Mouse optional. Modem optional. Laser printer optional. *Single User Price: $20.00*

Reviews
Vercruyssen, M. C., & Edwars, J. C. (1988). ANOVA/TT: Analysis of variance teaching template for Lotus 1-2-3. *Behavior, Research Methods, Instrumentation, and Computers, 20,* 349-354.

User Site References
Judy Hudnall, Research Assistant, National Institute Occupational Safety & Health, NIOSH, Division of Safety Research, 944 Chestnut-Ridge Road, Morgantown, WV, 26505, (304) 291-4801

Ross Pepper, Naval Ocean Systems Center, NOSC, Ocean Engineering Dw, Box 997, Kailua, HI, 96734, (808) 254-4409/4434
Mary Kay White, Lewis & Clark College, 9424 South West 54th Street, Portland, OR, (503) 244-6161

Anxiety and Personality Questionnaires

John Mueller
Burt Thompson

Educational Psychology Department
University of Calgary
Calgary, AL T2N 1N4 Canada
(403) 220-5664

Subjects see one question at a time and answer them true/false or pick a number on a rating scale. Scores are computed and stored in a separate data file. Administers questionnaires on state anxiety, trait anxiety, test anxiety, Thayer affect adjective checklist, self consciousness scale, and others. Instruction booklet included.

Classification: Personal Growth

Hardware Requirements and Price
Apple II+, IIe, IIc; 48 K; 1 disk drive. Requires DOS 3.3. *Single User Price: $1.00, send a blank disk*

Baffles & Baffles II

James A. Spain

Conduit
University of Iowa-Oakdale Campus
Iowa City, IA 52242
(319) 335-4100
(800) 365-9774

A simple interactive game that helps develop deductive reasoning and problem solving skills. The game begins by displaying a box laid out like a coordinate grid, in which a given number of baffles (deflectors) are hidden. The student's goal is to determine the baffle's location and tilt, and to mark them on the grid. By shooting from different positions, and analyzing the beam's deflections, the student develops hypothesis about the baffle's positions. Requires some method of scientific inquiry to be successful. Instruction booklet included.

Classification: Experimental Psychology

Hardware Requirements and Price
Apple II+, IIe, IIc; 48 K; 1 disk drive (5-1/4). Color display optional. *Single User Price: $60.00*

IBM PC, XT, AT, PS/2, & compatibles; 256 K; hard disk optional, 1 disk drive. Color display optional. *Single User Price: $60.00*

Basic Electrophysiology
James E. Randall

James E. Randall
609 South Jordan Avenue
Bloomington, IN 47401
(812) 855-1574

A tutorial that develops driving forces and currents across the axon membrane as ion concentrations are manipulated for three major ions. Pick stimulus voltage and duration and see plots of membrane potential, Na^+ and K^+ conductances, and the stimuli. Illustrates axon properties such as saltatory conduction. Pick axon size, distance between nodes, and threshold for excitation, and the program plots a schematic of an axon on the screen and volt-

age along the length of the axon. Instruction booklet included. Latest release 1991.

Classification: Physiological Psychology

Hardware Requirements and Price
IBM PC, XT, AT, PS/2, & compatibles; 512 K; hard disk optional; 1 disk drive (5-1/4). Graphic display required. *Single User Price: $8.00*

Behavior on a Disk
A. C. Catania
B. A. Matthews
E. Shimoff

CMS Software
P.O. Box 1514
Columbia, MD 21044-0514
(410) 730-7833

Ten interactive programs for courses in the psychology of learning including shaping, fading, verbal learning, memory span, cumulative records, reinforcement schedules, and problem solving. Detailed manual included. Latest release 1991.

Classification: Learning

Hardware Requirements and Price
IBM PC, XT, AT, PS/2, & compatibles; 64 K; 1 disk drive. CGA display. Not compatible with laser printer. *Single User Price: $8.95*

Behavioral Modification
Ann Gilchrist

Ann Gilchrist
Ulster County Community College
Stone Ridge, NY 12484

This full color program uses attractive graphic boxes to ask students multiple choice questions relating to the solution of everyday problems. Students are led step-by-step to the solution. If a wrong answer is selected, the program explains why the response is incorrect. Detailed manual included.

Classification: Personal Growth

Hardware Requirements and Price
IBM PC, XT, AT, PS/2, & compatibles; 360 K; hard disk optional; 1 disk drive. Color display required. *Single User Price: $35.00*

User Site References
Sharon Fitzgerald, Ulster City Community College, Stone Ridge, NY, 12484, (914) 687-5039
Janet Salanitri, Ulster City Community College, Stone Ridge, NY, 12484, (914) 687-5200
Barbara Sartorius, Ulster City Community College, Stone Ridge, NY, 12484, (914) 687-5039

Behavioral Sciences

Queue, Inc.
338 Commerce Drive
Fairfield, CT 06430
(203) 335-0906
(800) 232-2224
Fax: (203) 336-2481

An interactive tutorial that reviews psychology, sociology and anthropology. Instruction booklet included.

Classification: General Psychology

Hardware Requirements and Price
Apple II+, IIe, IIc; 48 K; 1 disk drive (5-1/4). *Single User Price: $34.95 (with management) $24.95 (without management)*

IBM PC, XT, AT, PS/2, & compatibles; 1 disk drive. *Single User Price: $34.95*

Macintosh, 128 K, 1 disk drive. *Single User Price: $34.95*

Biofeedback MicroLab

Paul Antonucci
Steve Schumacher
Lars Travers

Queue, Inc.
338 Commerce Drive
Fairfield, CT 06430
(203) 335-0906
(800) 232-2224
Fax: (203) 336-2481

Allows students (grades 8 to college) to use the computer to collect and analyze data, store records, and solve problems. This system includes a program disk, interface box, and sensors that measure heart rate, electrodermal activity, muscle tension, and skin temperature. Detailed manual included.

Classification: Physiological Psychology

Hardware Requirements and Price
Apple II+, IIe, IIc, IIgs; 64 K; 1 disk drive (5-1/4). Monochrome or color display. Requires DOS 3.3. Super Serial, Grappler, or Fingerprint card required. *Single User Price: $325.00*

Commodore, 1 disk drive. *Single User Price: $325.00*

Brain Hemisphere Information Processing

Joseph Dlhopolsky

Life Science Associates
1 Fenimore Road
Bayport, NY 11705-2115
(516) 472-2111
Fax: (516) 472-8146

Presents geometric or verbal stimuli randomly to left and right visual fields with machine language accuracy. Recall or recognition are dependent variable options. For psychology research and instruction. Instruction booklet included. Latest release 1990.

Classification: Physiological Psychology

Hardware Requirements and Price
IBM PC, XT, AT, PS/2, & compatibles; 640 K; hard disk optional; 1 disk drive. CGA display. *Single User Price: $295.00*

Brainscape

W. Jeffrey Wilson
Lynne A. Ostergren

Department of Psychological Sciences
Indiana University-Purdue
Fort Wayne, IN 46805

An adventure game in which students enter and explore the brain. The program is written in Turbo Pascal. Latest release January, 1991.

Classification: Physiological Psychology

Hardware Requirements and Price
IBM PC, XT, AT, PS/2, & compatibles; 128 K; hard disk optional; 1 disk drive. *Single User Price: Free, send diskette and postage-paid mailer to author.*

Reviews
Wilson, W. J., & Ostergren, L.A. (1986) Brainscape. *Behavior, Research Methods, Instrumentation, and Computers, 18,* 478-479.

Casper

William V. Chambers
James W. Grice

Department of Psychology
University of South Florida
8111 College Parkway
Fort Myers, FL 33919
(813) 432-5554

Lets students simulate questionnaires or multiple choice exams with user-friendly menu commands. Includes a variety of statistical analyses. Latest release 1990.

Classification: Experimental Psychology

Hardware Requirements and Price
IBM PC, XT, AT, PS/2, & compatibles; 640 K; hard disk optional; 2 disk drives. Graphic display required. *Single User Price: Free, send formatted disk and self-addressed, stamped envelope to W. Chambers.*

Reviews
Chambers, W.V. (1991). Casper: Educational psychometrics package. *Psychometrika, 56*(2), 349.

Catechollision

W. Jeffrey Wilson
Jennifer A. Cook

W. Jeffrey Wilson
Indiana-Purdue Fort Wayne
Department of Psychology
2101 Coliseum Boulevard East

Fort Wayne, IN 46805
(219) 481-6403

Catechollision is an arcade-type game that
teaches students about catecholamine synthesis. Tyrosine and enzymes responsible for the
synthesis fall from the top of the screen, and
the user must combine them to produce
dopamine, norepinephrine, and epinephrine.
Unused chemicals accumulate, and the game
ends when the screen gets too full. Has music,
sound effects, four levels of difficulty, manual
on disk. Saves high scores to disk. Instruction
booklet included. On-line help available. Latest release June, 1991.

Classification: Physiological Psychology

Hardware Requirements and Price
IBM PC, XT, AT, PS/2, & compatibles; 256 K;
hard disk optional; 1 disk drive. Hercules,
CGA, EGA, or VGA display. Requires DOS
2.0. *Single User Price: $25.00*

Reviews
Wilson, W. J., & Cook, J. (in press). Catechol-
    lision. *Behavior, Research Methods, Instru-
    mentation, and Computers.*

Catgen
Judith Kinnear

Conduit
University of Iowa-Oakdale Campus
Iowa City, IA 52242
(319) 335-4100
(800) 365-9774

A genetics simulation that allows students to
mate domestic cats of known genotypes. Students define these genotypes on the basis of up
to six gene loci affecting coat color and pattern.

The program then produces genetically valid
litters of kittens. In using Catgen, students
gain valuable experience in defining research
problems, controlling variables, analyzing and
interpreting data, and studying causal relationships. Detailed manual included.

Classification: Physiological Psychology

Hardware Requirements and Price
Apple II+, IIe, IIc; 64 K; 1 disk drive. Color
display optional. *Single User Price: $85.00*

IBM PC, XT, AT, PS/2, & compatibles; 256 K;
1 disk drive. Color display optional. *Single
User Price: $85.00 Network Price: $510.00*

Catlab
Judith Kinnear

Conduit
University of Iowa-Oakdale Campus
Iowa City, IA 52242
(319) 335-4100
(800) 365-9774

Program allows students to mate domestic cats
selected by coat color and pattern. Genetically
valid litters of kittens are then produced based
on these matings. Students not only learn
principles behind genetics transmission, they
also gain practice in scientific investigation–
defining and testing research problems, controlling variables, and analyzing and interpreting data. Detailed manual included.

Classification: Physiological Psychology

Hardware Requirements and Price
Apple II+, IIe, IIc; 48 K; hard disk optional; 1
disk drive. Color display recommended. *Single
User Price: $85.00*

IBM PC, XT, AT, PS/2, & compatibles; 128 K; 1 Mb hard disk optional; 1 disk drive. Color display recommended. *Single User Price: $85.00 Network Price: $510.00*

Circumgrids
William V. Chambers
James W. Grice

Department of Psychology
University of South Florida
8111 College Parkway
Fort Myers, FL 33919
(813) 432-5554

Circumgrids is used for the administration and analysis of repertory grids. User-friendly menu guides the user through factor analysis, and measures of logical consistency, integrative complexity, cognitive complexity, and other measures.

Classification: Statistics

Hardware Requirements and Price
IBM PC, XT, AT, PS/2, & compatibles; 640 K; hard disk optional; 1 disk drive. Printer required. *Single User Price: Free, send formatted disk and self-addressed, stamped envelope to W. Chambers.*

Reviews
Chambers, W. V., & Grize, J. W. (1986). Circumgrids: A repertory grid package for personal computers. *Behavior Research Methods, Instrumentation, & Computers, 18*(5), 468.

> **Statistics instructors will find additional programs of interest listed in the Statistics and Research Aids section of this directory.**

Classical Psychophysical Methods
Mark Wagner
Hiroshi Ono
Kenneth Ono

Conduit
University of Iowa-Oakdale Campus
Iowa City, IA 52242
(319) 335-4100
(800) 365-9774

Basic concepts and terms from psychophysics are presented, and students are shown how to use method of adjustment, method of constant stimuli, and method of limits. Learning objectives and operating instructions are included. On-line tutorial leads students through experiments and data analyses, presents questions, and allows students to design their own investigations. Detailed manual included.

Classification: Sensation and Perception

Hardware Requirements and Price
Apple II+, IIe, IIc, IIgs; 48 K; 1 disk drive. *Single User Price: $85.00*

IBM PC, XT, AT, PS/2, & compatibles; 256 K; 1 Mb hard disk optional. CGA, EGA, or VGA display. *Single User Price: $85.00 Network Price: $510.00*

Reviews
Wagner, M., Hiroshi, O., & Ono, K. (1988, October). Classical Psychophysical Methods, *Choice*, 693.

Clinical Interviews
Martin E. Rand
Joella M. Rand

Clinical Interviews
P.O. Box 69

Willard, NY 14588
(607) 869-5955

A simulation of an initial interview, this program provides practice in the counseling skills of reflecting, attending, and probing. Includes five different patients to interview. Detailed manual included. Latest release 1990.

Classification: Abnormal Psychology

Hardware Requirements and Price
Apple II, hard disk optional, 1 disk drive (5-1/4). Laser printer optional. *Single User Price: $150.00*

IBM PC, XT, AT, PS/2, & compatibles; 512 K; hard disk optional; 1 disk drive. Laser printer optional. *Single User Price: $150.00*

Reviews
Alperson, J. (1987). Clinical Interview: The mental health series. *Social Science Microcomputer Review, 5,* 383-386.
Piazza, N. J. (1986). Software review. *Computers in Human Behavior, 2,* 161-165.

Clinical Interviews: General Medical Surgical Series
Martin Rand
Joella Rand
Elizabeth Zwart

Clinical Interviews
P.O. Box 69
Willard, NY 14588
(607) 869-5955

An advanced interviewing program for use in general medical surgical (GMS) settings. Demonstrates the importance of psycho-social information in working with GMS patients. Of interest to advanced students in nursing, medicine, medical social work and health psychology. Detailed manual included. Latest release 1991.

Classification: Abnormal Psychology

Hardware Requirements and Price
IBM PC, XT, AT, PS/2, & compatibles; 512 K; 10 Mb hard disk required; 1 disk drive. Laser printer optional. *Single User Price: $150.00*

Reviews
Bolwell, C. (1991). Clinical interviews. *Microworld, 5*(4), 29.

CNS Mechanisms in Hearing
J. H. Casseday

Bio-Psych Educational Tools
P.O. Box 6436
Winston-Salem, NC 27109
(919) 759-0506

One of eight packages in the series "The Senses," this program employs high quality color images and animation to explain the processing of auditory information in brainstem (especially sound localization), and the neocortex, and the perception of sound. Interactive control via a mouse or the keyboard. 2 X 2 slides of major screen images are included. Detailed manual included. Latest release 1992.

Classification: Sensation and Perception

Hardware Requirements and Price
IBM PC, XT, AT, PS/2, & compatibles; 640 K; 10 Mb hard disk required; 2 disk drives. EGA display required. Mouse required. *Single User Price: $139.00 Network Price: $417.00*

CNS Mechanisms in Vision
James C. Walker

Bio-Psych Educational Tools
P.O. Box 6436
Winston-Salem, NC 27109
(919) 759-0506

Program uses animation and high quality color images to explain the circuitry and physiology of the visual areas of the brain (e.g., the thalamo-cortical visual pathway and superior colliculus). It is one of the programs in the series "The Senses." User controls the program through the use of a mouse or the keyboard. Slides, measuring 2 X 2, of important screen images are included. Detailed manual included. Latest release 1991.

Classification: Sensation and Perception

Hardware Requirements and Price
IBM PC, XT, AT, PS/2, & compatibles; 640 K; 10 Mb hard disk required; 2 disk drives. EGA display required. Mouse required. *Single User Price: $139.00 Network Price: $417.00*

User Site References
Don Balten, Department of Psychology, Lewis and Clark College, Portland, OR 97219

CNS Mechanisms of Feeling
Joel D. Greenspan

Bio-Psych Educational Tools
P.O. Box 6436
Winston-Salem, NC 27109
(919) 759-0506

Software uses high quality color graphics and animation to explain the representation of the body surface in the brain, the processing of somtosensory information (including pain), and the central integration of somatosensory information and motor control. Mouse or keyboard used for interactive control. Major screen images slides (2 x 2) included. Detailed manual included.

Classification: Sensation and Perception

Hardware Requirements and Price
IBM PC, XT, AT, PS/2, & compatibles; 640 K; 10 Mb hard disk required; 2 disk drives. EGA display required. Mouse required. *Single User Price: $139.00 Network Price: $417.00*

Cognitive Experimental Design & Testing System

Douglas B. Eamon
404 S. Buckingham Blvd.
Whitewater, WI 53190
(414) 473-8054

Allows students or instructor to create original experiments, run subjects, and collect data. No programming skills or experience required. Detailed manual included.

Classification: Experimental Psychology

Hardware Requirements and Price
Apple II+, IIe, IIc, IIgs; 64 K; hard disk optional; 1 disk drive. Printer required. Optional hardware clock. *Single User Price: $78.50*

Cognitive Psychology
John Mueller
Burt Thompson

AB i
2124 Kittendge, Suite 215

Berkeley, CA 94704
(510) 582-6343

This program contains projects similar to those in Keenen & Keller's (1980) package published by Conduit, but the topics are different. Students run themselves or others as subjects, then use the group's data to generate a class report. The projects involve a Posner-type same-different task, a Rosch-type typicality experiment, and a Bower-type mood congruence project. Detailed manual included.

Classification: Cognitive Psychology

Hardware Requirements and Price
Apple II+, IIe, IIc; 48 K; 1 disk drive (5-1/4). *Single User Price: $50.00 Site License: $300.00*

IBM PC, XT, AT, PS/2, & compatibles; 256 K; hard disk optional; 1 disk drive. *Single User Price: $50.00 Site License: $300.00*

Macintosh, 1 Mb, hard disk optional, 1 disk drive. *Single User Price: $50.00 Site License: $300.00*

Cognitive Psychology Programs
David J. Pittenger

Department of Psychology
Marietta College
Marietta, OH 45750-3031
(614) 374-4749

Programs demonstrate cognitive psychology concepts. Detailed manual included.

Classification: Cognitive Psychology

Hardware Requirements and Price
Commodore 64, 32 K, 1 disk drive. Color display required. *Single User Price: $10.00*

Commodore P.E.T. Model 8032, 32 K, 1 disk drive. Color display required. *Single User Price: $10.00*

Community Mental Health Model, Version 1.2
G. David Garrison

William C. Brown Publishers
2460 Kerper Blvd.
Dubuque, IA 52001
(319) 588-1451
(800) 351-7671

An example of regression-based simulation using real data. Change any variable (e.g., alcoholism rate) and see predicted effect. Instruction booklet included.

Classification: Statistics

Hardware Requirements and Price
IBM PC, XT, AT, PS/2, & compatibles; hard disk optional; 1 disk drive. *Single User Price: $32.50 Site License: $400.00*

Compliance
C. Michael Levy
Grant J. Levy

Life Science Associates
1 Fenimore Road
Bayport, NY 11705-2115
(516) 472-2111
Fax: (516) 472-8146

Demonstration modeled after the work of Asch whose tasks employed peer pressure to demonstrate conformity. The computer generates pressure for subjects to appear self-consistent. By requiring estimates of the number of dots shown briefly under different conditions of feedback, the program illustrates independence and compliance. Instruction booklet included.

Classification: Social Psychology

Hardware Requirements and Price
Apple II+, IIe, IIc; 64 K; 10 Mb hard disk optional; 1 disk drive (5-1/4). Monochrome or color display. *Single User Price: $40.00*

IBM PC, XT, AT, PS/2, & compatibles; 128 K; 20 Mb hard disk optional; 1 disk drive. CGA, EGA, or VGA display. *Single User Price: $40.00*

Computer Augmented Lecture Material (CALM): Excel™ Tools
Burrton Woodruff

Department of Psychology
Butler University
4600 Sunset Avenue
Indianapolis, IN 46208
(317) 283-9267

An EXCEL™-based lecture support. Each tool provides multiple screens illustrating quantitative topics. Designed to allow the instructor to project the screen during a lecture. All tools are interactive and the instructor can change parameters to illustrate theoretical basis of phenomena. Current tools include SDT model, CIE color stimulus specifications, magnitude estimation, and method of constant stimulus model. Instruction booklet included. Latest release September, 1991.

Classification: Experimental Psychology

Hardware Requirements and Price
Macintosh, 2 Mb, 20 Mb hard disk required. Color display recommended. Mouse required. Laser printer optional. Requires System 6 and Excel 2.2. Catalog requires Hypercard 2.0. *Single User Price: $10.00-$40.00 A Hypercard catalog is available for $1.00*

Computer Augmented Lecture Materials: Stat Stack
Burrton Woodruff

Department of Psychology
Butler University
4600 Sunset Avenue
Indianapolis, IN 46208
(317) 283-9267

An easy to use Hypercard 2.0 stack to support lecturing on elementary inferential statistics. Designed to provide the instructor with interactive screens that can be projected during a lecture. Generate univariate and bivariate samples, multiple samples that illustrate sampling distributions and Monte Carlo illustrations of Type 1 errors. Calculates one-way ANOVA (between and within), one-sample *t*-test, and one variable regression with scatterplot. Ideal for student use in lower-level, database experimental psychology courses. Instruction booklet included. Latest release September, 1991.

Classification: Statistics

Hardware Requirements and Price
Macintosh, 2 Mb, hard disk required. Mouse required. Laser printer optional. Requires System 6 and Hypercard 2.0. *Single User Price: $100.00/department*

Computer Lab in Memory and Cognition
Janice M. Keenan
Robert A. Keller

Conduit
University of Iowa-Oakdale Campus
Iowa City, IA 52242
(319) 335-4100
(800) 365-9774

Students participate as subjects in historically significant experiments in memory and cognition. Most of the programs store individual student data in a common class file and use it to calculate means and variances. Programs include levels of process, encoding specificity, semantic memory, sentence-picture verification, and constructive processes in prose comprehension. Student manual covers background, experimental design, and includes discussion questions. Detailed manual included.

Classification: Cognitive Psychology

Hardware Requirements and Price
Apple II+, IIe, IIc; 48 K; 2 disk drives. *Single User Price: $190.00*

IBM PC, XT, AT, PS/2, & compatibles; 256 K; 1 Mb hard disk optional; 2 disk drives. CGA, EGA, or VGA display. *Single User Price: $190.00 Network Price: $1,140.00*

Computer Simulations in Psychology
David J. Pittenger
Joseph D. Allen

Macmillan Publishing Co.
866 Third Avenue
New York, NY 10022
(800) 257-5755

Twenty programs demonstrate various color mixing and afterimage phenomena, the McCollough effect, optical illusions, learning and opponent-process theory, memory encoding and recognition, concept formation, prisoners dilemma, a brain model, and descriptive statistics. Detailed manual included. Latest release April, 1991.

Classification: General Psychology

Hardware Requirements and Price
IBM PC, XT, AT, PS/2, & compatibles; 128 K; hard disk optional; 2 disk drives. CGA display. Laser printer optional. Requires DOS 2.0. *Single User Price: Call publisher.*

Macintosh, hard disk optional, 2 disk drives. Graphics required. Laser printer optional. *Single User Price: Call publisher.*

Computer Simulations in Psychology, Second Edition
David J. Pittenger
Joseph D. Allen

Macmillan Publishing Co.
866 Third Avenue
New York, NY 10022
(800) 257-5755

Eighteen interactive computer simulations for class or lab use. Includes tutorials and experimental programs that engage students in simulated psychological experiments. Detailed manual included. Latest release 1990.

Classification: General Psychology

Hardware Requirements and Price
IBM PC, XT, AT, PS/2, & compatibles; 256 K; 720 K hard disk optional; 1 disk drive (5-1/4).

Hercules or color display required. Laser printer optional. Requires DOS 2.0. *Single User Price: $250.00 Available free to schools adopting textbook*

Macintosh, 512 K, hard disk optional, 1 disk drive (3-1/2). Mouse required. Laser printer optional. Requires System 6.0.3. *Single User Price: $250.00 Available free to schools adopting textbook*

Computerized Activities in Psychology IV (CAPS IV)

McGraw-Hill College Division
1221 Avenue of the Americas
New York, NY 10020
(800) 338-3987

This package presents 10 interactive computer-based learning modules in general psychology. Each module is designed to complement introductory psychology texts by providing fast-paced, hands-on activities, involving such concepts as left brain/right brain, word recognition, learning and reinforcement, memory, and insight. Instruction booklet included. Latest release 1989.

Classification: General Psychology

Hardware Requirements and Price
Apple II, 64 K, 1 disk drive (5-1/4). Requires DOS 3.3. *Single User Price: $29.95*

IBM PC, XT, AT, PS/2, & compatibles; 256 K; hard disk optional; 2 disk drives. Color display required. Requires DOS 2.0. *Single User Price: $29.95*

Computerized Cognitive Laboratory
David J. Pittenger
Bruce K. Britton

Department of Psychology
Marietta College
Marietta, OH 45750-3031
(614) 374-4749

Package of programs including free recall and recognition, Stroop test, optical illusions, movement programming, figure detection, language utilization, visual and name coding, and high-speed memory scanning. Detailed manual included.

Classification: Cognitive Psychology

Hardware Requirements and Price
Commodore, 64 K. *Single User Price: $10.00*

Reviews
Pittenger, D. J., & Britton, B. K. (1985). A computerized cognitive laboratory: A software package for the cognitive psychology laboratory class. *Behavior, Research Methods, Instrumentation, and Computers, 17,* 122-125.

Concept Formation: The Feature-Positive Effect
Donald E. Minty

Life Science Associates
1 Fenimore Road
Bayport, NY 11705-2115
(516) 472-2111
Fax: (516) 472-8146

The Feature-positive effect is a very robust phenomenon. In concept formation, the "feature," the stimulus element that defines the concept, may be present (feature-positive), or absent (feature-negative). In this demonstration, two series of trials are presented with identical pairs of stimuli. Students must decide which is the "correct" choice, with immediate feedback given. When the feature is positive, the vast majority of students will learn the concept within 30 trials. When the feature is negative, it is a near certainty that the concept will not be learned. The demonstration provides a basis for introducing concept-formation and for demonstrating the not-well-known feature-positive effect. Cumulative data are recorded. Detailed manual included.

Classification: Cognitive Psychology

Hardware Requirements and Price
Apple II, 64 K, 10 Mb hard disk optional, 1 disk drive (5-1/4). Monochrome or color display. *Single User Price: $40.00*

IBM PC, XT, AT, PS/2, & compatibles; 128 K; 20 Mb hard disk optional; 1 disk drive. CGA display. *Single User Price: $40.00*

Concepts of Probability
David A. Kravitz

CAUSE Project
Department of Psychology
University of Kentucky
Lexington, KY 40506
(606) 257-6839

Introduces students to the basic concepts of probability theory, including some definitions and the addition and multiplication rules. Elementary mathematics is assumed, but no

statistical knowledge is required. This is a set of linked programs written in Apple PILOT. Detailed manual included.

Classification: Statistics

Hardware Requirements and Price
Apple II+, IIe, IIc, IIgs; 48 K; 1 disk drive (5-1/4). *Single User Price: $20.00*

Conditioning
Ann Gilchrist

Ann Gilchrist
Ulster County Community College
Stone Ridge, NY 12484

This full color program uses attractive graphic boxes to ask students multiple choice questions about commonplace scenarios relating to classical and operant conditioning. The students are led, step by step, to the identification of the components of classical conditioning and the solution of problems requiring the application of operant conditioning. If students select a wrong answer, the program presents an explanation why the response is incorrect. Detailed manual included.

Classification: Learning

Hardware Requirements and Price
IBM PC, XT, AT, PS/2, & compatibles; 360 K; hard disk optional; 1 disk drive. Color display required. *Single User Price: $45.00*

User Site References
Barbara Budik, Ulster City Community College, Stone Ridge, NY, 12484, (914) 687-5104
Janet Salanitri, Ulster City Community College, Stone Ridge, NY, 12484, (914) 687-5200

Barbara Sartorius, Ulster City Community College, Stone Ridge, NY, 12484, (914) 687-5039

Conflict & Cooperation, Version 2.0 (Windows)
Joseph Oppenheimer
Mark Winer
Chad K. McDaniel

Wisc Ware
Academic Computing Center
University of Wisconsin
1210 W. Dayton Street
Madison, WI 53706
(608) 262-8167
(800) 543-3201

A social game construction kit. Expanding on the classic prisoners dilemma framework, this software allows students to author and then play out (either on one computer or a LAN) a wide variety of interactive decision-making scenarios constructed to represent political, business, or social situations in which participants vie for resource allocations. Instruction booklet included. On-line help available. Latest release 1988.

Classification: Social Psychology

Hardware Requirements and Price
IBM PC, XT, AT, PS/2, & compatibles; 512 K; 1.2 Mb hard disk optional; 1 disk drive. VGA display. Mouse required. Requires DOS 3.0. *Single User Price: $25.00 for members $75.00 for non-members*

Reviews
Peckens, R. G. (1989). Conflict and Cooperation Version 2.0. *Social Science Computer Review*, 7, 377-378.

Petry, F. (1990). Learning outcomes of game-theoretic computer simulation: An evaluation. *Social Science Computer Review*, 8, 367-377.

Consumer Behavior
C. Michael Levy

Life Science Associates
1 Fenimore Road
Bayport, NY 11705-2115
(516) 472-2111
Fax: (516) 472-8146

Demonstrates the selective interpretation and recall of the content of advertising copy. Eight short advertisements are presented followed by questions about them. The program analyzes percentages of correct identifications of claims that were, and were not made, and those that were indeterminate and implied. Instruction booklet included.

Classification: Industrial/Organizational

Hardware Requirements and Price
Apple II+, IIe, IIc; 64 K; 10 Mb hard disk optional; 1 disk drive (5-1/4). Monochrome or color display. *Single User Price: $40.00*

IBM PC, XT, AT, PS/2, & compatibles; 128 K; 20 Mb hard disk optional; 1 disk drive. CGA display required. *Single User Price: $40.00*

A Cooperative-Competitive Game
M. D. Morgan
D. McBride

Life Science Associates
1 Fenimore Road
Bayport, NY 11705-2115

(516) 472-2111
Fax: (516) 472-8146

Students of social psychology, gaming, bargaining, and conflict resolution have observed a general tendency for people to compete even when they could do much better by cooperating. This program, based on work by Deutsch and Krauss, puts each player in charge of a trucking company that transports goods to certain destinations via various routes, one of which is a one-way road. Players earn points depending on their time to reach destination which is, in turn, determined by an optimal combination of private versus cooperative strategies. Instruction booklet included.

Classification: Social Psychology

Hardware Requirements and Price
Apple II+, IIe, IIc; 64 K; 10 Mb hard disk optional; 1 disk drive (5-1/4). Monochrome or color display. *Single User Price: $40.00*

IBM PC, XT, AT, PS/2, & compatibles; 128 K; 20 Mb hard disk optional; 1 disk drive. CGA, EGA, or VGA display. *Single User Price: $40.00*

Datasim
Drake R. Bradley

Desktop Press
90 Bardwell Street
Lewiston, ME 04240
(207) 786-6180

A general purpose data simulator used to generate, analyze, and graph simulated datasets for a variety of research designs (one way, two way, and three way factorial designs, multivariate designs, table designs, etc.). The software comes with a built-in library of Datasim problems that generate simulated data for classic psychology studies. Instructors can use the software to create their own simulated datasets as well. Detailed manual included. On-line help available. Latest release April 7, 1991.

Classification: Statistics

Hardware Requirements and Price
IBM PC, XT, AT, PS/2, & compatibles; 640 K; hard disk optional; 1 disk drive. Monochrome, CGA, EGA, or VGA display. Mouse optional. Modem optional. Laser printer optional. Requires DOS 2.0. *Single User Price: $45.00*

Macintosh, 685 K, hard disk optional, 1 disk drive (3-1/2). Monochrome or color display. Mouse required. Modem optional. Laser printer optional. Requires System 6.0. *Single User Price: $55.00*

Reviews
Bradley, D. R. (1991). Anatomy of a DATA-SIM simulation: The Doob and Gross horn-honking study. *Behavior Research Methods, Instruments, & Computers*, *23*, 190-207.
Bradley, D. R., Senko, M.W., & Stewart, F. A. (1990). Statistical simulation on microcomputers. *Behavior Research Methods, Instruments, & Computers*, *22*, 236-246.
Bradley, D. R. (1989). A general purpose simulation program for statistics and research methods. In G. Garson & S. Nagel (Eds.), *Advances in social science and computers: Vol. 1*, (pp. 145-186). Greenwich, CT: JAI Press.

User Site References

David MacEwen, Department of Psychology, Mary Washington College, Fredericksburg, VA, 22401, (703) 899-4319

William Maki, Department of Psychology, North Dakota State University, Fargo, ND, 58105-5075, (701) 237-7053

Martin Richter, Department of Psychology, Lehigh University, Bethlehem, PA, 18015, (215) 758-3622

Demo-Graphics

Conduit
University of Iowa-Oakdale Campus
Iowa City, IA 52242
(319) 335-4100
(800) 365-9774

Presents current and historical demographic data for many nations and projects multinational populations given current trends. Facilitates the understanding of demographic dynamics and the impact of both real and simulated factors affecting the growth of world populations. Suitable for students beginning to learn population-resource relationships, as well as for graduate students who are ready to attempt computer simulations to test hypothesis about the effect of demographic variables. Detailed manual included.

Classification: Social Psychology

Hardware Requirements and Price
Apple II+, IIe, IIc; 48 K; hard disk optional; 1 disk drive. Color display recommended. *Single User Price: $95.00*

Digitized Nonobjects for the Macintosh

John O. Brooks III
Laura L. Bieber

VA Medical Center (151Y)
3801 Miranda Avenue
Palo Alto, CA 94304
(415) 493-5000

Digitized versions of Kroll and Potter's (1984) nonobjects are provided. There are a total of 88 nonobjects. Instruction booklet included.

Classification: Cognitive Psychology

Hardware Requirements and Price
Macintosh, 512 K, hard disk optional, 1 disk drive (3-1/2). *Single User Price: $6.00*

Reviews
Brooks, J. O. & Bieber, L. L. (1988). Digitized Nonobjects for use with the Apple Macintosh computer. *Behavioral Research Methods, Instruments & Computers, 20*, 433-434.

Digitized Pictorial Stimuli for the Macintosh

John O. Brooks III

VA Medical Center (151Y)
3801 Miranda Avenue
Palo Alto, CA 94304
(415) 493-5000

Program presents digitized versions of Snodgrass and Vanderwart's (1980) 260 line drawings. Instruction booklet included.

Classification: Cognitive Psychology

Hardware Requirements and Price
Macintosh, 512 K, hard disk optional, 1 disk drive. *Single User Price: $6.00*

Reviews
Brooks, J. O. (1985). Pictorial stimuli for the Apple Macintosh computer. *Behavioral Research Methods, Instruments & Computers, 17,* 409-410.

Discovering Psychology
C. Michael Levy
Grant J. Levy
Michael D. Morgan

Life Science Associates
1 Fenimore Road
Bayport, NY 11705-2115
(516) 472-2111
Fax: (516) 472-8146

A set of 15 computer programs covering a broad range of psychology topics at the introductory college or advanced high school level. Each program is independent and yields a brief interactive experience illustrating an important topic. The program records student responses at the keyboard and summarizes results at the end of the program. Detailed manual included. Latest release 1990.

Classification: General Psychology

Hardware Requirements and Price
Apple II, 64 K, 10 Mb hard disk optional, 1 disk drive (5-1/4). Monochrome or color display. *Single User Price: $450.00 Network Price: $1350.00*

IBM PC, XT, AT, PS/2, & compatibles; 128 K; 20 Mb hard disk optional; 1 disk drive. CGA display. *Single User Price: $495.00 Network Price: $1485.00*

Reviews
Beins, B. C. (1990). Computer software for introductory psychology courses. *Contemporary Psychology, 35,* 421-427.

Diskcovering Psychology and Computerized Study Guide
Thomas E. Ludwig
Richard O. Straub

Worth Publishers, Inc.
33 Irving Place
New York, NY 10003
(212) 475-6000
(800) 223-1715

A computerized version of the study guides that accompany Myer's books *Psychology, 3/e* and *Exploring Psychology.* Program includes questions that aid learning and reinforce understanding of progress tests, and analyses of results, and offers interactive assistance as needed. Instruction booklet included. Latest release January, 1992.

Classification: General Psychology

Hardware Requirements and Price
IBM PC, XT, AT, PS/2, & compatibles; 256 K; hard disk optional; 1 disk drive. *Single User Price: Call publisher*

Macintosh, 1 Mb, hard disk optional, 1 disk drive (3-1/2). *Single User Price: Call publisher*

DSM-III-R Tutorial Software
David C. Hayden
Michael J. Furlong

Psychoeducational Software
415-6 Via Rosa

Santa Barbara, CA 93110
(805) 964-1811

Clinical vignettes are used in an interactive tutorial to present the *DSM-III-R* (*Diagnostic and Statistical Manual of Mental Disorders*, 3rd ed., rev.) diagnostic system and clinical interview method. Printed feedback is provided for student and instructor. Latest release 1990. Instruction booklet included.

Classification: Abnormal Psychology

Hardware Requirements and Price
IBM PC, XT, AT, PS/2, & compatibles; 128 K; hard disk optional; 1 disk drive. Color display optional. Laser printer optional. Requires DOS 3.3. *Single User Price: $45.00*

Reviews
Hayden, D. C. (1990). A *DSM-III-R* computer tutorial for abnormal psychology. *Teaching of Psychology, 17*, 203-206.

The Ear
James C. Walker

Bio-Psych Educational Tools
P.O. Box 6436
Winston-Salem, NC 27109
(919) 759-0506

As one of eight packages in the series on "The Senses," this program utilizes high quality color images and animation to discuss the fundamental features of the auditory periphery. Mouse used for interactive control. 2 X 2 color slides of major screen images are included. Detailed manual included. Latest release 1986.

Classification: Sensation and Perception

Hardware Requirements and Price
IBM PC, XT, AT, PS/2, & compatibles; 640 K; hard disk optional; 1 disk drive. EGA display required. Mouse required. *Single User Price: $99.00 Network Price: $297.00*

Reviews
Walker, J. C. (1988, December). The Ear. *ASHA, 30*, 67.

User Site References
John Batson, Department of Psychology, Furman University, Poinselt Highway, Greenville, SC, 29613
Roger Dejmal, Science Department, Umpqua Community College, Roseburg, OR, 97470
George Mulford, University of Delaware, 222 South Chapel Street, Newark, DE, 19716

Ego Defense Mechanisms
Ann Gilchrist

Ann Gilchrist
Ulster County Community College
Stone Ridge, NY 12484

This full color program uses attractive graphic boxes to present 10 commonly cited ego defense mechanisms. After viewing these, students respond to four sets of examples of these defenses in the form of multiple choice questions. If an incorrect answer is selected, the program displays an explanation why the response is wrong. Detailed manual included.

Classification: Abnormal Psychology

Hardware Requirements and Price
IBM PC, XT, AT, PS/2, & compatibles; 360 K; hard disk optional; 1 disk drive. Color display required. *Single User Price: $25.00*

User Site References

Barbara Budik, Ulster City Community College, Stone Ridge, NY, 12484, (914) 687-5104

Janet Salanitri, Ulster City Community College, Stone Ridge, NY, 12484, (914) 687-5200

Barbara Sartorius, Ulster City Community College, Stone Ridge, NY, 12484, (914) 687-5039

Eliza II

Dynacomp, Inc.
The Dynacomp Office Building
178 Phillips Road
Webster, NY 14580
(716) 265-4040
(800) 828-6772

Simulates a session with a psychotherapist who analyzes the user's comments and responds accordingly. This program has the ability to provide realistic responses to statements. Features that have been added to Eliza include increasing the range of the dialogue, as well as less patterned responses. The entire exchange may be saved and recalled from disk. Sessions can be saved and continued later. Users can add their own BASIC code to extend Eliza's abilities. Instruction booklet included.

Classification: Abnormal Psychology

Hardware Requirements and Price
Apple II, 48 K, 1 disk drive (5-1/4). Laser printer optional. Requires DOS 3.3. *Single User Price: $19.95*

IBM PC, XT, AT, PS/2, & compatibles; 128 K; hard disk optional; 1 disk drive. Laser printer optional. *Single User Price: $19.95*

ESP: Precognition, Clairvoyance, & Telepathy
Joseph Dlhopolsky

Life Science Associates
1 Fenimore Road
Bayport, NY 11705-2115
(516) 472-2111
Fax: (516) 472-8146

Presents stimuli in precognition, clairvoyance and telepathy formats, and provides a statistical analysis of responses. Instruction booklet included.

Classification: Experimental Psychology

Hardware Requirements and Price
TRS-80, Model I, III, & IV; 48 K; hard disk optional; 1 disk drive. *Single User Price: $30.00*

Exam Builder

Precision People, Inc.
3452 North Ride Circle South
Jacksonville, FL 32223
(904) 262-1096
(800) 338-0710

Menu-driven test generation and storage system that allows options for editing test questions and subsequent test generation. Program provides for single and multiple subject tests, test item pool, test item review and editing, generation of answer keys, and password protection. The maximum number of items per test is 150, although test item pools may be larger. Detailed manual included.

Classification: Management

Hardware Requirements and Price

Apple II+, IIe, IIc, IIgs; 64 K; hard disk optional; 1 disk drive. Printer required. *Single User Price: $99.00*

IBM PC, XT, AT, PS/2, & compatibles; hard disk optional; 1 disk drive. Printer required. *Single User Price: $99.00*

Experimental Psychology Data Simulation

Oakleaf Systems
P.O. Box 472
Decorah, IA 52101
(319) 382-4320

Software simulates 25 experimental psychology situations. Students can use programs to obtain data to test hypotheses of their own or ones suggested by the instructor. They can also vary the value of independent variables and specify the number of replicate values to be simulated. Data can be analyzed without leaving the program. Instruction booklet included. Latest release January, 1990.

Classification: Experimental Psychology

Hardware Requirements and Price

Apple II, 64 K, hard disk optional, 1 disk drive. Lower case chip. *Single User Price: $69.95*

IBM PC, XT, AT, PS/2, & compatibles; hard disk optional; 1 disk drive. *Single User Price: $69.95*

Macintosh, hard disk optional, 1 disk drive. *Single User Price: $69.95*

Experimental Psychology Programs, Level 1

T. B. Perera
T. B. Perera, Jr.
John Brendel

Life Science Associates
1 Fenimore Road
Bayport, NY 11705-2115
(516) 472-2111
Fax: (516) 472-8146

A complete set of laboratory experiences for IBM and Apple II computers. Keyboard entry is required to select parameters and respond to stimuli. Offers extensive statistical analyses. Subjects include: auditory and visual reaction time; quantification of Muller-Lyer figure, horizontal/vertical, and Poggendorf illusions; line length and rectangle size judgments; concept formation; verbal learning; multiple field tach; visual illusion demonstrations; line length scaling; visual acuity; operant conditioning simulation; human maze learning; signal detection; delayed match-to-sample; levels of processing; auditory frequency thresholds; and psychophysical scaling of auditory frequency. Detailed manual included.

Classification: Experimental Psychology

Hardware Requirements and Price

Apple II, 64 K, 10 Mb hard disk optional, 1 disk drive (5-1/4). Monochrome or color display. *Single User Price: $450.00*

IBM PC, XT, AT, PS/2, & compatibles; 128 K; 20 Mb hard disk optional; 1 disk drive. CGA, EGA, or VGA display. *Single User Price: $450.00*

TRS-80, Model III & IV. Single User Price: $450.00

User Site References
Tom Bourbon, Stephen F. Austin State University, SFA Station, Nacodoches, TX, 74962, (409) 568-4402.

Experimental Psychology Programs, Level 2
T. B. Perera

Life Science Associates
1 Fenimore Road
Bayport, NY 11705-2115
(516) 472-2111
Fax: (516) 472-8146

Program for creating demonstrations and performing research that requires the computer to get information from or control some event in the environment. Level 2 programs require an interface that costs $189.00. Detailed manual included. Latest release 1989.

Classification: Experimental Psychology

Hardware Requirements and Price
Apple II+, IIe, IIc; 64 K; 10 Mb hard disk optional; 1 disk drive (5-1/4). Monochrome or color display. *Single User Price: $300.00*

IBM PC, XT, AT, PS/2, & compatibles; 128 K; 20 Mb hard disk optional; 1 disk drive. CGA, EGA, or VGA display. *Single User Price: $300.00*

> **Ninety-one of the 180 listings in this section are new programs not included in the second edition of this directory.**

Experimental vs. Correlational Research: A Question of Control
Michael Hubbard

CAUSE Project
Department of Psychology
University of Kentucky
Lexington, KY 40506
(606) 257-6839

The goal of this module is to teach students the difference between experimental and correlational research methods, various methods of experimental control, and how to distinguish between true experiments and non-experiments. Before using this module students should be familiar with causality, correlation, theoretical vs. applied research, and variables. This is a set of linked programs written in Apple PILOT. Detailed manual included.

Classification: Experimental Psychology

Hardware Requirements and Price
Apple II+, IIe, IIc, IIgs; 48 K; 2 disk drives (5-1/4). *Single User Price: $25.00*

Experiments and Personal Applications in Psychology

McGraw-Hill College Division
1221 Avenue of the Americas
New York, NY 10020
(800) 338-3987

Includes Eyewitness Testimony and Behavior Modification: A Personalized Plan, two inter active computer programs. Eyewitness Testimony explores how past experience and salient details can alter a witness' perception, why eyewitnesses have difficulty estimating time and duration, and how attorneys use common knowledge to create witness credibility. Behavior Modification allows students to develop an effective behavior modification plan. Instruction booklet included. Latest release 1989.

Classification: General Psychology

Hardware Requirements and Price
Apple II, 128 K, 1 disk drive (5-1/4). 80 column display required. Requires DOS 3.3. *Single User Price: $10.45*

IBM PC, XT, AT, PS/2, & compatibles; 128 K; hard disk optional; 2 disk drives. Requires DOS 2.0. *Single User Price: $10.45 (5-1/4" disk) $24.95 (3-1/2" disk)*

Experiments in Cognitive Psychology
Barbara Tversky

Office of Technology Licensing
857 Serra Street
Stanford University
Stanford, CA 94305-6225
(415) 723-0651

The package consists of 21 self-running classic experiments in attention, perception, memory, and thinking. Students select an experiment from a menu and run it themselves in 10-15 minutes. The program reports individual student data, group data, and the original data embedded in a discussion of the background and theories of the phenomenon. Students can print out the discussion, including data and references. Instruction booklet included. Latest release September, 1990.

Classification: Cognitive Psychology

Hardware Requirements and Price
Macintosh, 1.2 K, hard disk optional, 1 disk drive (3-1/2). Mouse required. Laser printer optional. Revision for System 7 and Hypercard 2 anticipated. *Single User Price: $400.00 (site license)*

Reviews
Collis, G. (1991). Review of Experiments in Cognitive Psychology. *Syllabus, 2*(2), 48-49.

Experiments in Human Physiology
Robert F. Tinker

Queue, Inc.
338 Commerce Drive
Fairfield, CT 06430
(203) 335-0906
(800) 232-2224
Fax: (203) 336-2481

Program allows students (grade 7 to college) to measure, record, and print heart rate, respiration rate, skin temperature, and response time data. Detailed manual included.

Classification: Physiological Psychology

Hardware Requirements and Price
Apple II+, IIe, IIc, IIgs; 64 K; 1 disk drive (5-1/4). Monochrome or color display. Printer required (Imagewriter). Not compatible with laser printer. Requires DOS 3.3. Requires Grappler or Fingerprint card to print graphics. *Single User Price: $275.00*

Expert System Tutorial (EST)

Dynacomp, Inc.
The Dynacomp Office Building
178 Phillips Road
Webster, NY 14580
(716) 265-4040
(800) 828-6772

Artificial intelligence (AI) programs that record the user's expertise in a particular subject
area so that non-experts can then use this information to make decisions by simply answer-
ing computer-generated questions. This particular system allows users to troubleshoot or
do a needs analysis. A stand-alone automobile
engine repair expert is included as an extended
example. Some typical uses for EST include
troubleshooting of automobiles, electronics,
and plumbing; choosing players for sports; fig-
uring the cheapest shipping scheme in a mail-
room; and so forth. Instruction booklet
included.

Classification: Cognitive Psychology

Hardware Requirements and Price
IBM PC, XT, AT, PS/2, & compatibles; 128 K;
hard disk optional; 1 disk drive. Laser printer
optional. *Single User Price: $29.95*

The Eye
James C. Walker

Bio-Psych Educational Tools
P.O. Box 6436
Winston-Salem, NC 27109
(919) 759-0506

The Eye is part of "The Senses" series. It uses
animation and high quality color graphics to

elucidate eye movements, accommodation, the
structure of the eye, retinal circuitry, photo
receptive fields. Program is controlled with a
mouse. Contains color slides (2 X 2) of the
more important screen images. Detailed manual included. Latest release 1990.

Classification: Sensation and Perception

Hardware Requirements and Price
IBM PC, XT, AT, PS/2, & compatibles; 640 K;
10 Mb hard disk required; 2 disk drives. EGA
display required. Mouse required. *Single User
Price: $159.00 Network Price: $477.00*

User Site References
George Mulford, University of Delaware, 222
    South Chapel Street, Newark, DE, 19716
Steve Southall, Department of Psychology,
    Lynchburg College, 1501 Lakeside Drive,
    Lynchburg, VA, 24501-3199
Joseph Sturr, Department of Psychology,
    Syracuse University, 430 Huntington Hall,
    Syracuse, NY, 13244-2340 (315) 443-2353

Eye Lines
Walter K. Beagley

Psychology Department
Alma College
Alma, MI 48801
(517) 463-3687

Eye Lines builds and runs experiments or
demonstrations that involve geometric image
manipulation. It uses the method of adjustment to measure perceived length, size, position, or angle of orientation of visual stimuli. It
can measure the magnitude of any variation on
the classic geometric illusions. Users create
line drawings, and then specify image name,

type of adjustment, and which lines to adjust. Mouse (or cursor keys) is used to manipulate the image. Includes a utility that sorts data into a variety of spreadsheet configurations. Detailed manual included. Tutorial program included.

Classification: Sensation and Perception

Hardware Requirements and Price
IBM PC, XT, AT, PS/2, & compatibles. CGA or EGA display. *Single User Price: $99.00 Multiple copy discounts available*

Macintosh, 1 Mb. Monochrome or color display. *Single User Price: $99.00 Multiple copy discounts available*

Factor Positive Effect, Version 1.0
William Kirk Richardson

William C. Brown Publishers
2460 Kerper Blvd.
Dubuque, IA 52001
(319) 588-1451
(800) 338-5578

This experiment generator is designed for courses in introductory psychology, research design, experimental psychology, and human learning. Subjects see two trigrams, one labeled "good," and the subject must decide what rule makes them "good." Nine variables are under the experimenter's control. Instruction booklet included. On-line help available. Latest release 1988.

Classification: Experimental Psychology

Hardware Requirements and Price
IBM PC, XT, AT, PS/2, & compatibles; 512 K; hard disk optional; 1 disk drive. *Single User Price: $37.50*

FIRM: Florida Interactive Modeler
C. Michael Levy
Marc Durnin

Conduit
University of Iowa-Oakdale Campus
Iowa City, IA 52242
(319) 335-4100
(800) 365-9774

A system for generating data for experimental designs. The system content is free and requires either prepackaged models, such as those distributed by Conduit, or ones written by the instructor. FIRM generates dependent variable measures, and, optionally, statistics and experimental costs. Can be used to simulate research or theory, or used in methods and statistics courses to generate data for analysis and interpretation. Detailed manual included.

Classification: Experimental Psychology

Hardware Requirements and Price
Apple II+, IIe, IIc; 48 K; hard disk optional; 2 disk drives. *Single User Price: $110.00 Quantity discounts available*

IBM PC, XT, AT, PS/2, & compatibles; 256 K; 1 Mb hard disk optional; 2 disk drives. CGA, EGA or VGA display. *Single User Price: $110.00 Quantity discounts available*

FIRM: Vol. I, Nature of Attitudes and Attitude Change
J. D. Elliot
T. K. Srull
M. W. Durnin

Conduit
University of Iowa-Oakdale Campus
Iowa City, IA 52242

(319) 335-4100
(800) 365-9774

Three data-generating models that simulate social psychological experiments dealing with attitudes and attitude change including counterattitudinal behavior, the sleeper effect, and persuasion. Students conduct experiments by entering the relevant experimental conditions and then observe, record and analyze the dependent measures generated. Detailed manual included.

Classification: Social Psychology

Hardware Requirements and Price
Apple II+, IIe, IIc; 48 K; 1 disk drive. Color display optional. Requires FIRM driver package ($110.00). *Single User Price: $150.00*

IBM PC, XT, AT, PS/2, & compatibles; 128 K; 1 Mb hard disk optional; 1 disk drive. Color display optional. Requires FIRM driver package ($110.00). *Single User Price: $150.00*

FIRM: Vol. II, Interpersonal Dynamics
J. D. Elliot
J. R. Walker
T. K. Srull

Conduit
University of Iowa-Oakdale Campus
Iowa City, IA 52242
(319) 335-4100
(800) 365-9774

Three data-generating models that simulate psychological experiments dealing with general problems in interpersonal dynamics including aggression, crowding, and conformity. Students conduct experiments by entering the experimental conditions relevant to a hypothesis into the model, and then observe, record, and analyze the dependent measures generated. Detailed manual included.

Classification: Social Psychology

Hardware Requirements and Price
Apple II+, IIe, IIc; 48 K; 1 disk drive. Requires FIRM driver package ($110.00). *Single User Price: $150.00*

IBM PC, XT, AT, PS/2, & compatibles; 256 K; 1 disk drive. CGA, EGA, or VGA display. Requires FIRM driver package ($110.00). *Single User Price: $150.00*

FIRM: Vol. III, Comparative Psychology
D. A. Dewsbury
C. J. Bartness
C. J. Rogers

Conduit
University of Iowa-Oakdale Campus
Iowa City, IA 52242
(319) 335-4100
(800) 365-9774

A series of models help students simulate research in comparative animal behavior. The volume consists of six models, each of which represents an area of active contemporary research. The models help students understand current literature in the field and will also give them a good background for their own work. Programs include: Deer Mouse, Behavior Genetics, Correlation, Enforced Interval, Imprinting, and Hormones and Aggression. Detailed manual included.

Classification: Animal Behavior

Hardware Requirements and Price
Apple II+, IIe, IIc; 48 K; 1 disk drive. Requires FIRM driver package ($110.00). *Single User Price: $175.00*

IBM PC, XT, AT, PS/2, & compatibles; 256 K; 1 disk drive. Requires FIRM driver package ($110.00). *Single User Price: $175.00*

Flash: Biofeedback
Greg Luterman
Mark Rochotte

Biosource Software
4 Sunrise Lane
Kirksville, MO 63501
(816) 665-5751

Tutorial program that reviews more than 800 biofeedback terms in 18 units. The areas include biofeedback theory, research contributions, clinical issues, electricity, hardware, human stress response, psychophysiological concepts, motor system, EMG instrumentation, neuromuscular applications, musculoskeletal applications, peripheral blood vessels, temperature instrumentation, the cardiovascular system, cardiovascular instrumentation, blood pressure applications, the nervous system, EEG instrumentation, CNS applications, the sudomotor system, electrodermal instrumentation, respiration, and pain. Instruction booklet included. Latest release 1991.

Classification: Physiological Psychology

Hardware Requirements and Price
Apple II, 64 K, hard disk optional, 1 disk drive (5-1/4). Monochrome or color display. Requires DOS 3.3. *Single User Price: $49.95 Site license available*

IBM PC, XT, AT, PS/2, & compatibles; 64 K; 1 disk drive. CGA, EGA, or VGA display. Requires DOS 2.0. *Single User Price: $49.95 Site license available*

User Site References
Robert Hoyt, University of Wisconsin-Stout, University Counseling Center-BF Lab, Menomonie, WI, 54751, (715) 232-2468
Ron Krebill, St. Louis University, St. Louis University Medical Center, 1221 S. Grand, St. Louis, MO, 63501, (314) 577-8703
Mark S. Schwartz, Mayo Clinic-Jacksonville, 4500 San Pablo Road, Jacksonville, FL, 32224, (904) 223-2000

Flash: The EEG
Greg Luterman
Mark Rochotte

Biosource Software
4 Sunrise Lane
Kirksville, MO 63501
(816) 665-5751

Flash: The EEG is an intelligent flash card program that teaches more than 250 learning objectives in five units. The areas covered include electroencephalograph (EEG) physiology, EEG wave forms, instrumentation, the international 10-20 electrode placement system, and clinical applications. Instruction booklet included. Latest release 1991.

Classification: Physiological Psychology

Hardware Requirements and Price
Apple II, 64 K, 20 Mb hard disk optional, 1 disk drive (5-1/4). Monochrome or color display. Modem optional. Laser printer optional. Requires DOS 3.3. *Single User Price: $49.95 Site license available*

IBM PC, XT, AT, PS/2, & compatibles; 64 K; 20 Mb hard disk optional; 1 disk drive. CGA, EGA, or VGA display. Modem optional. Laser printer optional. Requires DOS 2.0. *Single User Price: $49.95 Site license available*

User Site References
Robert Hoyt, University of Wisconsin-Stout, University Counseling Center-BF Lab, Menomonie, WI, 54751, (715) 232-2468
Ron Krebill, St. Louis University, University Medical Center, 1221 S. Grand, St. Louis, MO, 63501, (314) 577-8703
Mark S. Schwartz, Mayo Clinic-Jacksonville, 4500 San Pablo Road, Jacksonville, FL, 32224, (904) 223-2000

Flash: Human Brain
Greg Luterman
Mark Rochotte

Biosource Software
4 Sunrise Lane
Kirksville, MO 63501
(816) 665-5751

Tutorial program that reviews more than 250 brain structures in 10 units. The areas include the cerebral cortex, basal ganglia, limbic system, thalamus, hypothalamus, tectum, tegmentum, cerebellum, pons, and medulla. Instruction booklet included. Latest release 1991.

Classification: Physiological Psychology

Hardware Requirements and Price
Apple II, 64 K, 20 Mb hard disk optional, 1 disk drive (5-1/4). Monochrome or color display. Modem optional. Laser printer optional. Requires DOS 3.3. *Single User Price: $49.95 Site license available*

IBM PC, XT, AT, PS/2, & compatibles; 64 K; 20 Mb hard disk optional; 1 disk drive. CGA, EGA, or VGA display. Modem optional. Laser printer optional. Requires DOS 2.0. *Single User Price: $49.95 Site license available*

User Site References
Robert Hoyt, University of Wisconsin-Stout, University Counseling Center-BF Lab, Menomonie, WI, 54751, (715) 232-2468
Ron Krebill, St. Louis University, St. Louis University Medical Center, 1221 S. Grand, St. Louis, MO, 63501, (314) 577-8703
Mark S. Schwartz, Mayo Clinic-Jacksonville, 4500 San Pablo Road, Jacksonville, FL, 32224, (904) 223-2000

Flash: Human Stress
Greg Luterman
Mark Rochotte

Biosource Software
4 Sunrise Lane
Kirksville, MO 63501
(816) 665-5751

A flash card program that teaches more than 500 learning objectives in eight units. This package surveys stress concepts, personality, stress physiology, posture, respiration, stress disorders, stress interventions, and professional issues. Instruction booklet included. Latest release 1991.

Classification: Personal Growth

Hardware Requirements and Price
Apple II, 64 K, 20 Mb hard disk optional, 1 disk drive (5-1/4). Monochrome or color display. modem optional. Laser printer optional. Requires DOS 3.3. *Single User Price: $49.95 Site license available*

IBM PC, XT, AT, PS/2, & compatibles; 64 K; 20 Mb hard disk optional; 1 disk drive. CGA, EGA, or VGA display. Modem optional. Laser printer optional. Requires DOS 2.0. *Single User Price: $49.95 Site license available*

User Site References
Robert Hoyt, University of Wisconsin-Stout, University Counseling Center-BF Lab, Menomonie, WI, 54751, (715) 232-2468
Ron Krebill, St. Louis University Medical Center, 1221 S. Grand, St. Louis, MO, 63501, (314) 577-8703
Mark S. Schwartz, Mayo Clinic-Jacksonville, 4500 San Pablo Road, Jacksonville, FL, 32224, (904) 223-2000

Flash: Neurons
Greg Luterman
Mark Rochotte

Biosource Software
4 Sunrise Lane
Kirksville, MO 63501
(816) 665-5751

Program teaches more than 250 learning objectives in five units. The areas covered include neuron structure, types of neurons, electrical potentials, synaptic transmission, and neurotransmitters. Instruction booklet included. Latest release 1991.

Classification: Physiological Psychology

Hardware Requirements and Price
Apple II, 64 K, 20 Mb hard disk optional, 1 disk drive (5-1/4). Monochrome or color display. Modem optional. Laser printer optional. Requires DOS 3.3. *Single User Price: $49.95 Site license available*

IBM PC, XT, AT, PS/2, & compatibles; 64 K; 20 Mb hard disk optional; 1 disk drive. CGA, EGA, or VGA display. Modem optional. Laser printer optional. Requires DOS 2.0. *Single User Price: $49.95 Site license available*

User Site References
Robert Hoyt, University of Wisconsin-Stout, University Counseling Center-BF Lab, Menomonie, WI, 54751, (715) 232-2468
Ron Krebill, St. Louis University, University Medical Center, 1221 S. Grand, St. Louis, MO, 63501, (314) 577-8703
Mark S. Schwartz, Mayo Clinic-Jacksonville, 4500 San Pablo Road, Jacksonville, FL, 32224, (904) 223-2000

Games Research
Caryl E. Rusbult

CAUSE Project
Department of Psychology
University of Kentucky
Lexington, KY 40506
(606) 257-6839

This module will help students achieve a greater understanding of the use of games as a research method, including their advantages and limitations (including experimental control and internal vs. external validity). The module simulates the "Prisoner's Dilemma Game." Detailed manual included.

Classification: Social Psychology

Hardware Requirements and Price
Apple II+, IIe, IIc, IIgs; 48 K; 1 disk drive (5-1/4). *Single User Price: $20.00*

General Forecaster
Andrew R. Gilpin

William C. Brown Publishers
2460 Kerper Blvd.
Dubuque, IA 52001
(319) 588-1451
(800) 351-7671

Program allows users without programming knowledge to create simulations based on multiple regression. General Forecaster allows up to 17 variables to be analyzed simultaneously. The purpose of the program is to generate hypotheses or to demonstrate simple or cumulative effects of any variable on any other.

Classification: Experimental Psychology

Hardware Requirements and Price
IBM PC, XT, AT, PS/2, & compatibles. *Single User Price: $39.95 Site License: $400.00*

Genstat
Fred S. Halley

Socware, Inc.
1789 Colby Street
Brockport, NY 14420
(716) 352-1986

Creates data sheets for student use in lab work, homework, and testing. Genstat prints answer sheets with intermediate computations so instructors or lab assistants can quickly grade students' work. Program can be used by instructors to create materials for student use. Because students only use products created by Genstat and not the program itself, only one computer and one copy of Genstat is needed. Detailed manual included. Latest release November, 1990.

Classification: Statistics

Hardware Requirements and Price
IBM PC, XT, AT, PS/2, & compatibles; 512 K; hard disk optional; 1 disk drive. Monochrome display. Printer required. Laser printer optional. *Single User Price: $75.00*

Reviews
England, L. (1990). Genstat: A Student Data Generation System. *Teaching Sociology, 18*, 123-124.
Genstat: A student data generation system. (1990) *Social Science Computer Review, 8*, 472-473.

User Site References
Kichi Iwamoto, Santa Clara University, Department of Sociology and Anthropology, Santa Clara, CA, 95053, (408) 554-4510
Paul T. Murry, Sienna College, Department of Sociology and Social Work, Loudonville, NY, 12211, (518) 783-2305

Goal-Focused Interviewing, Volume I
Frank F. Maple
Lewis Kleinsmith

Conduit
University of Iowa-Oakdale Campus
Iowa City, IA 52242
(319) 335-4100
(800) 365-9774

Goal-Focused Interviewing helps students and mental health professionals enhance their interviewing skills. The program places the user in the position of an interviewer in hypothetical counseling situations. The interviewing approach illustrated in these simulations is based upon the premise that clarifying therapeutic goals is a crucial step in psychological counseling. Detailed manual included. On-line help available.

Classification: Personal Growth

Hardware Requirements and Price
IBM PC, XT, AT, PS/2, & compatibles; 512 K; 1 Mb hard disk optional. CGA, EGA, or VGA display. Laser printer optional. *Single User Price: $90.00*

Gottschaldt Hidden Figures Test
Edward Engel
David C. Lowe

CAUSE Project
Department of Psychology
University of Kentucky
Lexington, KY 40506
(606) 257-6839

Acquaints students with the Gottschaldt Hidden Figures Test, both as a theoretically significant perceptual phenomenon and as a test of field dependence-independence. Students obtain data on themselves, interpret it using norms, and answer discussion questions that assume a careful reading of the instructional material and some reflection on their own relevant experience. Detailed manual included.

Classification: Sensation and Perception

Hardware Requirements and Price
Apple II+, IIe, IIc, IIgs; 48 K; 1 disk drive (5-1/4). Color display required. *Single User Price: $20.00*

Grader
Michael E. Mills

Psytek Services
6401 West 81st Street
Los Angeles, CA 90045
(213) 670-4655
(800) 392-5454

Grader recommends letter grade cutoffs to instructors and assigns a grade for each student based on a consideration of both percentile ranking (grading on a curve) and percentage correct (content mastery). Instructors can modify program parameters to make grade cutoffs higher or lower. Detailed manual included. On-line help available. Latest release November 1, 1991.

Classification: Management

Hardware Requirements and Price
IBM PC, XT, AT, PS/2, & compatibles; 512 K; hard disk optional. Monochrome, CGA, EGA, or VGA display. Laser printer optional. *Single User Price: $29.00 Site License: $99.00 30-day money back guarantee*

Graphing Data
Susan M. Belmore

CAUSE Project
Department of Psychology
University of Kentucky
Lexington, KY 40506
(606) 257-6839

This module reduces fear of graphs and figures, teaches the student to read an experimental design from a graph of the data, introduces construction of graphs, and introduces the interpretation of main effects and interactions from graphs. Students should understand the concepts of independent variables and scales of measurement prior to using this program. This module is a set of linked programs written in Apple PILOT. Detailed manual included.

Classification: Experimental Psychology

Hardware Requirements and Price
Apple II+, IIe, IIc, IIgs; 48 K; 1 disk drive (5-1/4). Color display optional. *Single User Price: $25.00*

Hands-On Experimental Psychology
Bernard C. Beins

Psychology Department
Ithaca College
Ithaca, NY 14850
(607) 274-3304

Three programs involving gradually increasing levels of interaction for experimental psychology students. In a perceptual memory study, students use game paddles and follow instructions in drawing lines on the monitor. The second study involves students making a few experimental decisions regarding foreign language learning. During the third study, students enter, save and retrieve word lists. Students participate in real experimental paradigms involving abstract rule learning and visual search processes. Instruction booklet included.

Classification: Experimental Psychology

Hardware Requirements and Price
Apple II+, IIe, IIc, IIgs; 64 K; 1 disk drive. Printer required. One module requires game paddles. *Single User Price: $7.50*

Hansen-Predict

Dynacomp, Inc.
The Dynacomp Office Building
178 Phillips Road
Webster, NY 14580
(716) 265-4040
(800) 828-6772

Hansen-Predict is a self-learning, general purpose expert system. It is an artificial intelligence (AI) software package that allows users to impart their knowledge to the computer in a way that allows the computer to predict future outcomes of situations based on the information available at that time. By defining the input variables and possible outcomes, users can train the program to make decisions. Teaching is accomplished through the use of examples. With each example, Hansen-Predict examines the relationships between variables and outcomes, and refines its understanding of the situation. It deals with ambiguous and under-defined situations in a statistical manner, predicting the most likely outcome or decision. It can also treat clearly discontinuous variables. Hansen-Predict can be used for business or science, as well as for teaching the use of artificial intelligence and decision making. Instruction booklet included.

Classification: Cognitive Psychology

Hardware Requirements and Price
IBM PC, XT, AT, PS/2, & compatibles; 128 K; hard disk optional; 1 disk drive. Laser printer optional. Requires DOS 2.0. *Single User Price: $99.95*

The Human Brain: Neurons
Greg Luterman

Biosource Software
4 Sunrise Lane
Kirksville, MO 63501
(816) 665-5751

A review of neural structure, types of neurons, electrical potentials, synaptic transmission, and neurotransmitters. Instruction booklet included. Latest release 1989.

Classification: Physiological Psychology

Hardware Requirements and Price
Apple II, 64 K, 2 disk drives (5-1/4). Color display optional. Requires DOS 3.3. *Single User Price: $49.95*

Hypothesis Testing
David A. Kravitz
Meg M. Howard

CAUSE Project
Department of Psychology
University of Kentucky
Lexington, KY 40506
(606) 257-6839

Introduces the student to the basic concepts of scientific hypothesis testing. Before using this program, students should have an understanding of the mean as a measure of central tendency. This is a set of linked programs written in Apple PILOT. Detailed manual included.

Classification: Experimental Psychology

Hardware Requirements and Price
Apple II+, IIe, IIc, IIgs; 48 K; 1 disk drive (5-1/4). *Single User Price: $20.00*

ICISS: Integrated Comprehensive Instructional Support For Psychology
Joseph Coble
Man M. Sharma
John Gillam

Academic Computing
Clark Atlanta University
240 James P. Brawley Drive
Atlanta, GA 30314
(404) 880-8219

Create and modify question banks containing objective and free response questions. Generate multiple versions of class tests with the same degree of difficulty. Computerized review of each concept covered in general psychology courses. Administer simulated timed practice exams with immediate grading. Provides complete information about student progress. Detailed manual included. Latest release August, 1991.

Classification: Management

Hardware Requirements and Price
IBM PC, XT, AT, PS/2, & compatibles; 640 K; 10 Mb hard disk required. CGA display. Mouse optional. Modem optional. Not compatible with laser printer. *Single User Price: $770.00*

User Site References
Del Bice, Heritage College, 3240 Fort Road, Toppenish, WA, 98948, (509) 865-2244
Marilyn Molloy, Our Lady of the Lake University, 411 S.W. 24th Street, San Antonio, TX, 78207, (512) 434-6711

The Idea Generator

Dynacomp, Inc.
The Dynacomp Office Building
178 Phillips Road
Webster, NY 14580
(716) 265-4040
(800) 828-6772

A brainstorming tool that allows users to view problems or situations in new ways, thus enabling them to arrive at novel solutions. Useful for anyone who needs to solve problems. Using three stages (problem statement, idea generation, and evaluation), the program presents a structured, step-by-step approach to problem solving. Each stage helps users clarify their thoughts. Program is based on Gerald I. Nierenberg's book *The Art of Creative Thinking*. Instruction booklet included.

Classification: Industrial/Organizational

Hardware Requirements and Price
Apple II, 48 K, 1 disk drive (5-1/4). Laser printer optional. Requires DOS 3.3. *Single User Price: $159.95*

IBM PC, XT, AT, PS/2, & compatibles; 128 K; hard disk optional; 1 disk drive. Laser printer optional. Requires DOS 2.0. *Single User Price: $159.95*

Illusions Pack
Mark Cunningham

Grofter Publishing
4310 South Semoran, #690
Orlando, FL 32822

Contains six experiments for investigating illusions by means of three classical psychophysical methods. Includes the Mueller-Lyer illu-

sion, which can be studied with the method of average error or the method of constant stimuli. The Ponzo illusion is studied using the method of average error or the method of limits. The Poggendorff illusion can be studied using the method of limits or the method of constant stimuli. All programs use traditional methods to present the stimuli and to compute the psychophysical values. Detailed manual included.

Classification: Sensation and Perception

Hardware Requirements and Price
Apple II+, IIe, IIc, IIgs; 64 K; hard disk optional; 1 disk drive (5-1/4). Requires ProDOS. *Single User Price: $80.00*

IBM PC, XT, AT, PS/2, & compatibles; 256 K; hard disk optional; 1 disk drive (5-1/4). CGA display required. Requires DOS 2.1. *Single User Price: $80.00*

The Initial Psychiatric Interview: Module I, Units 1 & 2
Lee Biarnsfather
Paul Ware

Health Sciences Consortium
201 Silver Cedar Court
Chapel Hill, NC 27514
(919) 942-8731

Module I, Units 1 & 2, present an entire initial interview between a psychiatrist and a young woman. The woman has been referred to the psychiatrist by her doctor. Unit 1 consists of the first half of the interview, Unit 2 presents the second half. Detailed manual included. Latest release October 28, 1991.

Classification: Abnormal Psychology

Hardware Requirements and Price
IBM PC, XT, AT, PS/2, & compatibles; 640 K; 20 Mb hard disk required; 1 disk drive. IBM InfoWindows touch display monitor and videodisk player required. *Single User Price: $1,950.00*

InSight, Version 2–InColor

John A. Baro
Stephen Lehmkuhle
Michael A. Sesma

Intellimation
130 Cremona Drive
Santa Barbara, CA 93117
(800) 346-8355

A series of full-color interactive demonstrations and experiments in experimental psychology/vision science. Instruction booklet included. On-line help available. Latest release August, 1991.

Classification: Sensation and Perception

Hardware Requirements and Price
Macintosh, 4 Mb, 40 Mb hard disk required. 8-bit color, 640 X 480 minimum required. Mouse required. Laser printer optional. Requires System 6.05 or later. Hypercard 2.1 will be available in 1992. *Single User Price: $45.00 Lab Pack: $180.00*

User Site References
Randolph Blake, Department of Psychology, Vanderbilt University, 111 21st Avenue South, Nashville, TN, 37240, (615) 322-8515
Mark Fairchild, Center for Imaging Science, Rochester Institute of Technology, P.O. Box 9887, Rochester, NY, 14623, (716) 475-5988
S. Shea, School of Medicine, Southern Illinois University, Carbondale, IL, 62901, (618) 453-5861

Instructional Support Statistics, Version 2.0

David W. Abbott

Department of Psychology
University of Central Florida
Orlando, FL 32816
(407) 275-2547

For use by computer naive students along with their coursework in behavior science statistics and research methods. Data files can be easily generated and printed. Statistics include descriptives, *t*-test, ANOVA (with post hoc tests), bivariate and multiple correlation, regression, chi-square, contingency and fit, Wilcoxon signed-ranked test, and Mann-Whitney U-test. Instruction booklet included.

Classification: Statistics

Hardware Requirements and Price
IBM PC, XT, AT, PS/2, & compatibles; 256 K; 1 disk drive. *Single User Price: $9.95*

Integer Means and Variances

Barnard C. Beins

Department of Psychology
Ithaca College
Ithaca, NY 14850
(607) 274-3304

Program will generate data sets with a sample size and range of scores specified by the user. The means and variances will be integers. The user can specify whether variances should be based on the biased or unbiased estimator of the population variance. Listing available upon request. Instruction booklet included.

Classification: Statistics

Hardware Requirements and Price
Apple II+, IIe, IIc, IIgs; 48 K; 1 disk drive.
Single User Price: Free

Reviews
Beins, B. C. (1989). A BASIC program for generating integer means and variances. *Teaching of Psychology, 16,* 230-231.

Interact/Attitude
David Heise

William C. Brown Publishers
2460 Kerper Blvd.
Dubuque, IA 52001
(319) 588-1451
(800) 351-7671

Based on the affect-control theory, program is designed for the study of social relationships and roles. Software simulates man-woman, doctor-patient, and other relationships.

Classification: Social Psychology

Hardware Requirements and Price
IBM PC, XT, AT, PS/2, & compatibles. *Single User Price: $45.00 Site License: $400.00*

ISP: Interactive Statistical Programs
Spyros Makridakis
Robert L. Winkler

Lincoln Systems Corporation
P.O. Box 391
Westford, MA 01886
(508)-692-3910

Designed to help statistics students learn faster and more easily. The program is designed for use in an introductory statistics course, or as a refresher course for students or professionals wishing to improve their statistical skills. It is easy to use and allows students to learn statistics at their own pace. ISP covers more statistical subjects than are normally taught in a 1 year university course. The extensive collection of statistical functions is not only valuable pedagogically, but is useful in a wide variety of practical applications of statistics. ISP is available in either English or French. Instruction booklet and tutorial program included. Latest release August 15, 1991.

Classification: Statistics

Hardware Requirements and Price
IBM PC, XT, AT, PS/2, & compatibles; 512 K; hard disk optional; 2 disk drives. Laser printer optional. *Single User Price: $150.00 (commercial) $40.00 (academic)*

Reviews
Butler, D., & Neudecker, W. (1989). A comparison of inexpensive statistical packages for microcomputers running MS-DOS. *Behavior, Research Methods, Instrumentation, and Computers, 21,* 113-120.
Cargal, J. (1990). Reviews-ISP, *The UMAP Journal, 11*(4), 356-357.
Hays, R. D. (1989). Interactive statistical programs. *Social Science Computer Review, 7*(3), 473-476.

Item Analysis, Version 4.0
Charles F. Cicciarella

Persimmon Software
1910 Gemway Drive
Charlotte, NC 28216
(704) 398-1309

Extract analytic information about computer administered tests created using Test Writer. Detailed manual included.

Classification: Management

Hardware Requirements and Price
IBM PC, XT, AT, PS/2, & compatibles; 256 K; 5 Mb hard disk optional; 2 disk drives. Laser printer optional. *Single User Price: $149.00*

JMP Software

SAS Institute Inc.
SAS Campus Drive
Cary, NC 27513-2414
(919) 677-8000
Fax: (919) 677-8123

JMP Software, a stand-alone statistical visualization and exploratory program designed especially for the Macintosh, presents statistics in a graphical way so they can be visually understood and give the most insight. The software includes capabilities for univariate statistics and graphs, analysis of variance and multiple regression, quality control charts and statistics including Shewhart and Pareto charts, business graphs including line bar and pie charts with or without overlays, nonlinear model fitting, multivariate analysis, group processing, and non parametric tests. JMP Software uses a unified approach to statistics so it is complete and well-organized rather than an alphabet soup of methods. JMP In (a limited form of JMP) is available to students only. It is ideal for learning statistics. Detailed manual, on-line help and tutorial program included. Latest release October, 1991.

Classification: Statistics

Hardware Requirements and Price
Apple II, 2 Mb hard disk required, 1 disk drive (3-1/2). Mouse required. Modem optional. Laser printer optional. *Single User Price: $695.00 Network Price: $400.00-$500.00 per*

user Volume and academic discounts are available

Reviews
Custer, L. (1991). JMP-ing from data to understanding. *Macweek*, 85.

Kor
Mark Cunningham

Crofter Publishing
4310 South Semoran, #690
Orlando, FL 32822

A simulation and an experiment. The behavior of interest is a simple learning task–learning to draw a line of specific length, while blindfolded. Two subjects simultaneously draw their lines on the screen. Students can directly see the results of changes in levels of two independent variables. Kor quickly generates a lot of data, so it can be used as an aid in teaching statistics. Detailed manual included.

Classification: Experimental Psychology

Hardware Requirements and Price
Apple II+, IIe, IIc, IIgs; 64 K; hard disk optional; 1 disk drive. Requires ProDOS. *Single User Price: $30.00*

IBM PC, XT, AT, PS/2, & compatibles; 256 K; hard disk optional; 1 disk drive (5-1/4). CGA display required. Requires DOS 2.1. *Single User Price: $30.00*

Laboratory in Classical Conditioning
James O. Benedict

Conduit
University of Iowa-Oakdale Campus
Iowa City, IA 52242

(319) 335-4100
(800) 365-9774

Four simulations allow students to design and execute experiments in salivary conditioning, blocking effect, suppression ratio, and taste aversion. Students conduct simulated experiments by manipulating independent variables. The program then reports the results numerically and graphically. For each simulation, a student guide provides an overview of the research area, a description of the procedure and independent variables, and a list of discussion questions. Detailed manual included.

Classification: Learning

Hardware Requirements and Price
Apple II+, IIe, IIc, IIgs; 64 K; 1 disk drive. Color display optional. *Single User Price: $80.00*

IBM PC, XT, AT, PS/2, & compatibles; 256 K; 1 Mb hard disk optional; 1 disk drive. CGA, EGA, or VGA display. *Single User Price: $80.00*

Reviews
Anderson, D. E. (1987). Laboratory in Classical Conditioning, Version 3.3. *Social Science Microcomputer Review, 5,* 239.

Laboratory in Cognition and Perception
C. Michael Levy

Conduit
University of Iowa-Oakdale Campus
Iowa City, IA 52242
(319) 335-4100
(800) 365-9774

Exposes students to a variety of phenomena, theoretical points of view, and experimental designs. The package demonstrates the use of between-subject, within-subject, and mixed designs, explores the methodological decisions of a researcher, and extends students' knowledge of processes and phenomena in contemporary experimental psychology. Includes 11 different experiments. Detailed manual included.

Classification: Cognitive Psychology

Hardware Requirements and Price
Apple II+, IIe, IIc; 64 K; hard disk optional; 1 disk drive. Color display optional. *Single User Price: $145.00*

Laboratory in Cognition and Perception, Second Edition
C. Michael Levy
Sarah Ransdell

Conduit
University of Iowa-Oakdale Campus
Iowa City, IA 52242
(319) 335-4100
(800) 365-9774

Ensemble of 15 experimental simulations, ranging from problems in classical experimental psychology to modern concerns such as associative priming, implicit memory, lateralization of language, and reading. Experiments can be screened by the instructor or student in a demonstration mode and used to design quite elaborate experiments in the advanced project mode, although the primary focus is the "standard" laboratory mode in which students serve as their own subjects in replications of well-known experiments. Winner of the

Educon/Ncriptal 1989 Award for Best Psychology Software Detailed manual included.

Classification: Cognitive Psychology

Hardware Requirements and Price
IBM PC, XT, AT, PS/2, & compatibles; 256 K; 1 Mb hard disk optional; 2 disk drives. CGA, EGA, or VGA display. *Single User Price: $175.00 Network Price: $1,050 Quantity discounts available.*

Reviews
Psychology Software News, 1(3), 52.

Laboratory in Social Psychology
Joel Cooper

Wisc-Ware
Academic Computing Center
University of Wisconsin - Madison
1210 West Dayton Street
Madison, WI 53706
(608) 262-8167
(800) 543-3201

Five laboratory experiments for a large undergraduate course in social psychology, demonstrating classic experiments. Latest release March 1, 1991.

Classification: Social Psychology

Hardware Requirements and Price
IBM PC, XT, AT, PS/2, & compatibles; 640 K; CGA graphics adapter required. Mouse required. Requires DOS 2.2. Light pen, voice communications adapter, and earphones required. *Single User Price: $100.00 (Wisc-Ware member)*

Learning Theory Simulations
Joseph D. Allen

Department of Psychology
University of Georgia
Athens, GA 30602
(404) 542-3100

Graphics simulations of Rescorla-Wagner Model, Daly-Daly Model, Blough's Generalization Model, Hull's Generalization Model, and Solomon and Corbits Opponent-Process Model.

Classification: Learning

Hardware Requirements and Price
Commodore 64, 32 K, 1 disk drive. *Single User Price: $15.00*

Commodore P.E.T. Model 8032, 32 K, 1 disk drive. *Single User Price: $15.00*

Levels of Measurement: Nominal, Ordinal, Interval, Ratio
David A. Kravitz
Meg M. Howard

CAUSE Project
Department of Psychology
University of Kentucky
Lexington, KY 40506
(606) 257-6839

An introduction to the concept of measurement. Teaches the four levels of measurement commonly used in psychology. No mathematical sophistication beyond simple arithmetic is necessary. Assumes no special statistical knowledge. Set of linked programs written in Apple PILOT. Detailed manual included.

Classification: Statistics

Hardware Requirements and Price
Apple II+, IIe, IIc, IIgs; 48 K; 1 disk drive (5-1/4). *Single User Price: $20.00*

Life Course Simulation
Robert Leik
Ronald E. Anderson

McGraw-Hill College Division
1221 Avenue of the Americas
New York, NY 10020

Designed to teach students in sociology and social psychology courses how to apply abstract concepts of the family life cycle. Instruction booklet included. On-line help available.

Classification: Social Psychology

Hardware Requirements and Price
IBM PC, XT, AT, PS/2, & compatibles. Requires DOS 2.1. *Single User Price: Contact publisher.*

Listutor
Robert K. Leik
Peter J. Burke

Listutor
2403 South 9th Street
Minneapolis, MN 55406
(612) 338-0780

A computer tutorial in the use of Lisrel. Basic notation, all commands, and sample programs are provided in annotated form. Structural and measurement models can be created on the

screen. This is an instructional tool, not a front end to Lisrel. Instruction booklet included. On-line help available. Latest release March, 1991.

Classification: Statistics

Hardware Requirements and Price
IBM PC, XT, AT, PS/2, & compatibles; 250 K; hard disk optional. Hercules, CGA, EGA, or VGA display. *Single User Price: $47.50*

Maclaboratory for Psychology 2.0
Douglas L. Chute

Maclaboratory, Inc.
314 Exeter Road
Devon, PA 19333
(215) 688-3114

Maclaboratory for Psychology is an 18 disk set of research grade experimental applications, tutorials, and simulations. The package includes editors to create experiments with millisecond accuracy in reaction time, color perception, auditory perception and pitch, motor skills, hemispheric specialization, and other areas of human performance measurement. Other topics include: neuropsychology, survey research, and classical conditioning. On-line help available. Tutorial program included. Latest release September, 1991.

Classification: General Psychology

Hardware Requirements and Price
Macintosh, 2 Mb, 20 Mb hard disk required, 1 disk drive (3-1/2). Monochrome or color display. Mouse required. Modem optional. Laser printer optional. Requires System 6.0.7. *Single User Price: $189.90 Site licenses available*

Mapping the Visual Field

C. Michael Levy
Charles Collyer

Life Science Associates
1 Fenimore Road
Bayport, NY 11705-2115
(516) 472-2111
Fax: (516) 472-8146

Simulates a neurophysiological lab in which the scientist varies stimuli in the cat's visual field and records responses from cortical neurons. The functioning of "feature detecting neurons" is elaborated as is the general findings from Hubel and Wiesel's classic experiments. Instruction booklet included.

Classification: Sensation and Perception

Hardware Requirements and Price
Apple II+, IIe, IIc; 64 K; 10 Mb hard disk optional; 1 disk drive (5-1/4). Monochrome or color display. *Single User Price: $40.00*

IBM PC, XT, AT, PS/2, & compatibles; 128 K; 20 Mb hard disk optional; 1 disk drive. CGA display required. *Single User Price: $40.00*

Measures of Central Tendency

David C. Lowe
David A. Kravitz

CAUSE Project
Department of Psychology
University of Kentucky
Lexington, KY 40506
(606) 257-6839

Teaches students about the three primary measures of central tendency used in psychology–the mean, median, and mode. Requires no mathematical sophistication beyond simple arithmetic. An understanding of elementary algebra is desirable. This program is a set of linked programs written in Apple PILOT. Detailed manual included.

Classification: Statistics

Hardware Requirements and Price
Apple II+, IIe, IIc, IIgs; 48 K; 1 disk drive (5-1/4). *Single User Price: $20.00*

Measuring Subjective Experience

C. M. Levy
C. J. Levy

Life Science Associates
1 Fenimore Road
Bayport, NY 11705-2115
(516) 472-2111
Fax: (516) 472-8146

Three visual illusions are demonstrated and measured. Program includes vertical-horizontal, Muller-Lyer, and Pongo illusions. Instruction booklet included.

Classification: Sensation and Perception

Hardware Requirements and Price
Apple II, 64 K, 10 Mb hard disk optional, 1 disk drive (5-1/4). Monochrome or color display. *Single User Price: $40.00*

IBM PC, XT, AT, PS/2, & compatibles; 128 K; 20 Mb hard disk optional; 1 disk drive. CGA, EGA, or VGA display. *Single User Price: $40.00*

Micro Experimental Laboratory (MEL)
Walter Schneider

Psychology Software Tools, Inc.
511 Bevington Road
Pittsburgh, PA 15221
(412) 244-1908

An integrated software system for psychological research survey methods and statistics. Develop reaction time, questionnaire, and text comprehension experiments with the aid of MEL's advanced software tools that simplify user input and reduce learning and experiment development costs. A high-precision standard laboratory tool, this program can be used to write experiments incorporating graphics, music, animation, video tape and speech. Detailed manual, on-line help, and tutorial program included. Latest release September, 1990.

Classification: Experimental Psychology

Hardware Requirements and Price
IBM PC, XT, AT, PS/2, & compatibles; 640 K; 2.7 Mb hard disk required; 1 disk drive. Hercules, CGA, EGA, or VGA display. Laser printer optional. Requires DOS 3.0. Floating point chip recommended. *Single User Price: $695.00 Instructional Version: $495.00*

Reviews
Bulter, D. L. (1988). A critical evaluation of software for experiment development in research and teaching. *Behavior, Research Methods, Instrumentation, and Computers, 20,* 218-220.
Schneider, W. (1989) Micro Experimental Laboratory (MEL): An integrated software system for computerized experimentation for research and instruction on IBM PC compatible computers. *Behavior, Research Methods, Instrumentation, and Computers, 21,* 240-244

User Site References
Rich Carlson, Psychology Department, Penn State University, University Park, PA, 16802, (814) 863-1736
Patricia Mullins, Psychology Department, Catholic University, Washington, DC, 20064, (202) 319-5750

MEL Lab: Experiments in Perception, Cognition, Social Psychology & Human Factors
James St. James
Walter Schneider

Psychology Software Tools, Inc.
511 Bevington Road
Pittsburgh, PA 15221
(412) 244 1908

MEL Lab is an integrated system for teaching research methods. Students receive a textbook and disks containing 27 preprogrammed classic experiments in four areas of psychology. The instructor's guide and software provide answers to questions, automatic analysis of group data, and export to standard statistical packages. An experiment editor is provided to allow students to create their own experiments in a variety of experimental paradigms (reaction time, list learning, questionnaires, social bargaining, and human factors). Detailed manual included. Latest release August 16, 1991.

Classification: Experimental Psychology

Hardware Requirements and Price
IBM PC, XT, AT, PS/2, & compatibles; 512 K; hard disk optional; 1 disk drive. Hercules, CGA, EGA, or VGA display. Requires DOS

3.0. Non-interlaced VGA monitor recommended. *Single User Price: $99.00 (instructional version) $19.95 (student version)*

Reviews

St. James, J. (1989) The MEL Library in the undergraduate research methods course. *Behavior, Research Methods, Instrumentation, and Computers, 21,* 245-247.

St. James, J. & Schneider, W. (1991) Student MEL software support for instructors and teaching assistants in research methods course. *Behavior, Research Methods, Instrumentation, and Computers, 23,* 149-154.

User Site References

Hank Gorman, Austin College, Suite 61584, P.O. Box 1177, Sherman, TX, 75091-1177, (903) 813-2481

Jeff Graham, Division of Life Sciences, University of Toronto, Scarborough, ON, M1C 1A4, Canada, (416) 287-7399

Richard West, Psychology Department, James Madison University, Harrisonburg, VA, 22807, (703) 568-6502

Memory Techniques

C. Michael Levy

Grant J. Levy

Life Science Associates
1 Fenimore Road
Bayport, NY 11705-2115
(516) 472-2111
Fax: (516) 472-8146

Illustrates the use of two powerful methods, "loci" and "peg word" for enhancing the capacity to remember information that is typically forgotten quickly. This program can teach how mnemonic techniques are used and how they can be applied to practical situations such as learning academic material or preparing oral presentations. Instruction booklet included.

Classification: Cognitive Psychology

Hardware Requirements and Price
Apple II+, IIe, IIc; 64 K; 10 Mb hard disk optional; 1 disk drive (5-1/4). Monochrome or color display. *Single User Price: $40.00*

IBM PC, XT, AT, PS/2, & compatibles; 128 K; 20 Mb hard disk optional; 1 disk drive. CGA, EGA, or VGA display. *Single User Price: $40.00*

Mind Scope

Robert W. Henderson

West Publishing Company
50 West Kellogg Boulevard
P.O. Box 6452
St. Paul, MN 55164-1003
(612) 228-2500
(800) 328-9424

Twenty experiments on a wide variety of subjects including: blind spot mapping, towers of Hanoi, reaction time, contrast effects, sentence-picture completion, Stroop effect, Chimeric faces, schedules of reinforcement, mental paper folding, visual effects, neural conduction, scanning short-term memory, sensory homunculus, signal detection, human randomness, digit span, serial position effects, anxiety hierarchy, social dilemma, and semantic memory. Each exercise is a lab experiment that the student performs by himself or herself. The computer leads students through the tasks that make up the exercise, recording their performances as they go. This data is then printed out at the conclusion of the experiment. Because the data is taken from the student's actual performance, it is real, not simulated. The accompanying workbook includes a worksheet for each exercise. Each worksheet asks a series of leading questions that require students to interpret the data they generate. Student manuals sold separately. Detailed manual included.

Classification: General Psychology

Hardware Requirements and Price
IBM PC, XT, AT, PS/2, & compatibles; 320 K; hard disk optional; 1 disk drive. Requires DOS 2.0. *Single User Price: $300.00 (annual site license)*

Mnemonic Demonstration
Bernard C. Beins

Psychology Department
Ithaca College
Ithaca, NY 14850
(607) 274-3304

Two programs for learning foreign language vocabulary with the mnemonic keyboard technique. One is a miniature version of Atkinson and Raugh (1975) study using Russian words. The other involves German words with obvious (Milch=mik), non-obvious (Ave=meadow), or deceptive words (Gift=poison). A third program generates a demonstration of déjà vu in a word-memory format. Instruction booklet included.

Classification: Cognitive Psychology

Hardware Requirements and Price
Apple II, 16 K, hard disk optional, 1 disk drive (5-1/4). *Single User Price: $7.50*

Neurosys
Herbert Levitan

Zoology Department
University of Maryland
College Park, MD 20742
(301) 405-6930

Using a graphic simulation of the electrical behavior of a neuron, students can vary major conditions affecting nerve cell function, and can examine and record all the basic behavioral characteristics of real preparations. On-line help available. Tutorial program included. Latest release September, 1990.

Classification: Physiological Psychology

Hardware Requirements and Price
IBM PC, XT, AT, PS/2, & compatibles; 640 K. CGA, EGA, or VGA display. *Single User Price: $50.00 Network Price: $100.00*

Olfaction
James C. Walker

Bio-Psych Educational Tools
P.O. Box 6436
Winston-Salem, NC 27109
(919) 759-0506

One of eight packages in the series "The Senses." Program employs high quality color images and animation to describe the biochemistry of olfactory transduction, the functional neurology and plasticity of the olfactory system, and current research on the coding of odor quality. Interactive control achieved via a mouse or the keyboard. Program accompanied by 2 X 2 color slides of major screen images. Detailed manual included. Latest release 1991.

Classification: Sensation and Perception

Hardware Requirements and Price
IBM PC, XT, AT, PS/2, & compatibles; 640 K; 10 Mb hard disk required; 2 disk drives. EGA display required. Mouse required. *Single User Price: $159.00 Network Price: $477.00*

Op.Rat
Mark Cunningham

Crofter Publishing
4310 South Semoran, #690
Orlando, FL 32822

A simulation of operant conditioning in rats. On-screen rat may be used to demonstrate shaping, maintenance, extinction, discrimination-learning, and discrimination-reversal. Each student may have his or her own colony on disk. Screen display includes a cumulative recorder. Detailed manual included.

Classification: Learning

Hardware Requirements and Price
Apple II+, IIe, IIc, IIgs; 64 K; hard disk optional; 1 disk drive. Requires ProDOS. *Single User Price: $90.00*

IBM PC, XT, AT, PS/2, & compatibles; hard disk optional; 1 disk drive (5-1/4). CGA display required. Requires DOS 2.1. *Single User Price: $90.00*

Operant Conditioning Control
T. B. Perera

Life Science Associates
1 Fenimore Road
Bayport, NY 11705-2115

(516) 472-2111
Fax: (516) 472-8146

Operant chamber control program that supports 11 schedules of reinforcement, under experimenter control. Response and reinforcement data are continually displayed and updated on the screen during conditioning.

Classification: Learning

Hardware Requirements and Price
Apple II+, IIe. #530A interface required. *Single User Price: $75.00*

Paired Associates
Rosamond Gianutsos

Life Science Associates
1 Fenimore Road
Bayport, NY 11705-2115
(516) 472-2111
Fax: (516) 472-8146

Pairs of unrelated words are displayed for study. The user tries to learn the pairs so that the second word can be typed when the computer presents the first. The number of pairs and study time can be varied to change task difficulty. The exercise promotes associative verbal learning skills. Interference may be given between trials to prevent reliance on rote short-term memory.

Classification: Cognitive Psychology

Hardware Requirements and Price
Apple II, 64 K, 10 Mb hard disk optional, 1 disk drive (5-1/4). Monochrome or color display. *Single User Price: $50.00*

IBM PC, XT, AT, PS/2, & compatibles; 128 K; 20 Mb hard disk optional; 1 disk drive. CGA,

EGA, or VGA display. *Single User Price: $50.00*

The PC As A Laboratory Instrument
S. C. Fowler

Life Science Associates
1 Fenimore Road
Bayport, NY 11705-2115
(516) 472-2111
Fax: (516) 472-8146

A two-part package for use in the development of instrumentation skills, graduate training programs, and as a laboratory resource. Basic functions from Part I, Lab Assistant, may be implemented immediately. Refinements requiring editing or coding can be added under tutorial guidance from Part II, Lab Tutorial. Detailed manual included. Latest release 1989.

Classification: Experimental Psychology

Hardware Requirements and Price
IBM PC, XT, AT, PS/2, & compatibles; 512 K. Color display optional. *Single User Price: $345.00*

pcSTEREOSCOPE/Vision Lab
Dan Swift

Vision Research Graphics, Inc.
99 Madbury Road
Durham, NH 03824
(603) 868-2270

A sophisticated sensation/perception teaching laboratory. This hardware and software system achieves stereoscopic effects through electronic shutter glasses. Experiments and demonstrations include: illusions, spatial frequency shift, apparent size variation with disparity, length discrimination, apparent and relative motion, random dot stereograms, after-effects, kinetic depth effect, and subjective contours. Detailed manual included. On-line help available. Latest release March, 1991.

Classification: Sensation and Perception

Hardware Requirements and Price
IBM PC, XT, AT, PS/2, & compatibles; 640 K; 2 Mb hard disk optional; 1 disk drive. EGA or VGA display. Mouse optional. Not compatible with laser printer. Requires DOS 3.3. *Single User Price: $450.00 (pcSTEREOSCOPE hardware), $600.00 (Vision Lab software for one computer), $1,500.00 (Vision Lab software for an unlimited number of computers)*

User Site References
William Hayes, Psychology Department, Albion College, Albion, MI, 49224, (517) 629-0278

John Sparrow, Department of Psychology, SUNY College at Geneseo, Department of Psychology, Geneseo, NY, 14454, (716) 245-5202

David Westendorf, Psychology - MEMH - 216, University of Arkansas, Fayetteville, AR, 72701, (501) 575-4256

Perception: A Computerized Approach
Theodore T. Hirota

Life Science Associates
1 Fenimore Road
Bayport, NY 11705-2115
(516) 472-2111
Fax: (516) 472-8146

Using high-resolution EGA/VGA graphics, sound, movement and text, this program covers five categories of perception. Topics dealt with include energy, light and color, the visual system, demonstrations of visual phenomena, theory and methodology, and experiments in perception and psychophysics. Students may work independently or in groups using the programs and lab manuals. Detailed manual included. Latest release 1991.

Classification: Sensation and Perception

Hardware Requirements and Price
IBM PC, XT, AT, PS/2, & compatibles; 640 K; 5 Mb hard disk optional; 1 disk drive. EGA or VGA display. *Single User Price: $295.00 Network Price: $885.00 Individual programs available for $70.00*

Perceptual Identification Routines for the Macintosh
John O. Brooks III

VA Medical Center (151Y)
3801 Miranda Avenue
Palo Alto, CA 94304
(415) 493-5000

Routines that can be used with Microsoft BASIC for the Macintosh to perform standard perceptual identification techniques. Instruction booklet included.

Classification: Sensation and Perception

Hardware Requirements and Price
Macintosh, 1 Mb, hard disk optional, 1 disk drive. *Single User Price: $6.00*

Reviews
Brooks, J. O. (1987). Enhancing and degrading visual stimuli. *Behavioral Research Methods, Instruments, & Computers, 19*, 260-269.

Peripheral Somatosensory System
Joel D. Greenspan

Bio-Psych Educational Tools
P.O. Box 6436
Winston-Salem, NC 27109
(919) 759-0506

Program is part of the series "The Senses." High quality color images and animation are used to explain the structure and function of different types of cutaneous receptors and describe the transmission of impulses from the body surface to the central nervous system (CNS). Mouse is used for interactive control. Slides of important screen images (measuring 2 X 2) are part of the software package. Detailed manual included. Latest release 1987.

Classification: Sensation and Perception

Hardware Requirements and Price
IBM PC, XT, AT, PS/2, & compatibles; 640 K; 10 Mb hard disk required; 2 disk drives. EGA display. Mouse required. *Single User Price: $169.00 Network Price: $507.00*

User Site References
John Batson, Department of Psychology, Furman University, Poinselt Highway, Greenville, SC, 29613
Steve Southall, Lynchburg College, 1501 Lakeside Drive, Lynchburg, VA, 24501-3199

Piaget's Cognitive Operations
M.D. Morgan
D. McBride

Life Science Associates
1 Fenimore Road
Bayport, NY 11705-2115
(516) 472-2111
Fax: (516) 472-8146

A computerized version of a chemistry program used by Jean Piaget in his studies of intellectual development. The computer presents a simple lab in which colorless chemicals can be mixed in beakers. Subjects are asked to find all combinations that produce a colored result when mixed. Depending on the combinations tried, the program reports the use by subjects of formal operations, incomplete formal operations, advanced concrete operations, or concrete operations. Instruction booklet included.

Classification: General Psychology

Hardware Requirements and Price
Apple II+, IIe, IIc; 64 K; 10 Mb hard disk optional; 1 disk drive (5-1/4). Monochrome or color display. *Single User Price: $40.00*

IBM PC, XT, AT, PS/2, & compatibles; 128 K; 20 Mb hard disk optional; 1 disk drive. CGA, EGA, or VGA display. *Single User Price: $40.00*

Problem Solving Sets
C. Michael Levy
Grant J. Levy

Life Science Associates
1 Fenimore Road
Bayport, NY 11705-2115
(516) 472-2111
Fax: (516) 472-8146

A computer adaptation of the Luchins task that requires subjects to obtain a specific quantity of water by measuring with three different sized containers. The program demonstrates that after experience with a solution rule that works, few people use a simpler rule when the problem permits it. Instruction booklet included.

Classification: Cognitive Psychology

Hardware Requirements and Price
Apple II, 64 K, 10 Mb hard disk optional, 1 disk drive (5-1/4). Monochrome or color display. *Single User Price: $40.00 Network Price: $120.00*

IBM PC, XT, AT, PS/2, & compatibles; 128 K; 20 Mb hard disk optional; 1 disk drive. CGA display required. *Single User Price: $40.00 Network Price: $120.00*

The Psychiatric Interview Series, Module II
Lee Bairnsfather
Paul Ware

Health Sciences Consortium
201 Silver Cedar Court
Chapel Hill, NC 27514
(919) 942-8731

Interactive videodisk software presents selected segments from the initial interview between a psychiatrist and a young woman who was admitted to the psychiatric ward on the previous night after an attempted suicide. The program allows the student to place themselves in the role of psychiatrist by requiring them to answer questions or select responses related to the segments. Detailed manual included.

Classification: Abnormal Psychology

Hardware Requirements and Price
IBM PC, XT, AT, PS/2, & compatibles; 640 K; 20 Mb hard disk required; 1 disk drive. IBM InfoWindows touch display monitor and videodisk player required. *Single User Price: $1,300.00*

Psychlab

Elizabeth Levin
JoAnn Comito

Queue, Inc.
338 Commerce Drive
Fairfield, CT 06430
(203) 335-0906
(800) 232-2224
Fax: (203) 336-2481

A series of experiments in perception, memory, and learning that allow the student to be the experimenter or subject. Data can be collected, saved, and analyzed later. Detailed manual included.

Classification: Experimental Psychology

Hardware Requirements and Price
Apple II+, IIe, IIc, IIgs; 64 K; disk drive (5-1/4). *Single User Price: $49.95*

Psychological Disorders 1.0

Douglas L. Chute
Margaret E. Kliss

Maclaboratory, Inc.
314 Exeter Road
Devon, PA 19333
(215) 688-3114

A group of hypercard stacks that present case studies, diagnostic criteria, and diagnostic decision trees, based on the *DSM-III-R*. An accompanying introduction and laboratory manual are used to structure a self-discovery teaching approach for students in abnormal or clinical courses. Instruction booklet and tutorial program included. On-line help available. Latest release September, 1991.

Classification: Abnormal Psychology

Hardware Requirements and Price
Macintosh, 1 Mb, 20 Mb hard disk required, 1 disk drive (3-1/2). Monochrome or color display. Mouse required. Modem optional. Laser printer optional. Requires System 6.0.7. *Single User Price: $79.95*

Psychological Testing Demonstration

Bernard C. Beins

Department of Psychology
Ithaca College
Ithaca, NY 14850
(607) 274-3304

Program administers a bogus personality inventory designed to teach students about test administration, interpretation, and caution about accepting test results. Instruction booklet included.

Classification: Psychological Testing

Hardware Requirements and Price
Apple II+, IIe, IIc, IIgs; 16 K; hard disk optional; 1 disk drive. *Single User Price: $7.50*

Psychology On a Disk

E. Shimoff
B. A. Matthews
A. C. Catania

CMS Software
P.O. Box 1514
Columbia, MD 21044-0514
(410) 730-7833

A collection of interactive experiments for courses in general psychology. Programs include: horizontal-vertical illusion, goal-setting, guilt detection, shaping, problem solving, personality evaluation, social perception, cooperation and competition, memory span, and prejudice. New version with added programs will be available fall, 1992. Detailed manual included. Latest release 1990.

Classification: General Psychology

Hardware Requirements and Price
IBM PC, XT, AT, PS/2, & compatibles; 64 K; 1 disk drive. CGA display. Not compatible with laser printer. *Single User Price: $11.95*

Reviews
Hyten, C. (1989). A review of CMS software's psychology on a disk. *The Behavior Analyst, 12*, 227-232.

Psychotherapy
C. Michael Levy
Grant J. Levy

Life Science Associates
1 Fenimore Road
Bayport, NY 11705-2115
(516) 472-2111
Fax: (516) 472-8146

Based on Eliza, the program Weizenbaum at Massachusetts Institute of Technology (MIT) designed to illustrate artificial intelligence, Psychotherapy simulates a Rogerian therapy session. The subject "talks" to the therapist via the keyboard and the therapist "talks" back in a surprisingly intelligent and empathetic manner. Principles of the Rogerian method are illustrated as are rudiments of computer artificial intelligence. Instruction booklet included.

Classification: Abnormal Psychology

Hardware Requirements and Price
Apple II+, IIe, IIc; 64 K; 10 Mb hard disk optional; 1 disk drive (5-1/4). Monochrome or color display. *Single User Price: $40.00*

IBM PC, XT, AT, PS/2, & compatibles; 128 K; 20 Mb hard disk optional; 1 disk drive. CGA, EGA, or VGA display. *Single User Price: $40.00*

PsychSim II
Thomas E. Ludwig

Worth Publishers, Inc.
33 Irving Place
New York, NY 10003
(212) 475-6000
(800) 223-1715

Sixteen programs designed to simulate psychological processes or demonstrate classic experiments. Program modules include: neural messages, hemispheric specialization, cognitive development, the auditory system, visual illusions, classical conditioning, operant conditioning, maze learning, iconic memory, forgetting, hunger and the fat rat, mystery client, computer therapist, social decision making, descriptive statistics, and correlation. Programs are designed for individual or small group use. Note: Iconic memory program is not included in the Gray: Psychology package. Instruction booklet included.

Classification: General Psychology

Hardware Requirements and Price
IBM PC, XT, AT, PS/2, & compatibles; 256 K; hard disk optional; 1 disk drive. CGA, EGA,

or VGA display. Requires DOS 2.1. *Single User Price: $559.95 (nonadopters) Free to schools adopting Myer's book* Exploring Psychology *or Gray's book* Psychology.

Macintosh, 1 Mb, hard disk optional, 1 disk drive (3-1/2). Requires System 6.0.2. *Single User Price: $559.95 (nonadopters) Free to schools adopting Myer's book* Exploring Psychology *or Gray's book* Psychology.

Psychware
Robert S. Slotnick

West Publishing Company
50 West Kellogg Boulevard
P.O. Box 6452
St. Paul, MN 55164-1003
(612) 228-2500
(800) 328-9424

Psychware is a collection of 10 programs for general psychology that make complex concepts more concrete and manageable for students. It helps students become aware of the processes involved in analyzing data and making inferences. Faculty and student guides are included. Instruction booklet included.

Classification: General Psychology

Hardware Requirements and Price
Apple II+, IIe, IIc; 64 K; hard disk optional; 1 disk drive (5-1/4). *Single User Price: $249.95 Additional Support Package: $59.95 Substantial discount for users of West texts*

PsychWorld 2E
John C. Hay

McGraw-Hill College Division
1221 Avenue of the Americas

New York, NY 10020
(800) 338-3987

A set of interactive graphics simulations of classic experiments in psychology, designed for classroom or individual use. The modules include: split-brain syndrome, split-brain model, brain localization, sleep and dreams, classical conditioning, operant conditioning, short-term memory and chunking, color sensation, perception of space and motion, feature detection neurons, development in infancy, psychoanalysis of a dream, abnormal behavior, and statistical microworld. Detailed manual included. Latest release 1991.

Classification: General Psychology

Hardware Requirements and Price
Apple II+, IIe, IIc; 128 K; 2 disk drives (5-1/4). Monochrome display preferred. *Single User Price: $550.00 Substantial discounts to textbook-adopting schools*

IBM PC, XT, AT, PS/2, & compatibles; 512 K; hard disk optional; 1 disk drive. Color display required. Requires DOS 3.1. *Single User Price: $500.00 Substantial discounts to textbook-adopting schools*

Reinforcement Schedules
Michael Levy
Grant Levy

Life Science Associates
1 Fenimore Road
Bayport, NY 11705-2115
(516) 472-2111
Fax: (516) 472-8146

Reinforcement Schedules is a tool for learning the logic of the major schedules of reinforcement and for simulating the operation of the cumulative recorder. The program shows and defines fixed and variable interval and ratio schedules. It gives the user an opportunity to respond and see a response record for each schedule. Instruction booklet included.

Classification: Learning

Hardware Requirements and Price
Apple II, 64 K, 10 Mb hard disk optional, 1 disk drive (5-1/4). Monochrome or color display. *Single User Price: $40.00*

IBM PC, XT, AT, PS/2, & compatibles; 128 K; 20 Mb hard disk optional; 1 disk drive. CGA, EGA, or VGA display. *Single User Price: $40.00*

Release From P.I.
Susan M. Belmore

CAUSE Project
Department of Psychology
University of Kentucky
Lexington, KY 40506
(606) 257-6839

This module demonstrates the phenomenon of release from proactive interference, provides an example of methods used to study coding categories in human memory, and illustrates the advantages and disadvantages of within-subjects designs. Before using this module students should understand the concepts of independent and dependent variables, within-subjects variables, extraneous variables, and sequencing effects. The program allows students to act as subjects or experimenters. Detailed manual included.

Classification: Cognitive Psychology

Hardware Requirements and Price
Apple II+, IIe, IIc, IIgs; 48 K; 1 disk drive (5-1/4). *Single User Price: $20.00*

Rw Model
H. Lachnit
R. L. Schneider
O.V. Lipp

Department of Psychology
University of Giessen
6300 Giessen
Federal Republic of Germany, Germany
064017025437

Turbo Pascal program that simulates the Rescorla-Wagner model of classical conditioning. Instruction booklet included. Latest release 1988.

Classification: Learning

Hardware Requirements and Price
IBM PC, XT, AT, PS/2, & compatibles; 512 K; hard disk optional; 1 disk drive (5-1/4). Hercules graphics required. *Single User Price: $15.00*

Reviews
Lachnit, H., Schneider, R. L., & Lipp, O. V. (1988). RwModel: A program in Turbo Pascal for simulating predictions based on the Rescorla-Wagner model of classical conditioning. *Behavior, Research Methods, Instrumentation, and Computers, 20*, 413-415.

School Psychologist Simulation (SPS)
Morton Isaacs
Virginia Costenbader
Margery Reading-Brow

Psychology Department
Rochester Institute of Technology
One Lomb Memorial Drive
Rochester, NY 14623
(716) 475-2422

The user acts like a school psychologist, handling children referred for assessment. The user may conduct interviews with parents and teachers, observe classroom behavior, examine records, and can administer more than 50 tests to the child. The program automatically records the sequence of actions taken and the user's final report on the child that can be done in multiple-choice or written format. An instructor's aid program allows the instructor to alter all case material and many forms. Detailed manual included. Latest release November 20, 1991.

Classification: School Psychology

Hardware Requirements and Price
Macintosh, 500 K, 1 Mb hard disk optional, 1 disk drive (3-1/2). Mouse optional. Laser printer optional. *Single User Price: $125.00 Network Price: $350.00*

Self-Assessment in Biofeedback I and II
Greg Luterman
Mark Rochotte

Biosource Software
4 Sunrise Lane
Kirksville, MO 63501
(816) 665-5751

Two programs featuring multiple-choice test questions on theory, physiology, instrumentation, research, and clinical applications of biofeedback. Twenty-five question multiple-choice tests with immediate feedback can be randomly generated. Fifty- or one-hundred-question diagnostic comprehensive exams can also be created. Instruction booklet included. Latest release 1991.

Classification: Physiological Psychology

Hardware Requirements and Price
Apple II, 64 K, 2 disk drives (5-1/4). Color display optional. *Single User Price: $49.95*

IBM PC, XT, AT, PS/2, & compatibles; 128 K; 1 disk drive. Color display optional. *Single User Price: $49.95*

User Site References
Robert Hoyt, University of Wisconsin-Stoot, University Counseling Center, Menomonie, WI, 54751, (715) 232-2468

Self-Assessment in Psychology
Greg Luterman
Mark Rochotte

Biosource Software
4 Sunrise Lane
Kirksville, MO 63501
(816) 665-5751

An examination system that provides immediate student feedback. Includes mastery tests of learning, cognition, sensation, perception, comparative, personality, abnormal, clinical, developmental, social, history, measurement, and statistics content areas. Instruction booklet included. Latest release 1991.

Classification: General Psychology

Hardware Requirements and Price
Apple II, 64 K, 2 disk drives (5-1/4). Color display optional. Requires DOS 3.3. *Single User Price: $49.95 Site license available*

IBM PC, XT, AT, PS/2, & compatibles; 128 K; 1 disk drive. Color display optional. Requires DOS 2.0. *Single User Price: $49.95 Site license available*

User Site References
Michele Martel, Northeast Missouri State University, McClaen Hall 214, Kirksville, MO, 63501, (816) 785-4000

Self-Assessment in Stress Management
Greg Luterman
Mark Rochotte

Biosource Software
4 Sunrise Lane
Kirksville, MO 63501
(816) 665-5751

Self-Assessment in Stress Management contains 500 multiple-choice questions covering stress concepts, personality, stress physiology, stress disorders, and stress interventions. This product can be used to randomly select 10- or 25-question tests covering separate areas, or 50- or 100-question comprehensive exams. Performance is reported separately for each subject area.   Instruction booklet included. Latest release 1991.

Classification: Personal Growth

Hardware Requirements and Price
Apple II, 64 K, 20 Mb hard disk optional, 1 disk drive (5-1/4). Monochrome or color display. Modem optional. Laser printer optional. Requires DOS 3.3. *Single User Price: $49.95 Site license available*

IBM PC, XT, AT, PS/2, & compatibles; 64 K; 20 Mb hard disk optional; 1 disk drive. CGA display required.   Modem optional.   Laser

printer optional.   Requires DOS 2.0.   *Single User Price: $49.95 Site license available*

User Site References
Robert Hoyt, University of Wisconsin-Stout, University Counseling Center-BF Lab, Menomonie, WI, 54751, (715) 232-2468
Ron Krebill, St. Louis University Medical Center, 1221 S. Grand, St. Louis, MO, 63501, (314) 577-8703
Mark S. Schwartz, Mayo Clinic-Jacksonville, 4500 San Pablo Road, Jacksonville, FL, 32224, (904) 223-2000

Self-Guided Study Program (SGS)
Kathy Sexton-Radek

Elmhurst College
Department of Psychology
190 Prospect
Elmhurst, IL 60126
(708) 617-3587

A computerized, interactive study program that has features to allow students to track their study efforts, keep records of their grades and assignments, work on assignments on the computer and learn about access to Network systems at Elmhurst College. This program was written using Macintosh software to be consistent with typical Macintosh syntax. It uses a rolodex metaphor to organize information. Each segment of the program is represented by a card. The seven cards within the SGS program are introduction, communications, study development, academic calendar, study guide, to do list, and class progress. Detailed manual included.

Classification: Study Skills

Hardware Requirements and Price
Macintosh. *Single User Price: Contact author*

Shaping Behavior

C. Michael Levy
Grant J. Levy

Life Science Associates
1 Fenimore Road
Bayport, NY 11705-2115
(516) 472-2111
Fax: (516) 472-8146

Program's *globulus undulata* can be taught to move to a goal box. Students discover which variables determine how this new organism "learns." Instruction booklet included.

Classification: Learning

Hardware Requirements and Price
Apple II, 64 K, 10 Mb hard disk optional, 1 disk drive (5-1/4). Monochrome or color display. Printer optional. *Single User Price: $40.00*

IBM PC, XT, AT, PS/2, & compatibles; 128 K; 20 Mb hard disk optional; 1 disk drive. CGA display required. Printer optional. *Single User Price: $40.00*

Sibex-Inferential Statistics by Experimentation

Stephen Jarrell

William C. Brown Publishers
2460 Kerper Blvd.
Dubuque, IA 52001
(319) 588-1451
(800) 351-7671

Teaches the concepts of sampling distribution, confidence limits, probability levels, and hypothesis testing for population means. The user can input and save any data set as a population. Data files can be edited. Repeated samples can be generated automatically with and without replacement. Sample statistics are displayed, along with frequency distributions and histograms. Detailed manual included.

Classification: Statistics

Hardware Requirements and Price
IBM PC, XT, AT, PS/2, & compatibles; 256 K; hard disk optional; 1 disk drive. *Single User Price: $24.00 Site License: $400.00*

Siminteract

Donald E. Muir

William C. Brown Publishers
2460 Kerper Blvd.
Dubuque, IA 52001
(319) 588-1451
(800) 351-7671

A simulation system based on stimulus-response learning theory. Comes with several simulated experiments, or instructors can create their own. Simulations can pit students against each other, against the computer, or operate entirely automatically. Detailed manual included.

Classification: Learning

Hardware Requirements and Price
IBM PC, XT, AT, PS/2, & compatibles; 256 K; hard disk optional; 1 disk drive. *Single User Price: $30.00 Site License: $400.00*

Social Cognition

John Mueller
Burt Thompson

AB i
2124 Kittendge, Suite 215
Berkeley, CA 94704
(510) 582-6343

Four experiments allow students to participate as subjects, or recruit other students to serve as subjects, and then obtain group summary data to be used for class discussion or report writing. All experiments use a self-reference orienting task. Latency data and incidental memory measures are collected for items involved in the self-descriptiveness and other-descriptiveness decisions. Detailed manual included.

Classification: Social Psychology

Hardware Requirements and Price
Apple II+, IIe, IIc; 48 K; 1 disk drive (5-1/4). *Single User Price: $50.00 Site License: $300.00*

IBM PC, XT, AT, PS/2, & compatibles; 256 K; hard disk optional; 1 disk drive. *Single User Price: $50.00 Site License: $300.00*

Macintosh, 1 Mb, hard disk optional, 1 disk drive. *Single User Price: $50.00 Site License: $300.00*

Social Power Game

Robert Leik
Ronald E. Anderson

McGraw-Hill College Division
1221 Avenue of the Americas
New York, NY 10020

An instructional game designed to teach undergraduate students the nature and process of power relationships. Instruction booklet included. On-line help available.

Classification: Social Psychology

Hardware Requirements and Price
IBM PC, XT, AT, PS/2, & compatibles. Requires DOS 2.1. *Single User Price: Contact publisher.*

Sociology on a Disk

B. A. Matthews
E. Shimoff
A. C. Catania

CMS Software
P.O. Box 1514
Columbia, MD 21044-0514
(410) 730-7833

Nine interactive programs in sociology, including evolution of cooperation, social decision making, collective behavior, correlation, occupational prestige, and seriousness of crimes. The new version will be available in the fall of 1992. Detailed manual included. Latest release 1990.

Classification: Social Psychology

Hardware Requirements and Price
IBM PC, XT, AT, PS/2, & compatibles; 64 K; 1 disk drive. Not compatible with laser printer. *Single User Price: $11.95*

SPSS/PC+, Studentware

SPSS, Inc.
444 N. Michigan Avenue
Chicago, IL 60611

(312) 329-3500
(800) 543-6609

Student version of SPSS combines capabilities of SPSS-X and SPSS/PC+. Features immediate error checking, statistical glossary, and on-line help. Text book included. Can read and write SPSS/PC+ system files. Separate versions available for social sciences and business. Detailed manual included. On-line help available. Latest release 1991.

Classification: Statistics

Hardware Requirements and Price
IBM PC, XT, AT, PS/2, & compatibles; 512 K; hard disk optional; 2 disk drives. Hercules, CGA, EGA, or VGA display. Requires DOS 3.0. *Single User Price: $34.95*

Reviews
Butler, D. L., & Neudecker W. (1989). A comparison of inexpensive statistical packages for microcomputers running MS-DOS. *Behavior, Research Methods, Instrumentation, and Computers, 21,* 113-120.

Jurie, J. D. (1989). Working With SPSS/PC+ Studentware. *Social Science Computer Review, 7,* 311-314.

START: Tools for Experiments in Memory, Learning, Cognition, & Perception
Robert J. Gregory
Stephen A. Poffel

Conduit
University of Iowa-Oakdale Campus
Iowa City, IA 52242
(319) 335-4100
(800) 365-9774

START is a set of 15 programs that provide students with hands-on experience in designing and conducting psychological research. The package transforms the microcomputer into a set of specialized research tools that present stimuli and record responses–tools such as the tachistoscope, memory drum, reaction timer, visual stimulus display, and audio tape. The users guide included in the package describes each program, its operation, the research and literature related to it, and suggested projects for use. Detailed manual included.

Classification: Experimental Psychology

Hardware Requirements and Price
Apple II+, IIe, IIc, IIgs; 48 K; 2 disk drives. Color display optional. *Single User Price: $165.00*

IBM PC, XT, AT, PS/2, & compatibles; 256 K; 2 disk drives. Color display optional. *Single User Price: $165.00 Network Price: $990.00*

Reviews
Brown, J. (1988, May). START: Stimulus and response tools for experiments in memory, learning, cognition, and perception. *The Science Teacher,* 78.

Ricketts, C. L. (1987). START. *Social Science Microcomputer Review, 5*(4), 584.

Stat-Tutor
Jon Glase

Exceller Software Corporation
223 Langmuir Lab
Ithaca, NY 14850
(607) 257-5634
(800) 426-0444

Software system for introducing students to the use of statistics. Includes a series of interactive self-paced tutorials and a powerful, easy-to-use data analysis utility called Ministat. The tutorials cover major topics such as probability, hypothesis testing, descriptive statistics, the normal distribution, and experimental design. Detailed manual included.

Classification: Statistics

Hardware Requirements and Price
IBM PC, XT, AT, PS/2, & compatibles; hard disk required. CGA, EGA, or VGA display. Mouse optional. *Single User Price: $95.00 Network Price: $395.00*

Statistical Computation Package for Students
W. Kirk Richardson

McGraw-Hill College Division
1221 Avenue of the Americas
New York, NY 10020
(800) 338-3987

Designed for students enrolled in introductory psychology and other beginning behavioral science statistics courses. The program allows users to quickly calculate many of the standard statistical measurements commonly employed in behavioral science research. Instruction booklet included. Latest release 1989.

Classification: Statistics

Hardware Requirements and Price
IBM PC, XT, AT, PS/2, & compatibles; 256 K; hard disk optional; 1 disk drive. Monochrome or color display. Requires DOS 2.1. *Single User Price: $29.95*

Apple II, 128 K, 2 disk drives (5-1/4). Monochrome or color, 80-column display. Requires ProDOS. *Single User Price: $13.95*

Statistical Consultant
Robert P. Sechrist

William C. Brown Publishers
2460 Kerper Blvd.
Dubuque, IA 52001
(319) 588-1451
(800) 351-7671

Expert system designed to help researchers and students select the appropriate statistic for a given application.

Classification: Statistics

Hardware Requirements and Price
IBM PC, XT, AT, PS/2, & compatibles. *Single User Price: $32.50 Site License: $400.00*

Statistics Software for Microcomputers

Kern International, Inc.
575 Washington Street
P.O. Box 308
Pembroke, MA 02359
(617) 871-4982

A statistical package with 19 procedures used primarily for teaching statistics.

Classification: Statistics

Hardware Requirements and Price
IBM PC, XT, AT, PS/2, & compatibles; 256 K. Color display required. *Single User Price: $75.00*

Reviews
Quast, T. E. (1988). Statistics software for microcomputers. *Social Science Computer Review*, 6, 155-156.

Statistics Tutor: Tutorial & Computational Software for the Behavioral Sciences

Joseph D. Allen
David J. Pittenger

John Wiley & Sons
605 Third Avenue
New York, NY 10158-0012
(212) 850-6212

Program has two parts. Part 1 is a statistical tutorial containing interactive and graphical demonstration of distributions, histograms and polygons, correlation and regression, normal curve, central limit theorem, general linear additive model, power, interactions, and several probability functions. Part II is a complete statistical package containing a data editor and data analysis programs for descriptive statistics, F-tests, ANOVA (up to 9 variables), correlation and regression, chi square, and a statistics calculator. Detailed manual included. Latest release February 15, 1991.

Classification: Statistics

Hardware Requirements and Price
IBM PC, XT, AT, PS/2, & compatibles; 128 K; hard disk optional; 2 disk drives. CGA display. Laser printer optional. Requires DOS 2.0. *Single User Price: $21.95*

Statistics Tutorial

Joseph D. Allen

Department of Psychology
University of Georgia
Athens, GA 30602
(404) 542-3100

Four programs graphically demonstrate frequency distributions, areas under the normal curve, central limit theorem, and correlation and scatter plots.

Classification: Statistics

Hardware Requirements and Price
Commodore 64, 64 K, 1 disk drive. Color display required. *Single User Price: $15.00*

StatPatch

Mike Smithson

Intellimation Library for the Macintosh
130 Cremona Drive
P.O. Box 1922
Santa Barbara, CA 93116-1922
(805) 968-2291
(800) 346-8355

A tutorial on ANOVA, chi-square, probability, confidence intervals, significance testing, correlation, and regression. Detailed manual included. Latest release October 1, 1990.

Classification: Statistics

Hardware Requirements and Price
Macintosh, 20 K, 1 Mb hard disk optional, 2 disk drives. Mouse optional. Laser printer optional. Requires System 5.0 or later. *Single User Price: $45.00*

Stress and the Young Adult

Cambridge Career Products
P.O. Box 2153
Charleston, WV 25328-2153
(304) 744-9323
(800) 468-4227

This program enables students to assess and deal with stress in their lives. Instruction booklet included.

Classification: Personal Growth

Hardware Requirements and Price
Apple II, 48 K. *Single User Price: $69.95*

Stroop Effects
C. Michael Levy
Grant J. Levy

Life Science Associates
1 Fenimore Road
Bayport, NY 11705-2115
(516) 472-2111
Fax: (516) 472-8146

A computer version of the Stroop color-word test in which words are presented in various colors. A black and white version using numbers instead of words is included. Instruction booklet included.

Classification: Sensation and Perception

Hardware Requirements and Price
Apple II+, IIe, IIc; 64 K; 10 Mb hard disk optional; 1 disk drive (5-1/4). Color display optional. *Single User Price: $40.00*

IBM PC, XT, AT, PS/2, & compatibles; 128 K; 20 Mb hard disk optional; 1 disk drive. Color display optional. *Single User Price: $40.00*

Survey Sampling
G. Nigel Gilbert

Conduit
University of Iowa-Oakdale Campus
Iowa City, IA 52242

(319) 335-4100
(800) 365-9774

Program enables students to practice survey sampling and compare the merits of four different sampling designs: simple random, stratified, cluster, and quota. Students select the design and number of respondents, the program then samples the population and reports the results. Multiple surveys, with varying sample sizes and designs, can be conducted and the results can be compared. Program also reports on the costs of administering the surveys so students can consider the financial implications of their choices. Detailed manual included.

Classification: Experimental Psychology

Hardware Requirements and Price
Apple II+, IIe, IIc, IIgs; 48 K; 1 disk drive. *Single User Price: $90.00*

IBM PC, XT, AT, PS/2, & compatibles; 128 K; 1 disk drive. CGA, EGA, or VGA display. *Single User Price: $90.00*

Taste
Barry J. Davis

Bio-Psych Educational Tools
P.O. Box 6436
Winston-Salem, NC 27109
(919) 759-0506

Software package utilizes animation and high quality color graphics to describe the location, morphology, and response properties of gustatory and trigeminal receptors in the oral cavity. CNS projections of these receptors are also illustrated. User controls program through use of a mouse or the keyboard. Accompanying the program are 2 X 2 slides of major screen images. Detailed manual included. Latest release late 1992.

Classification: Sensation and Perception

Hardware Requirements and Price
IBM PC, XT, AT, PS/2, & compatibles; 640 K; 10 Mb hard disk required; 2 disk drives. EGA display required. Mouse required. *Single User Price: $159.00 Network Price: $477.00*

Teacher/Trainer Turned Author

Dynacomp, Inc.
The Dynacomp Office Building
178 Phillips Road
Webster, NY 14580
(716) 265-4040
(800) 828-6772

Creates courses with color and graphics. Built-in systems provide fast graphics production, including the ability to freely mix text and color graphics. Word processing system has instant editing and page playback. User controls page sequencing, branching, and loops. True/false, multiple choice, and fill-in the blank questions are supported with embedded student record keeping. Course playback features student log-on, log-off, and automatic reentry at the page of departure. Portable courses that play back without the authoring system can also be created. Three different menu-driven systems are available: System I: Starter, System II: Intermediate, and System III: Expert. Each represents three feature levels. Detailed manual and tutorial program included.

Classification: Management

Hardware Requirements and Price
IBM PC, XT, AT, PS/2, & compatibles; 128 K; hard disk optional; 1 disk drive. Laser printer optional. Requires DOS 2.0. *Single User Price: $89.95 (System I), $239.95 (System II), $374.95 (System III), $9.95 (Demo disk and literature)*

Testgen

John Gillam
Donald Norris
Man M. Sharma

Man M. Sharma
Department of Mathematics
Clark Atlanta University
240 James P. Brawley Drive
Atlanta, GA 30314
(404) 681-8219

Allows students to review course materials in the form of simulated timed practice tests or tests with immediate assistance in the form of hint and solution. Detailed manual included.

Classification: Study Skills

Hardware Requirements and Price
IBM PC, XT, AT, PS/2, & compatibles; 320 K; 10 Mb hard disk required. Mouse optional. Modem optional. Not compatible with laser printer. *Single User Price: $100.00*

User Site References
Del Bice, Heritage College, 3240 Fort Road, Toppenish, WA, 98948, (509) 865-2244
Marilyn Molloy, Our Lady of the Lake University, 411 S.W. 24th Street, San Antonio, TX, 78207, (512) 434-6711

The Academic Software section is dominated by programs appropriate for courses in experimental psychology ($N=31$), statistics ($N=27$), sensation and perception ($N=19$), and cognitive psychology ($N=18$).

Test Writer
Charles F. Cicciarella

Persimmon Software
1910 Gemway Drive
Charlotte, NC 28216
(704) 398-1309

Prepare and maintain files of test questions
and administer tests at the computer. Detailed
manual included.

Classification: Any course

Hardware Requirements and Price
IBM PC, XT, AT, PS/2, & compatibles; 256 K;
5 Mb hard disk optional; 2 disk drives. Printer
optional. Laser printer optional. Requires
DOS 3.0. *Single User Price: $149.00*

Topics in Research Methods: Main Effects and Interactions
Russell H. Fazio
Martin H. Backler

Conduit
University of Iowa-Oakdale Campus
Iowa City, IA 52242
(319) 335-4100
(800) 365-9774

Provides practice identifying independent
variable effects on a dependent variable in a
variety of designs. Five sections introduce
concepts including factorial design and its
notation, 2 x 2 designs and their main effects
and interactions, and 2 x 2 x 2 designs and their
two- and three-way interactions. Detailed
manual included.

Classification: Experimental Psychology

Hardware Requirements and Price
Apple II+, IIe, IIc, IIgs; 64 K; 1 disk drive.
Single User Price: $60.00

IBM PC, XT, AT, PS/2, & compatibles; 256 K;
1 Mb hard disk optional; 1 disk drive (3-1/2).
CGA, EGA, or VGA display. *Single User Price:
$60.00 Network Price: $360.00*

Topics in Research Methods: Power
Russell H. Fazio
Martin H. Backler

Conduit
University of Iowa-Oakdale Campus
Iowa City, IA 52242
(319) 335-4100
(800) 365-9774

Program uses simulated experiments to illustrate the concepts of power and error variance,
focusing on issues such as sample size, reliability, period of observation, homogeneity of
sample, sources of variation, matched pairs,
and repeated measures designs. Detailed
manual included.

Classification: Statistics

Hardware Requirements and Price
Apple II+, IIe, IIc, IIgs; 64 K, 1 disk drive.
Single User Price: $60.00

IBM PC, XT, AT, PS/2, & compatibles; 256 K;
1 Mb hard disk optional; 1 disk drive. CGA,
EGA, or VGA display. *Single User Price:
$60.00 Network Price: $360.00*

Reviews
Kallam, M. (1989). Topics in research methods: Power. *Social Science Computer Review, 7*, 123.

Topics in Research Methods: Survey Sampling

Russell H. Fazio
Martin H. Backler

Conduit
University of Iowa-Oakdale Campus
Iowa City, IA 52242
(319) 335-4100
(800) 365-9774

Simulation introduces concepts involved in surveys and sampling procedures. Students choose topics and specify sample size. Program produces samples and allows students to request stratified and simple random samples. Program conducts polls and displays responses for each alternative with confidence intervals. Detailed manual included.

Classification: Experimental Psychology

Hardware Requirements and Price
Apple II+, IIe, IIc, IIgs; 64 K; 1 disk drive (5-1/4). *Single User Price: $60.00*

IBM PC, XT, AT, PS/2, & compatibles; 256 K; 1 Mb hard disk optional; 1 disk drive. CGA, EGA, or VGA display. *Single User Price: $60.00 Network Price: $360.00*

Reviews
Fazio, R. H., & Backler, M. H. (1985). Topics in Research Methods: Survey Sampling. *Social Science Microcomputer Review, 3,* 392.

Tribbles Apple and Tribbles Revised IBM

R. Von Blum
T. M. Hursh
David G. Schwaegler

Conduit
University of Iowa-Oakdale Campus
Iowa City, IA 52242
(319) 335-4100
(800) 365-9774

Introduction to the scientific method. Students are told they are in a spaceship orbiting an alien planet. Each day they take photographs of the only visible inhabitants–small, round creatures called tribbles. Students search for relationships to explain shifts in patterns of the tribbles' location. Guides students to make detailed systematic observations, and practice hypothesis testing and other scientific methods. Detailed manual included.

Classification: Experimental Psychology

Hardware Requirements and Price
Apple II+, IIe, IIc; 48 K; 1 disk drive (5-1/4). *Single User Price: $50.00*

IBM PC, XT, AT, PS/2, & compatibles; 192 K; 1 Mb hard disk optional; 1 disk drive. *Single User Price: $50.00*

Vistat

Eugene Kroch
Glenn C. Slayden

Economics Hall
Bartley Hall
Villanova University
Villanova, PA 19085
(215) 645-6428

Vistat is short for visual statistics. It is designed to use visual feedback to teach mathematical statistics. Uses a friendly windows environment in which students learn the properties of statistical techniques and can explore and be guided through a wide range of applications. On-line help available. Latest release 1990.

Classification: Statistics

Hardware Requirements and Price
IBM PC, XT, AT, PS/2, & compatibles; 640 K; hard disk required. VGA display. Mouse required. Requires DOS 3.0 and Windows 2.0. *Single User Price: $10.00 Network Price: $50.00*

Visual Illusions: Scientific Problem Solving
Robert Tinker
Tim Barclay
Sean Nolan

Queue, Inc.
338 Commerce Drive
Fairfield, CT 06430
(203) 335-0906
(800) 232-2224
Fax: (203) 336-2481

Program uses six illusions to introduce students (grades 6 to college) to various experimental methods. Helps students learn how to pose questions; solve problems; design experiments; collect, analyze, and compare data; and draw conclusions. Illusions can be changed using the program's figure editor. Detailed manual included.

Classification: Experimental Psychology

Hardware Requirements and Price
Apple II+, IIe, IIc, IIgs; 64 K; 1 disk drive (5-1/4). Printer required. *Single User Price: $69.00*

Vote: A Social Choice Gaming System
Joseph Oppenheimer
Mark Winer
Chad K. McDaniel

Wisc Ware
Academic Computing Center
University of Wisconsin
1210 W. Dayton Street
Madison, WI 53706
(608) 262-8167
(800) 543-3201

A voting game construction kit that allows students to author then play (either on a single machine or over a LAN) a wide variety of interactive scenarios in which decisions are made by a voting process. Participation is useful as a training exercise, as an aid to developing empathic understanding of decision-making through role playing, and as a general learning and research tool for the analysis of behavior. Instruction booklet included. On-line help available. Latest release 1988.

Classification: Social Psychology

Hardware Requirements and Price
IBM PC, XT, AT, PS/2, & compatibles; 512 K; 1.2 Mb hard disk optional; 1 disk drive. VGA display. Mouse required. Requires DOS 3.2. *Single User Price: $25.00 (members), $75.00 (non-members)*

Which Statistic?
O. Zeller Robertson

William C. Brown Publishers
2460 Kerper Blvd.
Dubuque, IA 52001

(319) 588-1451
(800) 351-7671

Using a decision tree structure, the program guides students to the selection of an appropriate measure of significance or association.

Classification: Statistics

Hardware Requirements and Price
IBM PC, XT, AT, PS/2, & compatibles. *Single User Price: $24.00 Site License: $400.00*

Macintosh. *Single User Price: $20.00 Site License: $400.00*

Word Processor/Reference Help
Allen H. Wolach

Department of Psychology
Illinois Institute of Technology
Chicago, IL 60616
(312) 567-3500

The program provides a word processor that is designed to prepare manuscripts in APA (American Psychological Association) format coupled with an easily accessible menu system to help enter references. Detailed manual included. On-line help available.

Classification: Experimental Psychology

Hardware Requirements and Price
IBM PC, XT, AT, PS/2, & compatibles; 512 K; hard disk optional; 1 disk drive. Printer required. Laser printer optional. *Single User Price: $10.00, free with abbreviated manual*

The World of Sidney Slug and His Friends
Loren E. Acker
Bram C. Goldwater

Associates in Analysis of Behavior
16-2330 Harbor Road
Sidney, BC V8L 2P8 Canada
(604) 656-4209

Computer program that introduces the concepts of behavior, reinforcement, extinction, and punishment. Also simulates the use of differential reinforcement and shaping. Detailed manual and tutorial program included. On-line help available. Latest release October, 1991.

Classification: Learning

Hardware Requirements and Price
Apple II+, IIe; 64 K; hard disk optional; 1 disk drive (5-1/4). Requires Apple DOS. *Single User Price: $49.95 Network Price: $350.00*

IBM PC, XT, AT, PS/2, & compatibles; 256 K; hard disk optional; 1 disk drive. Requires DOS 2.0. *Single User Price: $49.95 Network Price: $350.00*

Macintosh, 64 K. *Single User Price: $49.95 Network Price: $350.00*

Reviews
Acker, L. E., Goldwater, B. C., & Agnew, J. L. (1990). Sidney Slug: A computer simulation for teaching shaping without an animal laboratory. *Teaching of Psychology, 17*(2), 130-132.

User Site References
G. Martin, University of Manitoba, Winnepeg, Manitoba, Canada

CLINICAL
SOFTWARE

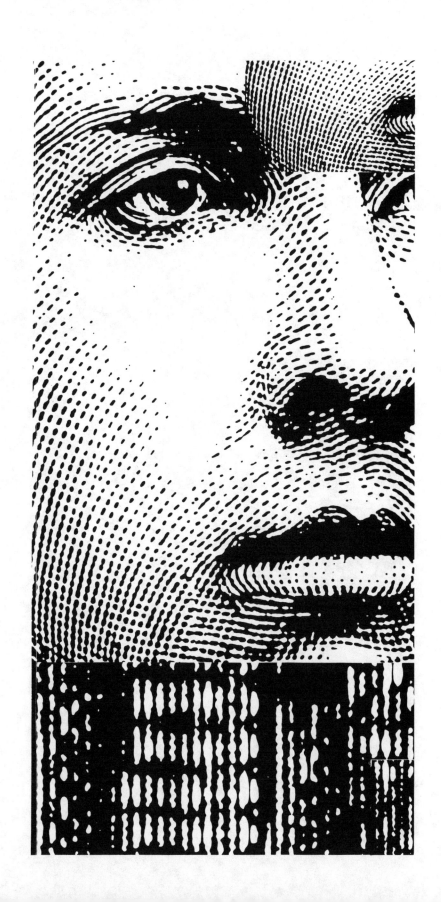

Accountability Plus

The Guidance Shoppe
2909 Brandemere Drive
Tallahassee, FL 32312
(904) 385-6717

Record keeping system for counselors; daily activities are tallied using either the quick log or detailed log. The quick log includes 11 categories, the detailed log includes the same categories, each broken down into subcategories. Information is password protected. Printed reports are available for any specified time period. The program calculates the total number of contracts and the total time and the percentage of time spent in each category. Detailed manual included.

Classification: Counseling Aid

Hardware Requirements and Price
Apple II, 48 K, 1 disk drive (5-1/4). *Single User Price: $79.95*

IBM PC, XT, AT, PS/2, & compatibles; 128 K; hard disk optional; 1 disk drive. *Single User Price: $89.90*

The Answer

The Guidance Shoppe
2909 Brandemere Drive
Tallahassee, FL 32312
(904) 385-6717

This information dissemination program answers the questions students ask over and over again. Personal topics and responses are entered using the built-in word processor. One touch commands and detailed help screens make it easy to use. Create data disks as needed. Printouts are available. Detailed manual included.

Classification: Counseling Aid

Hardware Requirements and Price
Apple II, 48 K, 1 disk drive (5-1/4). *Single User Price: $69.95*

IBM PC, XT, AT, PS/2, & compatibles; 1 disk drive. *Single User Price: $69.95*

Assessment of Career Decision Making

Western Psychological Services
12031 Wilshire Blvd.
Los Angeles, CA 90025
(213) 478-2061
(800) 648-8857

Program provides interpretation of the assessment that measures the strategies that people use in selecting a career. Feedback includes a group summary, a counselor's report, and a student's report. Each report provides interpretive information and a narrative description of the student's decision making style and his/her progress in making a career choice. Price depends upon the number of assessments. A teleprocessing service.

Classification: Career Counseling

Hardware Requirements and Price
Contact publisher for hardware options. *Single User Price: $75.00*

At Ease!

Giles D. Rainwater

Psychometric Software, Inc.
P.O. Box 1677
Melbourne, FL 32902-1677
(407) 729-6390
(800) 882-9811

Aids in learning and practicing relaxation. Contains seven techniques ranging from active to passive. Session lengths vary from 20 sec. to 20 min. Detailed manual included. Latest release 1985.

Classification: Relaxation Training

Hardware Requirements and Price
Apple II+, IIe, IIc, IIgs; 128 K; 1 disk drive (5-1/4). Monochrome display. Printer required. Will not run on hard drive. *Single User Price: $69.95*

IBM PC, XT, AT, PS/2, & compatibles; 10 Mb hard disk optional; 1 disk drive. Monochrome, CGA, EGA, or VGA display. Printer required. Can be run on Macintosh systems operating under SoftPC. *Single User Price: $69.95 Network Price: $69.95 plus $34.98 for each additional user*

BestChoice3

Sterling Castle
2532 Lincoln Blvd.
Marina del Rey, CA 90291
(213) 306-3020

Decision support software that bases conclusions on paired comparisons of alternatives. Employs user-identified judgment criteria and decision-makers. Detailed manual included.

On-line help available. Latest release December, 1990.

Classification: Industrial Consulting

Hardware Requirements and Price
IBM PC, XT, AT, PS/2, & compatibles; 256 K; 150 K hard disk optional. Mouse optional. Laser printer optional. *Single User Price: $99.00*

C-lect

Chronicle Guidance Publications, Inc.
Aurora Street Extension
P.O. Box 1190
Moravia, NY 13118-1190
(315) 497-0330
(800) 622-7284

A career guidance program that uses temperament and interest surveys to identify occupations. Detailed manual included. Latest release 1991.

Classification: Career Counseling

Hardware Requirements and Price
Apple II. Laser printer optional. *Single User Price: $900.00*

IBM PC, XT, AT, PS/2, & compatibles; 10 Mb hard disk required. Laser printer optional. *Single User Price: $900.00*

C-lect, Jr.

Chronicle Guidance Publications, Inc.
Aurora Street Extension
P.O. Box 1190
Moravia, NY 13118-1190

(315) 497-0330
(800) 622-7284

Self-assessment and career exploration program for grades 7 through 10. Detailed manual included.

Classification: Career Counseling

Hardware Requirements and Price
Apple II. *Single User Price: $199.90*

IBM PC, XT, AT, PS/2, & compatibles. *Single User Price: $199.90*

Career Counselor

Intellectual Software/Division of Queue
338 Commerce Drive
Fairfield, CT 06430
(203) 335-0906
(800) 232-2224
Fax: (203) 336-2481

By analyzing their likes and dislikes, Career Counselor helps users learn how to choose a satisfying career. Instruction booklet included.

Classification: Career Counseling

Hardware Requirements and Price
Apple II, 64 K. *Single User Price: $59.95*

Career Directions

Cambridge Career Products
P.O. Box 2153
Charleston, WV 25328-2153
(304) 744-9323
(800) 468-4227

Provides self and occupational exploratory activities that develop a profile of career interests and other interests and abilities. The program delineates specific occupations that relate to the profile, and involve users in developing specific plans to enter the occupation of their choice. Instruction booklet included. Latest release 1982.

Classification: Career Counseling

Hardware Requirements and Price
Apple II, 48 K, 2 disk drives (5-1/4). Not compatible with laser printer. *Single User Price: $89.00*

IBM PC, XT, AT, PS/2, & compatibles; 128 K; 2 disk drives. Not compatible with laser printer. *Single User Price: $89.00*

Career Directions Inventory (CDI)
Douglas N. Jackson

Sigma Assessment Systems, Inc.
P.O. Box 610984
Port Huron, MI 48061-0984
(800) 265-1285

On-site software administers and scores 100 triads of statements describing job-related activities, yielding a sex-fair profile of 15 basic interest scales. The CDI Extended Report contains profiles of the 15 basic interest scales, including similarity to 100 specialty groups, general occupational themes, 22 specialty clusters, as well as administrative indices. Interpretive paragraphs, associated with Department of Transportation (DOT) codes, for each of the three highest occupational classifications are also included. Per-test fees apply. Detailed manual included. On-line help available.

Classification: Career Counseling

Hardware Requirements and Price
IBM PC, XT, AT, PS/2, & compatibles; 256 K;
1 Mb hard disk optional; 1 disk drive. Laser
printer optional. *Single User Price: $75.00 (10
scorings), $150.00 (25 scorings), $112.50 (25
additional scorings)*

Career Exploration Series
Arthur Cutler
Francis Ferry
Robert Kauk
Robert Robinett

CFKR Career Materials, Inc.
11860 Kemper Road, Unit 7
Auburn, CA 95603
(916) 889-2357
(800) 525-5626

Six diskettes focus on specific occupational
fields, including agriculture, business, consumer education, design-art communication, and
industrial and health science. A series of
assessment questions are then used to generate
a career interest profile that is then matched
with jobs in each field. Job duties, pay range,
and employment outlook of each job title is
included. Latest release 1987.

Classification: Career Counseling

Hardware Requirements and Price
Apple II, 64 K, 1 disk drive. Not compatible
with laser printer. *Single User Price: $249.95
Network Price: $999.80*

IBM PC, XT, AT, PS/2, & compatibles; 64 K;
hard disk optional; 1 disk drive. Laser printer
optional. *Single User Price: $249.95*

Career Finder
Patricia E. Waldren
Marilyn E. Maze

Wintergreen Software, Inc.
P.O. Box 15899
New Orleans, LA 70175
(504) 899-0378
(800) 321-9479

Identifies appropriate occupations and compares them to the needs of the client. Detailed
manual included. On-line help available.
Latest release September, 1991.

Classification: Career Counseling

Hardware Requirements and Price
Apple II, 64 K, 2 disk drives (5-1/4). *Single
User Price: $239.00*

IBM PC, XT, AT, PS/2, & compatibles; 256 K;
hard disk optional; 1 disk drive. *Single User
Price: $239.00*

Macintosh, 1 Mb, 2 Mb hard disk required, 1
disk drive (3-1/2). Uses Hyper Card. *Single
User Price: $239.00*

User Site References
Jacqueline Goodman, Oakland Unified School
   District, 1025 Second Avenue, Portable 14,
   Oakland, CA, 94606, (510) 836-8316
Dr. Martin Nomko, Consultant, 5936 Chabe-
   lynn Terrace, Oakland, CA, 94618, (510)
   655-2777

**This Clinical Software section includes 43
programs for cognitive rehabilitation and 39
career counseling aids.**

Career Scan V

Opportunities for Learning, Inc.
Career Aids Division
941 Hickory Lane
Mansfield, OH 44901
(419) 589-1700
(800) 243-7116

Using an eight-item questionnaire, students search and explore over 800 occupations that match their interests and abilities.

Classification: Career Counseling

Hardware Requirements and Price
Apple II, 56 K, 1 disk drive (5-1/4). Laser printer optional. *Single User Price: $169.00*

IBM PC, XT, AT, PS/2, & compatibles. *Single User Price: $179.00*

CareerPoint
Zaney Lebowitz
Stephen Farrer

Conceptional Systems, Inc.
1100 Wayne Ave., 12th Floor
Silver Spring, MD 10910
(301) 589-1800

A comprehensive career development system featuring Holland's Self-Directed Search that helps the client set goals and develop an action plan. Latest release 1991.

Classification: Career Counseling

Hardware Requirements and Price
IBM PC, XT, AT, PS/2, & compatibles; 640 K. Color display required. Mouse optional. Printer required. *Single User Price: Contact publisher.*

CareerSearch

The Guidance Shoppe
2909 Brandemere Drive
Tallahassee, FL 32312
(904) 385-6717

A career exploration program that combines color graphics and sound with a 3-dimensional game format. The interactive format helps students explore 400 career areas. Written at the fifth grade reading level. Students get a list of their top 10 jobs in each of three educational categories (high school, vocational/2 year college, and 4 year college), their top three standard occupational classification (SOC) clusters, references to DOT and *Guide to Occupational Exploration* (GOE) codes, and more. Detailed manual included.

Classification: Career Counseling

Hardware Requirements and Price
Apple II, 1 disk drive (5-1/4). *Single User Price: $149.95 Lab pack: $295.00 (5 copies)*

IBM PC, XT, AT, PS/2, & compatibles; 1 disk drive. *Single User Price: $149.95 Lab pack: $295.00 (5 copies)*

CASSIP: Computer Assisted Study Skills Improvement Program
William F. Brown

WFB Enterprises
1225 19th Street
Beaumont, TX 77706
(409) 898-1983

A college presentation program that improves study skills and academic attitudes. Detailed manual included. Latest release July 1, 1990.

Classification: Career Counseling

Hardware Requirements and Price
Apple II, 48 K, hard disk optional, 1 disk drive (5-1/4). *Single User Price: $550.00*

IBM PC, XT, AT, PS/2, & compatibles; 72 K; hard disk optional; 1 disk drive (5-1/4). *Single User Price: $550.00*

User Site References
Dorothy Forristall, Director of Learning Skills, Lanar University, Beaumont, TX, 77710, (409) 880-8882

CCIS: Computerized Career Information System

Opportunities for Learning, Inc.
Career Aids Division
941 Hickory Lane
Mansfield, OH 44901
(419) 589-1700
(800) 243-7116

This two-part system presents a means to career exploration and career information. Includes a "career game" and "information files" for more data.   Detailed manual included.

Classification: Career Counseling

Hardware Requirements and Price
Apple II, 48 K, 2 disk drives (5-1/4). Laser printer optional. *Single User Price: $240.00*

IBM PC, XT, AT, PS/2, & compatibles; 64 K; 2 disk drives (5-1/4). Laser printer optional. *Single User Price: $240.00*

Clinical Assistant
James A. Kennedy

Kennedy Computing
26 Old Lincoln Street
Worchester, MA 01650
(508) 757-2266
(800) 535-5680

A computerized system for writing progress notes and reports, making *DSM-III-R* (*Diagnostic and Statistical Manual of Mental Disorders,* 3rd ed., rev.) diagnoses, tracking literature abstracts, and assisting with billing. This is an upgrade of the Psychiatric Assistant. It also contains a personal note pad and to do lists. It is designed for single and/or multi-disciplinary use. Detailed manual and tutorial program included.   On-line help available. Latest release February 15, 1992.

Classification: Counseling Aid

Hardware Requirements and Price
IBM PC, XT, AT, PS/2, & compatibles; 384 K; 10 Mb hard disk required; 1 disk drive. CGA, EGA, or VGA display.   Mouse optional. Modem optional.   Laser printer optional. Requires DOS 2.0. *Single User Price: $500.00 Network Price: $1,000.00 Demo Price: $15.00*

Reviews
Warren, B. (1990). Software reviews & computer news for physicians. *Physicians Financial News, 8*(15), 28.
Zarr, M. L. (1991). Software reviews. *American Journal of Psychotherapy, 45*(2), 299-300.

User Site References
Robert A. Ciottone, 48 Cedar Street, Worcester, MA, 01609, (508) 756-4825

Neil S. Kaye, Christiana Hospital, Newark, DE, 19718, (302) 655-5575

Ronald Parks, Woodbourne Center, 1301 Woodbourne Avenue, Baltimore, MD, 21239, (301) 433-1000

Cognitive Data Base, Vol. I

Giles D. Rainwater
Nancy Z. Spotz

Psychometric Software, Inc.
P.O. Box 1677
Melbourne, FL 32902-1677
(407) 729-6390
(800) 882-9811

Facilitates developing cognitive rehabilitation treatment regimes. Database contains 25 cross references including strategies, books, computer programs, and articles. User can add own resources and customize any reference. Program will be updated as new resources are identified. Detailed manual included. Latest release 1986.

Classification: Cognitive Rehab: General

Hardware Requirements and Price
IBM PC, XT, AT, PS/2, & compatibles; 128 K; 10 Mb hard disk required; 1 disk drive. Monochrome, CGA, EGA, or VGA display. Printer required. Laser printer optional. Can be run on Macintosh systems operating under SoftPC. *Single User Price: $69.50 Network Price: $69.50 plus $34.75 each additional user*

Cognitive Drills: Set I (Visual)

Richard C. Katz

Sunset Software
9277 E. Corrine Drive

Scottsdale, AZ 85260
(602) 451-0753

Eleven computer programs provide a variety of tasks involving attention, reaction time, visual field, visual scanning, visual discrimination, and memory skills, while requiring a minimum of overt language processing. Navigation through the programs is simple for patients. On-line help screens and a text editor increase the program's flexibility. Instruction booklet included. Latest release June 24, 1990.

Classification: Cognitive Rehab: General

Hardware Requirements and Price
Apple II, 64 K, 10 Mb hard disk optional, 1 disk drive (5-1/4). Laser printer optional. Requires ProDOS. *Single User Price: $99.95*

Cognitive Prescription, Vol. I

Giles D. Rainwater

Psychometric Software, Inc.
P.O. Box 1677
Melbourne, FL 32902-1677
(407) 729-6390
(800) 882-9811

Five cognitive rehabilitation modules address abilities assessed by tests in the Halstead-Reitan Neuropsychological Test Battery. Modules include: digit span, digit symbol, rhythm, tapping, and trails. Each module has strategies to improve performance, various levels of difficulty, immediate feedback, and automatic timing. Detailed manual included.

Classification: Cognitive Rehab: General

Hardware Requirements and Price
IBM PC, XT, AT, PS/2, & compatibles; 128 K; 10 Mb hard disk optional; 1 disk drive. Mono-

chrome, CGA, EGA, or VGA display. Printer required. Laser printer optional. Can be run on Macintosh systems operating under SoftPC. *Single User Price: $97.50 Network Price: $97.50 plus $48.75 each additional user*

Cogrehab, Vol. 1
Rosamond Gianutsos
Carol Klitzner

Life Science Associates
1 Fenimore Road
Bayport, NY 11705-2115
(516) 472-2111
Fax: (516) 472-8146

A software/handbook system for dealing with cognitive deficits resulting from strokes and other brain injuries. The seven programs in this core package can be used to help identify and treat memory and perceptual disorders. Included are a clinical guide and a search-a-word booklet that is used to identify attentional deficits and hemi-imperception. Detailed manual included. Latest release 1991.

Classification: Cognitive Rehab: General

Hardware Requirements and Price
Apple II, 64 K, 10 Mb hard disk optional, 1 disk drive (5-1/4). Monochrome or color display. *Single User Price: $250.00 Network Price: $750.00 Individual program modules are also available separately for $40.00 each.*

IBM PC, XT, AT, PS/2, & compatibles; 128 K; 20 Mb hard disk optional; 1 disk drive. CGA display. *Single User Price: $250.00 Network Price: $750.00 Individual program modules are also available separately for $40.00 each.*

Reviews
Burglass, M. (1984). Computer programs for cognitive rehabilitation. *Computing Physician, 2,* 11-12.

User Site References
Paula Sociedade, Newark Beth Israel Hospital, 201 Lyons Avenue, Newark, NJ, 07112, (201) 926-8491
Diane Wise, The Sinai Rehabilitation Center, Baltimore, MD, 21209, (301) 578-5626

Cogrehab, Vol. 2
Rosamond Gianutsos
Georgine Vroman
Pauline Matheson

Life Science Associates
1 Fenimore Road
Bayport, NY 11705-2115
(516) 472-2111
Fax: (516) 472-8146

Extension of the original Cogrehab package with a focus on detection and treatment of perceptual deficits. Includes five programs: line bisection, eye movement exercise, shape matching, search for the odd shape, and single and double simultaneous stimulation. Detailed manual included.

Classification: Cognitive Rehab: Visual

Hardware Requirements and Price
Apple II, 64 K, 10 Mb hard disk optional, 1 disk drive (5-1/4). Monochrome or color display. *Single User Price: $150.00 Network Price: $450.00*

Cogrehab, Vol. 3
Rosamond Gianutsos

Life Science Associates
1 Fenimore Ave
Bayport, NY 11705-2115
(516) 472-2111
Fax: (516) 472-8146

The programs in this series are for individuals with memory problems. They were designed to be used, with minimal supervision, by clients who can see a computer display and use a keyboard. Responses are usually typed on the keyboard, however, provision for switch input is available for Vismem. The program includes the Cogrehab "shell" that permits convenient setting of parameters, patient information, and storage of results on disk. Detailed manual included. Latest release 1990.

Classification: Cognitive Rehab: Memory

Hardware Requirements and Price
Apple II, 64 K, 10 Mb hard disk optional, 1 disk drive (5-1/4). Monochrome or color display. *Single User Price: $175.00 Network Price: $525.00*

IBM PC, XT, AT, PS/2, & compatibles; 128 K; 20 Mb hard disk optional; 1 disk drive. CGA display. *Single User Price: $175.00 Network Price: $525.00*

Cogrehab, Vol. 4
Linda Laatsch

Life Science Associates
1 Fenimore Road
Bayport, NY 11705-2115
(516) 472-2111
Fax: (516) 472-8146

Designed to provide three broad behavioral tasks: attention, scanning, and problem solving. Each set of tasks may be used for assessment and practice. Detailed manual included. Latest release 1988.

Classification: Cognitive Rehab: Attention

Hardware Requirements and Price
Apple II, 64 K, 10 Mb hard disk optional, 1 disk drive (5-1/4). Monochrome or color display. *Single User Price: $95.00*

IBM PC, XT, AT, PS/2, & compatibles; 128 K; 20 Mb hard disk optional; 1 disk drive. CGA display. *Single User Price: $95.00 Network Price: $285.00*

Cogrehab, Vol. 5
Rosamond Gianutsos

Life Science Associates
1 Fenimore Road
Bayport, NY 11705-2115
(516) 472-2111
Fax: (516) 472-8146

Software for the individual emerging from a coma into consciousness. A library of 10 programs help clients evaluate and treat the cognitive recovery of an emerging coma patient. A hierarchy of "milestones" guides the therapist and rationalizes the choice of programs. Milestones advance from single discrete responses to multi-switch response differentiation. The programs use sound and bold displays whenever possible. Detailed manual included. Latest release 1990.

Classification: Cognitive Rehab: General

Hardware Requirements and Price
Apple II, 64 K, 10 Mb hard disk optional, 1 disk drive (5-1/4). Monochrome or color display. *Single User Price: $200.00*

IBM PC, XT, AT, PS/2, & compatibles; 128 K; 20 Mb hard disk optional; 1 disk drive. CGA display. *Single User Price: $200.00*

Cogrehab, Vol. 6
Rosamond Gianutsos

Life Science Associates
1 Fenimore Road
Bayport, NY 11705-2115
(516) 472-2111
Fax: (516) 472-8146

This driving advisement system includes computer-based tasks that assess cognitive abilities necessary for the safe operation of a motor vehicle. Addresses choice and execution components of reaction time, response to complex processing demands, impulse control, ability to sustain performance, flexibility, eye-hand coordination, and judgment. Report displays the individual's scores graphically in comparison to scores of safe drivers. Detailed manual included. Latest release 1991.

Classification: Cognitive Rehab: General

Hardware Requirements and Price
Apple II, 64 K, 10 Mb hard disk optional, 1 disk drive (5-1/4). Monochrome or color display. *Single User Price: $1,200.00*

IBM PC, XT, AT, PS/2, & compatibles; 128 K; 20 Mb hard disk optional; 1 disk drive. CGA display. *Single User Price: $1,200.00*

User Site References
Amy Campbell, Gaylord Hospital, Gaylord Farm Road, Wallingford, CT, 06492, (203) 284-2800.
Cynthia Hock, St. Vincent Hospital, 1233 N. 30 Street, Billings, MT, 59101, (406) 657-7723.
Steven Rumble, 360 E. Southport Road, Suite A, Indianapolis, IN, 46227, (317) 782-1332.

Cogrehab Vol. 7, Quest
Rosamond Gianutsos

Life Science Associates
1 Fenimore Road
Bayport, NY 11705-2115
(516) 472-2111
Fax: (516) 472-8146

Quest is a method of presenting verbal problems and offering feedback on the individual's answers. A variety of formats is possible, including: true/false, multiple choice, sentence completion, short answer, and fill-ins. It is designed for independent or supervised use by persons engaged in rehabilitation of cognitive and associated information processing problems (e.g., aphasia) caused by brain injury, strokes, infections, tumors, or dementia. The areas covered are: word finding, retrieval from remote memory, comprehension, abstract thinking, logic and reasoning, and quantification. Includes a text editor and sample files. Detailed manual included.

Classification: Cognitive Rehab: Verbal

Hardware Requirements and Price
Apple II, 64 K, 10 Mb hard disk optional, 1 disk drive (5-1/4). Monochrome or color display. *Single User Price: $490.00*

IBM PC, XT, AT, PS/2, & compatibles; 128 K; 20 Mb hard disk optional; 1 disk drive. CGA display. *Single User Price: $490.00*

College Explorer, 1992

The College Board
College Board Publications
Box 886
New York, NY 10101-0886
(800) 323-7155

Software assists user in choosing a college by offering in-depth data on 2,700 colleges. Identify wanted college features to get a list of schools that meet the client's needs, then sort the list by size, SAT scores, cost, application due dates, and more. Detailed manual included. On-line help and tutorial program available. Latest release September, 1991.

Classification: Career Counseling

Hardware Requirements and Price
Apple II, 128 K, hard disk optional, 1 disk drive. Not compatible with laser printer. *Single User Price: $89.95 Network Price: $339.95*

IBM PC, XT, AT, PS/2, & compatibles; 256 K; hard disk optional; 1 disk drive. Laser printer optional. *Single User Price: $89.95 Network Price: $339.95*

Reviews
Software: High school. (1991). *Electronic Learning, 10*(4), 34.

Complex Attention Rehabilitation
Robert J. Sbordone
Steven Hall

Robert J. Sbordone, PhD, Inc.
7700 Irvine Center Drive
Suite 750
Irvine, CA 92708
(714) 753-7711

Program provides training in attentional tasks using a visual tracking system. Designed for use with cognitively impaired individuals. The program monitors patient's attentional behavior to determine when rest periods are needed. Detailed manual included.

Classification: Cognitive Rehab: Attention

Hardware Requirements and Price
Apple II, 48 K, 1 disk drive. Joystick required. Optional speech synthesizer. *Single User Price: $195.00*

Comprehensive Treatment Planner
John Rosenberg
Matthew Wolf

PsychoLogics
6323A Fairmount Avenue
El Cerrito, CA 94530
(510) 528-6244
(800) 528-6244

A menu-driven program that produces treatment plans that meet Joint Commission on Accreditation of Hospitals (JCAH) and insurance company standards. Symptoms, treatment goals, and objectives are organized by diagnostic categories and may be selected from comprehensive standard lists or lists defined by the user. Output files can be customized with comments or modified using word processing software. Ideal for use with psychiatric inpatients or outpatients under managed care. Preprinted custom forms are available.

Detailed manual included.   Latest release
March, 1992.

Classification: Counseling Aid

Hardware Requirements and Price
IBM PC, XT, AT, PS/2, & compatibles; 640 K;
hard disk optional; 1 disk drive.   Printer required. *Single User Price: $279.00*

Computer Assisted Career Selection

Educational Industrial Sales, Inc.
2225 Grant Road, Suite 3
Los Altos, CA 94024
(415) 969-5212
(800) 955-5570

This program assists in career planning by
matching job characteristics to occupations and
personality traits.

Classification: Career Counseling

Hardware Requirements and Price
Apple II. *Single User Price: $98.00*

Coping With Tests
Paul M. Insel
Carl Thoresen

Consulting Psychologists Press
3803 East Bayshore Road
Palo Alto, CA 94303
(415) 969-8901
(800) 624-1765

This program enables test-anxious students or
adults to assess their level of test anxiety and

reduce this anxiety using behavior modification. Detailed manual included.

Classification: Counseling Aid

Hardware Requirements and Price
Apple II, 64 K, 2 disk drives. *Single User Price:
$185.00 (counseling center), $65.00 (individual
student)*

IBM PC, XT, AT, PS/2, & compatibles; 64 K; 1
disk drive.   Requires DOS 2.0. *Single User
Price: $185.00 (counseling center), $65.00
(individual student)*

Corporate Culture Programs
Tom Janz

Multi-Health Systems, Inc.
908 Niagara Falls Blvd.
North Tonawanda, NY 14120-2060
(416) 424-1700
(800) 456-3003

Two modules (Checkup and Followup) apply
motivational principles to the workplace,
helping people understand how they manage
and are managed.   They point individuals
toward specific changes in their work culture
that will lead to a healthier, more productive
work unit. Detailed manual included.

Classification: Industrial Consulting

Hardware Requirements and Price
IBM PC, XT, AT, PS/2, & compatibles; 128 K;
hard disk optional; 1 disk drive.   Printer required. Laser printer optional. *Single User
Price: $675.00 Programs also available sepa-
rately for $350.00 each.*

Counselor's Notebook

The Guidance Shoppe
2909 Brandemere Drive
Tallahassee, FL 32312
(904) 385-6717

Record important student information for individual or group counseling sections. Precoded choices make entering data quick and easy. A window keeps relevant codes visible at the bottom of the screen. A comments section allows room for detailed information. Word processing capabilities make editing information easy. All information is password protected. Numerous printed reports are available. Detailed manual included.

Classification: Counseling Aid

Hardware Requirements and Price
Apple II, 48 K, 1 disk drive (5-1/4). *Single User Price: $79.95*

IBM PC, XT, AT, PS/2, & compatibles; 2 disk drives. *Single User Price: $89.95*

Datesim

George W. Holden
Stanley O. Gaines, Jr.

Department of Psychology
University of Texas
Austin, TX 78712
(512) 471-9228

Designed to examine the two social cognition processes that commonly occur in interpersonal relationships: acquiring information about another person and making decisions about that person. Instruction booklet included. Latest release June, 1989.

Classification: Counseling Aid

Hardware Requirements and Price
IBM PC, XT, AT, PS/2, & compatibles; 512 K; 20 Mb hard disk optional; 1 disk drive. Monochrome or color display. Laser printer optional. Requires DOS 3.2. *Single User Price: $15.00*

Daysim

George W. Holden
Kathy L. Ritchie

Department of Psychology
University of Texas
Austin, TX 78712
(512) 471-9228

A tool for collecting parents' behavioral self-reports and determining whether patterns of parental behavior can be identified. Instruction booklet included. Latest release June, 1989.

Classification: Counseling Aid

Hardware Requirements and Price
IBM PC, XT, AT, PS/2, & compatibles; 512 K; 20 Mb hard disk optional; 1 disk drive. Monochrome or color display. Laser printer optional. Requires DOS 3.2. *Single User Price: $15.00*

DOT Lookup
Janet Field

Elliott & Fitzpatrick, Inc.
1135 Cedar Shoals Drive
Athens, GA 30605
(404) 548-8161
(800) 843-4977

DOT Lookup allows the user to quickly display DOT codes, titles and worker traits by selecting DOT code, data-people-things (DPT) code, industrial designation, work field code, or a phrase from the DOT title. Scroll through the titles, select the title of interest and worker traits will appear on the screen. Information may be sent to a printer if desired. Instruction booklet included.

Classification: Career Counseling

Hardware Requirements and Price
IBM PC, XT, AT, PS/2, & compatibles; 512 K; 500 K hard disk optional; 1 disk drive. *Single User Price: $129.95*

EAP Management Module

Harting Associates, Inc.
8 Executive Drive, Suite 160
Fairview Heights, IL 62208-9916
(618) 632-3145
(800) 782-6785

Generates statistical report, referral analysis, analysis of discharges, and lists of cases open and closed. Detailed manual included. Latest release November 1, 1991.

Classification: Industrial Consulting

Hardware Requirements and Price
IBM PC, XT, AT, PS/2, & compatibles; 256 K; 10 Mb hard disk required; 1 disk drive. Modem optional. Printer required. Laser printer optional. *Single User Price: $995.00 Network Price: $1,200.00*

User Site References
Pat Benson, Peoples Gas, 122 South Michigan, Room 711, Chicago, IL, 60603, (312) 431-4620

Tobias Schreiber, Professional Management Consultant, Aiken Barnwell Community Mental Health, 115 Greenville Street SW, Aiken, SC, 29801, (803) 642-5007

Enjoy Your Job

The Guidance Shoppe
2909 Brandemere Drive
Tallahassee, FL 32312
(904) 385-6717

Looks at the activities the client enjoys and relates those activities to job satisfaction. Provides valuable insight and clues to self-understanding. Detailed manual included.

Classification: Career Counseling

Hardware Requirements and Price
IBM PC, XT, AT, PS/2, & compatibles; 1 disk drive. *Single User Price: $69.95*

Expert Ease

Dynacomp, Inc.
The Dynacomp Office Building
178 Phillips Road
Webster, NY 14580
(716) 265-4040
(800) 828-6772

An analysis tool that allows clients to analyze and refine their decision making processes. Using keyed in examples of previous decisions, the program creates a decision tree based on rules it derives from the examples, automatically eliminating redundancies and alerting the user to any inconsistencies. The system can be expanded, refined, or modified to fit any user. It can be used for anything that requires consistent, accurate problem solving or decision making. Possible applications include screening job applicants, validating expense claims, producing testing schedules, delegating responsibilities, advising on personal regulations, training, diagnosing medical problems, teaching and advising. Instruction booklet included.

Classification: Industrial Consulting

Hardware Requirements and Price
IBM PC, XT, AT, PS/2, & compatibles; 128 K; hard disk optional; 1 disk drive. Laser printer optional. *Single User Price: $395.00*

Exploracion de Carreras

Cambridge Career Products
P.O. Box 2153
Charleston, WV 25328-2153
(304) 744-9323
(800) 468-4227

This is a career exploration system in Spanish that lists 300 occupations. Detailed manual included.

Classification: Career Counseling

Hardware Requirements and Price
Apple II. *Single User Price: $295.00*

IBM PC, XT, AT, PS/2, & compatibles. *Single User Price: $295.00*

Explore the World of Work
Arthur Cutler
Francis Ferry
Robert Kauk
Robert Robinett

CFKR Career Materials, Inc.
11860 Kemper Road, Unit 7

Auburn, CA 95603
(916) 889-2357
(800) 525-5626

Program allows students to rate work activities and identify individual preferences. From this assessment, a bar graph and printout indicate job cluster preferences, culminating in a choice of one job for further exploration. This program is written on a fourth grade reading level and is designed especially for students in grades 4-6 and special education students. Detailed manual included. Latest release 1987.

Classification: Career Counseling

Hardware Requirements and Price
Apple II, 64 K, 1 disk drive. Printer required. *Single User Price: $89.95*

FactFile: Brief Facts and Jokes for Reading Stimulation
Richard C. Katz

Sunset Software
9277 E. Corrine Drive
Scottsdale, AZ 85260
(602) 451-0753

Program contains questions, facts, and jokes suitable for users who find reading difficult and unenjoyable. The 150 items are randomly selected. The user reads the question, thinks of an answer and presses any key to see the correct answer. The response is not evaluated and no other response is required as the task is intended to be a pleasant language activity that encourages and reinforces attention and reading behavior. Not copy protected. Instruction booklet included. Latest release June 24, 1990.

Classification: Cognitive Rehab: Verbal

Hardware Requirements and Price
Apple II+, IIe, IIc, IIgs; 48 K; 10 Mb hard disk optional; 1 disk drive (5-1/4). Not compatible with laser printer. Requires ProDOS. *Single User Price: $29.95*

Feeling Better

Dynacomp, Inc.
The Dynacomp Office Building
178 Phillips Road
Webster, NY 14580
(716) 265-4040
(800) 828-6772

An education program designed to help children reduce their feelings of anger, depression, anxiety, and guilt. It begins with a presentation about the nature of feelings and emotions so that the child will be able to label and identify them when they occur. It then presents a simple but powerful A > B > C method for the analysis of emotionally disturbing events, and shows the child how to feel less upset in response to those events. Interest is maintained by animation. Instruction booklet included.

Classification: Counseling Aid

Hardware Requirements and Price
Apple II, 48 K, 1 disk drive (5-1/4). Laser printer optional. Requires DOS 3.3. *Single User Price: $39.95*

Free Recall
Rosamond Gianutsos
Carol Klitzner

Life Science Associates
1 Fenimore Road

Bayport, NY 11705-2115
(516) 472-2111
Fax: (516) 472-8146

This test measures short- and long-term memory, and is used to diagnose and exercise memory retention. One module from Cogrehab.

Classification: Cognitive Rehab: Memory

Hardware Requirements and Price
Apple II, 64 K, 10 Mb hard disk optional, 1 disk drive (5-1/4). Monochrome or color display. *Single User Price: $40.00*

IBM PC, XT, AT, PS/2, & compatibles; 128 K; 20 Mb hard disk optional; 1 disk drive. CGA display required. *Single User Price: $40.00*

Goal Tracker-The Personal Success System
Michael E. Mills

Psytek Services
6401 West 81st Street
Los Angeles, CA 90045
(213) 670-4655
(800) 392-5454

Helps individuals assess their priorities and achieve their personal, educational, and career goals. The system includes an assessment and prioritization of personal goals, daily/weekly/monthly and/or yearly review of progress toward those goals in the form of graphs, and a focus on goals via graphical visualizations. In addition, a memory resident program is included that presents messages or flash card-type questions (and answers) from user created message files of quotes, things to do, motivational messages, material to memorize, and so forth. Messages are randomly selected and presented over currently running (non-windows) applications at various times. Detailed manual included. Latest release January, 1992.

Classification: Career Counseling

Hardware Requirements and Price
IBM PC, XT, AT, PS/2, & compatibles; 512 K; hard disk optional. Monochrome, CGA, EGA, or VGA display. Laser printer optional. 30-day money back guarantee. *Single User Price: $99.00*

Help-Assert
Judy I. Stewart

CATSco, Inc.
1531 Chapala Street, Suite 4
Santa Barbara, CA 93101-3060
(800) 522-8726
(800) 521-8726 (from Canada)

HELP-Assert interactively educates, trains, provides practice, motivates for positive change, and gives individual feedback for assertive and communication skills. Nine sessions include introduction, assessment, beliefs, techniques for change, behaviors, preparing others, and a summary. For individuals ages 15 years to adult. Instruction booklet and tutorial program included. Latest release 1991.

Classification: Counseling Aid

Hardware Requirements and Price
IBM PC, XT, AT, PS/2, & compatibles; 256 K; 1 Mb hard disk optional; 1 disk drive. Monochrome or CGA display. Laser printer optional. Requires DOS 2.1. *Single User Price: $395.00 (12 users), $495.00 (24 users) Network Price: $1,295.00 (unlimited use)*

Reviews
Sowers-Hoag, K. (1991). HELP-Stress, HELP-Assert, HELP-Esteem. *Computers in Human Services*, 8(2), 141.

User Site References
Joe Garms, University of Texas Medical Center, 1400 Wallace Boulevard, Arlington, TX, 79106, (806) 354-5463
Richard D. Stanton, Iroquois M.H.C., P.O. Box 332, Watseka, IL, 60970, (815) 432-5241
Wayne Theye, Ohio Northern University, Ada, OH, 45810, (419) 772-2190

Help-Esteem
Nancy L. Chaconas

CATSco, Inc.
1531 Chapala Street, Suite 4
Santa Barbara, CA 93101-3060
(800) 522-8726
(800) 521-8726 (from Canada)

HELP-Esteem is a cognitive-behavior based interactive, psycho-educational software program used as an adjunct to counseling and psychotherapy. The 11 session program teaches specific concepts, provides practice, and builds skills that assist people in developing strong, positive, and realistic self images. Available in youth or adult versions. Instruction booklet and tutorial program included. Latest release 1991.

Classification: Counseling Aid

Hardware Requirements and Price
IBM PC, XT, AT, PS/2, & compatibles; 256 K; 1 Mb hard disk optional; 1 disk drive. Monochrome or CGA display. Laser printer optional. Requires DOS 2.1. *Single User Price: $395.00 (12 users), $495.00 (24 users) Network Price: $1,295.00 (unlimited use)*

Reviews

Sowers-Hoag, K. (1991). HELP-Stress, HELP-Assert, HELP-Esteem. *Computers in Human Services*, 8(2), 141.

User Site References

Joe Garms, University of Texas Medical Center, 1400 Wallace Boulevard, Arlington, TX, 79106, (806) 354-5463

Richard D. Stanton, Iroquois M.H.C., P.O. Box 332, Watseka, IL, 60970, (815) 432-5241

Wayne Theye, Ohio Northern University, Ada, OH, 45810, (419) 772-2190

Help-Stress

Mark Johnson
Bert W. Shaw
Andy Winzelberg
Christianne Brems

CATSco, Inc.
1531 Chapala Street, Suite 4
Santa Barbara, CA 93101-3060
(800) 522-8726
(800) 521-8726 (from Canada)

HELP-Stress is a comprehensive, interactive stress management program that helps people learn how to control and manage stress. A 10 session format includes an assessment, relaxation, cognitive sources, environment, diet, exercise, stress inoculation, and a summary. Available in adult and youth (13-17 years) versions. Instruction booklet and tutorial program included. Latest release 1991.

Classification: Counseling Aid

Hardware Requirements and Price

IBM PC, XT, AT, PS/2, & compatibles; 256 K; 1 Mb hard disk optional; 1 disk drive. Monochrome or CGA display. Printer optional. Laser printer optional. Requires DOS 2.1.

Single User Price: $395.00 (12 users), $495.00 (24 users) Network Price: $1,295.00 (unlimited use)

Reviews

Sowers-Hoag, K. (1991). HELP-Stress, HELP-Assert, HELP-Esteem. *Computers in Human Services*, 8(2), 141.

User Site References

Joe Garms, University of Texas Medical Center, 1400 Wallace Boulevard, Arlington, TX, 79106, (806) 354-5463

Richard D. Stanton, Iroquois M.H.C., P.O. Box 332, Watseka, IL, 60970, (815) 432-5241

Wayne Theye, Ohio Northern University, Ada, OH, 45810, (419) 772-2190

Help-Think

Mark Johnson
Christianne Brems

CATSco, Inc.
1531 Chapala Street, Suite 4
Santa Barbara, CA 93101-3060
(800) 522-8726
(800) 521-8726 (from Canada)

Interactive, cognitive-behavioral psychoeducational software dealing with distorted thought patterns, irrational beliefs, and automatic thoughts. Nine sessions foster awareness, motivate, educate, and provide practical strategies for change. Available in youth and adult versions. Instruction booklet and tutorial program included. Latest release 1991.

Classification: Counseling Aid

Hardware Requirements and Price

IBM PC, XT, AT, PS/2, & compatibles; 256 K; 1 Mb hard disk optional; 1 disk drive. Monochrome or CGA display. Laser printer optional. Requires DOS 2.1. *Single User Price: $395.00 (12 users), $495.00 (24 users) Network Price: $1,295.00 (unlimited use)*

Reviews

Sowers-Hoag, K. (1991). HELP-Stress, HELP-Assert, HELP-Esteem. *Computers in Human Services, 8*(2), 141.

User Site References

Joe Garms, University of Texas Medical Center, 1400 Wallace Boulevard, Arlington, TX, 79106, (806) 354-5463

Richard D. Stanton, Iroquois M.H.C., P.O. Box 332, Watseka, IL, 60970, (815) 432-5241

Wayne Theye, Ohio Northern University, Ada, OH, 45810, (419) 772-2190

High School Career-Choice Planner

Arthur Cutler
Francis Ferry
Robert Kauk
Robert Robinett

CFKR Career Materials, Inc.
11860 Kemper Road, Unit 7
Auburn, CA 95603
(916) 889-2357
(800) 525-5626

Program is designed to help incoming high school students plan a 4-year high school program based upon a career interest assessment. The computer matches the student's questionnaire responses with 16 occupational groups and prints out the results. The report includes job entry information, suggested high school course planning, and a high school career-choice planning form. Instruction booklet included. Latest release 1987.

Classification: Career Counseling

Hardware Requirements and Price

Apple II, 64 K, 1 disk drive. Not compatible with laser printer. *Single User Price: $89.95 Network Price: $359.80*

IBM PC, XT, AT, PS/2, & compatibles; 64 K; hard disk optional; 1 disk drive. Laser printer optional. *Single User Price: $89.95 Network Price: $359.80*

Holidays

Richard C. Katz

Sunset Software
9277 E. Corrine Drive
Scottsdale, AZ 85260
(602) 451-0753

Spelling task that uses drawings and multi-level linguistic cueing to help patients learn to type and write the names of 10 holidays or any other target words determined by the teacher or clinician. Program provides a hierarchy of cues and, in response to errors, homework. Cues include anagrams, copying from memory, multiple-choice, and modeling. Performance saved on disk for later session and item analysis. Instruction booklet included. Latest release June 24, 1990.

Classification: Cognitive Rehab: Verbal

Hardware Requirements and Price

Apple II+, IIe, IIc, IIgs; 48 K; 10 Mb hard disk optional; 1 disk drive (5-1/4). Requires DOS 3.3. *Single User Price: $49.95*

How Did I Feel?

Barbara Benjamin
Dave Cantrell
Marilyn Jones

Peak Potential, Inc.
P.O. Box 1461
Loveland, CO 80539-1461
(303) 226-3576

Helps secondary school students recognize and label a broad range of feelings and identify which feelings might occur in a situation. Ten disks, 10 stories per disk. Allows exploration of typical feeling responses to situations, and practice in empathy. Topics include family, divorce and stepfamilies, friends, school, drugs and alcohol, and work. Detailed manual included. Latest release 1986.

Classification: Counseling Aid

Hardware Requirements and Price
Apple II, 48 K, hard disk optional, 1 disk drive. Modem optional. *Single User Price: $130.00*

Macintosh, hard disk optional, 1 disk drive (3-1/2). Mouse required. Modem optional. Laser printer optional. Requires Hyper Card 2.0 or higher. *Single User Price: $130.00*

Reviews
Benjamin, B. (1989). How did I feel? In G. R. Walz (Ed.), *Counseling software guide: A resource for the guidance and human development professions* (p. 321). Alexandria, VA: American Association for Counseling and Development.

User Site References
Patty Goldberg, Montgomery City Schools, 8512 Atwell Road, Potomac, MD, 20854, (301) 279-2620
Wes Mason, Santa Clara Office of Education, 100 Skyport Drive, San Jose, CA, 95115, (408) 299-4088
Nancy Meredith, Thompson School District R2-J, Loveland High School, Loveland, CO, 80538, (303) 667-5374

If You Drink
Scott Meier

Multi-Health Systems, Inc.
908 Niagara Falls Blvd.
North Tonawanda, NY 14120-2060
(416) 424-1700
(800) 456-3003

Helps teach adolescents and adults about alcohol use and abuse. Program contains an alcohol quiz, simulated breathalyzer test, test that examines attitudes towards drinking and driving, simulated party that calculates the party IQ, and a database of interactions between alcohol and 16 commonly prescribed medications. Detailed manual included.

Classification: Counseling Aid

Hardware Requirements and Price
Apple II, 256 K, hard disk optional, 1 disk drive. Laser printer optional. *Single User Price: $195.00*

IBM PC, XT, AT, PS/2, & compatibles; hard disk optional; 1 disk drive. *Single User Price: $195.00*

Reviews
Meier, S. T. (1988). Alcohol education through computer-assisted instruction. *Journal of Counseling and Development, 66,* 389-390.

Job Hunter's Survival Kit

The Guidance Shoppe
2909 Brandemere Drive
Tallahassee, FL 32312
(904) 385-6717

This package includes two interactive programs, Skill Analyzer and Resume Writer, that help students identify transferable job skills and write an effective resume while teaching a proven job search strategy. This program includes an instructional section, a choice of resume formats, editing features, and more. Appropriate for beginning job seekers or experienced professionals. Detailed manual included.

Classification: Career Counseling

Hardware Requirements and Price
Apple II, 48 K, 2 disk drives (5-1/4). *Single User Price: $149.95*

IBM PC, XT, AT, PS/2, & compatibles; 256 K; 2 disk drives. *Single User Price: $149.95*

Jump: Eye Movement Exercise
Rosamond Gianutsos
Georgine Vroman
Pauline Matheson

Life Science Associates
1 Fenimore Road
Bayport, NY 11705-2115
(516) 472-2111
Fax: (516) 472-8146

Computer-administered tool that provides eye-movement exercise in lateral scanning. The task requires horizontal scanning from a starting point that the subject locates before initiating a trial. Each trial consists of successive exposure to two stimuli, at opposite ends of the screen. The subject must decide whether they are the same or different. The exposure duration of the stimuli determines the scanning rate required.

Classification: Cognitive Rehab: Visual

Hardware Requirements and Price
Apple II, 64 K, 10 Mb hard disk optional, 1 disk drive (5-1/4). Monochrome or color display. *Single User Price: $40.00*

IBM PC, XT, AT, PS/2, & compatibles; 128 K; 20 Mb hard disk optional; 1 disk drive. CGA display required. *Single User Price: $40.00*

Keyboarder: Finding Letters & Numbers
Richard C. Katz

Sunset Software
9277 E. Corrine Drive
Scottsdale, AZ 85260
(602) 451-0753

Drill designed to help orient students and patients to the position of letters and numbers on the keyboard. A simple design, auditory and visual cues, and large-sized characters make the task particularly useful for young clients and hemiparetic and hemianopic patients. Results saved on disk. Errors printed out for practice. Instruction booklet included. Latest release June, 24 1990.

Classification: Cognitive Rehab: Verbal

Hardware Requirements and Price
Apple II+, IIe, IIc, IIgs; 48 K; 10 Mb hard disk optional; 1 disk drive (5-1/4). Not compatible with laser printer. Requires DOS 3.3. *Single User Price: $29.95*

Learning to Cope with Pressure
Hal Myers
Lawrence Klein
Patrick Bowman

Sunburst Communications
39 Washington Avenue
Pleasantville, NY 10570
(914) 796-5030
(800) 628-8897

This program uses biofeedback to help students learn to reduce stress and develop effective relaxation techniques. Detailed manual and tutorial program included. Latest release 1987.

Classification: Relaxation Training

Hardware Requirements and Price
Apple II, 48 K, hard disk optional, 1 disk drive (5-1/4). Color composite display required. Not compatible with laser printer. Requires DOS 3.3. Includes GSR device (biosensor) & cassette tape. *Single User Price: $99.00*

User Site References
Barbara Winters, Department Coordinator, Culver Community Jr/Sr High School, 701 N. School Street, Culver, IN, 46511, (219) 842-3391

LeisurePREF
Patsy B. Edwards

Constructive Leisure
511 North La Cienega Blvd., Suite 214
Los Angeles, CA 90048-2008
(310) 652-7389

Surveys interest in leisure activities, evaluates responses, categorizes them, and interprets the results for improving leisure or leisure/career guidance and development. Instruction booklet included. Latest release March, 1990.

Classification: Counseling Aid

Hardware Requirements and Price
Apple II, 128 K, hard disk optional, 1 disk drive (5-1/4). Not compatible with laser printer. *Single User Price: $45.00*

IBM PC, XT, AT, PS/2, & compatibles; 128 K; hard disk optional; 1 disk drive. Printer required. Not compatible with laser printer. *Single User Price: $45.00*

Macintosh, 128 K, hard disk optional, 1 disk drive (3-1/2). Not compatible with laser printer. *Single User Price: $45.00*

Reviews
Baumgartner, T. A., & Cicciarella, C. F. (1987). *Directory of computer software with application to physical education, exercise science, health, and dance II*. Alexandria, VA: AAHPERD Research Consortium Computer Network Committee, 21.
Winton, M. A. (1989). LeisurePREF. In G. R Walz (Ed.), *Counseling software guide: A resource the guidance and human development professions* (p. 351). Alexandria, VA: American Association for Counseling and Development.

Life/Time Manager
Giles D. Rainwater

Psychometric Software, Inc.
P.O. Box 1677
Melbourne, FL 32902-1677
(407) 729-6390
(800) 882-9811

The Life/Time Manager helps the client get control of their time by setting goals, prioritizing activities, and learning to use brainstorming techniques. The goal of the program is to help the client enjoy life more by working smarter, not harder. Detailed manual included. Latest release 1985.

Classification: Industrial Consulting

Hardware Requirements and Price
IBM PC, XT, AT, PS/2, & compatibles; 128 K; 10 Mb hard disk optional; 1 disk drive. Monochrome, CGA, EGA, or VGA display. Laser printer optional. Can be run on Macintosh systems operating under SoftPC. *Single User Price: $49.95 Network Price: $49.95 plus $24.98 for each additional user*

Line Bisection
Rosamond Gianutsos
Georgine Vroman
Pauline Matheson

Life Science Associates
1 Fenimore Road
Bayport, NY 11705-2115
(516) 472-2111
Fax: (516) 472-8146

Program designed to detect spatial hemi-imperception. The subject is presented with lines on the screen. Each line has a visual gap and the subject is instructed to adjust the gap, using the arrow keys, until it is in the exact middle of the line.

Classification: Cognitive Rehab: Visual

Hardware Requirements and Price
Apple II, 64 K, 10 Mb hard disk optional, 1 disk drive (5-1/4). Monochrome or color display. *Single User Price: $40.00*

IBM PC, XT, AT, PS/2, & compatibles; 128 K; 20 Mb hard disk optional; 1 disk drive. CGA, EGA, or VGA display. *Single User Price: $40.00 Network Price: $120.00*

LMA Plus 1990
Janet Field

Elliott & Fitzpatrick, Inc.
1135 Cedar Shoals Drive
Athens, GA 30605
(404) 548-8161
(800) 843-4977

The LMA Plus 1990 is valuable in routine DOT job matching and determining employability and wage loss for the injured worker, especially in cases involving compensation or liability issues. The job search feature allows the user to enter a client profile (worker traits) and match it against the DOT database to determine transferability of skills. The labor market access feature permits a pre- and post-injury assessment of an individual's access to jobs within a geographic area. Detailed manual included. Latest release 1989. Will be revised in Winter, 1992.

Classification: Career Counseling

Hardware Requirements and Price
IBM PC, XT, AT, PS/2, & compatibles; 640 K; 5 Mb hard disk required; 1 disk drive. Printer required. *Single User Price: $1,295.00*

The Magic Mirror
Ernest Kinnie

Blue Valley Software
29 Shepard Street
Walton, NY 13856
(800) 545-6172

Ideas and strategies to help users create a deeper understanding of the many forces affecting them. The roles can be as simple as the 4 or 5 moves between a customer and a check-out clerk, or as complex as the tortuous dance of the alcoholic and their co-dependent spouse. Helps explore new networks of belief and if change is needed it can be accomplished using the powerful techniques found here. The program keeps track of the client's progress. Latest release September, 1991.

Classification: Counseling Aid

Hardware Requirements and Price
IBM PC, XT, AT, PS/2, & compatibles; 2 disk drives. Monochrome or VGA display. Mouse optional. *Single User Price: $39.95*

Amiga, hard disk optional. Mouse required. *Single User Price: $39.95*

Major-Minor Finder
Arthur Cutler
Francis Ferry
Robert Kauk
Robert Robinett

CFKR Career Materials, Inc.
11860 Kemper Road, Unit 7
Auburn, CA 95603
(916) 889-2357
(800) 525-5626

Program helps students select a college major that matches their aptitudes and interests. Questions include level of education desired, general field of study, mathematics, verbal reasoning, and spatial perception. Students also indicate their desire to work with complex data, people, and things, and choose the environment in which they want to work. Instruction booklet included. Latest release 1988.

Classification: Career Counseling

Hardware Requirements and Price
Apple II, 128 K, 2 disk drives. Not compatible with laser printer. *Single User Price: $89.95 Network Price: $359.80*

IBM PC, XT, AT, PS/2, & compatibles; 128 K; hard disk optional; 2 disk drives. Laser printer optional. *Single User Price: $89.95 Network Price: $359.80*

Meet Yourself (As You Really Are)

Dynacomp, Inc.
The Dynacomp Office Building
178 Phillips Road
Webster, NY 14580
(716) 265-4040
(800) 828-6772

A guide that takes clients on a tour of the less well charted regions of their psyche, helping them discover new and unsuspected aspects of their personality. As individual character portraits unfold, problems are discussed and set against the background of some of the wider issues of life. These may have bearing on the client's case or throw light on questions of general interest and significance beyond that of immediate personal concerns. The format used is a mixture of questions and observations. The package consists of over 200 blocks of routines, not all of which are used in the analysis of any one individual. Each routine acts in conjunction with the client's personal text file. From the information that is stored in the text file and the answers to the questions, you will be guided to further questions or observations about your personality. Instruction booklet included.

Classification: Counseling Aid

Hardware Requirements and Price
Apple II, 48 K. Laser printer optional. *Single User Price: $39.95*

Memory Span
Rosamond Gianutsos
Carol Kiltzner

Life Science Associates
1 Fenimore Road
Bayport, NY 11705-2115
(516) 472-2111
Fax: (516) 472-8146

Program designed to help restore short-term storage capacity and to measure the subject's ability to concentrate on a task. The subject sees a list of words and must recall certain words, according to instructions that vary with each trial. Thirty words are presented in rounds of five lists each. This is one module from Cogrehab.

Classification: Cognitive Rehab: Memory

Hardware Requirements and Price
Apple II, 64 K, 10 Mb hard disk optional, 1 disk drive (5-1/4). Monochrome or color display. *Single User Price: $40.00*

IBM PC, XT, AT, PS/2, & compatibles; 128 K; 20 Mb hard disk optional; 1 disk drive. CGA display required. *Single User Price: $40.00*

Mental Rotations
C. M. Levy
C. J. Levy

Life Science Associates
1 Fenimore Road
Bayport, NY 11705-2115
(516) 472-2111
Fax: (516) 472-8146

Mental Rotations examines the client's ability to mentally rotate representations of physical objects. Instruction booklet included.

Classification: Cognitive Rehab: General

Hardware Requirements and Price
Apple II, 64 K, 10 Mb hard disk optional, 1 disk drive (5-1/4). Monochrome or color display. *Single User Price: $40.00*

IBM PC, XT, AT, PS/2, & compatibles; 128 K; 20 Mb hard disk optional; 1 disk drive. CGA, EGA, or VGA display. *Single User Price: $40.00*

Micro-Skills I and II
Marilyn E. Maze

Eureka
241 26th Street
Richmond, CA 94804
(510) 235-3883

An inventory of 72 transferable building-block skills developed specifically for identifying appropriate occupations using a computer. Detailed manual included. Latest release September, 1991.

Classification: Career Counseling

Hardware Requirements and Price
Apple II, 64 K, hard disk optional, 1 disk drive (5-1/4). *Single User Price: $490.00*

IBM PC, XT, AT, PS/2, & compatibles; 256 K; hard disk optional; 1 disk drive. *Single User Price: $490.00*

Neurobics
Ratko V. Tomic

Ocean Isle Software
697 Copa D'Oro
Marathon, FL 33050
(305) 743-4546

Neurobics is an aerobics workout for the mind that consists of six brain-teaser games designed to exercise short term memory, concentration, problem solving skills, spatial abilities, and deductive and inductive reasoning. It is useful for stress management and encourages creativity. Puzzles involving the left and right sides of the brain include involve pattern recognition, sequence memorization, transitional analysis, and math skills. The user may customize the game with an options menu and there are 25 levels of difficulty. Detailed manual included.

Classification: Counseling Aid

Hardware Requirements and Price
Apple II+, IIe, IIc, IIgs; hard disk optional; 1 disk drive. *Single User Price: $44.95*

IBM PC, XT, AT, PS/2, & compatibles; 256 K; hard disk optional; 1 disk drive. EGA or VGA display. *Single User Price: $44.95*

Number Series Problems
Linda Laatsch

Life Science Associates
1 Fenimore Road
Bayport, NY 11705-2115
(516) 472-2111
Fax: (516) 472-8146

Program provides practice solving a series of problems at two levels of difficulty. This task requires attention, discrimination, and logical thought. The user receives feedback and can choose to receive prompts. Scoring is performed separately for each type of series. Latest release 1988.

Classification: Cognitive Rehab: Attention

Hardware Requirements and Price
Apple II, 64 K, 10 Mb hard disk optional, 1 disk drive (5-1/4). Monochrome or color display. *Single User Price: $40.00 Network Price: $120.00*

IBM PC, XT, AT, PS/2, & compatibles; 128 K; 20 Mb hard disk optional; 1 disk drive. CGA, EGA, or VGA display. *Single User Price: $40.00 Network Price: $120.00*

Occupational Outlook on Computer (OOOC)
Arthur Francis
Francis Ferry
Robert Kauk

CFKR Career Materials, Inc.
11860 Kemper Road, Unit 7
Auburn, CA 95603
(916) 889-2357
(800) 525-5626

Designed as a career information delivery system, OOOC has all the vital information from the US Department of Labor (DOL) *Occupational Outlook Handbook*. It provides a database on almost 450 jobs and more than 1,000 related jobs. The user obtains quick access, with printout capabilities, to the nature of work, job outlook, earnings, related occupations, sources of additional information, and other data related to occupations. Instruction booklet included. Latest release 1991.

Classification: Career Counseling

Hardware Requirements and Price
Apple II, 128 K, 2 disk drives. Not compatible with laser printer. *Single User Price: $129.95 Network Price: $519.80*

IBM PC, XT, AT, PS/2, & compatibles; 720 K; hard disk optional; 2 disk drives. Mouse optional. Modem optional. Laser printer optional. *Single User Price: $129.95 Network Price: $519.80*

Over 50: Needs, Values, Attitudes
Patsy B. Edwards

Constructive Leisure
511 North La Cienega Blvd., Suite 214
Los Angeles, CA 90048-2008
(310) 652-7389

This interactive software is designed to enhance self-understanding and life/career/leisure planning through assessment and evaluation of the subject's personal needs, values, and attitudes. The program leads to improved relationships and increased adjustment to the present world. For agency/community/private counseling clients, business/industry personnel counselors, education, guidance centers, and mental health facilities. Instruction booklet included. Latest release April, 1990.

Classification: Counseling Aid

Hardware Requirements and Price
IBM PC, XT, AT, PS/2, & compatibles; 516 K; hard disk optional; 1 disk drive. Printer required. Not compatible with laser printer. *Single User Price: $75.00*

Macintosh, 516 K, hard disk optional, 1 disk drive. *Single User Price: $75.00*

Reviews
Rosen T. (1989). Over 50. In G. R. Walz (Ed.). *Counseling software guide: A resource for the guidance and human development professions* (p. 318). Alexandria, VA: American Association for Counseling and Development.

The PA: Marriage Communication Training Module
Gary Brainerd

Brainerd Psychological Association
595 East Colorado Blvd., #614
Pasadena, CA 91101
(818)-577-2666
(800) 441-2628

Aids in teaching a 10-12 week marital communication program. Rates couples' strengths and weaknesses in a variety of skills (message sending, listening, self-disclosure, affectional communication, problem solving, etc.). An optional display card allows use of two additional monitors which serve as feedback displays for the couple. Prints a variety of reports. Has group or classroom mode as well as an individual couple mode. Detailed manual included. On-line help available. Latest release January, 1992.

Classification: Counseling Aid

Hardware Requirements and Price
IBM PC, XT, AT, PS/2, & compatibles; 640 K; 1-5 Mb hard disk optional; 2 disk drives. EGA or VGA display. Mouse required. Modem optional. Laser printer optional. *Single User Price: $795.00 Special $950.00 card for extra displays optional, but highly recommended. A three day training program is available for $300.00.*

Paired Word Memory Task

Rosamond Gianutsos
Georgine Vroman
Pauline Matheson

Life Science Associates
1 Fenimore Road
Bayport, NY 11705-2115
(516) 472-2111
Fax: (516) 472-8146

Program administers a task that is designed to promote associative verbal learning skills. Pairs of unrelated words are presented. Later, when the computer displays one word of the pair, the subject must provide the second word. Interference may be given between trials to prevent reliance on rehearsal.

Classification: Cognitive Rehab: Memory

Hardware Requirements and Price
Apple II, 64 K, 10 Mb hard disk optional, 1 disk drive (5-1/4). Monochrome or color display. *Single User Price: $40.00*

IBM PC, XT, AT, PS/2, & compatibles; 128 K; 20 Mb hard disk optional; 1 disk drive. CGA, EGA or VGA display. *Single User Price: $40.00*

Personnel Policy Expert

Knowledge Point
1311 Clegg Street
Petaluma, CA 94954
(707) 762-0333
(800) 727-1133

An expert system for writing a complete personnel manual. Detailed manual included. Latest release November, 1991.

Classification: Industrial Consulting

Hardware Requirements and Price
IBM PC, XT, AT, PS/2, & compatibles; 512 K; 2.5 Mb hard disk required; 1 disk drive. Color display required. Printer required. *Single User Price: $495.00*

Reviews
Personal policy expert. (1990). *Social Science Microcomputer Review, 8,* 151-153.

Peterson's Career Options

Peterson's Guides, Inc.
P.O. Box 2123
Princeton, NJ 08543-2123
(609) 243-9111
(800) 338-3282

A comprehensive guidance and information package designed to help students and adults identify occupations suited to their interests, skills, and abilities. Provides occupational descriptions, related occupations, and information on career planning. Occupational profiles and a "why not" feature are provided. A separate interest assessment is available with scoring and interpretation done by the program. Latest release November, 1991.

Classification: Career Counseling

Hardware Requirements and Price
Apple II, 128 K, hard disk optional, 2 disk drives. Requires ProDOS. *Single User Price: $295.00*

IBM PC, XT, AT, PS/2, & compatibles, 256 K; hard disk optional; 2 disk drives. Laser printer optional. Requires DOS 3.3. *Single User Price: $295.00*

Peterson's College Selection Service

Peterson's Guides, Inc.
P.O. Box 2123
Princeton, NJ 08543-2123
(609) 243-9111
(800) 338-3282

Helps students and their families identify colleges that meet their needs. Detailed manual included. On-line help available. Latest release September, 1991.

Classification: Career Counseling

Hardware Requirements and Price
Apple II, 128 K, 2 disk drives. Requires Apple Pascal. *Single User Price: $159.00*

IBM PC, XT, AT, PS/2, & compatibles; 256 K; 750 K hard disk optional; 1 disk drive. Laser printer optional. Requires DOS 2.1. *Single User Price: $159.00*

Peterson's Financial Aid Service (FAS)

Peterson's Guides, Inc.
P.O. Box 2123
Princeton, NJ 08543-2123
(609) 243-9111
(800) 338-3282

Completes the calculations needed to analyze aid eligibility at selected colleges. Identifies government, private, and college aid for which students qualify. Detailed manual included. On-line help available. Latest release September, 1991.

Classification: Career Counseling

Hardware Requirements and Price
Apple II, 128 K, 2 disk drives. Requires Apple Pascal. *Single User Price: $195.00*

IBM PC, XT, AT, PS/2, & compatibles; 256 K; 750 K hard disk optional; 1 disk drive. Laser printer optional. Requires DOS 2.1. *Single User Price: $195.00 Network Price: Contact publisher.*

Reviews
Peterson's Financial Aid Service 1991, Media Evaluation Center. (January, 1991). *School Library Journal*, 46-47.
Peterson's Financial Aid Service 1991. (January, 1991). *Micro Reviews*.

The Planning Guide

The Guidance Shoppe
2909 Brandemere Drive
Tallahassee, FL 32312
(904) 385-6717

This program makes it easy to write yearly guidance plans or classroom lesson plans. The categories include goal statements, objectives, evaluation criteria, activities, resources available, and the date activities are completed. Powerful word processing commands allow easy insertion, deletion, and changing of information. Plans can be updated and reused. Printed reports are available. Detailed manual included.

Classification: Counseling Aid

Hardware Requirements and Price
Apple II, 48 K, 1 disk drive (5-1/4). *Single User Price: $79.95*

IBM PC, XT, AT, PS/2, & compatibles, 2 disk drives. *Single User Price: $89.95*

Practice Speech
Muriel Goldojarb

Sunset Software
9277 East Corrine Drive
Scottsdale, AZ 85260
(602) 451-0753

Program intended for laryngectomee and other speakers who need supplementary practice on rate, voice, and articulation. Users are required to read and repeat words and phrases displayed in large-sized letters. Program offers two preset time-control choices and several levels of difficulty according to time delay, stimulus length, and phonemic complexity. Program offers 13 different treatment sections offering up to 180 stimulus items divided into single words or linked together into phrases. Allows user to exit if fatigue is factor. Instruction booklet included. Latest release June, 24 1990.

Classification: Cognitive Rehab: Verbal

Hardware Requirements and Price
Apple II+, IIe, IIc, IIgs; 64 K; 10 Mb hard disk optional; 1 disk drive. Not compatible with laser printer. Requires DOS 3.3. *Single User Price: $49.95*

Problem-Solving I: Rehabilitation
Robert J. Sbordone
Steven Hall

Robert J. Sbordone, PhD, Inc.
7700 Irvine Center Drive
Suite 750
Irvine, CA 92718
(714) 753-7711

Program provides computer-based training in visual and spatial problem-solving skills for patients with impaired cognitive functioning. The program requires the examinee to move a small square on the monitor to a goal box using a joystick. The task increases in difficulty as the test taker's skills improve. Program monitors responsivity and determines when rest periods are needed and when a session should be terminated. The program maintains performance data over time and provides an analysis on request. Speech synthesizer option. Detailed manual included.

Classification: Cognitive Rehab: General

Hardware Requirements and Price
Apple II, 48 K, hard disk optional, 1 disk drive (5-1/4). Mouse optional. Modem optional. Laser printer optional. Joystick required. Speech synthesizer optional. *Single User Price: $195.00*

Problem-Solving II: Rehabilitation
Robert J. Sbordone
Steven Hall

Robert J. Sbordone, PhD, Inc.
7700 Irvine Center Drive
Suite 750
Irvine, CA 92708
(714) 753-7711

Improves planning skills to facilitate effective problem-solving and train the patient to plan and evaluate the consequences of future behavior. The tasks become increasingly difficult as the test taker's skills improve. Program monitors the patient's responses and determines when rest periods are needed. Maintains patient performance data over time and provides an analysis on request. Speech synthesizer option. Detailed manual included.

Classification: Cognitive Rehab: General

Hardware Requirements and Price
Apple II, 64 K, 1 disk drive. *Single User Price: $195.00*

Productivity Improvement Program Series (PIPS)
Charles E. Kozoll

MetriTech
111 North Market Street
Champaign, IL 61820
(217) 398-4868
(800) 747-4868

PIPS helps users develop skills in managing time, handling stress, communicating, motivating others, and training subordinates. On-line help available. Latest release 1991.

Classification: Industrial Consulting

Hardware Requirements and Price
IBM PC, XT, AT, PS/2, & compatibles; 256 K; hard disk optional; 1 disk drive. *Single User Price: $125.00*

The Psych-Assistant
Nancy L. Chaconas
Christianne Brems
Judy I. Stewart
Bert W. Shaw

CATSco
1531 Chapala Street, Suite 4
Santa Barbara, CA 93101-3060
(800) 522-8726
(800) 521-8726 (from Canada)

Helps patients with self esteem, assertiveness, stress management, and thinking skills. Consists of HELP-Menu and HELP-Esteem, Youth and Adult; HELP-Stress; HELP-Assert; and HELP-Think, Youth and Adult. (See individual listings for program details.) Detailed manual and tutorial program included. Latest release 1991.

Classification: Counseling Aid

Hardware Requirements and Price
IBM PC, XT, AT, PS/2, & compatibles; 256 K; 6 Mb hard disk required; 1 disk drive. Monochrome or CGA display. Laser printer optional. *Single User Price: $1,795.00 (12 users), $2,250.00 (24 users) Network Price: Contact publisher. Unlimited use.*

Reviews
Sowers-Hoag, K. (1991). HELP-Stress, HELP-Assert, HELP-Esteem. *Computers in Human Services, 8*(2), 141.

User Site References
Joe Garms, University of Texas Medical Center, 1400 Wallace Boulevard, Arlington, TX, 79106, (806) 354-5463
Richard D. Stanton, Iroquois M.H.C., P.O. Box 332, Watseka, IL, 60970, (815) 432-5241
Wayne Theye, Ohio Northern University, Ada, OH, 45810, (419) 772-2190

Reaction Time Measure of Visual Field
Rosamond Gianutsos
Carol Klitzner

Life Science Associates
1 Fenimore Road
Bayport, NY 11705-2115
(516) 472-2111
Fax: (516) 472-8146

Program can be used to detect slowed response to visual stimuli. Subject must press any key on the keyboard in response to the display of a number on the screen. The computer tracks response times and displays the results. Stimuli appear in different areas of the screen on each trial. This is one module from Cogrehab.

Classification: Cognitive Rehab: Visual

Hardware Requirements and Price
Apple II, 64 K, 10 Mb hard disk optional, 1 disk drive (5-1/4). Monochrome or color display. *Single User Price: $40.00*

IBM PC, XT, AT, PS/2, & compatibles; 128 K; 20 Mb hard disk optional; 1 disk drive. CGA display required. *Single User Price: $40.00*

School Discipline Manager (SDM)

Dynacomp, Inc.
The Dynacomp Office Building
178 Phillips Road
Webster, NY 14580
(716) 265-4040
(800) 828-6772

Keeps accurate and up-to-date records of discipline information. Data can be easily entered for each student and a running record is maintained to facilitate monthly discipline reports. SDM tracks 29 different infractions in up to 15 different locations. It includes date, type and location of infraction, teacher and administrator involved, and disposition. Reports include a single student's entire discipline record, all infractions for a particular teacher or administrator, the number of each type of infraction, two monthly suspension reports, letters to parents, mailing labels, homeroom lists, and school or class rosters. SDM can be used for parent conferences, in preparation for court, or to provide teachers with hard evi-

dence of discipline complaints. The small-school version accommodates 800 students, the large-school version 2,400 students. Instruction booklet included.

Classification: Counseling Aid

Hardware Requirements and Price
Apple II, 48 K, 1 disk drive (5-1/4). Laser printer optional. Requires DOS 3.3. *Single User Price: $199.95 (small school version), $249.95 (large school version) Demonstration Version: $25.00*

IBM PC, XT, AT, PS/2, & compatibles; 128 K; hard disk optional; 1 disk drive. Laser printer optional. *Single User Price: $199.95 (small school version), $249.95 (large school version) Demonstration Version: $25.00*

Searching for Shapes
Rosamond Gianutsos
Carol Klitzner

Life Science Associates
1 Fenimore Road
Bayport, NY 11705-2115
(516) 472-2111
Fax: (516) 472-8146

Designed to detect and treat differences in attention and responsiveness on the two sides of the visual field. Subject is presented with a matrix of abstract shapes on the screen with an empty box in the middle. When this box is filled, subject must locate the matching shape elsewhere in the matrix. The computer records search times for each trial and for both left-and-right-side targets and computes medians. This is one module from Cogrehab.

Classification: Cognitive Rehab: Attention

Hardware Requirements and Price
Apple II, 64 K, 10 Mb hard disk optional, 1 disk drive, (5-1/4). Monochrome or color display. *Single User Price: $40.00*

IBM PC, XT, AT, PS/2, & compatibles; 128 K; 20 Mb hard disk optional; 1 disk drive. CGA, EGA, or VGA display. *Single User Price: $40.00*

Self-Administered Free Recall
Rosamond Gianutsos

Life Science Associates
1 Fenimore Road
Bayport, NY 11705-2115
(516) 472-2111
Fax: (516) 472-8146

Program conducts a supra span memory exercise that practices the transfer of information into longer-term storage. Computer presents a list of words that the subject must then type. The computer automatically tabulates separate measures of short- and long-term storage using the Tulving and Colotla method. Serial position curves are plotted at the end of the session.

Classification: Cognitive Rehab: Memory

Hardware Requirements and Price
Apple II, 64 K, 10 Mb hard disk optional, 1 disk drive, (5-1/4). Monochrome or color display. *Single User Price: $50.00*

IBM PC, XT, AT, PS/2, & compatibles; 128 K; 20 Mb hard disk optional; 1 disk drive. CGA, EGA, or VGA display. *Single User Price: $50.00*

SIGI Plus

Sigi Plus Office
Educational Testing Service
Princeton, NJ 08541
(800) 257-SIGI

A computerized career planning program that shows people how to make decisions and guides them from unfocused ideas to practical career plans through a nine-step layering process.

Classification: Career Counseling

Hardware Requirements and Price
IBM PC, XT, AT, PS/2, & compatibles; 256 K; 10 Mb hard disk required; 1 disk drive. Laser printer optional. *Single User Price: Contact publisher.*

Six-Factor Automated Vocational Assessment System
Bruce Duthie

Precision People, Inc.
3452 North Ride Circle South
Jacksonville, FL 32223
(904) 262-1096
(800) 338-0710

The Six-Factor Automated Vocational Assessment System (SAVAS) is a vocational guidance system for adolescents and adults that matches client interest patterns with information about occupations listed in the US Department of Labor's *Occupational Outlook Handbook.* All 80 occupations represented in the system are arranged in order of similarity to the client's interest profile from SAVAS results, or information entered from other interest tests that use the six factors of Holland's vocational theory. The six factors represented are realistic, investigative, artistic, social, enterprising, and conventional. Detailed manual included.

Classification: Career Counseling

Hardware Requirements and Price
Apple II, 128 K, hard disk optional, 1 disk drive (5-1/4). Printer required. *Single User Price: $195.00*

IBM PC, XT, AT, PS/2, & compatibles; 256 K; hard disk optional; 1 disk drive. Printer required. *Single User Price: $195.00*

Slow Speech
Muriel Goldojarb

Sunset Software
9277 E. Corrine Drive
Scottsdale, AZ 85260
(602) 451-0753

Program intended for dysarthric and other speakers who need supplementary practice in articulatory precision as a function of reduced rate of speech. Users are required to read and repeat words and phrases displayed in large-sized letters on the screen. Program offers several levels of difficulty according to time delay, stimulus length, and phonemic complexity. There are 12 different treatment sections, with up to 180 stimulus items divided into single words or linked into phrases. Allows user to exit if fatigued or if time becomes a factor. Instruction booklet included. Latest release June 24, 1990.

Classification: Cognitive Rehab: Verbal

Hardware Requirements and Price
Apple II+, IIe, IIc, IIgs; 64 K; 10 Mb hard disk optional; 1 disk drive (5-1/4). Not compatible with laser printer. Requires DOS 3.3. *Single User Price: $49.95*

SPECTRUM-I
Larry A. Braskamp
Martin L. Maehr

MetriTech
111 North Market Street
Champaign, IL 61820
(217) 398-4868
(800) 398-4868

SPECTRUM-I measures four motivation factors: accomplishment, recognition, power, and affiliation. It's uses include selection, career planning, and pre-interview testing. Detailed manual included. Latest release 1987.

Classification: Career Counseling

Hardware Requirements and Price
IBM PC, XT, AT, PS/2, & compatibles; 256 K; hard disk optional; 1 disk drive. Laser printer optional. *Single User Price: $519.00*

Reviews
Mercadal, D. (1987, October). Review of SPECTRUM-I. *Psychologist's Software Club Newsletter*, 1-2.

Speech Ware 2.0
Douglas L. Chute

Maclaboratory, Inc.
314 Exeter Road
Devon, PA 19333
(215) 688-3114

An argumentative and prosthetic approach to computer use for individuals with communications difficulties and motor impairments. Speech Ware uses both synthesized and digitized sound and provides modules for telephone communication, and electrical appliance and circuit control. It serves as a model system for rehabilitation and prosthetic software. On-line help available. Tutorial program included. Latest release September, 1991.

Classification: Cognitive Rehab: Verbal

Hardware Requirements and Price
Macintosh, 2 Mb, 20 Mb hard disk required, 1 disk drive (3-1/2). Color display recommended. Mouse required. Modem optional. Laser printer optional. Requires System 7.0. *Single User Price: $49.95*

Speeded Reading of Word Lists
Rosamond Gianutsos
Carol Klitzner

Life Science Associates
1 Fenimore Road
Bayport, NY 11705-2115
(516) 472-2111
Fax: (516) 472-8146

Designed to diagnose and treat at least four basic functions of human visual information processing, including anchoring at margins, scanning horizontally, identification of words within peripheral span, and monitoring the periphery. The lists are presented in three different formats. This is one module from Cogrehab. Latest release 1988.

Classification: Cognitive Rehab: Visual

Hardware Requirements and Price
Apple II, 64 K, 10 Mb hard disk optional, 1 disk drive (5-1/4). Monochrome or color display. *Single User Price: $40.00*

IBM PC, XT, AT, PS/2, & compatibles; 128 K; 20 Mb hard disk optional; 1 disk drive. CGA, EGA, or VGA display. *Single User Price: $40.00 Network Price: $120.00*

Stress Management

Cambridge Career Products
P.O. Box 2153
Charleston, WV 25328-2153
(304) 744-9323
(800) 468-4227

Students or adults learn the importance of managing stress. Two versions available, one for students and another for adults. Instruction booklet included.

Classification: Counseling Aid

Hardware Requirements and Price
Apple II, 48 K. *Single User Price: $49.50*

IBM PC, XT, AT, PS/2, & compatibles. *Single User Price: $49.50*

Success on Stress-Computerized Stress Assessment

Dynacomp, Inc.
The Dynacomp Office Building
178 Phillips Road
Webster, NY 14580
(716) 265-4040
(800) 828-6772

A stress assessment designed to enable an organization to measure employee stress levels, determine types of coping responses being used, find out how well stress is handled, and provide information on how to work with stress. It can be used alone or as part of a stress management program. Each participant is given detailed, personalized information on their stress responses and an action plan with suggestions designed to improve negative coping behaviors. The program also rates each participant on the Optimal Human Perform-ance Scale. This scale graphically displays how well the individual has adapted his or her coping strategies to stress. Instruction booklet included.

Classification: Relaxation Training

Hardware Requirements and Price
IBM PC, XT, AT, PS/2, & compatibles; 128 K; hard disk optional; 1 disk drive. Laser printer optional. Requires DOS 2.0. *Single User Price: $69.95*

Sunset Software 3.5-Vol. I
Richard C. Katz

Sunset Software
9277 East Corrine Drive
Scottsdale, AZ 85260
(602) 451-0753

Five complete treatments programs are pre-sented: Understanding Questions II, Under-standing Sentences II, Understanding Stories II, Fact File, and Cognitive Drills: Set I (Visual Skills). (See individual listings for program details.) Instruction booklet included. Latest release June 24, 1990.

Classification: Cognitive Rehab: General

Hardware Requirements and Price
Apple II, 64 K, 10 Mb hard disk optional, 1 disk drive (3-1/2). Laser printer optional. Requires ProDOS. *Single User Price: $149.95*

System 2000 DOT Database

ValPar International Corp.
P.O. Box 5767
Tucson, AZ 85703-5767
(602) 293-1510
(800) 528-7070

System 2000 is a modular, integrated software system. This module provides access to the 12,885 job profiles contained in the *Dictionary of Occupational Titles, 4th Edition* (US DOL) using factors described in the *Handbook for Analyzing Jobs* (US DOL, 1972). Detailed manual included. On-line help available.

Classification: Career Counseling

Hardware Requirements and Price
IBM PC, XT, AT, PS/2, & compatibles; 640 K; 20 Mb hard disk required. CGA, EGA, or VGA display. Printer required. Laser printer optional.

System 2000 Work Hardening

ValPar International Corp.
P.O. Box 5767
Tucson, AZ 85703-5767
(602) 293-1510
(800) 528-7070

This a modular, integrated software system is used by occupational therapists and/or physical therapists to collect daily performance data from a variety of work simulation tasks and to generate progress reports. Detailed manual included. On-line help available.

Classification: Career Counseling

Hardware Requirements and Price
IBM PC, XT, AT, PS/2, & compatibles; 640 K; 20 Mb hard disk required. CGA, EGA, or VGA display. Printer required. Laser printer optional.

System 2000 Work History

ValPar International Corp.
P.O. Box 5767
Tucson, AZ 89703-5767
(602) 293-1510
(800) 528-7070

From an individual's previous jobs this modular, integrated software calculates a Worker Qualification Profile, using factors described in the *Handbook for Analyzing Jobs* (US DOL, 1972). The resulting factor list indicates the person's transferable job skills. Detailed manual included. On-line help available.

Classification: Career Counseling

Hardware Requirements and Price
IBM PC, XT, AT, PS/2, & compatibles; 640 K; 20 Mb hard disk required. CGA, EGA, or VGA display. Printer required. Laser printer optional. *Single User Price: Contact publisher.*

Tachistoscopic Reading
Rosamond Gianutsos

Life Science Associates
1 Fenimore Road
Bayport, NY 11705-2115

(516) 472-2111
Fax: (516) 472-8146

A visual memory exercise useful for people with attention deficit disorders, foveal imperception, or verbal apraxia. Task speed is adjusted by the computer for each subject. The program can print presented words and subject responses.

Classification: Cognitive Rehab: Visual

Hardware Requirements and Price
Apple II, 64 K, 10 Mb hard disk optional, 1 disk drive (5-1/4). Monochrome or color display. *Single User Price: $50.00*

IBM PC, XT, AT, PS/2, & compatibles; 128 K; 20 Mb hard disk optional; 1 disk drive. CGA, EGA, or VGA display. *Single User Price: $50.00*

TAP: Talent Assessment Program

Talent Assessment, Inc.
P.O. Box 5087
Jacksonville, FL 32247-5087
(904) 260-4102
(800) 634-1472

Measures the functional aptitudes of a client and links them to suggested types of work.

Classification: Career Counseling

Hardware Requirements and Price
Apple II, 360 K hard disk optional. Printer required. Laser printer optional. *Single User Price: $5,590.00*

IBM PC, XT, AT, PS/2, & compatibles; 256 K; 900 K hard disk optional. Printer required.

Laser printer optional. *Single User Price: $5,590.00*

User Site References
Marge Gazvoda, University of South Florida, Tampa, FL, 33620, (813) 974-3455
Ron Martens, Northern Lights College, 11401 8th Street, Dawson Creek, BC, Z1G 4G2, Canada, (604) 784-7510
Gary Meers, University of Nebraska, 518 East Nebraska Hall, Lincoln, NE 68858, (402) 472-2365

Task Master
Linda Laatsch

Life Science Associates
1 Fenimore Road
Bayport, NY 11705-2115
(516) 472-2111
Fax: (516) 472-8146

Enables users to design their own tasks in attention/arousal, scanning, memory, sequencing, pair identification, and reading. Therapists can set up individualized programs using their own or built-in stimuli. Tasks can be saved and reused. Detailed manual included. Latest release 1988.

Classification: Cognitive Rehab: General

Hardware Requirements and Price
Apple II, 64 K, 10 Mb hard disk optional, 1 disk drive (5-1/4). Monochrome or color display. Printer required. *Single User Price: $195.00*

IBM PC, XT, AT, PS/2, & compatibles; 128 K; 20 Mb hard disk optional; 1 disk drive. CGA, EGA, or VGA display. *Single User Price: $195.00*

Teenage Stress Profile
Lyle H. Miller
Alma Dell Smith
Bruce L. Mehler
Mark Appel

Queue, Inc.
338 Commerce Drive
Fairfield, CT 06430
(203) 335-0906
(800) 232-2224
Fax: (203) 336-2481

Identifies physical and psychological symptoms of teenage stress. After the user answers several sets of questions, the computer outlines specific problems experienced and makes suggestions on how to deal with the problems. Instruction booklet included.

Classification: Counseling Aid

Hardware Requirements and Price
Apple II+, IIe, IIc, IIgs; 64 K; 1 disk drive (5-1/4). *Single User Price: $99.00*

IBM PC, XT, AT, PS/2, & compatibles; 256 K; 1 Mb hard disk optional; 1 disk drive. *Single User Price: $99.00*

Thinkable

The Psychological Corporation
555 Academic Court
San Antonio, TX 78204-0952
(512) 299-1061
(800) 228-0752

A computer-delivered rehabilitation program that helps individuals recover vital cognitive skills impaired due to brain injury, disease, or developmental disorders. It assists with patient therapy by utilizing visual and auditory stimuli including photo-quality pictures, animation, graphics, and a life-like human voice. A touch-screen capability permits simple, direct interaction with the computer and non-verbal help screens show patients how to respond. Thinkable assists the clinician with case management by automatically collecting data from each therapy session. Detailed manual included.

Classification: Cognitive Rehab: General

Hardware Requirements and Price
IBM PC, XT, AT, PS/2, & compatibles; 2 Mb RAM; 60 Mb hard disk required; 1 disk drive. VGA with touch-sensitive display. Mouse required. Requires OS/2 version 1.3 and Thinkable convenience kit. *Single User Price: Contact publisher.*

Understanding Questions I
Richard C. Katz

Sunset Software
9277 E. Corrine Drive
Scottsdale, AZ 85260
(602) 451-0753

A reading comprehension program that presents questions that contrast a selected pair of "Wh-" question words (who, what, where, when, why, how). Three hundred multiple choice questions require the user to press the number key (1 or 2) that corresponds with the answer. Specific feedback is given on each response to facilitate learning. Bar and line graphs are presented to display current and past session performances. Data is saved on disk for later review by the clinician. Not copy-protected. Instruction booklet included. Latest release June 24, 1990.

Classification: Cognitive Rehab: Verbal

Hardware Requirements and Price
Apple II+, IIe, IIc, IIgs; 48 K; 10 Mb hard disk optional; 1 disk drive (5-1/4). Laser printer optional. Requires DOS 3.3. *Single User Price: $29.95*

Understanding Questions II: More Questions
Richard C. Katz

Sunset Software
9277 E. Corrine Drive
Scottsdale, AZ 85260
(602) 451-0753

Program presents reading comprehension questions that contrast a selected pair of "Wh-" question words (who, what, where, when, why, and how). Over 500 questions are included. Users responded to multiple choice questions by pressing the number key (1 or 2) that corresponds with the answer. Special options and specific feedback are provided to facilitate learning. Current and past performance data are displayed in bar and line graphs. Data is saved for later review. Instruction booklet included. Latest release June 24, 1990.

Classification: Cognitive Rehab: Verbal

Hardware Requirements and Price
Apple II+, IIe, IIc, IIgs; 64 K; 10 Mb hard disk optional; 1 disk drive (5-1/4). Laser printer optional. Requires ProDOS. *Single User Price: $49.95*

Understanding Sentences I: Finding Absurdities
Richard C. Katz
Leonard L. LaPointe

Sunset Software
9277 East Corrine Drive
Scottsdale, AZ 85260
(602) 451-0753

A reading comprehension program that presents an absurd sentence and asks the user to select the word in the sentence that does not make sense. Fifty sentence sets are included. All responses are multiple choice and require the user to press the number key (1 , 2, or 3) that corresponds with the answer. Feedback is provided for each response. Line and bar line graphs display information on current and past performances. Clients can save information for later review. Instruction booklet included. Latest release June 24, 1990.

Classification: Cognitive Rehab: Verbal

Hardware Requirements and Price
Apple II+, IIe, IIc, IIgs; 48 K; 10 Mb hard disk optional; 1 disk drive (5-1/4). Laser printer optional. Requires DOS 3.3. *Single User Price: $29.95*

Understanding Sentences II: Abstract Meaning
Richard C. Katz

Sunset Software
9277 East Corrine Drive
Scottsdale, AZ 85260
(602) 451-0753

Program presents a proverb or cliché and asks the user to select the correct meaning from a field of three. Sixty sets of proverbs and meanings are included. Users press a number key (1 , 2, or 3) in response to multiple choice

questions and receive feedback. Bar and line graphs outline current and past performances. Client scores can be saved for later review. Instruction booklet included. Latest release June 24, 1990.

Classification: Cognitive Rehab: Verbal

Hardware Requirements and Price
Apple II+, IIe, IIc, IIgs; 64 K; 10 Mb hard disk optional; 1 disk drive (5-1/4). Laser printer optional. Requires ProDOS. *Single User Price: $39.95*

Understanding Stories I
Richard C. Katz

Sunset Software
9277 E. Corrine Drive
Scottsdale, AZ 85260
(602) 451-0753

Enhances reading comprehension by presenting a short story and series of three questions. Fifty sets of stories and choices are included. Program presents multiple choice questions and the user responds by pressing the number key (1, 2, or 3) that corresponds with the appropriate statement. Each response is met with feedback. Information on the user is then plotted in bar and line graphs. The information can be saved for later perusal. Instruction booklet included. Latest release June 24, 1991.

Classification: Cognitive Rehab: Verbal

Hardware Requirements and Price
Apple II+, IIe, IIc, IIgs; 48 K; 10 Mb hard disk optional; 1 disk drive (5-1/4). Laser printer optional. Requires DOS 3.3. *Single User Price: $39.95*

Understanding Stories II: More Stories

Richard C. Katz

Sunset Software
9277 E. Corrine Drive
Scottsdale, AZ 85260
(602) 451-0753

Program contains 100 short stories, each with a series of three questions. All of the questions are multiple choice and require the user to press the number key (1 , 2, or 3) that corresponds with the statement that is true according to the story. Feedback is given for each response. Bar and line graphs display current and past performance scores. Data is saved for later review by the client. Instruction booklet included. Latest release June 24, 1990.

Classification: Cognitive Rehab: Verbal

Hardware Requirements and Price
Apple II+, IIe, IIc, IIgs; 64 K; 10 Mb hard disk optional; 1 disk drive (5-1/4). Laser printer optional. Requires ProDOS. *Single User Price: $49.95*

ValueSearch

The Guidance Shoppe
2909 Brandemere Drive
Tallahassee, FL 32312
(904) 385-6717

This interactive program uses three different types of value clarification activities to help students learn which work values are most important to them. The color graphics and game format make learning about values fun. The activities look at the same 12 work values using three different approaches. Each activity takes only 10-15 min to complete. The values comparison serves as a valuable counseling tool. Printouts are available. Detailed manual included.

Classification: Career Counseling

Hardware Requirements and Price
Apple II, 48 K, 1 disk drive (5-1/4). *Single User Price: $95.00 Lab Pack: $199.95 (5 copies)*

Visual Attention Task

Linda Laatsch

Life Science Associates
1 Fenimore Road
Bayport, NY 11705-2115
(516) 472-2111
Fax: (516) 472-8146

A set of vigilance activities that require the subject to respond to targets and inhibit responses to nontargets. The test administrator can choose the number of trials, stimulus exposure/nonexposure duration, stimulus type, and regular or randomized intervals between stimuli. Latest release 1988.

Classification: Cognitive Rehab: Attention

Hardware Requirements and Price
Apple II, 64 K, 10 Mb hard disk optional, 1 disk drive (5-1/4). Monochrome or color display. *Single User Price: $40.00 Network Price: $120.00*

IBM PC, XT, AT, PS/2, & compatibles; 128 K; 20 Mb hard disk optional; 1 disk drive. CGA display required. *Single User Price: $40.00 Network Price: $120.00*

Visual Memory Task
Rosamond Gianutsos

Life Science Associates
1 Fenimore Road
Bayport, NY 11705-2115
(516) 472-2111
Fax: (516) 472-8146

A visual memory practice task. The computer displays one or more irregular patterns within a checkerboard. After studying the display, the subject "paints" the pattern on the screen and the computer records the subject's performance. The task focuses on visual, non-verbal memory. The subject can choose simple or complex displays and increase the length of the series as improvement in visual memory occurs.

Classification: Cognitive Rehab: Memory

Hardware Requirements and Price
Apple II, 64 K, 10 Mb hard disk optional, 1 disk drive (5-1/4). Monochrome or color display. *Single User Price: $50.00*

IBM PC, XT, AT, PS/2, & compatibles, 128 K, 20 Mb hard disk optional, 1 disk drive. CGA display required. *Single User Price: $50.00*

Voc-Tech Quick Screener
Arthur Cutler
Francis Ferry
Robert Kauk
Robert Robinett

CFKR Career Materials, Inc.
11860 Kemper Road, Unit 7
Auburn, CA 95603
(916) 889-2357
(800) 525-5626

Student rate 14 voc-tech occupational groups and jobs within these occupational groups and the computer generates a decision-making printout. Designed for students who do not plan to complete a 4-year college program. Instruction booklet included. Latest release 1987.

Classification: Career Counseling

Hardware Requirements and Price
Apple II+, IIe; 64 K; 1 disk drive. Laser printer optional. *Single User Price: $89.95 Network Price: $359.80*

IBM PC, XT, AT, PS/2, & compatibles; 64 K; hard disk optional; 1 disk drive. Laser printer optional. *Single User Price: $89.95 Network Price: $359.80*

Word Memory Task
Rosamond Gianutsos

Life Science Associates
1 Fenimore Road
Bayport, NY 11705-2115
(516) 472-2111
Fax: (516) 472-8146

The computer displays a random list of words, one by one, the user then types in all of the words in order. The number of words and how long they appear are determined by the user. Current scores may be viewed at any time. The exercise is designed to improve the immediate span of verbal memory. Latest release 1990.

Classification: Cognitive Rehab: Memory

Hardware Requirements and Price
Apple II, 64 K, 10 Mb hard disk optional, 1 disk drive (5-1/4). Monochrome or color

display. *Single User Price: $50.00 Network Price: $150.00*

IBM PC, XT, AT, PS/2, & compatibles; 128 K; 20 Mb hard disk drive optional; 1 disk drive. CGA display required. *Single User Price: $50.00*

Work Activities Inventory

Cambridge Career Products
P.O. Box 2153
Charleston, WV 25328-2153

(304) 744-9323
(800) 468-4227

Assists students in evaluating their future goals in select areas of study. Instruction booklet included.

Classification: Career Counseling

Hardware Requirements and Price
Apple II, 48 K. *Single User Price: $79.00*

IBM PC, XT, AT, PS/2, & compatibles; 64 K. *Single User Price: $79.00*

TESTING
SOFTWARE

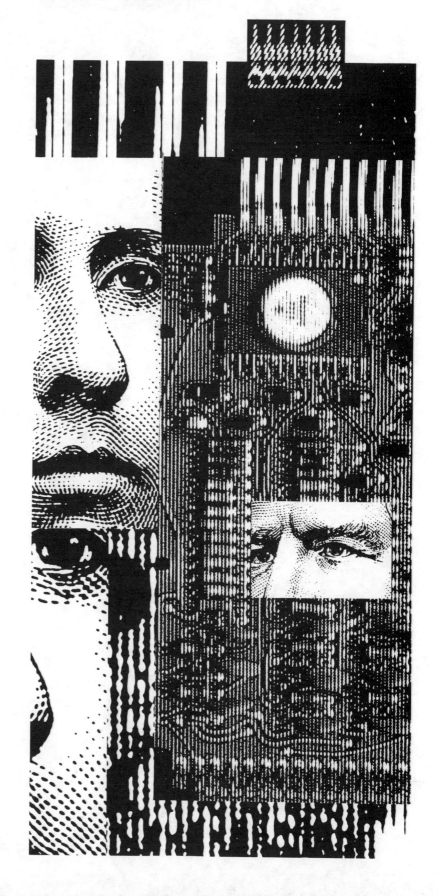

16PF-Forma C
Carlos Pal Hegedus

Psico-Iuris, S. A.
P.O. Box 1039 - Centro Colon
San Jose, 1007 Costa Rica
(506) 24-4416

Provides Sten scores and plots 16 primary personality traits along with a summary of each scale. Responses of the subjects are also printed. Unlimited use version. Detailed manual in available in Spanish. Tutorial program included. Latest release November, 1991.

Classification: 16PF (Interpretive report)

Hardware Requirements and Price
IBM PC, XT, AT, PS/2, & compatibles; 384 K; hard disk optional; 2 disk drives. Printer required. Laser printer optional. Requires DOS 3.1. *Single User Price: $250.00 Network Price: $600.00*

16PF Interpretive Report Generator
Michael E. Mills

Psytek Services
6401 West 81st Street
Los Angeles, CA 90045
(213) 670-4655
(800) 392-5454

Fully automated interpretive report generator. Reports may be exported to word processing programs and edited as desired. No per use fees. Sample report available on request. 30-day money back guarantee. Detailed manual included. Latest release March, 1992.

Classification: 16PF (Interpretive report)

Hardware Requirements and Price
IBM PC, XT, AT, PS/2, & compatibles; 512 K; hard disk optional. Monochrome, CGA, EGA, or VGA display. Laser printer optional. *Single User Price: $249.00 Site License: $349.00*

16PF: Karson Clinical Report, Version 3
Samuel Karson

Psychological Assessment Resources, Inc.
P.O. Box 998
Odessa, FL 33556
(800) 331-TEST

The Karson Clinical Report is an on-line administration, scoring and interpretation of the 16PF, Form A. The narrative report generated with this program produces charts showing scores in five significant diagnostic areas: primary personality traits, clinical signs and syndromes, interpersonal patterns, cognitive factors, and need patterns. Raw data is listed on the last page of the report. Detailed manual included. Latest release February 25, 1986.

Classification: 16PF (Administration and Interpretive report)

Hardware Requirements and Price
Apple II+, IIe; 64 K; 2 disk drives (5-1/4). *Single User Price: $170.00/$365.00*

IBM PC, XT, AT, PS/2, & compatibles; 256 K; hard disk optional; 2 disk drives or 1 disk drive and hard disk. Laser printer optional. *Single User Price: $170.00 (10 administrations) $365.00 (25 administrations)*

16PF Report
Giles D. Rainwater

Psychometric Software, Inc.
P.O. Box 1677
Melbourne, FL 32902-1677
(407) 729-6390
(800) 882-9811

The 16PF Report generates an automated interpretation of the Sixteen Personality Factor (16PF) questionnaire. A self-contained narrative report is printed, along with a test profile that graphically displays the 16PF Sten scores. Detailed manual included. Latest release 1984.

Classification: 16PF (Interpretive report)

Hardware Requirements and Price
Apple II+, IIe, IIc, IIgs; 64 K; 1 disk drive (5-1/4). Monochrome display. Printer required. Will not run on hard drive. *Single User Price: $97.50*

IBM PC, XT, AT, PS/2, & compatibles; 128 K; 10 Mb hard disk required. Monochrome, CGA, EGA, or VGA display. Laser printer optional. Can be run on Macintosh systems operating under SoftPC. *Single User Price: $97.50 Network Price: $48.75 each added user*

16PF Single-Page Report

Institute for Personality & Ability Testing
P.O. Box 188
Champaign, IL 61824-1188
(217) 352-4739
(800) 225-4728

Designed primarily for research applications, this concise scoring and interpretive program for the 16PF accepts raw scores and plots profiles for the primary scales. Scores for eight second-order personality scales, profile pattern code information, dissimulation scale scores, and item response data are also presented. Teleprocessing service. Instruction booklet included.

Classification: 16PF (Interpretive report)

Hardware Requirements and Price
1200 baud modem required. Printer required. Laser printer optional. *Price depends upon number of administrations.*

16PF Telxpress Software/License

Institute for Personality & Ability Testing (IPAT)
P.O. Box 188
Champaign, IL 61824-1188
(217) 352-4739
(800) 225-4728

Utility software for use with the Institute for Personality & Ability Testing's TeleTest Teleprocessing service. Provides access to 13 different IPAT interpretive reports. Allows batching client data off-line, reducing on-line connect times. Reports are produced using this program in conjunction with TeleTest. Instruction booklet included.

Classification: 16PF

Hardware Requirements and Price
IBM PC, XT, AT, PS/2, & compatibles; 1 disk drive. 1200 baud modem required. Printer required. Laser printer optional.

16PF/CL Clinical

AI Software, Inc.
P.O. Box 724
Wakefield, RI 02879
(401) 789-8660
(800) 272-2250

Prints a 2-4 page narrative interpretation including clinical, general, psychodiagnostic, occupational, and medical profiles. Detailed manual included.

Classification: 16PF (Interpretive report)

Hardware Requirements and Price
IBM PC, XT, AT, PS/2, & compatibles; 64 K; 1 disk drive. Printer required. Laser printer optional. Requires DOS 3.1. *Single User Price: $375.00*

3RT Test
Evelyn Lee Teng

University of Southern California
Department of Neurology (GNH 5641)

School of Medicine, 2025 Zonal Avenue
Los Angeles, CA 90033

This program presents three reaction time experiments. The three experiments are a simple RT (reaction time) task, a choice RT task, and a conditional RT task. Detailed manual included.

Classification: Neuropsychological Testing

Hardware Requirements and Price
IBM PC, XT, AT, PS/2, & compatibles. Hercules, CGA, or EGA display required. Monitor needs at least 500 x 230 pixel resolution. Mouse optional. Printer required. Laser printer optional. *Single User Price: $15.00*

Ability-Achievement Discrepancy
Davis C. Hayden
Mike Furlong

Southern Micro Systems
3545 S. Church Street
Burlington, NC 27216-2097
(919) 584-1661

Calculates the ability-achievement discrepancy and produces a report. Program assesses the degree of academic underachievement a student is experiencing. Provides a student profile comparison between ability test results and standardized achievement test results. Report provides correlations, discrepancy scores, and an interpretation of all scores. Detailed manual included. Latest release 1990.

Classification: Academic (Interpretive report)

Hardware Requirements and Price
Apple II, 1 disk drive. *Single User Price: $149.00*

IBM PC, XT, AT, PS/2, & compatibles; 512 K; 1 Mb hard disk optional; 1 disk drive. Not compatible with laser printer. *Single User Price: $149.00*

Reviews
Illovsky, M. (1989). Ability-Achievement Discrepancy. *Software for Testing,* 377.

Adaptive Behavior Inventory
Wayne P. Hresko
Paul Schlieve

Pro-Ed, Inc.
8700 Shoal Creek Blvd.
Austin, TX 78758-6897
(512) 451-3246

Uses the inventory completed by classroom teachers or other professional school staff to evaluate the daily living skills of school-age children in areas such as self-care, communication, social, academic, and occupational skills. Program generates a 4-page report that contains descriptive background information, various scores with descriptions, profiles, and significance testing for all subtests. Detailed manual included. Latest release 1986.

Classification: Academic (Interpretive report)

Hardware Requirements and Price
Apple II, 48 K, hard disk optional, 1 disk drive (5-1/4). *Single User Price: $79.00*

IBM PC, XT, AT, PS/2, & compatibles; 640 K; hard disk optional; 1 disk drive (5-1/4). *Single User Price: $79.00*

ADD-H Comprehensive Teachers' Rating Scale (ACTeRS), Second Ed.
Rina K. Ullmann
Esther K. Sleator
Robert L. Sprague

MetriTech
111 North Market Street
Champaign, IL 61820
(217) 398-4868
(800) 747-4868

Program intended for diagnosing and monitoring the behavior of the child who manifests an attention deficit (ADD) in the classroom. Includes 24 behavioral items relevant to the diagnosis of ADD with or without hyperactivity (AD-HD). Items are rated by the classroom teacher on a 5-point scale, with response categories ranging from "almost never" to "almost always." Items assess four factors: attention, hyperactivity, social skills, and oppositional. Detailed manual included. Latest release 1991.

Classification: Academic

Hardware Requirements and Price
IBM PC, XT, AT, PS/2, & compatibles; 256 K; hard disk optional; 1 disk drive. Laser printer optional. *Single User Price: $125.00 Manual: $10.00 100 Rating/Profile forms: $42.00*

Adolescent Diagnostic Screening Battery
James J. Smith
Joseph M. Eisenberg

Reason House
204 East Joppa Road, Suite 10
Towson, MD 21204
(301) 321-7270

A structured interview is administered to the 13- to 17-year old adolescent. This provides data that is independent of that given by the child's parent or guardian. A second questionnaire is completed by the clinician. Specific uses, applications, and suggestions are provided in a report that can be printed or displayed on the screen. Detailed manual included.

Classification: Academic (Administration and Interpretive report)

Hardware Requirements and Price
Apple II+, IIe; 64 K; hard disk optional; 1 disk drive. 80-column display required. *Single User Price: $195.00 Discount for APA Members $95.00*

IBM PC, XT, AT, PS/2, & compatibles; hard disk optional; 1 disk drive. *Single User Price: $195.00 Discount for APA Members: $95.00*

Adolescent Multiphasic Personality Inventory (AMPI)

Precision People, Inc.
3452 North Ride Circle South
Jacksonville, FL 32223
(904) 262-1096
(800) 338-0710

The purpose of the Adolescent Multiphasic Personality Inventory (AMPI) is to correct some of the deficiencies of the Minnesota Multiphasic Personality Inventory (MMPI) and other tests when used with adolescents. The strengths of the AMPI include: a single procedure for scoring, reading level at fourth grade, on-site scoring by hand or computer, short length (133 items), and scales that generally parallel MMPI scales. Recommended for adolescents ages 10-19. The AMPI has

three validity scales and 10 clinical scales. Instruction booklet included.

Classification: Personality Testing (Administration and Interpretive report)

Hardware Requirements and Price
Apple II, 128 K, hard disk optional, 1 disk drive (5-1/4). Printer required. Laser printer optional.

IBM PC, XT, AT, PS/2, & compatibles; 640 K; hard disk required; 1 disk drive. Printer required. Laser printer optional. *Single User Price: $495.00*

Adult Diagnostic Screening Battery
James J. Smith
Joseph M. Eisenberg

Reason House
204 East Joppa Road, Suite 10
Towson, MD 21204
(301) 321-7270

The adult patient and clinician each fill out a separate questionnaire and a report of the results is generated listing possible *DSM-III* (*Diagnostic and Statistical Manual of Mental Disorders*, 3rd ed., rev.) diagnoses. Reports can be printed or displayed on the screen. Detailed manual included.

Classification: Diagnostic Aid, DSM (Interpretive report)

Hardware Requirements and Price
Apple II+, IIe; 1 disk drive. 80 column display required. Discount for APA Members $95.00 *Single User Price: $195.00*

IBM PC, XT, AT, PS/2, & compatibles; 64 K; hard disk optional; 1 disk drive. *Single User*

Price: $195.00 Discount for APA Members: $95.00

Adult Personality Inventory
Samual E. Krug

The Test Agency International
Cournswood House, High Wycombe
Bucks, HP14 4NW England
44 240243384

English-cultural version of the Adult Personality Inventory for analyzing and reporting individual differences in personality, interpersonal style, and career preferences. Detailed manual included.

Classification: Personality Testing

Hardware Requirements and Price
IBM PC, XT, AT, PS/2, & compatibles; 512 K; 10 Mb 1 disk drive (5-1/4). EGA display. Requires DOS 3.0. *Single User Price: $750.00*

AI Offender Profile

AI Software, Inc.
P.O. Box 724
Wakefield, RI 02879
(401) 789-8660
(800) 272-2250

Specialized MMPI report for adults with a known criminal background. Report compares the patient's profile to the Megargee models and prints an interpretation based on the 2 closest fitting models to the profile type. Detailed manual included.

Classification: MMPI (Administration and Interpretive report)

Hardware Requirements and Price
IBM PC, XT, AT, PS/2, & compatibles; 193 K; hard disk required; 1 disk drive. Printer required. Laser printer optional. Requires DOS 3.1. *Single User Price: $250.00*

Alcadd Test
Morse P. Manson
George J. Huba

Western Psychological Services
12031 Wilshire Blvd.
Los Angeles, CA 90025
(213) 478-2061
(800) 648-8857

The Alcadd Test is a brief, 65-item scale that assesses drinking patterns and attitudes about alcohol that have been identified as characteristic of individuals who abuse alcohol. The test yields a total score and scores on five subscales that are reported graphically in a concise 2-page report. Teleprocessing service also available. Instruction booklet included.

Classification: Diagnostic Aid, Substance Abuse (Administration)

Hardware Requirements and Price
IBM PC, XT, AT, PS/2, & compatibles; 512 K; 1 Mb hard disk required; 1 disk drive. Printer required. Laser printer optional. Requires DOS 3.0. *Single User Price: $185.00*

Alcohol Assessment and Treatment Profile

Psychologistics, Inc.
P.O. Box 033896
Indialantic, FL 32903
(407) 259-7811

Program evaluates individuals with respect to drinking history, drinking patterns, reinforcement dimensions of drinking, beliefs about drinking, self-concept, and interpersonal relations. It is also prescriptive in nature, evaluating level of motivation for treatment, and providing relevant treatment recommendations based upon the individual's personal drinking patterns and life situations. The 3-4 page narrative report may be printed or written to a text file. Software permits unlimited uses. Detailed manual included. Latest release 1985.

Classification: Diagnostic Aid, Substance Abuse (Interpretive report)

Hardware Requirements and Price
IBM PC, XT, AT, PS/2, & compatibles; 128 K; hard disk optional; 1 disk drive. Printer required. Laser printer optional. Requires DOS 2.0. *Single User Price: $200.00 20 AATP Questionnaire: $20.00*

Macintosh, 512 K, hard disk optional, 1 disk drive (3-1/2). Printer required. *Single User Price: $200.00 20 AATP Questionnaire: $20.00*

Alcohol Use Inventory (AUI)
J. L. Horn
K. W. Wanberg
F. M. Foster

National Computer Systems, Inc.
P.O. Box 1416
Minneapolis, MN 55440
(800) 627-7271

Creates an inventory based on the theory that distinct conditions are found among persons broadly considered alcoholic. Describes different ways individuals use alcohol, major benefits derived from use, negative conse-

quences associated with use, and individual's expressed degree of concern. Requires Microtest Assessment System. Detailed manual included.

Classification: Diagnostic Aid, Substance Abuse

Hardware Requirements and Price
IBM PC, XT, AT, PS/2, & compatibles; 512 K; 10 Mb hard disk required; 1 disk drive. Monochrome, CGA, EGA, or VGA display. Modem optional. Printer required. Laser printer optional. Requires DOS 3.1. *Single User Price: Contact publisher*

API/Career Profile
Samuel E. Krug

MetriTech
111 North Market Street
Champaign, IL 61820
(217) 398-4868
(800) 747-4868

This program administers, scores, and generates immediate test results for the 21 scales and validity checks provided by the Adult Personality Inventory. The Career Profile program offers immediate comparison of 38 empirically based occupational decision models and up to 62 other models created by the administrator, providing a total comparison score for each occupation. The program generates a 7-9 page report. Detailed manual included. Latest release 1991.

Classification: Vocational Testing (Administration and Interpretive report)

Hardware Requirements and Price
IBM PC, XT, AT, PS/2, & compatibles; hard disk optional; 1 disk drive. Laser printer

optional. *Single User Price: $250.00 (25 administrations)*

Apticom
Jeffrey A. Harris
Howard Dansky

Vocational Research Institute
1528 Walnut Street, Suite 1502
Philadelphia, PA 19102
(800) 874-5387
Fax: (215) 875-0198

Desktop microcomputer with software designed specifically for assessing individual aptitudes, job interests, language, and mathematics skills. Provides method for creating a personal employment potential profile. Unit is self-scoring, self-timing, and completely portable. Capable of printing test results, transmitting data over phone lines, or downloading test score results to a personal computer. Report lists work groups of high interest for which the test taker is aptitudinally qualified and lists selected exemplary job titles within those work groups based on math and language scores. Detailed manual included. Latest release 1986.

Classification: Vocational Testing (Administration and Interpretive report)

Hardware Requirements and Price
1200 baud modem optional. RS-232 Serial Interface. *Single User Price: $5,750.00*

Reviews
Botterbusch, K. F. (1987). Vocational assessment and evaluation systems: A comparison. *Materials Development Center, University of Wisconsin-Stout*, 31-38.
Gucawa, B., Splete, H., & Stum, D. (1985). Vocational assessment systems: A review of

Apticom, MESA, & SAGE. *Michigan Personnel & Guidance Journal, 1,* 16.

User Site References
Marty Chance, Coordinator of Vocational Supplemental Services, Colorado Department of Corrections, Pre Release Center Box 4444, Canyon City, CO 81215-4444, (719) 275-4181 ext. 3689.
Don Hardesty, Center Coordinator, Baltimore County Public Schools, Community Career Center, 8200 Old Philadelphia Road, Baltimore, MD 21237, (301) 887-0133.
Lia Kennedy, Director of Operations, Bucks County Office of Employment and Training, 4259 Swamp Road, Daylestown, PA 18901, (215) 340-2020.

Aptitude Interest Measure
United States Employment Service

National Computer Systems, Inc.
P.O. Box 1416
Minneapolis, MN 55440
(800) 627-7271

Interpretive report integrates information from the United States Employment Service (USES) Interest Inventory and the General Aptitude Test Battery. Scores in 12 interest areas are related to aptitude scores by reference to 66 work groups. Thirteen-page report includes both graphical and verbal analyses of the test scores and provides specific suggestions for additional readings about job descriptions and educational/training requirements. Two-page counselor's report is also provided that summarizes the basic score data. Price depends upon number of reports generated. Detailed manual included.

Classification: Vocational Testing (Interpretive report)

Hardware Requirements and Price
Mail-in service only.

Areas of Change Computer Program
Robert Weiss

Multi-Health Systems, Inc.
908 Niagara Falls Blvd.
North Tonawanda, NY 14120-2060
(416) 424-1700
(800) 456-3003

Administrative, scoring, and interpretive program that assesses the amount of change a couple desires to bring about in their relationship. Report provides information on the total amount of change sought and areas of agreement and disagreement. Questionnaire responses are organized using affection, instrumental, and companionship scales. Sold with 50 administrations. Detailed manual included.

Classification: Diagnostic Aid (Administration and Interpretive report)

Hardware Requirements and Price
IBM PC, XT, AT, PS/2, & compatibles; 256 K; hard disk optional; 1 disk drive. Printer required. Laser printer optional. *Single User Price: $130.00*

Arion II Teleprocessing Service

National Computer Systems, Inc.
P.O. Box 1416
Minneapolis, MN 55440
(800) 627-7271

Permits scoring and interpretation of National Computer Systems (NCS) assessment instruments using a telephone hookup to NCS. Client takes psychological tests using written materials and office staff types responses at the computer keyboard. Data is transmitted to NCS where it is scored, interpreted, and a report is generated. The report is transmitted from NCS to the client's office and is printed on his or her equipment. Specific tests are listed separately in this directory. Price is based upon number of administrations. Detailed manual included.

Classification: Testing Utility

Hardware Requirements and Price
IBM PC, XT, AT, PS/2, & compatibles; 256 K; 1 Mb hard disk optional; 1 disk drive. Monochrome, CGA, EGA, or VGA display. 300-9600 baud modem required. Printer required. Laser printer optional.

An Augmented BASIC Program for Exploring Subtest Combination Short Forms
Leslie Atkinson
Glen Yoshida

2 Surrey Place
Surrey Place Centre
Toronto, ON M5S 2C2 Canada
(416) 925-5141

Abbreviated scales often involve administering a subset of tests from the full scale, and then using the obtained score to estimate the score which would have been obtained if the entire scale had been administered. Tellegen and Briggs (1967) provided formulae for determining the reliability, validity, and standard deviations of this type of short form. Atkinson and Yoshida (1989) described a BASIC program for making the requisite reliability and validity calculations. This is an augmented program that includes computation of standard deviations. On-line help available. Latest release October, 1991.

Classification: Intelligence Testing (Administration)

Hardware Requirements and Price
IBM PC, XT, AT, PS/2, & compatibles; 640 K; 100 K hard disk optional; 1 disk drive (5-1/4). Mouse optional. Modem optional. Laser printer optional. *Single User Price: Free*

Reviews
Atkinson, L., & Yoshida, G. (1991). An augmented BASIC program for exploring subtest combination short forms. *Educational and Psychological Assessment, 51*, 639-640.

Automated Child/Adolescent Social History (ACASH)
Mark Rohde

National Computer Systems, Inc.
P.O. Box 1416
Minneapolis, MN 55440
(800) 627-7271

On-line administered social history designed to gather information about life events and current circumstances of children and adolescents. Requires Microtest Assessment System. Detailed manual included.

Classification: Diagnostic Aid, Children and Adolescents (Administration and Interpretive report)

Hardware Requirements and Price
IBM PC, XT, AT, PS/2, & compatibles; 512 K; 10 Mb hard disk required; 1 disk drive. Monochrome, CGA, EGA, or VGA display. Printer

required. Laser printer optional. Requires DOS 3.1 and NCS Scorbox interface.

Automated Social History-ASH Plus
Joseph A. Waldron

Anderson Publishing Company
P.O. Box 1576
Cincinnati, OH 45201
(513) 421-4142
(800) 582-7295

Produces reports covering the most important areas of a subject's social and personal functioning. Generates five useful reports summarizing 401 client questions. ASH Plus can be administered on-line with the ability to add comments to any question, or can be administered off-line with disposable question/answer booklets and scannable answer sheets. Detailed manual included.

Classification: Diagnostic Aid, History (Administration and Interpretive report)

Hardware Requirements and Price
IBM PC, XT, AT, PS/2, & compatibles; 640 K; hard disk required. Printer required. Laser printer optional. *Single User Price: $345.00*

AutoPACL
Brian P. Robbins

21st Century Assessment
P.O. Box 608
South Pasadena, CA 91031
(818) 441-0614
(800) 374-2100

AutoPACL is the authorized software edition of Stephen Stracks Personality Adjective Check List (PACL). The PACL is a comprehensive, objective measure of eight basic personality styles as outlined by Millon, intended for use with normal adults. It also features a problem indicator (PI) scale measuring aspects of Millon's three more severe personalities. The Basic AutoPACL program allows you to administer and score the PACL, and display and print PACL profiles. AutoPACL with Interpretive Narratives additionally produces interpretive narrative reports, clinical research, and personnel applications. Detailed manual included. On-line help available. Latest release 11/91.

Classification: Personality Testing (Administration and Interpretive report)

Hardware Requirements and Price
IBM PC, XT, AT, PS/2, & compatibles; 384 K; 1 Mb hard disk optional; 1 disk drive. Mouse optional. Laser printer optional. Requires DOS 2.0. *Single User Price: $395.00 (AutoPACL with Interpretive Narratives), $10.00 (demo program), $195.00 (basic program without narratives)*

AutoSCID II
Michael First
Miriam Gibbon
Janet Williams
Robert Spitzer

Multi-Health Systems, Inc.
908 Niagara Falls Blvd.
North Tonawanda, NY 14120-2060
(416) 424-1700
(800) 456-3003

Combines patient interview and expert system for *DSM-II-R* (*Diagnostic and Statistical Manual of Mental Disorders*, 2nd ed., rev.) Axis II diagnosis. Can be used directly by patients and/or information can be entered after a patient interview. This program includes a computerized version of the Structured Clinical Interview for *DSM-II-R*, Axis II (SCID II, Personality Disorders) and the SCID-II Personality Questionnaire. Co-published with the American Psychiatric Association. Detailed manual included. Latest release 1991.

Classification: Diagnostic Aid, DSM (Administration and Interpretive Report)

Hardware Requirements and Price
IBM PC, XT, AT, PS/2, & compatibles; 512 K; hard disk required; 1 disk drive. Printer required. Laser printer optional. *Single User Price: $450.00*

Reviews
Schlosser, B. (1991). Computer assistance for diagnosing *DSM-III-R* personality disorders. *Journal of Personality Assessment, 57*, 199-201.

Baker Student Adaptation to College Questionnaire (SACQ)
Robert W. Baker
Bohdan Siryk
George J. Hueba

Western Psychological Services
12031 Wilshire Blvd.
Los Angeles, CA 90025
(213) 478-2061
(800) 648-8857

The SACQ is a 67-item, self-report, Likert-type scale that can be administered individually or in group settings. Designed to measure the effectiveness of a student's adjustment to college, the SACQ can be completed in approximately 20 min. The SACQ diskette administers, scores, and interprets the questionnaire. Teleprocessing service also available. Instruction booklet included.

Classification: Diagnostic Aid (Administration and Interpretive report)

Hardware Requirements and Price
IBM PC, XT, AT, PS/2, & compatibles; 512 K; 1 Mb hard disk required; 1 disk drive. Printer required. Laser printer optional. Requires DOS 3.0. *Single User Price: $185.00*

Barclay Classroom Assessment System (BCAS)

Western Psychological Services
12031 Wilshire Blvd.
Los Angeles, CA 90025
(213) 478-2061
(800) 648-8857

Scoring and interpretation report for data collected from self, peers, and teacher. Makes recommendations about general referrals, learning handicaps, gifted, problem areas, classroom problems, vocational awareness, peer tutoring candidates, contracting candidates, temperament patterns, achievement problems, factor scores, comparison of total ratings, achievement summary, and recommendations. Teleprocessing service.

Classification: Diagnostic Aid, Children and Adolescents (Interpretive report)

Basic Personality Inventory
Douglas N. Jackson

Sigma Assessment Systems, Inc.
P.O. Box 610984
Port Huron, MI 48061-0984
(800) 265-1285

On-site software administers and scores a 240 item, multi-phasic personality inventory intended for use with both normal and clinical adult and adolescent populations. The Summary Report contains a profile of the 11 BPI substantive clinical scales and the one critical item scale. The Clinical Report also contains scale descriptions and an interpretive validity paragraph. An Interpretive Report is under development. Per-test fees apply. Detailed manual included. On-line help available.

Classification: Personality Testing (Administration and Interpretive report)

Hardware Requirements and Price
IBM PC, XT, AT, PS/2, & compatibles; 256 K; 1 Mb hard disk optional; 1 disk drive. Laser printer optional. *Single User Price: $150.00 (first 25 scorings), $112.50 (25 additional scorings), $75.00 (10 additional scorings)*

Beck Interpretive Software

The Psychological Corporation
555 Academic Court
San Antonio, TX 78204-0952
(512) 299-1061
(800) 228-0752

Scores and interprets the Beck Anxiety Inventory, Beck Depression Inventory, Beck Hopelessness Scale, and Beck Scale of Suicide Ideation. Scannable answer sheets work with the program to make data input easy and accurate. Printed reports reflect the experience of staff at the Center for Cognitive Therapy in profile analysis and critical item discussion. An optional, but suggested scanner for reading the answer sheets is the NCS 3000 or compatible. Detailed manual included. On-line help available. Latest release August, 1992.

Classification: Personality Testing (Interpretive report)

Hardware Requirements and Price
IBM PC, XT, AT, PS/2, & compatibles; 640 K; hard disk optional; 2 disk drives. Laser printer optional.

Behaviordyne In House
Joseph C. Finney
Charles D. Auvenshine
Roger W. Sward

Behaviordyne, Inc.
P.O. Box 10994
Palo Alto, CA 94303-0992
(415) 857-0111
(800) 627-2673

Reports for the MMPI or the California Psychological Inventory (CPI) may be obtained in 14 formats. All reports include fully annotated *DSM-III* or *DSM-II* (ICD-90) diagnoses ranked according to probability of application. Instruction booklet included. On-line help available. Latest release 1991.

Classification: Personality Testing (Interpretive report)

Hardware Requirements and Price
IBM PC, XT, AT, PS/2, & compatibles; 512 K; 2 Mb hard disk required; 1 disk drive. Printer required. Laser printer optional. Requires DOS 2.0. *Single User Price: Contact publisher, per test fee applies*

User Site References
Raymond D. Elish, Raymond D. Elish, Inc., 9197 White Oaks Circle, Brecksville, OH, 44141-1654, (216) 526-4442
William J. Fiester, Vice President, Behaviordyne Psychological Corporation, 994 San Antonio Avenue, Palo Alto, CA, 94303-4951, (415) 857-0712

Behaviordyne On Line System
Joseph C. Finney
Charles D. Auvenshine

Behaviordyne, Inc.
P.O. Box 10994
Palo Alto, CA 94303
(415) 857-0111
(800) 627-2673

Computer reports for the MMPI or the CPI can be obtained in a brief or long form. All reports include fully annotated and properly classified *DSM-III* diagnoses ranked according to probability of application. *DSM-II* (ICD-90) diagnoses are available as an option. Data communication time is less than 1 min per report. Teleprocessing service. Instruction booklet included. On-line help available. Latest release 1992.

Classification: Personality Testing (Interpretive report)

Hardware Requirements and Price
IBM PC, XT, AT, PS/2, & compatibles; 384 K; hard disk required; 1 disk drive. 300-1200 baud modem required. Printer required. Laser printer optional. Requires DOS 2.0. Card reader may be used for data input. *Single User Price: $200.00 plus per test fee*

Bender Report
Giles D. Rainwater
L. Michael Wanaker

Psychometric Software, Inc.
P.O. Box 1677
Melbourne, FL 32902-1677

(407) 729-6390
(800) 882-9811

This program facilitates scoring and furnishes a detailed interpretation of the Bender Gestalt test. The program provides scoring and interpretation of both child and adult protocols. Detailed manual included. Latest release 1984.

Classification: Personality Testing (Interpretive report)

Hardware Requirements and Price
Apple II+, IIe, IIc, IIgs; 64 K; hard disk optional; 1 disk drive (5-1/4). Monochrome display. Printer required. Will not run on hard drive. *Single User Price: $149.95*

IBM PC, XT, AT, PS/2, & compatibles; 128 K; 10 Mb hard disk optional; 1 disk drive. Monochrome, CGA, EGA, or VGA display. Printer required. Laser printer optional. Can be run on Macintosh systems operating under SoftPC. *Single User Price: $199.95 Network Price: $199.95 plus $99.98 for each additional user*

Brief Computerized Stress Inventory (CSI)

Allan N. Press
Lynn Osterkamp

Preventive Measures, Inc.
1115 West Campus Road
Lawrence, KS 66044
(913) 842-5078

The Brief CSI assesses 16 life-style areas. This 115-item assessment generates an 8-page individualized profile plus graph, that can be the basis for discussion with a professional or can be given to the respondent without interpretation. The scales have high reliability and validity. This 20-min assessment can be computer-administered or responses from the 6-page, written questionnaire can be entered by an operator in approximately 90 sec. Price includes unlimited use and permission for unlimited duplication of the Brief CSI questionnaire. Detailed manual included. Latest release December, 1990.

Classification: Diagnostic Aid, Stress (Administration and Interpretive Report)

Hardware Requirements and Price
Apple II, 64 K. 80 column display required. Printer required. Laser printer optional. Some limitations compared to other computers. *Single User Price: $300.00 Trial Package $35.00*

IBM PC, XT, AT, PS/2, & compatibles; 256 K; hard disk optional; 1 disk drive. Printer required. Laser printer optional. *Single User Price: $300.00 Trial Package $35.00*

Macintosh, 256 K, 1 disk drive (3-1/2). Printer required. Laser printer optional. *Single User Price: $300.00 Trial Package $35.00*

Reviews
Essman, W. B. (1986). A software review newsletter. *Diskovery, 4*, 1-2.
Lichtenstein, G. A. (1987). Software review: Computerized Stress Inventory. *Computer News for Physicians, 5*, 10.

User Site References
Frank Gilbert, WellPlan, Inc., 617 East Elm, Salina, KS 67401, (913) 825-8224
Jack Hartje, Hartje Stress Clinic, 1826 University Blvd., West, Jacksonville, FL 32217, (904) 737-5821
Marc Zimmer, Biofeedback and Psychotherapy Center, Five Sunrise Plaza, Valley Stream, NY 11581, (516) 825-5005

Brief Symptom Inventory (SCORBSI) 3.0

Leonard R. Derogatis

Clinical Psychometric Research, Inc.
P.O. Box 619
Riderwood, MD 21139
(301) 321-6165
(800) 245-0277

Program designed to score the Brief Symptom Inventory (BSI), the 53-item brief form of the Symptom Distress Checklist, Revised (SCL-90-R). Input may be from keyboard, disk, or NCS scanner. Output consists of the 53 raw item scores by dimension, raw and area T scores for the nine primary symptom dimensions and three global scores, and a full page graphic profile of the scores in standardized format. Narrative report module also available. Detailed manual included.

Classification: Diagnostic Aid (Administration and Interpretive report)

Hardware Requirements and Price

IBM PC, XT, AT, PS/2, & compatibles; 64 K; hard disk optional; 1 disk drive. Laser printer optional. *Single User Price: $2.75-$3.50 per use with narrative, $.75-$1.75 per use without narrative*

California Psychological Inventory

Harrison G. Gough

Consulting Psychologists Press
3803 East Bayshore Road
Palo Alto, CA 94303
(415) 969-8901
(800) 624-1765

Administers, scores, and generates reports for the CPI. Allows on-line administration or response entry by scanner or clinical input. Detailed manual and tutorial program included. On-line help available.

Classification: CPI (Administration and Interpretive report)

Hardware Requirements and Price

IBM PC, XT, AT, PS/2, & compatibles; 640 K; hard disk required; 2 disk drives (3-1/2). *Single User Price: The initial system is $400.00. The initial system with a 5-year lease is $800.00. The initial system with a 10-year lease is $1000.00. Each additional software set is $50.00, and the annual lease fee is $125.00. Call for report prices.*

California Psychological Inventory Interpretive Report

Michael E. Mills
Matthew Wolf

Psytek Services
6401 West 81st Street
Los Angeles, CA 90045
(213) 670-4655
(800) 392-5454

Fully automated interpretive report generator. Includes separate sections for single scale interpretations, profile interpretations, personality typology, and special scales and indices. Interpretive statements describe leadership, interpersonal style, creativity, and social orientation. Reports may be imported to word processing programs. Sample report available on request. 30-day money back guarantee. Detailed manual included. Latest release September 1, 1991.

Classification: CPI (Interpretive report)

Hardware Requirements and Price
IBM PC, XT, AT, PS/2, & compatibles; 512 K; hard disk optional. Monochrome, CGA, EGA, or VGA display. Laser printer optional. *Single User Price: $249.00 Site License: 349.00 No per use fees*

California Verbal Learning Test-Research Edition

The Psychological Corporation
555 Academic Court
San Antonio, TX 78204-0952
(512) 299-1061
(800) 228-0752

Assesses verbal learning and memory deficits in the elderly and the neurologically impaired. Measures how learning occurs or fails to occur, in addition to the amount of verbal material learned. Test measures an individual's ability to learn a list of 16 words (4 words in each of 4 semantic categories) over five trials. A second list of 16 words is then presented for one trial, immediately followed by free and category-cued recall of the first list. After a 20 min delay, these are assessed again. Detailed manual included.

Classification: Neuropsychological Testing (Administration and Interpretive report)

Hardware Requirements and Price
Apple II+, IIe; 64 K; 2 disk drives. Printer required. *Single User Price: $168.00*

IBM PC, XT, AT, PS/2, & compatibles; 256 K; hard disk optional; 2 disk drives. Printer required. *Single User Price: $168.00*

California Verbal Learning Test (CVLT), Scoring and Administration Software

Dean C. Delis
Joel Kramer
Edith Kaplan

The Psychological Corporation
555 Academic Court
San Antonio, TX 78204-0952
(512) 299-1061
(800) 228-0752

A scoring and administration system that produces graphic representations of test data and automatically calculates over 25 critical parameters of learning and memory. The software scores tests administered with or without the computer-assisted administration system. With computer-assisted administration, the examiner enters the examinee's responses directly into the computer during administration, and the results are automatically scored. With paper and pencil administration, responses can be keyed into the computer later for computer scoring. Detailed manual included. Latest release 1987.

Classification: Intellectual Function Test (Administration and Interpretive Report)

Hardware Requirements and Price
Apple II+, IIe; 64 K; 2 disk drives (5-1/4). Laser printer optional. *Single User Price: $185.00*

IBM PC, XT, AT, PS/2, & compatibles; 320 K; hard disk optional; 2 disk drives (5-1/4). Laser printer optional. *Single User Price: $185.00*

Canfield Learning Styles Inventory (LSI)

Albert A. Canfield
George J. Huba
Christian P. Gruber

Western Psychological Services
12031 Wilshire Blvd.
Los Angeles, CA 90025
(213) 478-2061
(800) 648-8857

The LSI assesses learning styles among students by measuring the individual ways each person prefers to learn. The inventory consists of 30 ranked items, is untimed, and takes approximately 15 min to administer. Norms for the LSI are based on male and female adults and junior and senior high school students. Teleprocessing service also available. Instruction booklet included.

Classification: Personality Testing

Hardware Requirements and Price
IBM PC, XT, AT, PS/2, & compatibles; 512 K; 1 Mb hard disk required; 1 disk drive. Printer required. Laser printer optional. Requires DOS 3.0. *Single User Price: $185.00*

Card: Computer Assisted Reading Diagnostics

Ronald P. Carver

Reverac Publications, Inc.
207 West 116 Street
Kansas City, MO 64114
(816) 941-3313

Can administer 10 diagnostic tests, score them, interpret their results, diagnose three types of disabilities, three types of handicaps, and prescribes treatments for each problem. Detailed manual included.

Classification: Diagnostic Aid (Administration and Interpretive report)

Hardware Requirements and Price
IBM PC, XT, AT, PS/2, & compatibles; 256 K; hard disk optional. Printer required. Laser printer optional. *Single User Price: $275.00*

Career Assessment Program

Educational Technologies, Inc.
1007 Whitehead Road Extension
Trenton, NJ 08638
(609) 882-2668
(800) 882-4384

A combination of the ABCD (Aptitude Based Career Decision) and IBCD (Interest Based Career Decision) tests. These aptitude and interest tests are anchored to the Department of Labor databases and deliver probabilities for success in 66 work groups that cover 12,000 different jobs. The ABCD test will provide an ability-to-benefit report and both tests will match the client to local training programs. The programs can be purchased as separate tests or as a complete career assessment program. Detailed manual included. On-line help available. Latest release September 10, 1991.

Classification: Vocational Testing (Interpretive report)

Hardware Requirements and Price
IBM PC, XT, AT, PS/2, & compatibles; 495 K; 2 Mb hard disk optional; 1 disk drive. Graphic display required. Mouse optional. 1200 baud modem optional. Printer required (Epson compatible). Laser printer optional. Requires DOS 3.0.

User Site References

Wayne Brock, North Technical Educational Center, 7071 Garden Road, Riviera Beach, FL, 33404, (407) 881-4600

Charles Thomas, Director, Cumberland County Employment & Training, 72 N. Pearl Street, Bridgeton, NJ, 08302, (609) 451-8920

Kimberly Thomas, Director, Stars Program, Lewis Eubanks AVTS, 1621 Maple Avenue, Midwest City, OK, 73110, (405) 737-4461

Career Assessment Inventory-Enhanced Version
Charles B. Johansson

National Computer Systems, Inc.
P.O. Box 1416
Minneapolis, MN 55440
(800) 627-7271

A vocational interest assessment tool that identifies level of educational training required. Appropriate for individuals seeking career options but are uncertain as to how much schooling they want to pursue. On-line administration is possible with per test fee. Requires Microtest Assessment System. Detailed manual included.

Classification: Vocational Testing (Administration and Interpretive report)

Hardware Requirements and Price
IBM PC, XT, AT, PS/2, & compatibles; 512 K; 10 Mb hard disk required; 1 disk drive. Monochrome, CGA, EGA, or VGA display. Printer required. Laser printer optional. Requires DOS 3.1.

Career Assessment Inventory-Vocational Version
Charles B. Johnson

National Computer Systems, Inc.
P.O. Box 1416
Minneapolis, MN 55440
(800) 627-7271

A vocational interest assessment tool for use with individuals planning to enter occupations requiring little or no post-secondary education. On-line administration is possible with Microtest Assessment System. Per test fee. Detailed manual included.

Classification: Vocational Testing (Administration and Interpretive report)

Hardware Requirements and Price
IBM PC, XT, AT, PS/2, & compatibles; 512 K; 10 Mb hard disk required; 1 disk drive. Monochrome, CGA, EGA, or VGA display. Printer required. Laser printer optional. Requires DOS 3.1.

Career Directions Inventory (CDI)

Sigma Assessment Systems, Inc.
P.O. Box 610984
Port Huron, MI 48061-0984
(800) 265-1285

Allow easy administration and scoring of the Career Directions Inventory. Three different report formats are available. Detailed manual included. On-line help available.

Classification: Vocational Testing (Administration and Interpretive report)

Hardware Requirements and Price
IBM PC, XT, AT, PS/2, & compatibles; 320 K;
1 Mb hard disk optional; 1 disk drive. Laser
printer optional. Requires DOS 2.0.

Category Test Computer Program 3.0

James Choca

Multi-Health Systems, Inc.
908 Niagara Falls Blvd.
North Tonawanda, NY 14120-2060
(416) 424-1700
(800) 456-3003

Administers and scores adult version of the
Category Test. Draws figures of Halstead-
Reitan Category Test on screen, accepts keyboard answers, gives immediate feedback, and
computes scores including a perseveration
index. Detailed manual included.

Classification: Neuropsychological Testing
(Administration and Interpretive report)

Hardware Requirements and Price
IBM PC, XT, AT, PS/2, & compatibles; 256 K;
hard disk optional; 1 disk drive. Color display
required. Laser printer optional. *Single User
Price: $195.00*

CDS Profile III Management Development Profile

Computer Diversified Services
11104 W. Airport Blvd., 108
Stafford, TX 77477
(800) 843-8829

Generates personality-based narrative descriptions useful for the selection, training, and
development of managers, sales personnel, life
insurance agents, and other employees. Forms
C and D of the 16PF are used as a basis for all
computer-generated printouts. On-site service
is provided via a software lease arrangement
and teleprocessing service is provided via a
toll-free telephone number. Instruction booklet included.

Classification: 16PF (Interpretive report)

Hardware Requirements and Price
Contact publisher for equipment options and
prices. Printer required. Laser printer
optional.

User Site References
Michael S. Haro, 16850 Diana Lane, Houston,
    TX, 77058 (713) 488-5460
John D. Hezel, President, Hezel & Associates,
    8918 Tesoro Drive, #417, San Antonio, TX,
    78217, (800) 443-6143
Ronald Trego, 3403 N. Fitzburgh, #200,
    Dallas, TX, 75204, (800) 548-5916

Century Diagnostics Computer Interpreted Rorschach

Irvin H. Perline

Century Diagnostics, Inc.
2101 East Broadway, Suite 22
Tempe, AZ 85282
(602) 966-6006

Uses Klopfer techniques for Rorschach administration and scoring. Program produces 6-
8 page report containing interpretive statements, a keyword summary graph, and narrative summary page. Price based upon number
of administrations. Detailed manual included.
Latest release 1987.

Classification: Rorschach (Interpretive report)

Hardware Requirements and Price
IBM PC, XT, AT, PS/2, & compatibles; 256 K; hard disk optional; 2 disk drives (5-1/4). Hercules, EGA, CGA, or VGA display. Printer required. Laser printer optional. *Single User Price: Price based on the number of administrations*

Certify! DOS 3.3 and DOS 5.0
American Training International

SRA/London House
9701 W. Higgins Road
Rosemont, IL 60618
(708) 292-1900
(800) 221-8378

Certify! DOS 3.3 is a testing and training program. Certify! DOS 5.0 is available as a training package only. Instruction booklet included.

Classification: Vocational Testing (Administration)

Hardware Requirements and Price
IBM PC, XT, AT, PS/2, & compatibles; 512 K. *Single User Price: $149.95*

Chemical Dependency Assessment Profile

Psychologistics, Inc.
P.O. Box 033896
Indialantic, FL 32903
(407) 259-7811

The profile evaluates all types of chemical dependency and polydrug abuse covering chemical use history, patterns of use, reinforcement dimensions of use, beliefs about use, self-concept, and interpersonal relations. The 4-5 page narrative report may be printed or written to a text file. Software permits unlimited uses. Detailed manual included. Latest release 1989.

Classification: Diagnostic Aid, Substance Abuse (Interpretive report)

Hardware Requirements and Price
IBM PC, XT, AT, PS/2, & compatibles; 128 K; hard disk optional; 1 disk drive. Printer required. Requires DOS 2.0. *Single User Price: $295.00 CDAP questionnaires: $20.00 (package of 20)*

Macintosh, 512 K, hard disk optional, 1 disk drive (3-1/2). Printer required. *Single User Price: $295.00 CDAP checklists: $20.00 (package of 20)*

Child & Adolescent Diagnostic Scales (CADS)
Bruce Duthie

Precision People, Inc.
3452 North Ride Circle South
Jacksonville, FL 32223
(904) 262-1096
(800) 338-0710

CADS is a unique set of rating scales that employ criterion referenced methodology as well as traditional norming and can be related to the *DSM-III-R*. Included are scales that measure attention-deficit hyperactivity disorder, oppositional defiant disorder, identity disorder, substance abuse disorder, overanxious disorder, eating disorders, and major depression. This self-report measure takes only 10-15 min to self-administer. Software administers, scores, and interprets. Instruction booklet included.

Classification: Diagnostic Aid, Children and Adolescents (Administration and Interpretive report)

Hardware Requirements and Price
IBM PC, XT, AT, PS/2, & compatibles; 640 K; hard disk required; 1 disk drive. Printer required. Laser printer optional. *Single User Price: $295.00*

Child Diagnostic Screening Battery
James J. Smith
Joseph M. Eisenberg

Reason House
204 East Joppa Road, Suite 10
Towson, MD 21204
(301) 321-7270

Structured interview with parent, guardian, or informed adult, provides the data used to diagnose a child aged 2-17 years. Specific uses, applications, and suggestions are provided in a report that can be printed or displayed on the screen.

Classification: Diagnostic Aid, Children and Adolescents (Administrative and Interpretive report)

Hardware Requirements and Price
IBM PC, XT, AT, PS/2, & compatibles; hard disk optional; 1 disk drive. *Single User Price: $195.00 Discount for APA Members: $95.00*

Children's Personality Questionnaire Narrative Report

Institute for Personality & Ability Testing
P.O. Box 188
Champaign, IL 61824-1188

(217) 352-4739
(800) 225-4728

Program provides a narrative report for the Children's Personality Questionnaire, that includes significant personality characteristics, as well as the individual's projected levels of creativity and anticipated achievement in 10 school-related areas. Teleprocessing service.

Classification: Diagnostic Aid, Children and Adolescents (Interpretive report)

Hardware Requirements and Price
IBM PC, XT, AT, PS/2, & compatibles. 1200 baud modem required. Printer required. Laser printer optional. *Single User Price: Price depends on the number of administrations.*

Children's Personality Questionnaire Narrative Report

Psychological Testing Service
213 East Sugnet
Midland, MI 48640
(517) 631-9463
Fax: (517) 631-9419

This interpretive system analyzes profile patterns, scale combinations, and individual factor scales. The results are presented in narrative form under sections for interpersonal relationships, coping with stress, independence, determination and decisiveness, and intelligence. The program is bundled together with the High School Personality Questionnaire. Requires entry of Sten scores. Instruction booklet included. Latest release April, 1991.

Classification: Diagnostic Aid, Children and Adolescents (Interpretive report)

Hardware Requirements and Price
IBM PC, XT, AT, PS/2, & compatibles; 256 K; hard disk optional; 1 disk drive. Printer required. Laser printer optional. *Single User Price: $195.00*

Children's State-Trait Anxiety Inventory Computer Program
Charles Spielberger

Multi-Health Systems, Inc.
908 Niagara Falls Blvd.
North Tonawanda, NY 14120-2060
(416) 424-1700
(800) 456-3003

On-line administration of the Children's State-Trait Anxiety Inventory for upper elementary or junior high school children. Program instantly scores and graphs the results, with a report that includes a listing of item responses and a brief listing of raw, percentile, and normalized *t*-scores. Detailed manual included.

Classification: Diagnostic Aid Children and Adolescents (Administration and Interpretive report)

Hardware Requirements and Price
Apple II, 256 K, hard disk optional, 1 disk drive (5-1/4). Printer required. *Single User Price: $100.00 (50 Administrations)*

IBM PC, XT, AT, PS/2, & compatibles; hard disk optional; 1 disk drive. Printer required. Laser printer optional. *Single User Price: $100.00 (50 administrations)*

> **Testing Software is the largest section of this directory, containing 363 listings.**

Chronic Pain Battery
Stephen Levitt

Multi-Health Systems, Inc.
908 Niagara Falls Blvd.
North Tonawanda, NY 14120-2060
(416) 424-1700
(800) 456-3003

Collects medical, psychological, social, and behavioral information. Price based upon number of administrations. Program produces a 6-10 page report summarizing findings. Instruction booklet included.

Classification: Diagnostic Aid

Hardware Requirements and Price
IBM PC, XT, AT, PS/2, & compatibles; 256 K; hard disk optional; 2 disk drives. Printer required. Laser printer optional.

Clinical Analysis Questionnaire

Institute for Personality & Ability Testing
P.O. Box 188
Champaign, IL 61824-1188
(217) 352-4739
(800) 225-4728

Computer interpretation for simultaneous measurement of both normal and pathological personality characteristics. Teleprocessing service. Instruction booklet included. On-line help available.

Classification: Personality Testing (Interpretive report)

Hardware Requirements and Price
IBM PC, XT, AT, PS/2, & compatibles; 1200 baud modem required. Printer required.

Laser printer optional. *Single User Price: Depends upon the number of administrations.*

Clinical Analysis Questionnaire (CAQ)
Raymond B. Cattell

National Computer Systems, Inc.
P.O. Box 1416
Minneapolis, MN 55440
(800) 627-7271

This program combines diagnostic assessment of deviant behavior with the measurement of a patient's normal coping skills. Requires Arion II Teleprocessing service. Detailed manual included.

Classification: Diagnostic Aid

Hardware Requirements and Price
Contact publisher for equipment options. Hard disk optional. Modem required. Printer required.

Clinical Analysis Questionnaire (CAQ), Version 3

Psychological Assessment Resources, Inc.
P.O. Box 998
Odessa, FL 33556
(800) 331-TEST

Program administers, scores, and interprets the 16PF. Sten scores are provided for 16 scales and 12 dimensions in the psychopathology domain and nine second-order scale scores. The 6-8 page report consists of primary personality characteristics of significance, broad influence patterns, other clinical indicators, vocational observations, and occupational fitness projections. Raw data is listed on the last page of the report. Detailed manual included. Latest release April 28, 1989.

Classification: 16PF (Administration and Interpretive report)

Hardware Requirements and Price
IBM PC, XT, AT, PS/2, & compatibles; 256 K; hard disk optional; 2 disk drives or 1 disk drive and hard disk. Laser printer optional. *Single User Price: $195.00 (10 Administrations)*

Comprehensive Computerized Stress Inventory
Allan N. Press
Lynn Osterkamp

Preventive Measures, Inc.
1115 West Campus Road
Lawrence, KS 66044
(913) 842-5078

The Comprehensive CSI assesses over 30 lifestyle areas. This 400+ item assessment generates a 16-page individualized profile plus graph that can be the basis for discussion with a professional or can be given to the respondent without interpretation. The 60-min assessment can be computer-administered or responses from the 19-page written questionnaire can be entered by an operator in approximately 4 min. Price includes unlimited use and unlimited permission to duplicate the Comprehensive CSI questionnaire for professional use. Detailed manual included. Latest release January, 1991.

Classification: Diagnostic Aid, Stress (Administration and Interpretive report)

Hardware Requirements and Price
Apple II, 64 K, hard disk optional, 80 column display required. Printer required. Laser printer optional. Some limitations compared to other computers. *Single User Price: $325.00 (unlimited use) Trial Package $35.00*

IBM PC, XT, AT, PS/2, & compatibles; 256 K; hard disk optional; 1 disk drive. Printer required. Laser printer optional. *Single User Price: $325.00 (unlimited use) Trial Package $35.00*

Macintosh, 256 K, hard disk optional, 1 disk drive (3-1/2). Printer required. Laser printer optional. *Single User Price: $325.00 (unlimited use) Trial Package $35.00*

Reviews
Essman, W. B., (1986). A software review newsletter. *Diskovery, 4,* 1-2.
Lichtenstein, G. A., (1987). Computerized Stress Inventory, computer news for physicians. *Software Review, 5,* 10.

User Site References
Frank Gilbert, WellPlan, Inc., 617 East Elm, Salina, KS, 67401, (913) 825-8224
Jack Hartje, Hartje Stress Clinic, 1826 University Blvd. West, Jacksonville, FL, 32217, (904) 737-5821
Marc Zimmer, Biofeedback and Psychotherapy Center, Five Sunrise Plaza, Valley Stream, NY, 11581, (516) 825-5005

Comprehensive Personality Profile (CPP)
Larry L. Craft

Behaviordyne, Inc.
P.O. Box 10994
Palo Alto, CA 94303

(415) 857-0111
(800) 627-2673

Narrative report interpretation of the CPP, an 88-item questionnaire that measures basic personality traits as they relate to job requirements. Traits measured are emotional intensity, interaction, recognition, motivation, sensitivity, assertiveness, trust, exaggeration, ego drive, interpersonal warmth, stability, empathy, objectivity, independence, aggressiveness, decisiveness, tolerance, and efficiency. Software produces a choice of three narrative reports: selection, supervision, or self-report. Instruction booklet included. Latest release 1989.

Classification: Personality Testing (Interpretive report)

Hardware Requirements and Price
IBM PC, XT, AT, PS/2, & compatibles; 256 K; hard disk optional; 2 disk drives. Printer required. Key disk required. *Single User Price: $150.00 Per-test fee applies*

Compuscore for the Battelle Developmental Inventory
Chris Lamb

DLM Teaching Resources
One DLM Park
Allen, TX 75002
(800) 527-4747

Provides all available scores for the full battery or the screening test. Detailed manual included. Latest release 1991.

Classification: Intellectual Function Test

Hardware Requirements and Price
Apple II, 128 K, 1 disk drive. Requires Pro-DOS. *Single User Price: $115.00*

Compuscore for the Woodcock Spanish Psycho-Educational Battery (Bateria)

DLM Teaching Resources
One DLM Park
Allen, TX 75002
(800) 527-4747

Scores up to 20 subjects at a time, producing all cluster scores available. Detailed manual included. Latest release 1989.

Classification: Woodcock-Johnson (Interpretive report)

Hardware Requirements and Price
IBM PC, XT, AT, PS/2, & compatibles; 256 K; hard disk optional. Printer required. Requires DOS 2.1. *Single User Price: $159.00*

Compuscore for the Woodcock Johnson Psycho-Educational Battery-Revised
Chris Lamb

DLM Teaching Resources
One DLM Park
Allen, TX 75002
(800) 527-4747

Compuscore for the Woodcock Johnson Psycho-Educational Battery-Revised (WJ-R) provides all scores for the individual tests, as well as all possible clusters. All three types of discrepancies can be calculated, and profiles can be plotted with a graphics printer. Detailed manual included. On-line help available. Latest release 1991.

Classification: Woodcock-Johnson (Interpretive report)

Hardware Requirements and Price
Apple II, 128 K, 1 disk drive. Mouse optional. Modem optional. Laser printer optional. Requires ProDOS. Must have enhanced ROM chip. *Single User Price: $195.00*

IBM PC, XT, AT, PS/2, & compatibles; 384 K; hard disk optional; 1 disk drive. Mouse optional. Modem optional. Laser printer optional. Requires DOS 2.1. *Single User Price: $195.00*

Compuscore: ICAP
Bradley Hill

DLM Teaching Resources
One DLM Park
Allen, TX 75002
(800) 527-4747

Scores the Inventory for Client and Agency Planning. Detailed manual included. Latest release 1988.

Classification: Diagnostic Aid

Hardware Requirements and Price
IBM PC, XT, AT, PS/2, & compatibles; 256 K; hard disk optional; 1 disk drive. Printer required. Requires DOS 2.1. *Single User Price: $159.00*

Compuscore: WJ/SIB Subtest Norms
Chris Lamb

DLM Teaching Resources
One DLM Park
Allen, TX 75002
(800) 527-4747

Scoring program for all subtests of the Woodcock Johnson (WJ) and/or the Scales of Independent Behavior (SIB). Detailed manual included. Latest release 1988.

Classification: Diagnostic Aid (Interpretive report)

Hardware Requirements and Price
Apple II+, IIe, IIc; 128K; 1 disk drive (5-1/4). Printer required. *Single User Price: $159.00*

IBM PC, XT, AT, PS/2, & compatibles; 256 K; hard disk optional; 1 disk drive. Printer required. Requires DOS 2.1. *Single User Price: $159.00*

Computer-Generated Bender Clinical Assessment
John J. Trifiletti

Precision People, Inc.
3452 North Ride Circle South
Jacksonville, FL 32223
(904) 262-1096
(800) 338-0710

The Computer Generated Bender Clinical Assessment is designed to provide psychodynamic, neuropsychological, and personality formulations for the Bender-Gestalt Test. This program was developed on the basis of interpretive data derived from Koppitz and Hutt clinical systems. The clinical factor criteria and definitions are provided in the program. All clinical rating criteria and interpretive formulations are provided on a 1-2 page narrative report which can appear on the screen or printer. Detailed manual included.

Classification: Personality Testing

Hardware Requirements and Price
Apple II+, IIe, IIc, IIgs; 1 disk drive. Printer required. *Single User Price: $249.00*

IBM PC, XT, AT, PS/2, & compatibles; 64 K; hard disk optional; 1 disk drive. Printer required. *Single User Price: $249.00*

Computerized Assessment of Intelligibility of Dysarthric Speech
Kathryn Youkstory
David Beakelman
Charles Traynor

Pro-Ed, Inc.
8700 Shoal Creek Blvd.
Austin, TX 78758-6897
(512) 451-3246

Clinical software version of AIDS that provides scoring for quantifying of single-word intelligibility, sentence intelligibility, and speaking rates. Program automatically and randomly selects 50 words and 20 sentences from hundreds of stimuli contained in the program. All data is automatically stored and scored. Detailed manual included. Latest release 1984.

Classification: Intellectual Function Test (Administration and Interpretive report)

Hardware Requirements and Price
Apple II, 48 K, hard disk optional, 1 disk drive (5-1/4). *Single User Price: $149.00*

Conners Rating Scales Computer Program
C. Keith Conners

Multi-Health Systems, Inc.
908 Niagara Falls Blvd.
North Tonawanda, NY 14120-2060
(416) 424-1700
(800) 456-3003

Assessment instrument useful for clinical and research work with hyperactive children. Contains all four Conners Rating Scales for children: including the parent and teacher long and short forms. Allows for direct input of responses by teachers or parents. Detailed manual included.

Classification: Diagnostic Aid, Children and Adolescents (Administration and Interpretive report)

Hardware Requirements and Price
IBM PC, XT, AT, PS/2, & compatibles; 256 K; hard disk optional; 1 disk drive. Printer required. Laser printer optional. *Single User Price: $145.00 (50 administrations)*

Counseling Feedback Report (CFR)

Institute for Personality & Ability Testing
P.O. Box 188
Champaign, IL 61824-1188
(217) 352-4739
(800) 225-4728

The report uses high school personality questionnaire data and generates a report that promotes productive, client-focused dialogue between a counselor and an adolescent. The CFR presents feedback in a manner that adolescents find interesting and non-threatening. This is a teleprocessing service. Instruction booklet included.

Classification: Personality Testing (Interpretive report)

Hardware Requirements and Price
IBM PC, XT, AT, PS/2, & compatibles; 1200 baud modem required. Printer required. Laser printer optional. *Single User Price: Depends upon the number of administrations*

CPB/Score Report Processing Software
Stephen R. Levitt
Michael W. McKinney

Pain Resource Center, Inc.
P.O. Box 2836
Durham, NC 27705
(919) 286-9180
(800) 542-PAIN

Menu-driven scoring program for the Chronic Pain Battery that produces a narrative report describing aspects of the patient's pain problem along with recommendations for further action. Incorporates the SCL-90 R for psychological screening. Answer sheets are compatible with Sentry 3000 and Scantron 1400 optical scanners. Instruction booklet included. Latest release October, 1990.

Classification: Diagnostic Aid (Interpretive report)

Hardware Requirements and Price
IBM PC, XT, AT, PS/2, & compatibles; 256 K; hard disk optional; 2 disk drives. Laser printer optional. *Single User Price: $13.00-16.50 per test.*

CPI Interpretive Report
Matthew Wolf
Michael Mills

PsychoLogics
6323A Fairmount Avenue
El Cerrito, CA 94530
(510) 528-6244
(800) 528-6244

Produces interpretive reports for the CPI (1987 Version). Interprets single scales, profiles, personality typology, and special scales and indices in 2-4 pages. Assesses personality, behavior, and social style for use in counseling evaluation and selection. Scoring materials and sample reports available from test publisher. Program is available for limited use. Files can be customized in virtually any word-processor. Detailed manual included. Latest release November, 1991.

Classification: CPI (Interpretive report)

Hardware Requirements and Price
IBM PC, XT, AT, PS/2, & compatibles; 640 K; hard disk optional; 1 disk drive. Printer required. Laser printer optional. Program is encrypted, but not copy protected. *Single User Price: $249.00 Network Price: $339.00*

User Site References
William Kea, U.S. Penitentiary, 3901 Klein Boulevard, Lompoc, CA, 93435, (805) 735-2771 ext. 421

W. Pearce McCall, Compuguide, Inc., P.O. Box 210823, Columbia, SC, 29221, (803) 781-7306

Chris Perry, Psychological Screening Unit, California State Personnel Board, MS-47, P.O. Box 944201, Sacramento, CA, 94244, (916) 653-1258

CPP Software System

Consulting Psychologists Press
3803 East Bayshore Road
Palo Alto, CA 94303
(415) 969-8901
(800) 624-1765

Administration, scoring, and interpretation system for CPP's Strong Interest Inventory,

CPI, and the Myers-Briggs Type Indicator. On-line help available. Tutorial program included.

Classification: Diagnostic Aid (Interpretive report)

Hardware Requirements and Price
IBM PC, XT, AT, PS/2, & compatibles; 640 K; hard disk required. *Single User Price: The initial system with a 5 year lease is $800.00. The initial system with a 10 year lease is $1,000.00. Each additional software set is $50.00 and the annual lease fee is $125.00. Call for report prices*

CRT Skills Test
Science Research Associates

London House/SRA
9701 W. Higgins Road
Rosemont, IL 60018
(708) 292-1900
(800) 221-8378

The CRT Skills Test consists of three timed sections that can be administered in combination. Part 1 assesses speed and accuracy of entering alphanumeric data. Part 2 measures speed of entering numeric data. Part 3 assesses ability to retrieve customer files and answer customer questions. Detailed manual included. Latest release 1990.

Classification: Vocational Testing (Administration)

Hardware Requirements and Price
IBM PC, XT, AT, PS/2, & compatibles; 256 K. CGA display. Requires DOS 2.1. *Single User Price: $175.00*

D-48 (Dominoes Test)
Carlos Pal Hegedus

Psico-Iuris, S.A.
P.O. Box 1039 - Centro Colon
San Jose, 1007 Costa Rica
(506) 24-4416

Scores and gives the percentile rank, correct and incorrect answers, percentages, and prints the subjects responses along with personal information. Detailed manual in Spanish and tutorial program included. Latest release November, 1991.

Classification: Intellectual Function Test (Interpretive report)

Hardware Requirements and Price
IBM PC, XT, AT, PS/2, & compatibles; 128 K; hard disk optional; 1 disk drive. Laser printer optional. Requires DOS 3.1. *Single User Price: $150.00 Network Price: $450.00*

Decision Tree

Forest Hospital & Foundation
555 Wilson Lane
Des Plaines, IL 60016-4794
(708) 635-4100

Decision Tree provides decision making trees based on symptoms that lead to a diagnosis. Eight broad psychiatric categories are automated in this BASIC program. Very helpful in teaching diagnostic decision making.

Classification: Diagnostic Aid

Hardware Requirements and Price
IBM PC, XT, AT, PS/2, & compatibles; 560 K. *Single User Price: $49.95*

Decisionbase
Phillip W. Long

Suite 8110-420, 264 H Street
Blaine, WA 98230
(604) 876-2254

Decisionbase diagnoses more than 200 *DSM-III-R* psychiatric disorders and automates treatment planning. It permits the patient, informant, or therapist to quickly generate a full psychiatric report, diagnostic assessment, treatment plan, and progress note. Program automatically graphs and statistically analyzes the patient's progress. Decisionbase Plus includes the above plus search and retrieval of 3,000 journal abstracts. Detailed manual included.

Classification: Diagnostic Aid DSM

Hardware Requirements and Price
IBM PC, XT, AT, PS/2, & compatibles; 640 K; 10 Mb hard disk required; 1 disk drive. Laser printer optional. *Single User Price: $595.00 (Decisionbase) $695.00 (Decisionbase Plus)*

Reviews
Long, P. W. (1988). Decisionbase. *Journal of the American Medical Association*, *260*(1), 105.

User Site References
Ted Cardwell, Cardwell Human Development Resources, #200-333 25th Street East, Saskatoon, Saskatoon, Canada, 57K OL4, (306) 242-1010.
George Cloutier, Route 1, Box 88, Silesia, MT, 59080, (406) 962-3142.
Alvin E. Murphy, 850 W. Hind Drive, Suite 121, Hondulu, HI, 96821, (808) 377-5420.

Derogatis Sexual Functioning Inventory (SCORDSFI)
Leonard R. Derogatis

Clinical Psychometric Research, Inc.
P.O. Box 619
Riderwood, MD 21139
(301) 321-6165
(800) 245-0277

Microcomputer program designed to score the Derogatis Sexual Functioning Inventory (DSFI) from keyboard or disk input. Computer output includes 255 raw item scores by subtest; 10 dimension, 3 global raw, area T-scores; and the DSFI graphic profile plotted against standard norms. Detailed manual included.

Classification: Diagnostic Aid (Administration and Interpretive Report)

Hardware Requirements and Price
IBM PC, XT, AT, PS/2, & compatibles; 64 K; hard disk optional; 1 disk drive. Printer required. *Single User Price: $200.00*

Derogatis Sexual Functioning Inventory (ADMNDSFI)
Leonard R. Derogatis

Clinical Psychometric Research, Inc.
P.O. Box 619
Riderwood, MD 21139
(301) 321-6165
(800) 245-0277

Program administers and scores the DSFI from keyboard or disk input. Computer output includes 255 raw item scores by subtest; 10 dimension, 3 global raw area T-scores; and the

DSFI graphic profile plotted against standard norms. Detailed manual included.

Classification: Diagnostic Aid (Administration and Interpretive report)

Hardware Requirements and Price
IBM PC, XT, AT, PS/2, & compatibles; 64 K; hard disk optional; 1 disk drive. *Single User Price: $6.00-8.00 (per use) Price depends upon number of administrations*

Derogatis Stress Profile (DSP)
Leonard R. Derogatis

Clinical Psychometric Research, Inc.
P.O. Box 619
Riderwood, MD 21139
(301) 321-6165
(800) 245-0277

Program to score the Derogatis Stress Profile (DSP). Input may be from keyboard, disk, or scanner. Output consists of 77 item raw scores, 11 dimension, 3 domain, and 2 global raw and area T-scores, and a full page graphic profile. Detailed manual included.

Classification: Diagnostic Aid (Administration and Interpretive report)

Hardware Requirements and Price
IBM PC, XT, AT, PS/2, & compatibles; 64 K; hard disk optional; 1 disk drive. Laser printer optional. *Single User Price: $200.00*

Detroit Tests of Learning Aptitude-Adult (DTLA-A) Software Scoring & Report System
Brian R. Bryant

Pro-Ed, Inc.
8700 Shoal Creek Blvd.
Austin, TX 78758-6897
(512) 451-3248

Suitable for ages 16-79. The program converts raw scores into standard scores and percentile ranks and generates composite scores. Compares composite performance for significant intra-ability differences. Makes comparisons between DTLA-A performance and achievement. Test performance allow for additional intra-individual discrepancy analyses. Provides a multi-page printout. Detailed manual included. Latest release 1991.

Classification: Academic (Interpretive report)

Hardware Requirements and Price
Apple II, 48 K, hard disk optional, 1 disk drive (5-1/4). *Single User Price: $98.00*

IBM PC, XT, AT, PS/2, & compatibles; 640 K; hard disk optional; 1 disk drive (5-1/4). *Single User Price: $98.00*

Detroit Tests of Learning Aptitude-Primary, Second Edition
Brian R. Bryant

Pro-Ed, Inc.
8700 Shoal Creek Blvd.
Austin, TX 78758-6897
(512) 451-3246

Lets the user enter scores for each subtest and the total score or the child's item-by-item responses. Both options convert raw scores to standard scores and percentiles, and compare performance across domains. The program allows the user to enter achievement test scores for an intra-individual discrepancy analysis. A 2-page printout suitable for inclu-

sion in the child's permanent record is generated. Detailed manual included. Latest release 1991.

Classification: Academic (Interpretive report)

Hardware Requirements and Price
Apple II, 48 K, hard disk optional, 1 disk drive (5-1/4). *Single User Price: $98.00*

IBM PC, XT, AT, PS/2, & compatibles; 640 K; hard disk optional; 1 disk drive (5-1/4). *Single User Price: $98.00*

Detroit Tests of Learning Aptitude-3 Software Scoring and Report System
Brian R. Bryant

Pro-Ed, Inc.
8700 Shoal Creek Blvd.
Austin, TX 78758-6897
(512) 451-3246

Program converts student raw Detroit test scores into standard scores and percentile ranks, and generates four domain scores: linguistic, cognitive, attention, and motor. Comparisons between domain scores and achievement test performance permits an individual discrepancy analysis. The program provides a 2-page printout suitable for inclusion in the student's records. Detailed manual included. Latest release 1991.

Classification: Academic (Interpretive report)

Hardware Requirements and Price
Apple II, 48 K, hard disk optional, 1 disk drive (5-1/4). *Single User Price: $98.00*

IBM PC, XT, AT, PS/2, & compatibles; 640 K; hard disk optional; 1 disk drive (5-1/4). *Single User Price: $98.00*

Developmental History Checklist, Version 3

Edward H. Dougherty
John A. Schinka

Psychological Assessment Resources, Inc.
P.O. Box 998
Odessa, FL 33556
(800) 331-TEST

User inputs responses to items from the Developmental History Checklist (DHC) booklet which was designed to be completed by a parent, guardian, or clinician, for children aged 5-12. The 2-4 page report discusses the following content areas: presenting information, personal information/family background, early developmental history, educational history, medical history/health status, family history, and current behavior/relationships. Report may be edited using a word processor. Comes with a package of 25 DHC booklets. Detailed manual included. Latest release April 26, 1990.

Classification: Diagnostic Aid, Children and Adolescents (Interpretive report)

Hardware Requirements and Price

IBM PC, XT, AT, PS/2, & compatibles; 256 K; hard disk optional; 2 disk drives or 1 disk drive and hard disk. Laser printer optional. *Single User Price: $295.00*

Developmental History Report

Giles D. Rainwater
Bonnie Batter Slade

Psychometric Software, Inc.
P.O. Box 1677
Melbourne, FL 32902-1677

(407) 729-6390
(800) 882-9811

This program presents an automated structured interview that gathers comprehensive developmental information and generates a written narrative. Information is obtained about areas relevant for a child's psychological assessment, including pregnancy, birth, development, health, family, education, and behavior. Detailed manual included. Latest release 1984.

Classification: Diagnostic Aid, Children and Adolescents (Interpretive report)

Hardware Requirements and Price

Apple II+, IIe, IIc, IIgs; 64 K; hard disk optional; 1 disk drive (5-1/4). Monochrome display. Printer required. Will not run on hard drive. *Single User Price: $95.95*

IBM PC, XT, AT, PS/2, & compatibles; 128 K; 10 Mb hard disk optional; 1 disk drive. Monochrome, CGA, EGA, or VGA display. Printer required. Laser printer optional. Can be run on Macintosh systems operating under SoftPC. *Single User Price: $195.95 Network Price: $195.95 plus $97.98 for each additional user*

Developmental Profile II (DP-II)

Gerald Alpern
Thomas Boll
Marsha Shearer

Western Psychological Services
12031 Wilshire Blvd.
Los Angeles, CA 90025
(213) 478-2061
(800) 648-8857

The Developmental Profile II assesses a child's development from birth to 9 years of age. It consists of an inventory of 186 "yes-no" items that can be answered in 20-40 min. The DP-II is normed on developmental age in the areas of physical age, self-help age, social age, academic age, and communication age. Teleprocessing service also available. Instruction booklet included.

Classification: Diagnostic Aid, Children and Adolescents

Hardware Requirements and Price
IBM PC, XT, AT, PS/2, & compatibles; 512 K; 1 Mb hard disk required; 1 disk drive. Printer required. Laser printer optional. Requires DOS 3.0. *Single User Price: $185.00 Price depends on number of administrations*

Diagnostic Achievement Test for Adolescents
Wayne P. Hresko
Paul Schlieve

Pro-Ed, Inc.
8700 Shoal Creek Blvd.
Austin, TX 78758-6897
(512) 451-3246

Generates a 4-page report that contains descriptive background information, raw scores, standard scores, percentiles, descriptions for each subtest, standard score sums, percentiles, descriptions for all composites and quotients, profiles for subtests and composites, and significance tests of comparisons among all composites. Detailed manual included. Latest release 1986.

Classification: Diagnostic Aid, Children and Adolescents (Interpretive report)

Hardware Requirements and Price
Apple II, 48 K, hard disk optional, 1 disk drive (5-1/4). *Single User Price: $79.00*

IBM PC, XT, AT, PS/2, & compatibles; 640 K; hard disk optional; 1 disk drive (5-1/4). *Single User Price: $79.00*

Diagnostic Achievement Battery-Second Edition (DAB-2)
Wayne P. Hresko
Paul L. Schlieve

Pro-Ed, Inc.
8700 Shoal Creek Blvd.
Austin, TX 78758-6897
(512) 451-3246

Program uses the Diagnostic Achievement Battery Second Edition for 6- to 14-year-olds to generate descriptive background information, raw scores, standard scores, percentiles and descriptions for each subtest, standard score sums, percentiles, and descriptions for all composites and quotients, profiles for subtests and composites, and significance tests of comparisons among all composites. Detailed manual included. Latest release 1990.

Classification: Diagnostic Aid, Children & Adolescents (Interpretive report)

Hardware Requirements and Price
Apple II, 48 K, hard disk optional, 1 disk drive (5-1/4). *Single User Price: $79.00*

IBM PC, XT, AT, PS/2, & compatibles; 640 K; hard disk optional; 1 disk drive (5-1/4). *Single User Price: $79.00*

Diagnostic Interview for Children & Adolescents, Revised: Child/Adolescent

Barbara Herjanic
Wendy Reich
Zila Welner

Multi-Health Systems, Inc.
908 Niagara Falls Blvd.
North Tonawanda, NY 14120-2060
(416) 424-1700
(800) 456-3003

Program contains the entire interviewing process and allows direct administration to the child or adolescent. Software automatically branches to the proper questions while conducting the interview and identifies all *DSM-III-R* diagnostic categories met by the patient. Additional inclusion/exclusion for the diagnoses are identified. Detailed manual included. Latest release 1991.

Classification: Diagnostic Aid, DSM (Administration and Interpretive report)

Hardware Requirements and Price
IBM PC, XT, AT, PS/2, & compatibles; 640 K; hard disk required; 1 disk drive. Printer required. *Single User Price: $450.00*

Diagnostic Interview for Children & Adolescents, Revised: Parent

Barbara Herjanic
Wendy Reich
Zila Welner

Multi-Health Systems, Inc.
908 Niagara Falls Blvd.
North Tonawanda, NY 14120-2060
(416) 424-1700
(800) 456-3003

Microcomputer interviewing program allows direct administration to the parent. The program automatically branches to the proper questions while conducting the interview and identifies all *DSM-III-R* diagnostic categories met. Detailed manual included. Latest release 1991.

Classification: Diagnostic Aid, DSM (Administration and Interpretive report)

Hardware Requirements and Price
IBM PC, XT, AT, PS/2, & compatibles; 640 K; 5 Mb hard disk required; 1 disk drive. Printer required. Laser printer optional. *Single User Price: $450.00*

Diagnostic Inventory of Personality & Symptoms

Bruce Duthie

Precision People, Inc.
3452 North Ride Circle South
Jacksonville, FL 32223
(904) 262-1096
(800) 338-0710

The Diagnostic Inventory of Personality and Symptoms (DIPS) is a brief test of psychopathology built from items predictive of abnormality. The DIPS has 171 items and is quickly administered. Criterion for items is based on the *DSM-III-R* diagnostic criteria. Eleven Axis I scales measure major diagnostic clusters. Axis II disorders are collapsed into three major categories: withdrawn character (WC), immature character (IC), and neurotic character (NC). A recent study achieved a 70% hit rate for primary discharge diagnosis. This diagnosis of the 11 major *DSM-III-R* Axis I categories compares favorably to the MMPIs best ever hit rate of 65%. Construct validity has been demonstrated via factor analysis-three main factors of neurotic, psychotic, and characterological emerge. Instruction booklet included.

Classification: Diagnostic Aid, DSM (Administration and Interpretive report)

Hardware Requirements and Price
IBM PC, XT, AT, PS/2, & compatibles; 640 K; hard disk required; 1 disk drive. Printer required. *Single User Price: $495.00*

Differential Aptitude Tests: Computerized Adaptive Edition

The Psychological Corporation
555 Academic Court
San Antonio, TX 78204-0952
(512) 299-1061
(800) 228-1061

Individually tailored, computer administered implementation of the Differential Aptitude Tests and accompanying Career Planning Questionnaire. The computer selects the items that are most appropriate in terms of ability level the student being tested. When administration is complete, the program automatically scores and produces an individualized score report. Testing is self-paced and continuously monitored by the computer. The program allows for administration of selected portions of the battery as well. Per-test fee. Detailed manual included.

Classification: Vocational Testing (Administration and Interpretive report)

Hardware Requirements and Price
Apple II+, IIe, IIc; 64 K; 2 disk drives. Printer required. *Single User Price: $117.50*

IBM PC, XT, AT, PS/2, & compatibles; 256 K; hard disk optional. Printer required. *Single User Price: $117.50*

Differential Diagnostics

Forest Hospital & Foundation
555 Wilson Lane
Des Plaines, IL 60016-4794
(708) 635-4100

To be used with most Ashton-Tate products, this adaptable database file provides assistance ruling-in or ruling-out various biological conditions that mimic psychological disorders (e.g., hypoparathyroidism vs affective disorders). A symptom check list is also provided for structuring patient interviews. On-line symptom definitions, syndromal components, and documentation complete the package.

Classification: Diagnostic Aid

Hardware Requirements and Price
IBM PC, XT, AT, PS/2, & compatibles; 560 K; hard disk optional. *Single User Price: $49.95*

Digit-Digit Test II
Robert J. Sbordone
Steven Hall

Robert J. Sbordone, Ph.D., Inc.
7700 Irvine Center Drive
Suite 750
Irvine, CA 92708
(714) 753-7711

Fully automated, interactive, serial testing of complex attentional skills utilizing randomly generated test stimuli. Intended for use with normal, brain injured, and cognitively impaired individuals. The program presents the subject with an attentional task under control and test conditions. Comparison between the two formats permits the examiner to determine whether the test-taker's performance reflects cortical and/or subcortical dysfunction. Examinee records are automatically maintained. Detailed manual included.

Classification: Neuropsychological Testing

Hardware Requirements and Price
Apple II, 48 K, 1 disk drive. *Single User Price: $250.00*

Drug Store Applicant Inventory (DSAI)

London House/SRA
9701 W. Higgins Road
Rosemont, IL 60018
(708) 292-1900
(800) 221-8378

The DSAI is used for screening job applicants for front-end cashiers at drug stores and supermarket drug store departments. Requires ITAC/PC, an IBM-PC or compatible test scoring and reporting program that scores and generates reports for this and other London House test systems. Instruction booklet included.

Classification: Vocational Testing (Interpretive report)

Hardware Requirements and Price
IBM PC, XT, AT, PS/2, & compatibles; 512 K; 10 Mb hard disk required; 1 disk drive. Printer required. Requires DOS 2.2. *Single User Price: $7.00-$14.50 per test, based on number of administrations.*

DSM-III Diagnostic Screening Batteries
James J. Smith
Joseph M. Eisenberg

Reason House
204 East Joppa Road, Suite 10
Towson, MD 21204
(301) 321-7270

Child, adolescent, or adult versions of the *DSM-III* diagnostic screening batteries can be administered on-line or with paper and pencil. Has five axis *DSM-III* capability. Detailed manual included.

Classification: Diagnostic Aid, DSM (Administration and Interpretive report)

Hardware Requirements and Price
IBM PC, XT, AT, PS/2, & compatibles; hard disk optional; 1 disk drive. Printer required. *Single User Price: $195.00 Discount for APA Members: $95.00*

DSM-III-R On Call

Precision People, Inc.
3452 North Ride Circle South
Jacksonville, FL 32223
(904) 262-1096
(800) 338-0710

Computerized version of the *DSM-III-R* that enables the user to obtain diagnostic information. The user can find *DSM-III* information quickly, automatically cross-reference, search by diagnostic description, category, code number, or scan the diagnostic list. Program will display and print the requested information. Detailed manual included.

Classification: Diagnostic Aid, DSM

Hardware Requirements and Price
IBM PC, XT, AT, PS/2, & compatibles; 150 K; hard disk required; 1 disk drive. *Single User Price: $100.00*

DTLA-2 Report
John Trifiletti

Precision People, Inc.
3452 North Ride Circle South
Jacksonville, FL 32223
(904) 262-1096
(800) 338-0710

Diagnostic program for the Detroit Tests of Learning Aptitude. Basic demographic data is input from the keyboard along with standard scores on each of the subtests completed by the examinee. The program then prints demographic data, a standard scores table, profile of standard scores, composite quotient table, and narrative report of findings. Detailed manual included.

Classification: Diagnostic Aid (Interpretive report)

Hardware Requirements and Price
Apple II+, IIe, IIc, IIgs; 1 disk drive. Printer required. *Single User Price: $199.00*

IBM PC, XT, AT, PS/2, & compatibles; 64 K; hard disk optional; 1 disk drive. Printer required. *Single User Price: $249.00*

Dtree: The Electronic DSM III-R
Michael B. First
Janet B.W. Williams
Robert L. Spitzer

Multi-Health Systems, Inc.
908 Niagara Falls Blvd.
North Tonawanda, NY 14120-2060
(416) 424-1700
(800) 456-3003

An expanded and annotated computerized implementation of *DSM III-R* decision trees for differential diagnosis. Dtree facilitates the learning of diagnostic logic by allowing the clinician to interactively apply this logic to case vignettes or actual clinical material. Contains six decision trees for psychosis, organic, mood, anxiety, somatoform, and substance abuse disorders. Co-published with the American Psychiatric Association. Detailed manual included.

Classification: Diagnostic Aid, DSM

Hardware Requirements and Price
IBM PC, XT, AT, PS/2, & compatibles; 256 K; 5 Mb hard disk required; 1 disk drive. Laser printer optional. *Single User Price: $395.00*

Reviews
Alex, N. (1990). Dtree. *Journal of the American Medical Association, 264,* 2810-2811.
Zarr, M. (1990). Psychiatric software reviews. *American Journal of Psychotherapy, 43,* 308-309.

Dyadic Adjustment Scale: Computer Version
Graham Spanier

Multi-Health Systems, Inc.
908 Niagara Falls Blvd.
North Tonawanda, NY 14120-2060
(416) 424-1700
(800) 456-3003

A self-report measure designed to determine the degree of dissatisfaction couples are experiencing in their relationship. Optional on-line administration. Brief interpretive statements are generated. Each person's responses can be saved on a disk for future reference or research. Detailed manual included.

Classification: Diagnostic Aid (Administration and Interpretive report)

Hardware Requirements and Price
Apple II, 256 K, hard disk optional, 1 disk drive (5-1/4). Printer required. *Single User Price: $100.00 (50 administrations)*

IBM PC, XT, AT, PS/2, & compatibles; hard disk optional; 1 disk drive. Printer required. Laser printer optional. *Single User Price: $100.00 (50 administrations)*

EAP Alcohol/Drug Assessment Module
James J. Harting
Harting Associates, Inc.
8 Executive Drive, Suite 160
Fairview Heights, IL 62208-9916
(618) 632-3145
(800) 782-6785

Computer-administer interview or use pencil and paper. Prints report that lists identifying information, notes positive symptoms, evaluates depression, determines psychoactive substance use disorder, provides DSM III-R label, and provides a plan of action including level of care. Detailed manual included. Latest release October 1, 1991.

Classification: Diagnostic Aid, Substance Abuse (Interpretive report)

Hardware Requirements and Price
IBM PC, XT, AT, PS/2, & compatibles; 256 K; 10 Mb hard disk required; 1 disk drive. Mouse optional. Modem optional. Laser printer optional. *Single User Price: $495.00 Network Price: $795.00*

User Site References
Troy Cole, Methodist Outreach, Inc. 2009 Lamar, Memphis, TN, 38114, (901) 276-5401

Sarah Harrless, ARS, Inc., 2701 Jefferson Avenue, Birmingham, AL, 35211, (205) 923-6552

Eating Disorder Inventory-2, Version 4
David M. Garner

Psychological Assessment Resources, Inc.
P.O. Box 998
Odessa, FL 33556
(800) 331-TEST

Administration, scoring, and interpretive program. Program produces a profile of the individual's test results compared to both normal and patient normative groups. Detailed manual included. Latest release November 7, 1990.

Classification: Diagnostic Aid (Administration and Interpretive report)

Hardware Requirements and Price
IBM PC, XT, AT, PS/2, & compatibles; 256 K; hard disk optional; 2 disk drives or 1 disk drive and hard disk. Laser printer optional. *Single User Price: $225.00 (50 administrations)*

Emotional Problems Scales (EPS), Version 1

H. Thompson Prout
Douglas C. Strohmer

Psychological Assessment Resources, Inc.
P.O. Box 998
Odessa, FL 33556
(800) 331-TEST

User enters item responses or raw scale scores for the BRS (Behavior Rating Scales) or SRI (Self Report Inventory). The program produces normative-based, interpretive hypotheses for each scale; a profile of T scores; and a listing of the associated raw and percentile scores. The EPS was designed to assess emotional and behavioral problems in clients with mild retardation or borderline intellectual abilities: The computer report may be sent to a text file for editing with a word processor. Detailed manual included. Latest release June 15, 1991.

Classification: Diagnostic Aid (Interpretive report)

Hardware Requirements and Price
IBM PC, XT, AT, PS/2, & compatibles; 256 K; hard disk optional; 2 disk drives or 1 disk drive and hard disk. Laser printer optional. *Single User Price: $295.00*

Employee Attitude Inventory

London House/SRA
9701 W. Higgins Road
Rosemont, IL 60018
(708) 292-1900
(800) 221-8378

A test battery that can be used to assess theft behavior, theft attitudes, tendency toward substance abuse, job burnout, and job dissatisfaction among employees. Teleprocessing service. Detailed manual included.

Classification: Vocational Testing

Hardware Requirements and Price
IBM PC, XT, AT, PS/2, & compatibles; 512 K; hard disk optional; 2 disk drives. Only sold in conjunction with the publisher's test books.

Review
McDaniel, M. A., & Jones, J. W. (1986). A meta-analysis of the validity of the Employee Attitude Inventory theft scales. *Journal of Business and Psychology, 1*(1), 31-50.

Employment Productivity Index

London House/SRA
9701 W. Higgins Road
Rosemont, IL 60018
(708) 292-1900
(800) 221-8378

Paper-and-pencil test designed to aid in hiring productive employees. Measures an applicant's tendencies toward dependability, interpersonal cooperation, and drug avoidance. A safety scale is also available. Composite scales give an overall rating of the applicant, balanced for total applicant productivity. Per-test fee. Teleprocessing service also available. Detailed manual included.

Classification: Vocational Testing, (Interpretive report)

Hardware Requirements and Price
IBM PC, XT, AT, PS/2, & compatibles; 512 K;
hard disk optional; 2 disk drives. Only sold in
conjunction with publisher test books

Endler Multidimensional Anxiety Scales (EMAS)

Western Psychological Services
12031 Wilshire Blvd.
Los Angeles, CA 90025
(213) 478-2061
(800) 648-8857

Based on Endler's interaction model of personality, EMAS includes three brief self-report
scales. EMAS-S measures state anxiety, assessing both physiological and cognitive responses.
EMAS-T measures trait anxiety in socially
evaluative, physically dangerous, new or ambiguous, and routine situations. EMAS-P
measures the sense of situational threat; that
is, the respondent's perception of the nature
and degree of threat in his or her immediate
situation. The scales are usually given as a set,
although the EMAS-S can be used separately.
All three can be administered to individuals or
groups in just 25 min. EMAS is useful for
evaluating test anxiety, panic attacks, phobias,
post-traumatic stress disorder, and generalized
anxiety disorder. Detailed manual included.

Classification: Diagnostic Aid

Hardware Requirements and Price
IBM PC, XT, AT, PS/2, & compatibles; 512 K;
1 Mb hard disk required; 1 disk drive. *Single
User Price: $150.00*

Executive Profile Survey

Institute for Personality & Ability Testing
P.O. Box 188
Champaign, IL 61824-1188
(217) 352-4739
(800) 225-4728

Profile measures attitudes, values, and beliefs
of individuals compared with over 2,000 top-
level executives. The report provides a non-
technical description of those dimensions most
important in business, management, and
executive settings. Teleprocessing service.
Requires Telxpress service option.

Classification: Industrial Consulting (Interpretive report)

Hardware Requirements and Price
Contact publisher for equipment options. 1200
baud modem required. Printer required.
Laser printer optional. *Single User Price:
Depends upon the number of administrations*

FIRO-B: Software
Judith A. Waterman

Consulting Psychologists Press
3803 East Bayshore Road
Palo Alto, CA 94303
(415) 969-8901
(800) 624-1765

Software administers and scores the FIRO-B
and prints general comments and a narrative
report based on the client's results. Disk
provides 100 client administrations and 1 trial

run for administrators. Counselor's segment features client editing and review, quick interpretation, and scoring.

Classification: Personality Testing (Administration and Interpretive report)

Hardware Requirements and Price
IBM PC, XT, AT, PS/2, & compatibles; 256 K; 1 disk drive. *Single User Price: $165.00*

FIRO-B: Interpretive Report, Version 3
Leo R. Ryan

Psychological Assessment Resources, Inc.
P.O. Box 998
Odessa, FL 33556
(800) 331-TEST

By entering the six scale scores from the FIRO-B, users obtain four-part interpretive reports. The user enters scores from a completed FIRO-B booklet. Detailed manual included.

Classification: Personality Testing (Interpretive report)

Hardware Requirements and Price
IBM PC, XT, AT, PS/2, & compatibles; 256 K; hard disk optional; 2 disk drives or 1 disk drive and hard disk. Laser printer optional. *Single User Price: $225.00 (unlimited use)*

Four Score: Computer Scoring Program for the Stanford-Binet, Fourth Edition
Elizabeth Delaney
Thomas Hopkins
Richard Grantham
Arthur Bernard

The Riverside Publishing Company
8420 Bryn Mawr
Chicago, IL 60631
(312) 693-0040
(800) 323-9540

A computer assisted program for scoring the Stanford-Binet, Fourth Edition. Detailed manual and tutorial program included. Latest release April, 1991.

Classification: Stanford-Binet (Interpretive report)

Hardware Requirements and Price
IBM PC, XT, AT, PS/2, & compatibles; 512 K; 250 K hard disk optional; 1 disk drive. Color display recommended. Laser printer optional. *Single User Price: $294.00*

User Site References
Robert Clark, National Louis University, 2840 Sheridan Road, Evanston, IL, 60201-1996, (708) 256-5150 ext. 2014

Functional Capacity Checklist
Janet E. Field

Elliott & Fitzpatrick, Inc.
1135 Cedar Shoals Drive
Athens, GA 30605
(404) 548-8161
(800) 843-4977

Program designed to determine how clients view their own physical functioning. There are 165 items that reflect a wide variety of physical functions on 22 areas such as standing, sitting, walking, and so forth. Items are answered using a 6-point scale. A summary of the 22 functional areas may be printed, in addition to a listing of all questions and corresponding responses.   Instruction booklet included. Latest release 1991.

Classification: Diagnostic Aid

Hardware Requirements and Price
IBM PC, XT, AT, PS/2, & compatibles; 512 K; 500 K hard disk optional; 1 disk drive. Printer required. *Single User Price: $99.95*

General Aptitude Test Battery (GATB)

United States Employment Service

National Computer Systems, Inc.
P.O. Box 1416
Minneapolis, MN 55440
(800) 627-7271

An aptitude test developed specifically for vocational counseling in employment services and schools. Measures nine major aptitudes and skills required for occupational success. Requires GATB Test Scoring software. Detailed manual included.

Classification: Vocational Testing (Interpretive report)

Hardware Requirements and Price
IBM PC, XT, AT, PS/2, & compatibles; 512 K; hard disk optional; 1 disk drive (5-1/4). Monochrome display. Printer required. Laser printer optional. Sentry 3000 Scanner optional.

Giannetti On-Line Psychosocial History (GOLPH)

Ronald A. Giannetti

National Computer Systems, Inc.
P.O. Box 1416

Minneapolis, MN 55440
(800) 627-7271

On-line administered interview designed to gather information about an individual's life history and current circumstances. Program includes a follow-up summary to assist with subsequent interviews and *DSM-III-R* diagnostic classifications. Requires Microtest Assessment System. Instruction booklet included.

Classification: Diagnostic Aid, History (Administration and Interpretive report)

Hardware Requirements and Price
IBM PC, XT, AT, PS/2, & compatibles; 512 K; 10 Mb hard disk required; 1 disk drive. Monochrome, CGA, EGA, or VGA display. Printer required. Laser printer optional. Requires DOS 3.1.

Guilford-Zimmerman Temperment Survey (GZTS)

J.P. Guilford
Wayne S. Zimmerman

National Computer Systems, Inc.
P.O. Box 1416
Minneapolis, MN 55440
(800) 627-7271

The GZTS measures normal personality and temperment. It provides a nonclinical description for use in personnel selection, counseling, and research. Requires Microtest Assessment System or Arion II Teleprocessing service. Detailed manual included.

Classification: Personality Testing

Hardware Requirements and Price
IBM PC, XT, AT, PS/2, & compatibles; 512 K; 10 Mb hard disk required; 1 disk drive.

Monochrome, CGA, EGA, or VGA display. 300-2400 baud modem optional. Printer required. Laser printer optional. Requires DOS 3.1.

H-T-P Clinical Report
John J. Trifiletti
Precision People, Inc.
3452 North Ride Circle South
Jacksonville, FL 32223
(904) 262-1096
(800) 338-0710

The computer generated House-Tree-Person (H-T-P) clinical assessment is designed to handle clinical data generated from the H-T-P technique. The program organizes clinical criteria based on objective definitions of H-T-P projective protocol. The clinician enters the raw scores based on objective clinical criteria. The program then performs all necessary operations to provide clinical hypotheses concerning personality dynamics and prognosis for therapy and treatment. Two-page clinical narrative report can appear on the screen or printer. Detailed manual included.

Classification: House-Tree-Person (Interpretive report)

Hardware Requirements and Price
Apple II, 1 Mb, hard disk optional, 1 disk drive (5-1/4). Printer required. Laser printer optional. *Single User Price: $249.00*

IBM PC, XT, AT, PS/2, & compatibles; 640 K; hard disk optional; 1 disk drive. Printer required. Laser printer optional. *Single User Price: $249.00*

Halstead Category Test-A Computer Version
Michael Hill

Precision People, Inc.
3452 North Ride Circle South
Jacksonville, FL 32223
(904) 262-1096
(800) 338-0710

Computer-administered instrument used as a primary test of diffuse brain dysfunction and as one item in the Halstead-Reitan Neuropsychological Test Battery. The client observes a series of graphic displays designed to test for problem solving, hypothesis generation and modification, and the ability to profit from experience. Detailed manual included.

Classification: Neuropsychological Testing (Administration)

Hardware Requirements and Price
Apple II+, IIe, IIc, IIgs; 64 K; hard disk optional; 1 disk drive. Color display optional. Printer required. *Single User Price: $199.00*

IBM PC, XT, AT, PS/2, & compatibles; hard disk optional; 1 disk drive. Monochrome display required. *Single User Price: $199.00*

Halstead-Reitan Hypothesis Generator
Bruce Duthie

Precision People, Inc.
3452 North Ride Circle South
Jacksonville, FL 32223
(904) 262-1096
(800) 338-0710

Processes data from the Halstead-Reitan and the Wechsler intelligence scales into clinically useful hypotheses concerning the patient's neurological status. The program determines which of the following cognitive abilities are impaired: general intellectual ability, learning capacity, mental efficiency, verbal ability, remote memory, and academic achievement. The program also presents data using Reitans's conceptual model of patients with impaired functioning. The program evaluates pre morbid IQ using seven different models. Detailed manual included.

Classification: Neuropsychological Testing (Interpretive report)

Hardware Requirements and Price
IBM PC, XT, AT, PS/2, & compatibles; 256 K; hard disk optional; 1 disk drive. Printer required. *Single User Price: $195.00*

Handwriting Analyst
Garth Michaels
Marilyn Maze
Dorothy Hodos

Wintergreen Software, Inc.
P.O. Box 15899
New Orleans, LA 70175
(504) 899-0378
(800) 321-9479

This program asks 57 multiple choice questions about a persons handwriting and produces a 3-8 page description of the writer's personality. Detailed manual included. On-line help available. Latest release 1989.

Classification: Personality Testing

Hardware Requirements and Price
Apple II, 64 K, hard disk optional, 1 disk drive (5-1/4). *Single User Price: $69.95*

IBM PC, XT, AT, PS/2, & compatibles; 256 K; hard disk optional; 1 disk drive. *Single User Price: $69.95*

Macintosh, 512 K, hard disk optional, 1 disk drive (3-1/2). *Single User Price: $69.95*

Hermann: The Rorschach Assistant
James Choca
Dan Garside

Multi-Health Systems, Inc.
908 Niagara Falls Blvd.
North Tonawanda, NY 14120-2060
(416) 424-1700
(800) 456-3003

Helps with the scoring and/or administration of the Rorschach protocol. Detailed manual included.

Classification: Rorschach (Administration and Interpretive report)

Hardware Requirements and Price
IBM PC, XT, AT, PS/2, & compatibles; hard disk optional; 1 disk drive. Laser printer optional. *Single User Price: $125.00*

High School Personality Questionnaire Narrative Report

Psychological Testing Service
213 East Sugnet
Midland, MI 48640
(517) 631-9463
Fax: (517) 631-9419

This interpretive system analyzes profile patterns, scale combinations, and individual factor scales. The results are presented in narrative form under sections for interpersonal relationships, coping with stress, independence, determination and decisiveness, and intelligence. There is also a career profile, indicating the Holland themes most associated with the overall personality configuration. The program is bundled together with the Children's Personality Questionnaire. Requires entry of Sten scores. Instruction booklet included. Latest release April, 1991.

Classification: Diagnostic Aid, Children and Adolescents (Interpretive report)

Hardware Requirements and Price
IBM PC, XT, AT, PS/2, & compatibles; 256 K; hard disk optional; 1 disk drive. Printer required. Laser printer optional. *Single User Price: $195.00*

High School Personality Questionnaire Narrative Report

Institute for Personality & Ability Testing
P.O. Box 188
Champaign, IL 61824-1188
(217) 352-4739
(800) 225-4728

This program is intended to guide institutional personnel, counselors, and school psychologists working with students. The report is built around 14 personality dimensions, and several other broad trait patterns. The program helps spot potential dropouts and drug users, and identify psychological factors that may contribute to low school achievement. Teleprocessing service.

Classification: Diagnostic Aid, Children and Adolescents (Interpretive report)

Hardware Requirements and Price
IBM PC, XT, AT, PS/2, & compatibles. 1200 baud modem required. Printer required. Laser printer optional. *Single User Price: Contact publisher, depends on number of administrations*

Hilson Adolescent Profile (HAP)
Robin E. Inwald

Hilson Research, Inc.
P.O. Box 239, 82-28 Abingdon Road
Kew Gardens, NY 11415
(718) 805-0063

A behaviorally-oriented personality measure geared specifically to identify and predict delinquent and/or troubled behavior in adolescents. Includes scales for alcohol use, drug use, educational difficulties, depression/suicide potential, frustration tolerance, and homelife conflicts. Reports include HAP critical items and three profile graphs comparing tested individual with juvenile offenders, clinical inpatients and "normal" adolescents. Detailed manual included. Latest release August, 1990.

Classification: Diagnostic Aid, Children and Adolescents

Hardware Requirements and Price
IBM PC, XT, AT, PS/2, & compatibles; 256 K; 2 Mb hard disk required; 2 disk drives. Mouse optional. 1200 baud modem required. Printer required. Laser printer optional. Scanner optional. *Single User Price: $90.00 Processing fees based on the number of tests scores each month*

Hilson Career Satisfaction Index (HCSI)
Robin E. Inwald

Hilson Research, Inc.
P.O. Box 239, 82-28 Abingdon Road
Kew Gardens, NY 11415
(718) 805-0063

Designed to measure on-the-job stress symptoms, anger/hostility patterns, and satisfaction with supervisors and career progress. Report includes full computerized narrative report (clinical and/or self-development), HCSI critical items for follow-up evaluation, two profile graphs comparing the tested individuals scores with those of employees and candidates for promotion, scale/content area descriptions, true/false item responses, and an item tag-word print-out. Detailed manual included. Latest release August, 1990.

Classification: Vocational Testing (Interpretive report)

Hardware Requirements and Price
IBM PC, XT, AT, PS/2, & compatibles; 256 K; 2 Mb hard disk required; 2 disk drives. Mouse optional. 1200 baud modem required. Printer required. Laser printer optional. Scanner optional. *Single User Price: $90.00 Processing fees based on the number of tests scored per month*

Hilson Personnel Profile/Success Quotient (HPP/SQ)
Robin E. Inwald

Hilson Research, Inc.
P.O. Box 239, 82-28 Abingdon Road
Kew Gardens, NY 11415
(718) 805-0063

Assesses behavioral patterns and characteristics related to "success" in the working world. A measure of individual strengths and positive features useful for pre-employment screening and in-house staff training programs. A 150-item, paper-pencil, true-false instrument that measures candor, achievement history, social ability, "winner's image," initiative, and potential for success. Also includes content areas such as extroversion, popularity, sensitivity, drive, and competitive spirit. Detailed manual included. Latest release August, 1990.

Classification: Vocational Testing (Interpretive report)

Hardware Requirements and Price
IBM PC, XT, AT, PS/2, & compatibles; 256 K; 2 Mb hard disk required; 2 disk drives. Mouse optional. 1200 baud modem required. Laser printer required. Scanner optional. *Single User Price: $90.00 (Processing fee based on the number of tests scored per month.)*

Hilson Research Remote System Software (HRRSS™)
Robin E. Inwald
Henry Hurwitz, Jr.
Joel Rosner

Hilson Research, Inc.
P.O. Box 239, 82-28 Abingdon Road
Kew Gardens, NY 11415
(718) 805-0063

Immediate test-scoring system that works on any IBM PC with a modem. Used in conjunction with other Hilson Research products. Detailed manual included. Latest release August, 1990.

Classification: Testing Utility

Hardware Requirements and Price
IBM PC, XT, AT, PS/2, & compatibles; 256 K; 2 Mb hard disk required; 2 disk drives. Mouse optional. 1200 baud modem required. Printer required. Laser printer optional. Scanner optional. *Single User Price: $90.00*

HRB Norms Program, Version 1
Robert K. Heaton
Igor Grant
Charles G. Matthews

Psychological Assessment Resources, Inc.
P.O. Box 998
Odessa, FL 33556
(800) 331-TEST

Based on the book *Comprehensive Norms for an Expanded Halstead-Reitan Battery: Demographic Corrections, Research Findings, and Clinical Applications* (1991), this program converts raw test scores into scaled and T scores for any combination of the 54 test measures. Output consists of scaled scores, T scores, and profiles of T scores. The report can be formatted as a text file for editing with a word processor. Raw, scaled, and T scores can also be saved as an ASCII data file to facilitate research and statistical analyses. Detailed manual included. Latest release June 15, 1991.

Classification: Neuropsychological Testing (Interpretive report)

Hardware Requirements and Price
IBM PC, XT, AT, PS/2, & compatibles; 256 K; hard disk optional; 2 disk drives or 1 disk drive and hard disk. Laser printer optional. *Single User Price: $295.00*

Hudson Education Skills Inventory (HESI)
Brian R. Bryant
Floyd G. Hudson

Pro-Ed, Inc.
8700 Shoal Creek Blvd.
Austin, TX 78758-6897
(512) 451-3246

Allows user to input student information and generate a report concerning where testing with the HESI should begin. A printed instructional planning form is produced for each student, detailing background data, test performance, and goals and objectives in basic skills areas. Detailed manual included. Latest release 1989.

Classification: Academic (Interpretive report)

Hardware Requirements and Price
Apple II, 48 K, hard disk optional, 1 disk drive (5-1/4). *Single User Price: $79.00*

IBM PC, XT, AT, PS/2, & compatibles; 640 K; hard disk optional; 1 disk drive (5-1/4). *Single User Price: $79.00*

Human Resource Inventory

London House/SRA
9701 W. Higgins Road
Rosemont, IL 60018
(708) 292-1900
(800) 221-8378

Paper-and-pencil test designed to aid in hiring productive employees. Measures an applicant's attitudes in areas such as organizational adjustment, work performance, interpersonal cooperation, drug avoidance, and safety. Per-test fee. Teleprocessing service also available. Detailed manual included.

Classification: Vocational Testing (Interpretive report)

Hardware Requirements and Price
IBM PC, XT, AT, PS/2, & compatibles; 512 K; hard disk optional; 2 disk drives. *Sold only in conjunction with the publisher's test books.*

Idare
Carlos Pal Hegedus

Psico-Iuris, S.A.
P.O. Box 1039 - Centro Colon
San Jose, 1007 Costa Rica
(506) 24-4416

Scores the State-Trait Anxiety Inventory and gives raw-, percentile-, and T-scores on both scales. Instruction booklet and tutorial program included. Latest release November, 1991.

Classification: Diagnostic Aid (Interpretive report)

Hardware Requirements and Price
IBM PC, XT, AT, PS/2, & compatibles; 128 K; hard disk optional; 1 disk drive. Laser printer optional. Requires DOS 3.1. *Single User Price: $100.00 Network Price: $400.00*

InSight W.P. Reporting System
Martine J. Robards

PsychoLogics
6323A Fairmount Avenue
El Cerrito, CA 94530

(510) 528-6244
(800) 528-6244

This interpretation program for the Myers-Briggs Type Indicator (MBTI) produces a 10-13 page report for each of the 16 MBTI types. Each report provides an overall description of the type (with attention to information processing, judgment, and interpersonal style) and a special section on work style. Supplementary temperament-based reports describe styles of managers and employees as well as relationship styles. Reports can be customized with a word processor or used directly with clients individually or in groups. The report is appropriate for use in career and other counseling, training, and organizational development. References are available upon request. Detailed manual included. Latest release October, 1991.

Classification: Myers-Briggs (Interpretive report)

Hardware Requirements and Price
IBM PC, XT, AT, PS/2, & compatibles; 640 K; hard disk optional; 2 disk drives. Printer required. Laser printer optional. *Single User Price: $239.00 License permits unlimited use on 1 or more computers*

Macintosh, hard disk optional, 2 disk drives. Printer required. *Single User Price: $239.00 License permits unlimited use on 1 or more computers*

Intake Evaluation Report Clinician, Version 3.0

Psychologistics, Inc.
P.O. Box 033896
Indialantic, FL 32903
(407) 259-7811

This program is designed to provide a computer generated summary of the clinician's initial evaluation of the client. The report may be printed out or written to a text file. The narrative report organizes information in a manner useful for case conceptualization and treatment planning. Software permits unlimited uses. Detailed manual included. Latest release 1984.

Classification: Diagnostic Aid (Interpretive report)

Hardware Requirements and Price
Apple II+, IIe, IIc; 48 K; hard disk optional; 1 disk drive (5-1/4). Printer required. Requires DOS 3.3. *Single User Price: $250.00 20 IER checklists $15.00*

IBM PC, XT, AT, PS/2, & compatibles; 128 K; hard disk optional; 1 disk drive. Printer required. Requires DOS 2.0. *Single User Price: $250.00 20 IER checklists $15.00*

Macintosh, 512 K, hard disk optional, 1 disk drive (3-1/2). Printer required. 20 IER checklists $15.00. *Single User Price: $250.00*

International Testing System (ITS)

Saville & Holdsworth, Ltd.
575 Boylston Street
Boston, MA 02116
(617) 236-1550
(800) 899-7451

Allows users to administer a computer battery of Saville and Holdsworth, Ltd. (SHL) tests (The Occupational Personality Questionnaire OPQ, Verbal Critical Reasoning, Numerical Critical Reasoning) that were developed and normed for managers and professionals in business. Administration can be in any one of 12 languages. ITS takes candidates' scores and produces Expert System Narrative Reports in any of the 12 languages. Administration and report generation can also be done in different languages. Reports produced on site by the personal computer use norms that are specific to each country. Narrative reports interpret 30 work relevant personality scales and ability scores. Over 60 supplemental scales can also be generated. Report length can be customized. Detailed manual included. Latest release November 1, 1991.

Classification: Vocational Testing (Administration and Interpretive report)

Hardware Requirements and Price
IBM PC, XT, AT, PS/2, & compatibles; 640 K; 8 Mb hard disk required; 1 disk drive. Mouse optional. Modem optional. Printer required. Laser printer required. Per administration or report charge depends on volume. *Single User Price: $295.00 Network Price: $295.00*

Interpersonal Styles Inventory (ISI)
Maurice Lorr
Richard P. Youniss
George J. Huba

Western Psychological Services
12031 Wilshire Blvd.
Los Angeles, CA 90025
(213) 478-2061
(800) 648-8857

The ISI measures the way in which individuals 14 years and older relate to others. The inventory contains 300 true-false statements, that are usually completed in less than 30 min. In addition to being a general interpersonal personality battery, the ISI also evaluates style of impulse control and modes of dealing with work and play. Teleprocessing service also available. Instruction booklet included.

Classification: Diagnostic Aid

Hardware Requirements and Price
IBM PC, XT, AT, PS/2, & compatibles; 512 K; 1 Mb hard disk required; 1 disk drive. Printer required. Laser printer optional. Requires DOS 3.0. *Single User Price: $235.00*

Inventory for Counseling and Development (ICD)
Norman S. Giddan
F. Reid Creech
Victor R. Lovell

National Computer Systems, Inc.
P.O. Box 1416
Minneapolis, MN 55440
(800) 627-7271

Multiscale inventory used for counseling college students with vocational, educational, and personal problems. Inventory helps identify strengths and coping skills, considering personal, social, and academic functioning. The complete report presents scores and suggests the orientation and direction that remediation activities might take. Per-test fee. On-line administration is possible with Microtest Assessment System. Detailed manual included.

Classification: Diagnostic Aid (Administration and Interpretive report)

Hardware Requirements and Price
IBM PC, XT, AT, PS/2, & compatibles; 512 K; 10 Mb hard disk required; 1 disk drive. Monochrome, CGA, EGA, or VGA display. Modem optional. Printer required. Laser printer optional. Requires DOS 3.1. *Single User Price: Per-test fee*

Inwald Personality Inventory (IPI)
Robin E. Inwald

Hilson Research, Inc.
P.O. Box 239, 82-28 Abingdon Road
Kew Gardens, NY 11415
(718) 805-0063

Comprehensive psychological screening test designed and validated for law enforcement, correction, and security officer candidates. Includes full IPI computerized narrative report with written evaluation, IPI critical items, IPI personality profile graph, and IPI critical items printout. Program has 26 scales including: job difficulties, absence abuse, loner type, drugs, alcohol, trouble with law and society, lack of assertiveness, undue suspiciousness, and hyperactivity. Detailed manual included. Latest release August, 1990.

Classification: Vocational Testing (Interpretive report)

Hardware Requirements and Price
IBM PC, XT, AT, PS/2, & compatibles; 256 K; 2 Mb hard disk required; 2 disk drives. Mouse optional. 1200 baud modem required. Printer required. Laser printer optional. Scanner optional. *Single User Price: $90.00 Processing fee depends on the number of monthly administrations*

Inwald Survey 3 (IS3tm)
Robin E. Inwald

Hilson Research, Inc.
P.O. Box 239, 82-28 Abingdon Road
Kew Gardens, NY 11415
(718) 805-0063

System for screening out negative qualities of job applicants. Includes full computerized narrative report, items for follow-up evaluation, personality profile graph, true-false item responses, and item tag-word print-out. Scales for this 128-item test include guardedness, alcohol use, drug use, trouble with the law/society, job difficulties, and absence abuse. The overall score and critical items for follow-up evaluation score are also plotted on the personality profile graph. Processing fee based on the number of tests scored per month. Detailed manual included. Latest release August, 1990.

Classification: Vocational Testing (Interpretive report)

Hardware Requirements and Price
IBM PC, XT, AT, PS/2, & compatibles; 256 K; 2 Mb hard disk required; 2 disk drives. Mouse optional. 1200 baud modem required. Printer required. Laser printer optional. Scanner optional. *Single User Price: $90.00*

IQ Test Interpretation-Adult
John Trifiletti

Precision People, Inc.
3452 North Ride Circle South
Jacksonville, FL 32223
(904) 262-1096
(800) 338-0710

Program interprets the results on the Wechsler Adult Intelligence Scale-Revised (WAIS-R) and presents educational, vocational, and clinical recommendations. Detailed manual included.

Classification: WAIS (Interpretive report)

Hardware Requirements and Price
Apple II+, IIe, IIc, IIgs. *Single User Price: $295.00*

IBM PC, XT, AT, PS/2, & compatibles; 64 K; hard disk optional; 1 disk drive. *Single User Price: $295.00*

IQ Test Interpretation-Clinical
John Trifiletti

Precision People, Inc.
3452 North Ride Circle South
Jacksonville, FL 32223
(904) 262-1096
(800) 338-0710

Interprets results on the Wechsler Intelligence Scale for Children-Revised and gives both clinical and educational recommendations. The report provides a list of the client's strengths and weaknesses compared to the general population, the client's expected level of ability, and interpretation of the three major Wechsler Intelligence Scale for Children-Revised (WISC-R) factors (verbal comprehension, freedom from anxiety, and perceptual organization). Detailed manual included.

Classification: WISC (Interpretive report)

Hardware Requirements and Price
Apple II+, IIe, IIc, IIgs; 1 disk drive. *Single User Price: $295.00*

IBM PC, XT, AT, PS/2, & compatibles; 64 K; hard disk optional; 1 disk drive. *Single User Price: $295.00*

Jackson Personality Inventory
Douglas N. Jackson

Sigma Assessment Systems, Inc.
P.O. Box 610984
Port Huron, MI 48061-0984
(800) 265-1285

On-site administration, scoring, and reporting software designed to yield a set of scores for personality traits of normal functioning individuals. Scales include anxiety, risk taking, and tolerance. Particularly useful with individuals of average to above average intelligence. The basic report provides a profile of scores on all scales, along with validity information. Per test fees apply. Detailed manual included. On-line help available.

Classification: Personality Testing (Administration and Interpretive report)

Hardware Requirements and Price
IBM PC, XT, AT, PS/2, & compatibles; 256 K; 1 Mb hard disk optional; 1 disk drive. Laser printer optional. *Single User Price: $150.00 (first 25 scorings) or $75.00 (first 10 scorings) $112.50 (25 additional scorings)*

Jackson Vocational Interest Survey (JVIS)
Douglas N. Jackson

Sigma Assessment Systems, Inc.
P.O. Box 610984
Port Huron, MI 48061-0984
(800) 265-1285

Program designed to help high school, college, and adult populations with career planning and educational guidance. This forced-choice inventory is written on a 7th grade reading level. The Basic Report graphically displays 34 scores from the interest scales. The Extended Report includes a profile of 10 general occupational themes, a profile of similarity to 17 educational fields, a ranking of 32 occupational groups, validity scales, and a narrative summary. Per-test fees apply. Detailed manual included. On-line help available.

Classification: Vocational Testing (Administration and Interpretive report)

Hardware Requirements and Price
IBM PC, XT, AT, PS/2, & compatibles; 256 K; 1 Mb hard disk optional; 1 disk drive. Laser printer optional. *Single User Price: $150.00 (first 25 scorings) or $75.00 (first 10 scorings) $112.50 (25 additional scorings)*

Jesness Behavior Checklist Computer Program
Carl F. Jesness

Multi-Health Systems, Inc.
908 Niagara Falls Blvd.
North Tonawanda, NY 14120-2060
(416) 424-1700
(800) 456-3003

This 80-item scale measures 14 bipolar behavioral tendencies among adolescents. An observer form can be used for ratings by counselors, therapists, teachers, and probation or correction officers. A self-appraisal form is also included. The program administers and scores the checklist and prints the results. Detailed manual included.

Classification: Diagnostic Aid, Children and Adolescents (Administration)

Hardware Requirements and Price
IBM PC, XT, AT, PS/2, & compatibles; 256 K; hard disk optional; 1 disk drive. Printer required. Laser printer optional. *Single User Price: $160.00 (50 administrations)*

Jesness Inventory Narrative Report

Psychological Testing Service
213 East Sugnet
Midland, MI 48640
(517) 631-9463
Fax: (517) 631-9419

This program analyzes the 10 standard scales and Asocial Index to produce narrative interpretive reports. The areas assessed by the program (including social maladjustment, values, and aggressiveness) are particularly useful in the evaluation of adolescents with behavioral and emotional problems. Requires entry of standard scores. Instruction booklet included. Latest release April, 1991.

Classification: Diagnostic Aid, Children and Adolescents (Interpretive report)

Hardware Requirements and Price
IBM PC, XT, AT, PS/2, & compatibles; 256 K; hard disk optional; 1 disk drive. Printer required. Laser printer optional. *Single User Price: $195.00*

Jesness Inventory of Adolescent Personality Computer Program
Carl F. Jesness

Multi-Health Systems, Inc.
908 Niagara Falls Blvd
North Tonawanda, NY 14120-2060
(416) 424-1700
(800) 456-3003

Administers, scores, and interprets the Jesness Inventory of Adolescent Personality. Designed for youth aged 8-18. Scales include social maladjustment, withdrawal, value orientation, immaturity, and denial. Includes I-level classi-

fication and a narrative report. Detailed manual included.

Classification: Diagnostic Aid, Children and Adolescents (Administration and Interpretive report)

Hardware Requirements and Price
IBM PC, XT, AT, PS/2, & compatibles; 256 K; hard disk optional; 1 disk drive. Printer required. Laser printer optional. *Single User Price: $175.00*

JOB-O
Arthur Cutler
Francis Ferry
Robert Kauk
Robert Robinett

CFKR Career Materials, Inc.
11860 Kemper Road, Unit 7
Auburn, CA 95603
(916) 889-2357
(800) 525-5626

Self-administering career exploration instrument that employs 18 variables to which students respond on a 1-2-3 continuum. The variables cover educational aspirations, job fields of interest, and preferred working conditions. Responses are matched with 144 of the most popular job titles and over 800 related job titles. Instruction booklet included. Latest release 1991.

Classification: Vocational Testing (Administration and Interpretiver report)

Hardware Requirements and Price
Apple II, 64 K, 1 disk drive. Not compatible with laser printer. *Single User Price: $89.95 Network Price: $359.80*

IBM PC, XT, AT, PS/2, & compatibles; hard disk optional; 1 disk drive. Laser printer optional. *Single User Price: $89.95 Network Price: $359.80*

JOB-O A (Advanced)
Arthur Cutler
Francis Ferry
Robert Kauk

CFKR Career Materials, Inc.
11860 Kemper Road, Unit 7
Auburn, CA 95603
(916) 889-2357
(800) 525-5626

Helps the user assess skills and interests in making career decisions. JOB-O A uses simple assessment questions relating to job interests and skills. The user makes personal choices about preferred work interest areas, length of training time, basic educational skills, preferred working conditions, physical demands of jobs, and job requirements. JOB-O A is recommended for clients from the 10th grade through adult. Instruction booklet included. Latest release 1991.

Classification: Vocational Testing (Administration and Interpretive report)

Hardware Requirements and Price
IBM PC, XT, AT, PS/2, & compatibles; 128 K; hard disk optional; 2 disk drives. Mouse optional. Modem optional. Laser printer optional. *Single User Price: $99.95 Network Price: $399.80*

Some of the programs described in the Clinical Software section can also be used for psychological assessment.

Karson Clinical Report (KCR) for the 16PF

Institute for Personality & Ability Testing
P.O. Box 188
Champaign, IL 61824-1188
(217) 352-4739
(800) 225-4728

Computer interpretation of the 16PF for clinical applications and treatment planning. Teleprocessing service. Price depends upon the numbers of administrations.

Classification: 16PF (Interpretive report)

Hardware Requirements and Price
IBM PC, XT, AT, PS/2, & compatibles. 1200 baud modem required. Printer required. Laser printer optional. *Single User Price: Call publisher*

Kaufman Assessment Battery for Children-ASSIST
Alan S. Kaufman
Nadeen L. Kaufman

American Guidance Service
4201 Woodland Road
Circle Pines, MN 55014-1796
(612) 786-4343
(800) 328-2560

Automated system for scoring and interpreting the Kaufman Assessment Battery for Children. Obtains derived scores and generates profiles showing an individual's strengths and weaknesses. The program provides interpretive data including: standard scores, confidence intervals on standard scores, national and/or sociocultural percentile ranks, percentile intervals corresponding to the confidence intervals, age equivalents, descriptive classifications, and global scale comparisons. Detailed manual included.

Classification: Academic (Interpretive report)

Hardware Requirements and Price
Apple II, 48 K, 2 disk drives (5-1/4). *Single User Price: $115.00*

Kaufman Test of Educational Achievement ASSIST
Alan S. Kaufman
Nadeen L. Kaufman

American Guidance Service
4201 Woodland Road
Circle Pines, MN 55014-1796
(612) 786-4343
(800) 328-2560

Converts raw scores into derived scores, summarizes student performance, and offers teaching objectives for remedial instruction. Provides diagnostic information for reading, mathematics, total test and subtests. The ASSIST reports standard scores, age or grade equivalents, and percentile ranks in a narrative or chart format. Features include area and subtest comparisons, error analysis and word lists. Detailed manual included. On-line help available.

Classification: Academic (Interpretive report)

Hardware Requirements and Price
Apple II, 128 K, 2 disk drives. *Single User Price: $115.00*

IBM PC, XT, AT, PS/2, & compatibles; 256 K; hard disk optional; 2 disk drives. *Single User Price: $115.00*

Key Math-Revised ASSIST
Austin J. Connolly

American Guidance Service
4201 Woodland Road
Circle Pines, MN 55014-1796
(612) 786-4343
(800) 328-2560

Converts raw scores into derived scores, summarizes student performance, and offers suggestions for remedial instruction. Provides diagnostic information at four levels: total test, subtest, area, and domain. The ASSIST reports standard scores, age or grade equivalents, and percentile ranks. Detailed manual included. On-line help available.

Classification: Academic (Interpretive report)

Hardware Requirements and Price
Apple II+, IIe, IIc, IIgs; 128 K; 2 disk drives. *Single User Price: $125.00*

IBM PC, XT, AT, PS/2, & compatibles; 256 K; hard disk optional; 2 disk drives. *Single User Price: $125.00*

Kinetic Family Drawing Tests: Computer Analysis
Joseph M. Eisenberg
James J. Smith

Reason House
204 East Joppa Road, Suite 10
Towson, MD 21204
(301) 321-7270

Program designed to facilitate scoring and analysis of the Kinetic Family Drawing Tests. Analysis is structured according to specific family members and issues pertaining to those members. Detailed manual included.

Classification: Personality Testing (Interpretive report)

Hardware Requirements and Price
IBM PC, XT, AT, PS/2, & compatibles; 64 K; hard disk optional; 1 disk drive. Printer required. *Single User Price: $395.00 Discount for APA Members: $195.00*

Law Enforcement Assessment and Development Report (LEADR)

Institute for Personality & Ability Testing
P.O. Box 188
Champaign, IL 61824-1188
(217) 352-4739
(800) 225-4728

Computer interpretation of the 16PF and the Clinical Analysis Questionnaire for effective officer selection in law enforcement settings. Teleprocessing service.

Classification: 16PF (Interpretive report)

Hardware Requirements and Price
Contact publisher for equipment options. 1200 baud modem required. Printer required. Laser printer optional. *Single User Price: depends on number of administrations,contact publisher*

Life Space Analysis Profile (LSAP)
John W. Baker

XICOM, Inc.
Sterling Forest
Tuxedo, NY 10987

(914) 351-4735
(800) 759-4266

An interactive self-assessment instrument that creates a customized profile of an individual's level of satisfaction and adaptability to change for 18 areas of their life. Analyzes the degree of integration and/or polarization in each area, and assesses the balance between the needs of the self, home & family and work. Detailed manual included.

Classification: Diagnostic Aid

Hardware Requirements and Price
IBM PC, XT, AT, PS/2, & compatibles; 640 K; hard disk optional. Laser printer optional. *Single User Price: $40.00 Additional diskettes $20.00*

LNNB Scoring & Interpretation Program
Charles Vella

140 Moffitt Street
San Francisco, CA 94131
(415) 929-5210

Provides Luria-Nebraska Neuropsychological Battery (LNNB) scores for 106 scales and clinical interpretive statements. Output to printer. Instruction booklet included. Latest release January, 1991.

Classification: Neuropsychological Testing (Interpretive report)

Hardware Requirements and Price
IBM PC, XT, AT, PS/2, & compatibles; 64 K; hard disk required; 1 disk drive (5-1/4). Printer required. *Single User Price: $200.00*

Louisville Behavior Checklist (LBC)
Lovick C. Miller

Western Psychological Services
12031 Wilshire Blvd.
Los Angeles, CA 90025
(213) 478-2061
(800) 648-8857

The LBC measures social and emotional behavior of children 4 through 17 years of age,
with separate norms for sex and age group.
The checklist is composed of 164 true-false
items that are completed by a child's parent or
guardian in about 20 min. The items are easy
to understand and address a broad range of
behaviors symptomatic of childhood psychopathology. Price depends on number of administrations. Teleprocessing service also available. Instruction booklet included.

Classification: Diagnostic Aid, Children and
Adolescents

Hardware Requirements and Price
Apple II+, IIe, IIc, IIgs; 48 K; 1 disk drive.
Printer required. Laser printer optional.
Single User Price: $180.00

IBM PC, XT, AT, PS/2, & compatibles; 512 K;
1 Mb hard disk required; 1 disk drive. Printer
required. Laser printer optional. Requires
DOS 3.0. *Single User Price: $180.00*

LSI Stylus
J. Clayton Lafferty

Human Synergistics, Inc.
39819 Plymouth Road
Plymouth, MI 48187
(313) 459-1030

Allows users to assess their personal and
management styles and learn methods to
improve problem areas. Companion program
evaluates the user from the perspective of
his/her co-workers and subordinates and
makes recommendations for improving problem areas through the comparison of self-
perception to perception by others.

Classification: Industrial Consulting

Hardware Requirements and Price
IBM PC, XT, AT, PS/2, & compatibles; 256 K;
2 disk drives. Requires DOS 2.0. *Single User
Price: $240.00*

Luria Nebraska Scoring System
Dana LeTendre

Precision People, Inc.
3452 North Ride Circle South
Jacksonville, FL 32223
(904) 262-1096
(800) 338-0710

Program for organizing and reporting scores
on the LNNB. Raw and T-scores are provided
for 14 Profile scales, 10 localization scales, and
30 experimental/factor-derived scales. T-
scores that exceed critical levels are highlighted. Four-page report lists item responses
for each of the scored scales. Detailed manual
included.

Classification: Neuropsychological Testing
(Interpretive report)

Hardware Requirements and Price
Apple II+, IIe, IIc, IIgs; 64 K; hard disk op-
tional; 1 disk drive. Printer required. *Single
User Price: $250.00*

IBM PC, XT, AT, PS/2, & compatibles; hard disk optional; 1 disk drive. Printer required. *Single User Price: $250.00*

Luria-Nebraska Neuropsychological Battery (LNNB)
Charles J. Golden
Thomas A. Hammeke
Arnold D. Purisch

Western Psychological Services
12031 Wilshire Blvd.
Los Angeles, CA 90025
(213) 478-2061
(800) 648-8857

The LNNB is a multidimensional test battery designed to assess a broad range of neuropsychological dysfunction in adults and children. The computer program is designed as an advanced scoring aid that computes and profiles T-scores and formats tables of a client's relative strengths and weaknesses. Price depends on number of administrations. IBM version provides scoring and interpretation. Apple version provides scoring only. Teleprocessing service also available. Instruction booklet included.

Classification: Neuropsychological Testing (Interpretive report)

Hardware Requirements and Price
Apple II+, IIe, IIc, IIgs; 48 K; 1 disk drive. 80-column display required. Printer required. *Single User Price: $225.00*

IBM PC, XT, AT, PS/2, & compatibles; 512 K; 1 Mb hard disk required; 1 disk drive. Printer required. Laser printer optional. Requires DOS 3.0. *Single User Price: $250.00*

Management Readiness Profile (MRP)

London House/SRA
9701 W. Higgins Road
Rosemont, IL 60018
(708) 292-1900
(800) 221-8378

The MRP helps companies make accurate selection, placement, and promotion decisions concerning entry-level supervisory and management positions in service or manufacturing environments. The MRP evaluates candidates in the following areas: management interest, leadership, energy level, practical thinking, management responsibility, and interpersonal skills. A Management Readiness Index combines the results into a single score that reflects a person's overall fit with a managerial role. Detailed manual included.

Classification: Vocational Testing (Interpretive report)

Hardware Requirements and Price
IBM PC, XT, AT, PS/2, & compatibles; 512 K; hard disk optional; 2 disk drives.

Manson Evaluation
Morse P. Manson
George J. Huba

Western Psychological Services
12031 Wilshire Blvd.
Los Angeles, CA 90025
(213) 478-2061
(800) 648-8857

The Manson Evaluation identifies alcoholics or alcohol-abuse-prone individuals by measuring seven personality characteristics: anxiety, depressive fluctuation, emotional sensitivity, resentfulness, incompleteness, aloneness, and interpersonal relations. It is a 72-item test that is easily administered in 5 to 10 min and is rapidly scored and interpreted. Teleprocessing service also available. Instruction booklet included.

Classification: Diagnostic Aid, Substance Abuse

Hardware Requirements and Price
IBM PC, XT, AT, PS/2, & compatibles; 512 K; 1 Mb hard disk required; 1 disk drive. Printer required. Laser printer optional. Requires DOS 3.0. *Single User Price: $185.00*

Marital Satisfaction Inventory (MSI)
Douglas K. Snyder
David Lachar

Western Psychological Services
12031 Wilshire Blvd.
Los Angeles, CA 90025
(213) 478-2061
(800) 648-8857

The MSI identifies for each spouse the nature and extent of marital distress along nine dimensions of the relationship. The MSI computer program administers the test on line or scores and interprets a previous administration, performs comparative analyses, and prints a descriptive report. Teleprocessing service also available. Instruction booklet included.

Classification: Diagnostic Aid (Interpretive report)

Hardware Requirements and Price
IBM PC, XT, AT, PS/2, & compatibles; 512 K; 1 Mb hard disk required; 1 disk drive. Printer required. Laser printer optional. Requires DOS 3.0. *Single User Price: $185.00 Price depends on number of administrations*

The Marks MMPI Adolescent Clinical Report
Phillip A. Marks
Richard W. Lewak

Western Psychological Services
12031 Wilshire Blvd.
Los Angeles, CA 90025
(213) 478-2061
(800) 648-8857

This program functions as a professional consultation to mental health practitioners. The user enters the client's T-scores, and the program provides a comprehensive clinical interpretation of MMPI results. Instruction booklet included.

Classification: MMPI (Interpretive report)

Hardware Requirements and Price
IBM PC, XT, AT, PS/2, & compatibles; 512 K; 1 Mb hard disk required; 1 disk drive. Printer required. Laser printer optional. Requires DOS 3.0. *Single User Price: $150.00*

The Marks MMPI Adolescent Feedback and Treatment Report
Phillip A. Marks
Richard W. Lewak

Western Psychological Services
12031 Wilshire Blvd.

Los Angeles, CA 90025
(213) 478-2061
(800) 648-8857

This program gives an individualized interpretation of MMPI results, based on adolescent norms and T-scores entered by the user. It provides interpretive information for both the clinician and the client. Instruction booklet included.

Classification: MMPI (Interpretive report)

Hardware Requirements and Price
IBM PC, XT, AT, PS/2, & compatibles; 512 K; 1 Mb hard disk required; 1 disk drive. Printer required. Laser printer optional. Requires DOS 3.0. *Single User Price: $130.00*

The Marks MMPI and MMPI-2 Adult Clinical Report
Phillip A. Marks
Richard W. Lewak
Gerald E. Nelson

Western Psychological Services
12031 Wilshire Blvd.
Los Angles, CA 90025
(213) 478-2061
(800) 648-8857

This program functions as a professional consultation to mental health practitioners. The user enters the client's T-scores, and the program provides a comprehensive clinical interpretation of MMPI or MMPI-2 (Minnesota Multiphasic Personality Inventory-2) results. Instruction booklet included.

Classification: MMPI (Interpretive report)

Hardware Requirements and Price
IBM PC, XT, AT, PS/2, & compatibles; 512 K; 1 Mb hard disk required; 1 disk drive. Printer required. Laser printer optional. Requires DOS 3.0. *Single User Price: $150.00*

The Marks MMPI and MMPI-2 Adult Feedback and Treatment Report
Phillip A. Marks
Richard W. Lewak
Gerald E. Nelson

Western Psychological Services
12031 Wilshire Blvd.
Los Angeles, CA 90025
(213) 478-2061
(800) 648-8857

This report profiles the client's K-corrected T-scores for the validity, clinical, and special scales. It notes the client's code type and tells the clinician whether or not test results are valid. Treatment suggestions are provided. The second part of the report is addressed to the client, and offers self-help suggestions. Instruction booklet included.

Classification: MMPI (Interpretive report)

Hardware Requirements and Price
IBM PC, XT, AT, PS/2, & compatibles; 512 K; 1 Mb hard disk required; 1 disk drive. Printer required. Laser printer optional. Requires DOS 3.0. *Single User Price: $130.00*

Marriage Counseling Report (MCR)

Institute for Personality & Ability Testing
P.O. Box 188
Champaign, IL 61824-1188

(217) 352-4739
(800) 225-4728

Computer interpretation of the 16PF for exploration of marital relationships from a counseling perspective. Teleprocessing service. Instruction booklet included.

Classification: 16PF (Interpretive report)

Hardware Requirements and Price
IBM PC, XT, AT, PS/2, & compatibles. 1200 baud modem required. Printer required. Laser printer optional. *Single User Price: Depends upon the number of administrations*

McDermott Multidimensional Assessment of Children

The Psychological Corporation
555 Academic Court
San Antonio, TX 78204-0952
(512) 299-1061
(800) 228-0752

Comprehensive system of over 100 integrated computer programs that use test results, behavioral data, and demographic variables to produce objective classifications of childhood normality and exceptionally. The program can also assist in the development of IEPs. Disks provide 50 or 100 classification and/or program design uses.

Classification: Diagnostic Aid, Children and Adolescents (Interpretive report)

Hardware Requirements and Price
Apple II+, IIe, IIc; 48 K; 1 disk drive. Printer required. *Single User Price: $198.00 (includes 10 administrations) Per test fee*

IBM PC, XT, AT, PS/2, & compatibles; 256 K; 2 disk drives. Printer required. *Single User Price: $198.00 (includes 10 administrations) Per test fee*

Memory Assessment Scales (MAS), Version 1
J. Michael Williams

Psychological Assessment Resources, Inc.
P.O. Box 998
Odessa, FL 33556
(800) 331-TEST

User enters raw subtest and verbal process scores and the program calculates MAS Summary Scales scores and the Global Memory Scale score. It lists raw and percentile scores with associated normative scale, or standard scores for MAS age, education, and US census norms. Generates interpretive hypotheses that address overall memory functioning, functional memory areas, and specific subtest performance within functional memory areas. This report can be created as a text file for editing with a word processor. Detailed manual included. Latest release July 1, 1991.

Classification: Neuropsychological Testing (Interpretive report)

Hardware Requirements and Price
IBM PC, XT, AT, PS/2, & compatibles; 256 K; hard disk optional; 2 disk drives or 1 disk drive and hard disk. Laser printer optional. *Single User Price: $295.00*

Readers interested in vocational testing programs should also examine career counseling programs in the clinical software chapter.

Menstrual Distress Questionnaire (MDQ)

Rudolf H. Moos
George J. Huba

Western Psychological Services
12031 Wilshire Blvd.
Los Angeles, CA 90025
(213) 478-2061
(800) 648-8857

The MDQ is a 47-item self-report inventory for use in the diagnosis and treatment of premenstrual and menstrual symptoms. It identifies the kind and intensity of symptoms during each phase of the menstrual cycle and can help researchers and clinicians identify the effect of therapeutic interventions. Teleprocessing service also available. Instruction booklet included.

Classification: Diagnostic Aid

Hardware Requirements and Price
IBM PC, XT, AT, PS/2, & compatibles; 512 K; 1 Mb hard disk required; 1 disk drive. Printer required. Laser printer optional. Requires DOS 3.0. *Single User Price: $240.00*

Mental Status Checklist-Adolescent, Version 3

Edward Dougherty
John A. Schinka

Psychological Assessment Resources, Inc.
P.O. Box 998
Odessa, FL 33556
(800) 331-TEST

The user inputs item responses from the Mental Status Checklist-Adolescent (MSC) booklet which consists of 170 items typically included in a comprehensive mental status examination of adolescents. The report may be generated as a text file for editing with a word processor. The narrative covers presenting problems, behavioral and physical descriptions, emotional state, mental status, health and habits, legal issues/aggressive behavior, recreation, family/peer relationships, developmental status, academic performance, and recommendations. Detailed manual included. Latest release March 22, 1989.

Classification: Diagnostic Aid, Children and Adolescents (Interpretive report)

Hardware Requirements and Price
IBM PC, XT, AT, PS/2, & compatibles; 256 K; hard disk optional; 2 disk drives or 1 disk drive and hard disk. Laser printer optional. *Single User Price: $295.00*

Mental Status Checklist-Adult, Version 3

John A. Schinka

Psychological Assessment Resources, Inc.
P.O. Box 998
Odessa, FL 33556
(800) 331-TEST

Item responses from the MSC-Adult booklet (which consists of 120 items typically included in a comprehensive mental status examination of adults) are inputted. Data entry takes about 5 min and the report can be generated as a text file for editing with a word processor. The report covers presenting problems, behavioral and physical descriptions, emotional state, mental status, health and habits, legal issues/ aggressive behavior, current living situations, diagnoses, treatment, and disposition. Detailed manual included. Latest release March 10, 1989.

Classification: Diagnostic Aid (Interpretive report)

Hardware Requirements and Price
IBM PC, XT, AT, PS/2, & compatibles; 256 K; hard disk optional; 2 disk drives or 1 disk drive and hard disk. Laser printer optional. *Single User Price: $295.00*

Meyer-Kendall Assessment Survey (MKAS)

Henry D. Meyer
Edward L. Kendall

Western Psychological Services
12031 Wilshire Blvd.
Los Angeles, CA 90025
(213) 478-2061
(800) 648-8857

The MKAS is a multifaceted instrument designed to measure a number of personal attributes important to managerial success and performance. Consisting of 105 true-false items, the MKAS can be administered in about 15 min and assesses a number of different clinical and control scales. Teleprocessing service. Detailed manual included.

Classification: Vocational Testing

Hardware Requirements and Price
Contact publisher for equipment options. Modem required. *Single User Price: Depends upon number of administrations*

MICROTEST Assessment System

National Computer Systems, Inc.
P.O. Box 1416

Minneapolis, MN 55440
(800) 627-7271

Permits administration, scoring, and interpreting of NCS assessment instruments using a personal computer. Client takes psychological tests using written materials and standard answer forms. Forms are scanned by the Sentry 3000 scanner or key-entered. Scores, interpretations, and reports are generated with a connected personal computer. An interactive testing capability also exists. Specific tests are listed separately in this directory. Detailed manual included.

Classification: Testing Utility (Administration and Interpretive report)

Hardware Requirements and Price
IBM PC, XT, AT, PS/2, & compatibles; 512 K; hard disk required; 1 disk drive. Printer required. Laser printer optional. Requires DOS 3.1. NCS ScorBox Interface, Sentry 3000 Scanner optional. *Single User Price: Based upon number of administrations*

Millon Adolescent Personality Inventory Narrative Report

Psychological Testing Service
213 East Sugnet
Midland, MI 48640
(517) 631-9463
Fax: (517) 631-9419

This interpretive system uses a complex set of decision rules to analyze profile patterns, various scale combinations, and single scales. The results are presented in narrative form and divided into test-taking behavior, personality patterns, expressed concerns, and behavioral correlates sections. Requires entry of final base rate scores. (Note that hand-scoring materials may not be available and that scoring options for this test are very limited.) Instruction booklet included. Latest release April, 1991.

Classification: Millon (Interpretive report)

Hardware Requirements and Price
IBM PC, XT, AT, PS/2, & compatibles; 256 K; hard disk optional; 1 disk drive. Printer required. Laser printer optional. *Single User Price: $295.00*

Millon Adolescent Personality Inventory-Guidance (MAPI)
Theodore Millon
Catherine J. Green
Robert B. Meagher

National Computer Systems, Inc.
P.O. Box 1416
Minneapolis, MN 55440
(800) 627-7271

The clinical interpretive report deals with the major features of the adolescent's personality, individual styles of expression, scholastic behavior, and flags potential problem areas. Requires Microtest Assessment System. Detailed manual included.

Classification: Millon (Interpretive report)

Hardware Requirements and Price
IBM PC, XT, AT, PS/2, & compatibles; 512 K; 10 Mb hard disk required; 1 disk drive. Monochrome, CGA, EGA, or VGA display. Modem optional. Printer required. Laser printer optional. Requires DOS 3.1. Sentry 3000 Scanner optional. *Single User Price: Depends upon the number of administrations*

Millon Adolescent Personality Inventory-Clinical (MAPI)
Theodore Millon
Catherine J. Green
Robert B. Meagher

National Computer Systems, Inc.
P.O. Box 1416
Minneapolis, MN 55440
(800) 627-7271

This clinical interpretive report is designed for adolescents seen in private practice and mental health treatment settings. It includes a narrative that synthesizes scale profiles. Requires Microtest Assessment System. Detailed manual included.

Classification: Millon

Hardware Requirements and Price
IBM PC, XT, AT, PS/2, & compatibles; 512 K; 10 Mb hard disk required; 1 disk drive. Monochrome, CGA, EGA, or VGA display. Modem optional. Printer required. Laser printer optional. Requires DOS 3.1. Sentry 3000 Scanner optional. *Single User Price: Depends upon the number of administrations*

Millon Behavioral Health Inventory Interpretive Report
Michael E. Mills

Psytek Services
6401 West 81st Street
Los Angeles, CA 90045
(213) 670-4655
(800) 392-5454

Fully automated interpretive report generator. Reports may be exported to word processing programs. No per use fees. Sample report available on request. 30-day money back guarantee. Detailed manual included. Latest release June 1, 1991.

Classification: Diagnostic Aid (Interpretive report)

Hardware Requirements and Price
IBM PC, XT, AT, PS/2, & compatibles; 512 K; hard disk optional. Monochrome, CGA, EGA, or VGA display. Laser printer optional. *Single User Price: $149.00 Site License: $249.00*

Millon Behavioral Health Inventory (MBHI)
Theodore Millon
Catherine J. Green
Robert B. Meagher

National Computer Systems, Inc.
P.O. Box 1416
Minneapolis, MN 55440
(800) 627-7271

A psychodiagnostic instrument to assess psychological factors affecting physically ill and behavioral health patients. Requires Microtest Assessment System. Detailed manual included.

Classification: Diagnostic Aid

Hardware Requirements and Price
IBM PC, XT, AT, PS/2, & compatibles; 512 K; 10 Mb hard disk optional; 1 disk drive. Monochrome, CGA, EGA, or VGA display. Modem optional. Printer required. Laser printer optional. Requires DOS 3.1. Sentry 3000 Scanner optional. *Single User Price: Depends upon the number of administrations*

Millon Clinical Multiaxial Inventory II (MCMI-II)
Theodore Millon

National Computer Systems, Inc.
P.O. Box 1416
Minneapolis, MN 55440
(800) 627-7271

A brief measure of personality disorders and clinical syndromes, designed to be compatible with the official *DSM-III-R* diagnostic system. Requires Microtest Assessment System. Detailed manual included.

Classification: Diagnostic Aid

Hardware Requirements and Price
IBM PC, XT, AT, PS/2, & compatibles; 512 K; 10 Mb hard disk required; 1 disk drive. Monochrome, CGA, EGA, or VGA display. Modem optional. Printer required. Laser printer optional. Requires DOS 3.1. Sentry 3000 Scanner optional. *Single User Price: Depends upon the number of administrations*

Millon Clinical Multiaxial Inventory-II: Narrative Report

Psychological Testing Service
213 East Sugnet
Midland, MI 48640
(517) 631-9463
Fax: (517) 631-4919

This interpretive system uses a complex set of decision rules to analyze profile patterns, various scale combinations, and individual scales. The results are presented in narrative form, with sections for clinical syndromes (Axis I disorders), personality patterns (Axis II disorders), and clinical-personality interaction. The program is bundled with the MCMI Narrative Report. Requires entry of final base rate scores. Instruction booklet included. Latest release June, 1991.

Classification: Millon (Interpretive report)

Hardware Requirements and Price
IBM PC, XT, AT, PS/2, & compatibles; 256 K; hard disk optional; 1 disk drive. Printer required. Laser printer optional. *Single User Price: $395.00*

Mini-SCID
Michael First
Miriam Gibbon
Janet Williams
Robert Spitzer

Multi-Health Systems, Inc.
908 Niagara Falls Blvd.
North Tonawanda, NY 14120-2060
(416) 424-1700
(800) 456-3003

Abbreviated computerized version of the Structured Clinical Interview for *DSM-III-R* (SCID). Software administers interview directly to the patient. No limit on number of patients. Co-published with the American Psychiatric Association. Detailed manual included. Latest release 1990.

Classification: Diagnostic Aid, DSM (Administration and Interpretive report)

Hardware Requirements and Price
IBM PC, XT, AT, PS/2, & compatibles; hard disk optional; 1 disk drive. Printer required. Laser printer optional. *Single User Price: $295.00*

Reviews
Bennett, B. (1990). Innovative software program assists diagnostic process. *Illinois Psychologist, 29*(3), 26-34.

The Minnesota Report: Adult Clinical System Interpretive Report (MMPI-2)
Starke R. Hathaway
J. Charnley McKinley

National Computer Systems, Inc.
P.O. Box 1416
Minneapolis, MN 55440
(800) 627-7271

Provides pertinent clinical information based on research with the original MMPI Clinical and Validity Scales as well as on special scales and indices developed for the MMPI-2. Specially tailored reports are available for six different settings. Requires Microtest Assessment System or Arion II Teleprocessing service. Detailed manual included.

Classification: MMPI

Hardware Requirements and Price
IBM PC, XT, AT, PS/2, & compatibles; 512 K; 10 Mb hard disk required; 1 disk drive. 300-2400 baud modem optional. Printer required. Laser printer optional. Requires DOS 3.1. *Single User Price: Contact publisher*

The Minnesota Report: Personnel Selection System Interpretive Report (MMPI-2)
James N. Butcher

National Computer Systems, Inc.
P.O. Box 1416

Minneapolis, MN 55440
(800) 627-7271

Designed to identify individuals emotionally unsuitable for high-risk, high-stress positions. Specialized reports are available for the following occupations: law enforcement, firefighter, airline or military flight crew member, air traffic controller, nuclear power plant operator, medical school and graduate mental health program applicant, and seminarian. Requires Microtest Assessment Software or Arion II Teleprocessing service. Detailed manual included. Latest release July, 1991.

Classification: MMPI (Interpretive report)

Hardware Requirements and Price
IBM PC, XT, AT, PS/2, & compatibles; 512 K; 10 Mb hard disk required; 1 disk drive. 300-2400 baud modem optional. Printer required. Laser printer optional. Requires DOS 3.1. *Single User Price: Contact publisher.*

MMPI Adolescent Interpretive System, Version 3
Robert P. Archer

Psychological Assessment Resources, Inc.
P.O. Box 998
Odessa, FL 33556
(800) 331-TEST

Program operates from T-score input and provides a profile and interpretive report based on the clinical scales and several frequently scored research scales. Interpretive information is based on research with adolescents. Detailed manual included. Latest release August 2, 1988.

Classification: MMPI (Interpretive report)

Hardware Requirements and Price
Apple II+, IIe; 64 K; 2 disk drives (5-1/4). *Single User Price: $325.00*

IBM PC, XT, AT, PS/2, & compatibles; 256 K; hard disk optional; 2 disk drives or 1 disk drive and hard disk. Laser printer optional. *Single User Price: $325.00*

The MMPI Adult Interpretive System, Version 4
Robert C. Brown
Roger Greene

Psychological Assessment Resources, Inc.
P.O. Box 998
Odessa, FL 33556
(800) 331-TEST

Provides a single scale and configural interpretation of over 90 MMPI scales including the validity and clinical scales, frequently scored research scales, Harris and Lingoes subscales, Serkownek subscales, Wiggins Content Scales, the Tryon, Stein, and Chu Cluster scales, and the Test-Taking Scales. User inputs T-scores and the program (containing data for over 100 code types) produces interpretive statements based on *DSM-III-R* categories. Detailed manual included. Latest release January 2, 1990.

Classification: MMPI (Interpretive report)

Hardware Requirements and Price
Apple II+, IIe; 128 K; 2 disk drives (5-1/4). Not compatible with laser printer. *Single User Price: $425.00*

IBM PC, XT, AT, PS/2, & compatibles; 256 K; hard disk optional; 2 disk drives or 1 disk drive and hard disk. Laser printer optional. *Single User Price: $425.00*

Caldwell Report for the MMPI

Caldwell Report
1545 Sawtelle Boulevard, Suite 14
Los Angeles, CA 90025
(213) 478-3133

MMPI interpretation program includes a library of over 25,000 statements and produces a narrative report that incorporates sections dealing with test-taking attitude, symptoms, personality characteristics, diagnostic impression, and treatment considerations. Specific treatment considerations evaluated include suicide risk, which medication (if any) to use, transference problems, and points for interview focus. Teleprocessing service.

Classification: MMPI (Interpretive report)

Hardware Requirements and Price
Contact publisher for equipment options. Modem required. *Single User Price: Contact publisher*

MMPI Mini Mult
Carlos Pal Hegedus

Psico-Iuris, S.A.
P.O. Box 1039 - Centro Colon
San Jose, 1007 Costa Rica
(506) 24-4416

Scores, plots a graphic profile, and calculates raw and T-scores from the short form of the MMPI called the Mini Mult. Unlimited use version. Detailed manual in Spanish. Detailed manual included. Latest release November, 1991.

Classification: MMPI (Interpretive report)

Hardware Requirements and Price
IBM PC, XT, AT, PS/2, & compatibles; 128 K; hard disk optional; 1 disk drive.   Hercules graphics required.   Laser printer optional. Requires DOS 3.1. *Single User Price: $250.00 Network Price: $800.00*

The Minnesota Report: Adult Clinical System (MMPI)
James N. Butcher

National Computer Systems, Inc.
P.O. Box 1416
Minneapolis, MN 55440
(800) 627-7271

This program generates a MMPI report with tailored interpretations based on a wide range of individual demographics and institutional settings. Requires Arion II Teleprocessing or Microtest Assessment Software.   Detailed manual included.

Classification: MMPI (Interpretive report)

Hardware Requirements and Price
IBM PC, XT, AT, PS/2, & compatibles; 512 K; hard disk optional; 1 disk drive. Modem required. Printer required. *Single User Price: Per test fee, contact publisher*

MMPI Report
Giles D. Rainwater

Psychometric Software, Inc.
P.O. Box 1677
Melbourne, FL 32902-1677
(407) 729-6390
(800) 882-9811

The MMPI Report generates an automated interpretation of the MMPI. The interpretation is based on adult research. The user can print profiles, clinical scale by scale analyses, supplemental scales, and references. Detailed manual included. Latest release 1984.

Classification: MMPI (Interpretive report)

Hardware Requirements and Price
Apple II, 64 K, 1 disk drive (5-1/4). Monochrome display. Printer required. Will not run on hard drive. *Single User Price: $149.95*

IBM PC, XT, AT, PS/2, & compatibles; 256 K; 10 Mb hard disk optional; 2 disk drives. Monochrome, CGA, EGA, or VGA display. Printer required. Laser printer optional. Can be run on Macintosh systems operating under SoftPC. *Single User Price: $395.95 Network Price: $395.95 plus $197.98 for each additional user*

MMPI-2 Adult Interpretive System Version 1
Roger L. Greene
Robert C. Brown, Jr.

Psychological Assessment Resources, Inc.
P.O. Box 998
Odessa, FL 33556
(800) 331-TEST

User enters T scores from the MMPI-2 and the program produces an interpretive report. Configural interpretations for the validity and clinical scales are taken from a database of over 100 different 1-, 2- and, 3-point MMPI-2 code types. Individual scale interpretations are printed for supplementary, content, Harris-Lingoes, and Wiener-Harmon scales. Interpretive hypotheses address presenting problems, symptoms, personality characteristics, self-concept, interpersonal relationships, prognosis, and diagnostic possibilities based on *DSM-III-R* codes. Detailed manual included. Latest release April 23, 1990.

Classification: MMPI (Interpretive report)

Hardware Requirements and Price
IBM PC, XT, AT, PS/2, & compatibles; 256 K; hard disk optional; 2 disk drives or 1 disk drive and hard disk. Laser printer optional. *Single User Price: $425.00*

Reviews
Nicholas, D. S. (1991). Software review: MMPI-2 microgenie? *Journal of Personality Assessment, 56*(3), 545-546.

MMPI-2 Extended Score Report
Starke R. Hathaway
J. Charnley McKinley

National Computer Systems, Inc.
P.O. Box 1416
Minneapolis, MN 55440
(800) 627-7271

The MMPI-2 Extended Score Report is a restandardized version of the original MMPI. Designed to assess major personality characteristics that reflect the social and personal adjustment factors that are indicative of disabling psychological abnormality. This report contains scores for more than 80 scales. Requires Microtest Assessment System or Arion II Teleprocessing service. Detailed manual included. Latest release July, 1991.

Classification: MMPI (Interpretive report)

Hardware Requirements and Price
IBM PC, XT, AT, PS/2, & compatibles; 512 K; 10 Mb hard disk required; 1 disk drive. 300-

2400 baud modem optional. Printer required. Laser printer optional. Requires DOS 3.1.

(MMPI-2) The Minnesota Report: Adult Clinical System Interpretive Report
James N. Butcher

National Computer Systems, Inc.
P.O. Box 1416
Minneapolis, MN 55440
(800) 627-7271

The MMPI-2 Adult Clinical System Interpretive Report provides pertinent clinical information based on research with the original MMPI Clinical and Validity Scales as well as special scales and indices developed for the MMPI-2. Specially tailored reports are available for six different settings. Microtest Assessment System or Arion II Teleprocessing service. Detailed manual included. Latest release July, 1991.

Classification: MMPI (Interpretive report)

Hardware Requirements and Price
IBM PC, XT, AT, PS/2, & compatibles; 512 K; 10 Mb hard disk required; 1 disk drive. 300-2400 baud modem optional. Printer required. Laser printer optional. Requires DOS 3.1. *Single User Price: Contact publisher.*

MMPI-2 Narrative Report

Psychological Testing Service
213 East Sugnet
Midland, MI 48640
(517) 631-9463
Fax: (517) 631-9419

This interpretation system applies a complex set of decision rules to analyze profile patterns, various scale combinations, and individual scales. The interpretive capability ranges from extremely pathological to modest elevations and variations. The program also features a context-sensitive interpretation of the new validity scales, clinical subscales, and additional scales, resulting in a extended report. The program requires entry of T-scores. There are flexible options to enter only the basic scales or additional groups of scales. Instruction booklet included. Latest release June, 1991.

Classification: MMPI (Interpretive report)

Hardware Requirements and Price
IBM PC, XT, AT, PS/2, & compatibles; 256 K; hard disk optional; 1 disk drive. Printer required. Laser printer optional. *Single User Price: $295.00*

MMPI-2 Report
Giles D. Rainwater

Psychometric Software, Inc.
P.O. Box 1677
Melbourne, FL 32902-1677
(407) 729-6390
(800) 882-9811

The MMPI-2 Report generates an automated interpretation of the MMPI-2. The interpretation is based on adult research. The user can print profiles, clinical scale by scale analyses, supplemental scales and references. Detailed manual included. Latest release 1991.

Classification: MMPI (Interpretive report)

Hardware Requirements and Price
IBM PC, XT, AT, PS/2, & compatibles; 256 K; 10 Mb hard disk optional; 2 disk drives.

Printer required. Can be run on Macintosh systems running under SoftPC *Single User Price: $395.95*

MMPI-83 Adolescent
Bruce Duthie
Ken Vincent

Precision People, Inc.
3452 North Ride Circle South
Jacksonville, FL 32223
(904) 262-1096
(800) 338-0710

Works with adolescent norms developed at the Mayo Clinic. The program scores the MMPI 399, Form R and the group form. Over 120 scales and indices are graphed and named using the new adolescent norms. Critical item numbers are provided. The interpretation is completely new, employing a system of cluster coding based on a group of 300 adolescent patients hospitalized from 1982-1986. Probability levels are given for interpretive statements. Instruction booklet included.

Classification: MMPI (Interpretive report)

Hardware Requirements and Price
IBM PC, XT, AT, PS/2, & compatibles; 640 K; hard disk required; 1 disk drive. Printer required. Laser printer optional. *Single User Price: $295.00*

Macintosh, 1 Mb, hard disk required, 1 disk drive (3-1/2). Printer required. Laser printer optional. *Single User Price: $395.00*

MMPI-83, Version 2.1: Behavioral Medicine Report
Bruce Duthie
Ken R. Vincent

Precision People, Inc.
3452 North Ride Circle South
Jacksonville, FL 32223
(904) 262-1096
(800) 338-0710

The Behavioral Medicine Report includes a MMPI-83 scoring system that evaluates 122 MMPI scales including frequently scored scales, Harris subscales, Serkownek subscales, Wiggins content scales, TSC cluster scales, personality disorder scales, Weiner-Harmon subtle-obvious subscales, and forensic scales. The 3 original validity and 10 clinical scales require entry of T scores. The report provides profile validity statements and *DSM-III* diagnostic hypotheses. Medical concerns, such as response to surgery, drug abuse potential, chronic pain and many others are addressed. Instruction booklet included.

Classification: MMPI (Interpretive report)

Hardware Requirements and Price
IBM PC, XT, AT, PS/2, & compatibles; 640 K; hard disk required; 1 disk drive. Printer required. Laser printer optional. *Single User Price: $195.00*

Macintosh, 1 Mb, hard disk required, 1 disk drive (3-1/2). Printer required. Laser printer optional. *Single User Price: $295.00*

MMPI-83, Version 2.1: Forensic Report
Bruce Duthie
Ken R. Vincent

Precision People, Inc.
3452 North Ride Circle South
Jacksonville, FL 32223
(904) 262-1096
(800) 338-0710

The Forensic Report is paired with the new MMPI-83, Version 2.1: Scoring Report to produce the MMPI-83 Forensic Report. The report has six sections: profile validity, general forensic profile, prisoner profile, child molester profile, homicide profile, and psychiatric diagnostic hypotheses. Instruction booklet included.

Classification: MMPI (Interpretive report)

Hardware Requirements and Price
IBM PC, XT, AT, PS/2, & compatibles; 640 K; hard disk required; 1 disk drive. Printer required. Laser printer optional. *Single User Price: $195.00*

Macintosh, 1 Mb, hard disk required, 1 disk drive (3-1/2). Printer required. Laser printer optional. *Single User Price: $295.00*

MMPI-83, Version 2.1: Scoring and Interpretation System
Bruce Duthie
Ken Vincent

Precision People, Inc.
3452 North Ride Circle South
Jacksonville, FL 32223
(904) 262-1096
(800) 338-0710

This system provides both scoring and interpretation for the MMPI given to adolescent and adult clients. Scores the MMPI 399, Form R, and the Group Form. Over 120 scales and indices are reported including the dissimulation index, Goldberg index, post-traumatic stress disorder scale, Grayson critical items, Lachar and Wrobel critical items, Koss and Butcher critical items, Caldwell critical items, CNS critical items, frequently scored scales,

Harris subscales, Serkownek subscales, Wiggins content scales, TSC cluster scales, personality disorder scales, Weiner-Harmon subtle-obvious subscales, and forensic scales. T-scores must be entered for the original 3 validity and 10 clinical scales. The software has unlimited use, and many different report options that can be stored for word processing. Instruction booklet included.

Classification: MMPI (Interpretive report)

Hardware Requirements and Price
IBM PC, XT, AT, PS/2, & compatibles; 640 K; hard disk required; 1 disk drive. Printer required. Laser printer optional. *Single User Price: $195.00*

Macintosh, 1 Mb, hard disk required, 1 disk drive (3-1/2). Printer required. Laser printer optional. *Single User Price: $295.00*

MOS Short-Form Health Survey
Ron D. Hays

Hays Consultants
19524 Normandale
Cerritos, CA 90701
(213) 860-0868

Administers and scores the 20-item MOS Short-Form Health Survey. The program is available from the author. Instruction booklet included.

Classification: Diagnostic Aid, Health (Administration and Interpretive report)

Hardware Requirements and Price
IBM PC, XT, AT, PS/2, & compatibles; 256 K; hard disk optional; 1 disk drive (5-1/4). *Single User Price: Free, send diskette*

Motivation Analysis Test

Institute for Personality & Ability Testing
P.O. Box 188
Champaign, IL 61824-1188
(217) 352-4739
(800) 225-4728

Scoring and interpretive program plots scores on five basic drives (caution, set, self-assertion, aggressiveness and self-indulgence) and on five areas of interest that mature and develop through learning (career, affection, dependency, responsibility, and self-fulfillment). Overall drive level, satisfaction level, degree of conflict, and total motivational strength are also reported. Teleprocessing service. Requires Telxpress service option. Instruction booklet included.

Classification: Personality Testing (Interpretive report)

Hardware Requirements and Price
IBM PC, XT, AT, PS/2, & compatibles. 1200 baud modem required. Printer required. Laser printer optional. *Single User Price: Depends upon the number of administrations*

Multidimensional Aptitude Battery (MAB)
Douglas N. Jackson

Sigma Assessment Systems, Inc.
P.O. Box 610984
Port Huron, MI 48061-0984
(800) 265-1285

On-site software administers any combination of five verbal aptitude and five performance aptitude subtests. Program scores results and reports both IQ and percentile figures. The basic report consists of a verbal profile, performance subtest, and full scale scores. The extended report adds detailed subtest descriptions to these profiles, while the clinical report contains an interpretation of the IQ results. Detailed manual included. On-line help available.

Classification: Intelligence Testing (Administration and Interpretive report)

Hardware Requirements and Price
IBM PC, XT, AT, PS/2, & compatibles; 256 K; 1 Mb hard disk optional; 1 disk drive. Laser printer optional. *Single User Price: $150.00 (first 25 scorings) or $75.00 (first 10 scorings) plus $112.50 (25 additional scorings)*

Multiscore Depression Inventory (MDI)
David J. Berndt
George J. Huba

Western Psychological Services
12031 Wilshire Blvd.
Los Angeles, CA 90025
(213) 478-2061
(800) 648-8857

The MDI is a 118-item, self-report questionnaire designed to measure the severity of depression and depressive features in adolescents and adults. An overall assessment of severity of depression is reflected in a total score, as well as 10 relevant subscores. Teleprocessing service and mail-in computer scoring is also available (1 day turnaround). Teleprocessing service. Instruction booklet included.

Classification: Personality Testing (Interpretive report)

Hardware Requirements and Price
IBM PC, XT, AT, PS/2, & compatibles; 512 K; 1 Mb hard disk required; 1 disk drive. Printer required. Laser printer optional. Requires DOS 3.0. *Single User Price: $290.00 Price depends on number of administrations*

Multiscore Depression Inventory: WPS Test Report
David J. Berndt

Western Psychological Services
12031 Wilshire Blvd.
Los Angeles, CA 90025
(213) 478-2061
(800) 648-8857

Administers, scores, and interprets the Multiscore Depression Inventory. Instruction booklet included.

Classification: Personality Testing (Administration and Interpretive report)

Hardware Requirements and Price
IBM PC, XT, AT, PS/2, & compatibles; 512 K; hard disk required; 1 disk drive. Printer required. Laser printer optional. Requires DOS 3.0. *Single User Price: $290.00 (25 administrations)*

My Real Feelings About School
Richard R. Boersma
William Fournier

Edumetrics Publishers
P.O. Box 1234
Steamboat Plaza, CO 80488
(303) 879-5663

Students (third through eight grades) evaluate their school experience along six dimensions, communicating their individual and class-wide needs to counselors, school psychologists, and school climate personnel. Manual of intervention strategies included. Detailed manual and tutorial program included. Latest release January, 1992.

Classification: Vocational Testing (Administration)

Hardware Requirements and Price
Apple II, 64 K, hard disk optional, 1 disk drive (5-1/4). Monochrome display. Printer required. Laser printer optional. Requires Apple II. *Single User Price: $140.00*

IBM PC, XT, AT, PS/2, & compatibles; 640 K; hard disk optional. Monochrome or CGA display. Mouse optional. Printer required. Laser printer optional. Requires DOS 3.3. *Single User Price: $185.00*

User Site References
Paul Grull, Pfeiffer Elementary School, Jefferson County Public Schools, Denver West Office Park, Golden, CO, 80312

Myers-Briggs Type Indicator Interpretive Report
Michael E. Mills

Psytek Services
6401 West 81st Street
Los Angeles, CA 90045
(213) 670-4655
(800) 392-5454

Fully automated interpretive report generator. Includes separate sections for single scale interpretations, profile interpretations, and personality typology. Interpretive statements describe leadership, interpersonal style, creativity, and social orientation. Reports may be exported to word processing software for further editing. No per use fee. Sample report available on request. 30-day money back guarantee. Detailed manual included. Latest release June 1, 1991.

Classification: Myers-Briggs (Interpretive report)

Hardware Requirements and Price
IBM PC, XT, AT, PS/2, & compatibles; 512 K; hard disk optional. Monochrome, CGA, EGA, or VGA display. Laser printer optional. *Single User Price: $145.00 Site License: $245.00*

Myers-Briggs Type Indicator Narrative Report for Organizations

Consulting Psychologists Press
3803 East Bayshore Road
Palo Alto, CA 94303
(415) 969-8901
(800) 624-1765

Describes how a client's personality type fits into an organization. Used primarily for team building, career and management development, organizational development, and placement. The Narrative Report for Organizations (NRO) identifies the client's strengths, clarifies his or her management style, and highlights areas for development. On-line help available. Tutorial program included.

Classification: Myers-Briggs (Interpretive report)

Hardware Requirements and Price
IBM PC, XT, AT, PS/2, & compatibles; 640 K; hard disk required. Price includes MBTI board kit and a 1 year lease. *Single User Price: $400.00*

Myers-Briggs Type Indicator

Isabel Briggs Myers
Katharine C. Briggs

Consulting Psychologists Press
3803 East Bayshore Road
Palo Alto, CA 94303
(415) 969-8901
(800) 624-1765

On-line administration and scoring software for the Myers-Briggs. The user may select which form of the test will be administered. A brief beginning tutorial familiarizes the user with the keyboard and format.On-line help available. Tutorial program included.

Classification: Myers-Briggs (Administration and Interpretive report)

Hardware Requirements and Price
IBM PC, XT, AT, PS/2, & compatibles; 640 K; hard disk required. *Single User Price: The initial system with a 5 year lease is $800.00. The initial system with a 10 year lease is $1000.00. Each additional software set is $50.00 and the annual lease fee is $125.00*

Narrative Score Report

Institute for Personality & Ability Testing
P.O. Box 188
Champaign, IL 61824-1188
(217) 352-4739
(800) 225-4728

Computer interpretation of the 16PF for counseling and guidance settings. Teleprocessing service. Instruction booklet included.

Classification: 16PF (Interpretive report)

Hardware Requirements and Price
IBM PC, XT, AT, PS/2, & compatibles. 1200 baud modem required. Printer required. Laser printer optional. *Single User Price: Depends upon on the number of administrations*

NEO Personality Inventory: Computer, Version 4
Paul T. Costa
Robert R. McCrae

Psychological Assessment Resources, Inc.
P.O. Box 998
Odessa, FL 33556
(800) 331-TEST

Administration, scoring, and interpretive program for the NEO Personality Inventory. Narrative report is generated which addresses stability of personality configuration, response to stress, somatization, vocational interests, and personality traits. Detailed manual included. Latest release January 27, 1989.

Classification: Personality Testing (Administration and Interpretive Report)

Hardware Requirements and Price
Apple II+, IIe; 64 K; 2 disk drives (5-1/4). *Single User Price: $250.00 (50 administrations)*

IBM PC, XT, AT, PS/2, & compatibles; 256 K; hard disk optional; 2 disk drives or 1 disk drive and hard disk. Laser printer optional. *Single User Price: $250.00 (50 administrations)*

Occupational Report
Brian Bolton

Arkansas Research & Training Center
P.O. Box 1358
Hot Springs, AR 71902-1779
(501) 624-4411

Menu-driven program designed for use by rehabilitation professionals in field and facility settings. Uses raw scores from USES Interest Inventory and either the General Aptitude Test Battery (GATB) or Nonreader Aptitude Test Battery (NATB). The report includes a list of suitable occupational areas, graphic profiles of interest areas, aptitude scales ranked in standard score order, and a comparison of the examinee's aptitude profile with requirements for 66 groups of occupations. This program is only sold to recognized vocational rehabilitation agencies and facilities. Detailed manual included.

Classification: Vocational Testing (Interpretive report)

Hardware Requirements and Price
IBM PC, XT, AT, PS/2, & compatibles; 640 K; hard disk optional; 1 disk drive (5-1/4). Printer required. Laser printer optional. *Single User Price: $12.50*

Occupational Stress Inventory (OSI): Computer Version, Version 1
Samuel H. Osipow
Arnold Spokane

Psychological Assessment Resources, Inc.
P.O. Box 998
Odessa, FL 33556
(800) 331-TEST

On-line administration, scoring, and interpretation of the 140-item OSI. User may choose to enter responses or raw scale scores from a completed OSI rating sheet. The program calculates percentile and T scores for the 14 OSI scales and produces professional and client reports. The professional report contains an interpretive summary and detailed analysis of the OSI scales. The 8-12 page client report reviews the OSI scales and provides feedback on scores with suggestions for reducing stress, relieving strain, and increasing coping skills. Detailed manual included. Latest release December 15, 1989.

Classification: Diagnostic Aid, Stress (Administration and Interpretive reports)

Hardware Requirements and Price
IBM PC, XT, AT, PS/2, & compatibles; 256 K; hard disk optional; 2 disk drives or 1 disk drive and hard disk. Laser printer optional. *Single User Price: $275.00 (25 administrations)*

Ohio Vocational Interest Survey: Second Edition (OVIS II)

The Psychological Corporation
555 Academic Court
San Antonio, TX 78204-0952
(512) 299-1061
(800) 228-0752

Program is designed to help students from grade 7 through college and adults with educational and vocational plans. OVIS II combines an interest inventory with the occupational Career Planning Questionnaire and Local Survey. Two full-color sound filmstrips assist in administering and interpreting the test. Detailed manual included.

Classification: Vocational Testing (Interpretive report)

Hardware Requirements and Price
Apple II+, IIe, IIc, IIgs. Printer required. *Single User Price: $220.00 Per test fee*

OPQ Expert System

Saville & Holdsworth, Ltd.
575 Boylston Street
Boston, MA 02116
(617) 236-1550
(800) 899-7451

The Occupational Personnel Questionnaire (OPQ) is a computer or paper and pencil administered personality questionnaire, developed and normed for use with managers and professionals in business. The OPQ Expert System takes raw scores from an OPQ administration and produces a detailed narrative report that interprets the 30 work relevant scales of the OPQ. The program also produces 60 supplemental scales that cover team type, leadership/subordinate style, selling/ influencing style, as well as management interests in terms of skills and functional areas. It can also integrate scores from Saville and Holdsworth's verbal and numerical critical reasoning tests. Detailed manual included. Latest release November 1, 1991.

Classification: Industrial Consulting (Administration and Interpretive report)

Hardware Requirements and Price
IBM PC, XT, AT, PS/2, & compatibles; 640 K; 2 Mb hard disk required; 1 disk drive. Mouse optional. Modem optional. Laser printer optional. *Single User Price: $295.00 Per report charge depends upon number of administrations*

Organization Survey

London House/SRA
9701 W. Higgins Road
Rosemont, IL 60018
(708) 292-1900
(800) 221-8378

Paper-and-pencil survey provides employers with feedback about how employees feel about company operations, supervisory effectiveness, quality and amount of communication, job satisfaction, and compensation. A customized survey can be developed for special applications. Computer scoring produces three types of reports: company comparison to national norms, group comparison, and a summary report. Teleprocessing service.

Classification: Industrial Consulting (Interpretive report)

Hardware Requirements and Price
Contact publisher for equipment options. Modem required. *Single User Price: Contact publisher*

PACE
Lisa K. Barclay
James R. Barclay

MetriTech
111 North Market Street
Champaign, IL 61820
(217) 398-4868
(800) 747-4868

PACE is a behavioral rating instrument for identifying learning skills deficits in preschool children. Can be used for screening, evaluation, and program planning. Detailed manual included. Latest release 1988.

Classification: Academic (Administration)

Hardware Requirements and Price
Apple II, 64 K, hard disk optional, 2 disk drives. Laser printer optional. *Single User Price: $180.00*

IBM PC, XT, AT, PS/2, & compatibles; 256 K; hard disk optional; 1 disk drive. Laser printer optional. *Single User Price: $180.00*

Peabody Individual Achievement Test-Revised ASSIST
Frederick C. Morkwardt, Jr.

American Guidance Service
4201 Woodland Road
Circle Pines, MN 55014-1796
(612) 786-4343
(800) 328-2560

Converts raw scores into derived scores, summarizes student performance, and offers subtest comparisons. Provides diagnostic information for total reading, subtests, and total test. The ASSIST reports standard scores, age or grade equivalents, and percentile ranks in a narrative or chart format. Detailed manual included. On-line help available.

Classification: Academic (Interpretive report)

Hardware Requirements and Price
Apple II, 128 K, 2 disk drives. *Single User Price: $115.00*

IBM PC, XT, AT, PS/2, & compatibles; 256 K; hard disk optional; 2 disk drives. *Single User Price: $115.00*

Peer Interaction Profile (PIP)

Richard R. Boersma
William Fournier

Edumetrics Publishers
P.O. Box 1234
Steamboat Plaza, CO 80488
(303) 879-5663

A departure from standard sociometric methods, the PIP uses photocopied pictures and colorful sort boxes to yield complete peer data on all children within a classroom, plus graphs and text describing social dynamics. First through eighth grades. Detailed manual included. Latest release November, 1989.

Classification: Diagnostic Aid, Children and Adolescents

Hardware Requirements and Price
Apple II, 64 K, hard disk optional, 2 disk drives (5-1/4). Monochrome display. Printer required. Laser printer optional. *Single User Price: $185.00*

Reviews
Boersma, R. R. (1990). Bottom of the pecking order. *The Peer Facilitator Quarterly*, 6(4), 8-9.

User Site References
Stuart Horsfall, Sopris West Research, Northern Colorado B.O.C.E.S., Longmont, CO, 80501
Ann D. Wright, SoRoCo School District, P.O. Box 97, Yampa, CO, 80467, (303) 638-4558

Personal Career Development Profile

Institute for Personality & Ability Testing
P.O. Box 188
Champaign, IL 61824-1188

(217) 352-4739
(800) 225-4728

System offers a professionally developed computer interpretation of the 16PF for career exploration and personal development. The report organizes relevant information about individual strengths, behavioral attributes, and gratifications useful for developing personal career objectives. Teleprocessing service.

Classification: 16PF (Interpretive report)

Hardware Requirements and Price
IBM PC, XT, AT, PS/2, & compatibles. 1200 baud modem required. Printer required. Laser printer optional. *Single User Price: $150.00 Price depends upon the number of administrations*

Personal Experience Inventory (PEI)

Ken Winters
George Henly
Western Psychological Services
12031 Wilshire Blvd.
Los Angeles, CA 90025
(213) 478-2061
(800) 648-8857

Designed to help clinicians in the identification, referral, and treatment of problems associated with teenage drug and alcohol abuse. Self-report inventory is divided into problem severity scales and psychosocial scales. Teleprocessing service. Detailed manual included.

Classification: Diagnostic Aid, Substance Abuse

Hardware Requirements and Price
IBM PC, XT, AT, PS/2, & compatibles; 512 K; 1 Mb hard disk required; 1 disk drive. Modem

and printer required. Laser printer optional. Requires DOS 3.0. *Single User Price: $270.00 Price depends upon number of administrations*

Personal History Checklist-Adolescent, Version 3
Edward H. Dougherty
John A. Schinka

Psychological Assessment Resources, Inc.
P.O. Box 998
Odessa, FL 33556
(800) 331-TEST

User inputs responses to 120 items of the Personal History Checklist for Adolescents booklet, which was designed to be completed by the adolescent (aged 13-17; seventh-grade reading level) or by the clinician. The 2-4 page report covers presenting problems, personal information/family background, developmental history, educational history, occupational history, health and habits, family history, and current situation. Output may be created as a text file for word processor editing. Detailed manual included. Latest release August 1, 1989.

Classification: Diagnostic Aid, Children and Adolescents (Interpretive report)

Hardware Requirements and Price
IBM PC, XT, AT, PS/2, & compatibles; 256 K; hard disk optional; 2 disk drives or 1 disk drive and hard disk. Laser printer optional. *Single User Price: $295.00 (includes 25 PHC-Adolescent booklets)*

Personal History Checklist-Adult, Version 3
John A. Schinka

Psychological Assessment Resources, Inc.
P.O. Box 998
Odessa, FL 33556
(800) 331-TEST

Responses to items in the Personal History Checklist for Adults (a booklet designed to be completed by the client or by the clinician during routine intake procedures) are inputted by the user. The 2-4 page narrative covers presenting problems, family background, childhood and adolescence, educational/occupational history, medical history/status, family history, and current situation. Output may be created as a text file for word processor editing. Detailed manual included. Latest release January 9, 1990.

Classification: Diagnostic Aid, History (Interpretive report)

Hardware Requirements and Price
IBM PC, XT, AT, PS/2, & compatibles; 256 K; hard disk optional; 2 disk drives or 1 disk drive and hard disk. Laser printer optional. *Single User Price: $295.00 (includes 25 PHC-Adult booklets)*

Personality Assessment Inventory (PAI): Computer Version, Version 1
Leslie C. Morey

Psychological Assessment Resources, Inc.
P.O. Box 998
Odessa, FL 33556
(800) 331-TEST

Online administration, scoring, and interpretation of the PAI (344 items). The program calculates scores for all 22 PAI scales and subscales resulting in a 6-8 page interpretive report that contains raw scores, T scores, and profiles for all scales and subscales. The report also includes sections addressing test validity, clinical features, interpersonal behavior, treatment considerations, diagnostic possibilities, and critical items. Detailed manual included. Latest release August 15, 1991.

Classification: Personality Testing (Administration and Interpretive report)

Hardware Requirements and Price
IBM PC, XT, AT, PS/2, & compatibles; 256 K; hard disk optional; 2 disk drives or 1 disk drive and hard disk. Laser printer optional. *Single User Price: $295.00 (20 administrations) $545.00 (50 administrations)*

Personality Assessment Inventory (PAI): Interpretive Report, Version 1
Leslie C. Morey

Psychological Assessment Resources, Inc.
P.O. Box 998
Odessa, FL 33556
(800) 331-TEST

User enters raw scores from a completed PAI answer sheet (no scoring keys are required) to obtain a 6-8 page interpretive report containing T scores and profiles for all 22 PAI scales and subscales. Also included are sections on test validity, clinical features, interpersonal behavior, treatment considerations, diagnostic possibilities, and critical items. Detailed manual included. Latest release August 15, 1991.

Classification: Personality Testing (Interpretive report)

Hardware Requirements and Price
IBM PC, XT, AT, PS/2, & compatibles; 256 K; hard disk optional; 2 disk drives or 1 disk drive and hard disk. Laser printer optional. *Single User Price: $395.00 (unlimited use)*

Personality Inventory for Children-Revised Narrative Report

Psychological Testing Service
213 East Sugnet
Midland, MI 48642
(517) 631-9463
Fax: (517) 631-9419

This program analyzes single scale elevations and combinations to produce complete narrative reports. The reports are organized into sections for validity, general impressions, family environment, school achievement, interpersonal relations, behavioral and emotional problems, and somatic complaints. Requires entry of T-scores. Instruction booklet included. Latest release April, 1991.

Classification: Diagnostic Aid, Children and Adolescents (Interpretive report)

Hardware Requirements and Price
IBM PC, XT, AT, PS/2, & compatibles; 256 K; hard disk optional; 1 disk drive. Printer required. Laser printer optional. *Single User Price: $195.00*

Personality Inventory for Children (PIC)
Robert D. Wirt
David Lachar
James E. Klinedinst

Western Psychological Services
12031 Wilshire Blvd.
Los Angeles, CA 90025
(213) 478-2061
(800) 648-8857

PIC provides comprehensive and clinically relevant descriptions of child behavior, affect, cognitive status, and family characteristics in children, ages 3 through 16 years. The inventory consists of up to 600 true-false items that are answered by a parent or surrogate. Teleprocessing service also available. Instruction booklet included.

Classification: Diagnostic Aid, Children and Adolescents (Administration and Interpretive report)

Hardware Requirements and Price
Apple II+, IIe, IIc, IIgs; 48 K; 1 disk drive. Printer required. *Single User Price: $185.00 Price depends on number of administrations*

IBM PC, XT, AT, PS/2, & compatibles; 512 K; hard disk required; 1 disk drive. Printer required. Laser printer optional. Requires DOS 3.0. *Single User Price: $225.00 Price depends on number of administrations*

Personality Research Form
Douglas N. Jackson

Sigma Assessment Systems, Inc.
P.O. Box 610984
Port Huron, MI 48061-0984
(800) 265-1285

On-site administration, scoring, and reporting software designed to yield a set of scores for personality traits broadly relevant to normal functioning individuals. The basic report provides a profile of scores on all scales, while the extended report adds narrative text, scale descriptions, percentile profile with validity information, and interpretive text outlining the implications of the test scores for preferred work environments and styles of interaction. Per-test fees apply. Detailed manual included. On-line help available.

Classification: Personality Testing (Interpretive report)

Hardware Requirements and Price
IBM PC, XT, AT, PS/2, & compatibles; 256 K; 1 Mb hard disk optional; 1 disk drive. Laser printer optional. *Single User Price: $150.00 (first 25 administrations) or $75.00 (10 administrations) plus $112.50 (25 additional administrations)*

Personnel Selection Inventory

London House/SRA
9701 W. Higgins Road
Rosemont, IL 60018
(708) 292-1900
(800) 221-8378

Paper-and-pencil test written at the sixth grade reading level. Evaluates applicants' tendencies toward such traits as: honesty, nonviolence, drug abuse, emotional stability, safety consciousness, tenure, work values, supervision attitudes, customer relations, productivity, responsibility, and math/cash handling skills. Software scoring package or Teleprocessing service. Detailed manual included.

Classification: Vocational Testing (Interpretive report)

Hardware Requirements and Price
IBM PC, XT, AT, PS/2, & compatibles; 512 K; hard disk optional; 2 disk drives. *Single User Price: Contact publisher. Only sold in conjunction with test books; per test fee*

Reviews
O Bannon, R. M., Goldinger, L. A., & Appleby, G.S. (1989). *Honesty and integrity testing: A practical guide.* Applied Information Resources: Atlanta, GA.

PIAT-80 Diagnostics

John Trifiletti

Precision People, Inc.
3452 North Ride Circle South
Jacksonville, FL 32223
(904) 262-1096
(800) 338-0710

Computerized program that translates results of the Peabody into meaningful educational strategies and produces a 6-page report in less than 5 min. Program converts raw scores to grade equivalents for all subtests. By entering items missed on the math subtest, the following reports are also produced: correct and incorrect items, percent correct, an error matrix that organizes Peabody items, and behavioral objectives for incorrect items. Detailed manual included.

Classification: Diagnostic Aid (Interpretive report)

Hardware Requirements and Price
Apple II+, IIe, IIc, IIgs; 1 disk drive. *Single User Price: $149.00*

IBM PC, XT, AT, PS/2, & compatibles; 64 K; hard disk optional; 1 disk drive. *Single User Price: $149.00*

PICApad II: Computerized Report Generating Program

Richard C. Katz
Bruce E. Porch

Sunset Software
9277 E. Corrine Drive
Scottsdale, AZ 85260
(602) 451-0753

A program for entry of scores and computing of mean scores and percentiles for the Porch Index of Communicative Ability (PICA). Instruction booklet included. Latest release June 24, 1990.

Classification: Intellectual Function Test (Interpretive report)

Hardware Requirements and Price
Apple II+, IIe, IIc, IIgs; 128 K; 10 Mb hard disk optional; 1 disk drive. 80-column display required. Printer required (Imagewriter). Requires ProDOS. *Single User Price: $249.95*

Piers-Harris Children's Self Concept Scale (PHCSC)

Ellen V. Piers
Dale B. Harris
Robert Zachary

Western Psychological Services
12031 Wilshire Blvd.
Los Angeles, CA 90025
(213) 478-2061
(800) 648-8857

The PHCSC is a brief, self-report measure designed to aid in the assessment of self-concept in children and adolescents, grades 4 through 12. Consisting of 80 "yes-no" items, the Piers-Harris diskette administers, scores, and prints a narrative report on each individual tested. Teleprocessing service also available. Instruction booklet included.

Classification: Personality Testing (Administration and Interpretive report)

Hardware Requirements and Price
IBM PC, XT, AT, PS/2, & compatibles; 512 K; 1 Mb hard disk required; 1 disk drive. Printer required. Laser printer optional. Requires

DOS 3.0. *Single User Price: $250.00 Price depends on the number of administrations*

Please Understand Me

Cambridge Career Products
P.O. Box 2153
Charleston, WV 25328-2153
(304) 744-9323
(800) 468-4227

This software package helps determine psychological type, temperament type, career interest and information about the client's interpersonal, social, and domestic relationships. Detailed manual included. Latest release 1986.

Classification: Diagnostic Aid

Hardware Requirements and Price
Apple II, 64 K, 2 disk drives (5-1/4). Not compatible with laser printer. *Single User Price: $89.00*

IBM PC, XT, AT, PS/2, & compatibles; 256 K; hard disk optional; 2 disk drives. Laser printer optional. *Single User Price: $89.00*

PMS Analysis, Version 1.0
Terrance G. Lichtenwald

Happ Electronics, Inc.
3680 North Main Street
Oshkosh, WI 54901
(414) 231-5128

Menu-driven, premenstrual syndrome (PMS) analysis and self-help tool. Includes daily symptom charting, detailed symptom analysis, medical and psychological questionnaire and report, and PMS progress assessment. Per-

sonalized symptom recommendations report features suggestions for diet, exercise, and stress management. Program provides symptom charts, graphs, and statistical and pattern analysis. Includes extensive reference section and help screens. Detailed manual and tutorial program included. On-line help available.

Classification: Diagnostic Aid (Interpretive report)

Hardware Requirements and Price
Apple II, hard disk optional, 1 disk drive. *Single User Price: $69.00*

IBM PC, XT, AT, PS/2, & compatibles; hard disk optional; 1 disk drive. *Single User Price: $69.00 Professional Office Version: $250.00*

Projective Drawing Tests: Computer Analysis
Joseph M. Eisenberg
James J. Smith

Reason House
204 East Joppa Road, Suite 10
Towson, MD 21204
(301) 321-7270

Designed to facilitate scoring and analysis of the House-Tree-Person Drawing and Human Figure Drawing Tests. Program allows for clinical observations, choice of two tests, and inclusion of personalized text. Detailed manual included.

Classification: House-Tree-Person (Interpretive report)

Hardware Requirements and Price
Apple II, 64 K, hard disk optional, 2 disk drives (5-1/4). Printer required. *Single User Price: $395.00 Discount for APA Members: $195.00*

IBM PC, XT, AT, PS/2, & compatibles; 1 disk drive. Printer required. *Single User Price: $395.00 Discount for APA Members: $195.00*

Projective Drawing Tests: Computer Analysis-School Version
Joseph M. Eisenberg
James J. Smith

Reason House
204 East Joppa Road, Suite 10
Towson, MD 21204
(301) 321-7270

Designed to facilitate scoring and analysis of the House-Tree-Person Drawing and Human Figure Drawing Tests for use in school testing of students aged 2-19. Program allows for clinical observations, choice of two tests, and inclusion of personalized text. Detailed manual included.

Classification: House-Tree-Person (Interpretive report)

Hardware Requirements and Price
Apple II, 64 K, hard disk optional, 2 disk drives (5-1/4). Printer required. *Single User Price: $395.00 Discount for APA Members: $195.00*

IBM PC, XT, AT, PS/2, & compatibles; 1 disk drive. Printer required. *Single User Price: $395.00 Discount for APA Members: $195.00*

Projective Drawing Tests
Joseph M. Eisenberg
James J. Smith
Stuart C. Burman

Reason House
204 East Joppa Road, Suite 10

Towson, MD 21204
(301) 321-7270

Program assists in the scoring of the House-Tree-Person and Human Drawing Tests. Using scoring determinants provided by the system, the administrator calculates three digit codes. When entered, these codes yield hypotheses grouped into 13 categories, and prints a narrative report. Detailed manual included.

Classification: House-Tree-Person (Interpretive report)

Hardware Requirements and Price
Apple II, 256 K, hard disk optional, 2 disk drives (5-1/4). Printer required. *Single User Price: $395.00 Discount for APA Members: $195.00*

IBM PC, XT, AT, PS/2, & compatibles; hard disk optional; 2 disk drives. Printer required. *Single User Price: $395.00 Discount for APA Members: $195.00*

Projective Drawings: Computer Analysis

AI Software, Inc.
P.O. Box 724
Wakefield, RI 02879
(401) 789-8660
(800) 272-2250

Facilitates the scoring and interpretive analysis of the House-Tree-Person and Human Figure Drawing Tests. The program provides a clinical observations section that can be customized and an interpretive narrative covering 13 topics. Detailed manual included.

Classification: House-Tree-Person (Interpretive report)

Hardware Requirements and Price
IBM PC, XT, AT, PS/2, & compatibles; 1 disk drive. Printer required. *Single User Price: $395.00*

Psych Report Writer, Version 2.1
Shayen A. George
Jack T. Raver

Psych Support Systems
Marine Bank Building, Suite #308
Box 710
Sharon, PA 16146
(412) 983-1131
(800) 776-0519

Writes an integrated psychological report that can be edited with any word processing program. The following tests can be incorporated into the report: Wechsler Preschool and Primary Scale of Intelligence-Revised (WPPSI-R), WISC-R, WAIS-R, Standford-Binet Fourth Edition, any combination of Achievement Tests, Bender Visual-Motor Gestalt, Visual-Motor Integration (VMI), Visual-Motor Integration, Third Revision (VMI-3R), Goodenough-Harris, Vineland Adaptive Behavior Scales, Scales of Independent Behavior, and WISC-III (Wechsler Intelligence Scale for Children, 3rd ed.). Detailed manual included. On-line help available.

Classification: Testing Utility (Interpretive report)

Hardware Requirements and Price
Apple II, 64 K, hard disk optional, 2 disk drives. Printer required. *Single User Price: Contact publisher.*

IBM PC, XT, AT, PS/2, & compatibles; 640 K; hard disk optional; 1 disk drive. Printer required. *Single User Price: Contact publisher.*

User Site References
John Garlock, Psychologist, 18 North Wilde Yaupon, The Woodlands, TX, 77381, (713) 363-0648

Ted Walbourn, Psychologist, Fulton N.Y. City Schools, 59 Bakeman Street, Fulton, NY, 13069, (313) 593-5520

Sally Zubyk, Psychologist, Youngstown Public Schools, 20 W. Wood Street, Youngstown, OH, 44501, (216) 744-6900

Psychiatric Diagnostic Interview, Revised (PDI-R)
Ekkehard Othmer
Elizabeth C. Penick
Barbara J. Powell

Western Psychological Services
12031 Wilshire Blvd.
Los Angeles, CA 90025
(213) 478-2061
(800) 648-8857

Structured diagnostic interview based upon clinical criteria compatible with both the *DSM-III* and *DSM-III-R*. Program generally takes 15-30 min for normals and about 1 hr for those with two or more syndromes. Accurately identifies whether an individual is currently suffering, or ever has suffered from any of 17 major established psychiatric disorders, in addition to four derived syndromes. Program proceeds to appropriate questions, scores items, and prints a report. Instruction booklet included.

Classification: Diagnostic Aid, DSM (Administration and Interpretive report)

Hardware Requirements and Price
IBM PC, XT, AT, PS/2, & compatibles; 640 K, 1 Mb hard disk required; 1 disk drive. Printer required. Requires DOS 3.1. Requires

Microsoft Windows/286 v. 2.11 or above. *Single User Price: $215.00*

Psychological Resources Report

Herbert W. Eber

Psychological Resources, Inc.
74 Fourteenth Street, N.W.
Atlanta, GA 30309
(404) 892-3000
(800) 969-5777

Accepts answer sheet input by keyboard or scanner. Scores, norms, profiles, and interprets user-defined tests batteries including most Institute for Psychological and Ability Testing (IPAT) instruments, any form of the 16PF, Clinical Analysis Questionnaire, Motivation Analysis Test, Vocational Interest Measure, and other special purpose tests. Keyboard entry can include numeric data from intelligence, aptitude, and achievement tests. Data are integrated into one or more reports, each addressed to a specific issue. User selects reports from available options that include standard clinical assessment, vocational issues, public safety candidate evaluation, implications for health maintenance, pain management, control and security of inmates, offenders, and others. Detailed manual included. Latest release June, 1991.

Classification: Testing Utility (Interpretive report)

Hardware Requirements and Price
IBM PC, XT, AT, PS/2, & compatibles; 192 K; 5 Mb hard disk required; 1 disk drive. 2400 baud modem required. Printer required. Laser printer optional. Requires DOS or OS/2. Volume discounts available. *Single User Price: $35 (per administration)*

User Site References
Nichole Benton, Psychological Service & Employee Assistance, 75 Piedmont Avenue, NE, Suite 434, Atlanta, GA, 30303, (404) 658-7731

Shirley Fifer, Magnolia Psychological Group, 6887 Magnolia Avenue, Riverside, CA, 92506, (714) 787-0960

Jennifer Kelly, Southeastern Pain Institute, 340 Boulevard, NE, Suite 210, Atlanta, GA, 30312, (404) 653-4621

Psychological/Psychiatric Status Interview

Psychologistics, Inc.
P.O. Box 033896
Indialantic, FL 32903
(407) 259-7811

This program is designed for the on-line computer administration of an initial psychological/psychiatric interview. A 3-5 page report may be printed or written to a text file. The program interviews the patient with respect to presenting problems, current living situation, mental status, biological/medical status, interpersonal relations, and socialization. Software permits unlimited uses. Detailed manual included. Latest release 1988.

Classification: Diagnostic Aid (Administration and Interpretive report)

Hardware Requirements and Price
IBM PC, XT, AT, PS/2, & compatibles; 128 K; hard disk optional; 1 disk drive. Printer required. Requires DOS 2.1. *Single User Price: $250.00*

Macintosh, 512 K, hard disk optional, 1 disk drive (3-1/2). Printer required. *Single User Price: $250.00*

Psychological/Social History Report
Giles D. Rainwater
Debora Silver Coe

Psychometric Software, Inc.
P.O. Box 1677
Melbourne, FL 32902-1677
(407) 729-6390
(800) 882-9811

The Psychological/Social History Report conducts a structured psychological intake interview and prints a narrative report. It also generates an important responses section. This section allows the clinician to determine where more in depth evaluation is needed. Detailed manual included. Latest release 1984.

Classification: Diagnostic Aid, History (Administration)

Hardware Requirements and Price
Apple II+, IIe, IIc, IIgs; 64 K; hard disk optional; 1 disk drive (5-1/4). Monochrome display. Printer required. Will not run on hard disk drive. *Single User Price: $195.95*

IBM PC, XT, AT, PS/2, & compatibles; 128 K; 10 Mb hard disk optional; 1 disk drive. Monochrome, CGA, EGA, or VGA display. Printer required. Laser printer optional. Can be used on Macintosh systems operating under SoftPC. *Single User Price: $295.95 Network Price: $295.95 plus $147.98 for each additional user*

Reviews
Schlosser, B. (1990). Computer-assisted practice. *Independent Practitioner, 9*(3), 5.

Readers interested in software for neuropsychological testing should also examine the cognitive rehabilitation software described in the Clinical Software section.

Psychosocial Adjustment to Illness Scale (PAIS)
Leonard R. Derogatis
Clinical Psychometric Research, Inc.

P.O. Box 619
Riderwood, MD 21139
(301) 321-6165
(800) 245-0277

Program designed to score both the interview and self-report version of the PAIS. Seven primary domain scores and the overall adjustment to illness score are calculated and may be converted into standardized score (area T-score) formats in terms of any of the currently available norm groups: renal dialysis, cardiac bypass, lung cancer, acute burn, essential hypertension, mixed cancer, and diabetes. Detailed manual included.

Classification: Diagnostic Aid, Health (Interpretive report)

Hardware Requirements and Price
IBM PC, XT, AT, PS/2, & compatibles; 64 K; hard disk optional; 1 disk drive. Laser printer optional. *Single User Price: $160.00*

Q-Fast

StatSoft, Inc.
2325 East 13th Street
Tulsa, OK 74104
(918) 583-4149
Fax: (918) 583-4376

Q-Fast is a menu-driven survey administration system that accepts subject responses from the keyboard and checks them for formal correctness. It scores results and saves them for further analysis or prints them in a formatted report. The user may create cumulative files of raw or summary scores. Files may be accessed with other programs. Detailed manual included.

Classification: Testing Utility (Administration)

Hardware Requirements and Price
Apple II, 64 K, hard disk optional, 1 disk drive. Requires ProDOS. *Single User Price: $299.00*

IBM PC, XT, AT, PS/2, & compatibles; 256 K; hard disk optional; 1 disk drive. Laser printer optional. Requires DOS 2.1. *Single User Price: $299.00*

Macintosh, 512 K, hard disk optional, 1 disk drive (3-1/2). Requires System 5.1 or higher. *Single User Price: $299.00*

Quality of Life Computer Program
David Evans
Wendy Cope

Multi-Health Systems, Inc.
908 Niagara Falls Blvd.
North Tonawanda, NY 14120-2060
(416) 424-1700
(800) 456-3003

Measures quality of life directly from clients and scores and interprets their responses. Detailed manual included.

Classification: Diagnostic Aid (Administration and Interpretive report)

Hardware Requirements and Price
IBM PC, XT, AT, PS/2, & compatibles; 256 K; hard disk optional; 1 disk drive. Printer required. Laser printer optional. *Single User Price: $125.00*

QuestMake
Giles D. Rainwater

Psychometric Software, Inc.
P.O. Box 1677
Melbourne, FL 32902-1677
(407) 729-6390
(800) 882-9811

QuestMake allows the user to develop test administration and scoring programs. After the program is completed, responses from an answer sheet can be entered. The program calculates raw scores, corrected raw scores, and T-scores. Detailed manual included. Latest release 1984.

Classification: Testing Utility (Administration and Interpretive report)

Hardware Requirements and Price
Apple II+, IIe, IIc, IIgs; 64 K; 1 disk drive (5-1/4). Monochrome display. Printer required. Will not run on hard disk drive. *Single User Price: $149.95*

IBM PC, XT, AT, PS/2, & compatibles; 128 K; 10 Mb hard disk optional; 1 disk drive. Monochrome, CGA, EGA, or VGA display. Printer required. Laser printer optional. Can be run on Macintosh systems operating under SoftPC *Single User Price: $149.95 Network Price: $149.95 plus $74.98 for each additional user*

Quick Computerized Stress Inventory
Allan N. Press
Lynn Osterkamp

Preventive Measures, Inc.
1115 West Campus Road
Lawrence, KS 66044
(913) 842-5078

Measures a person's satisfaction and sources of stress. Assesses 11 major sources of life satisfaction and stress, along with recent shifts in overall life satisfaction and stress, and the ability to make life-style changes. The 30-item assessment generates a 2-page individualized profile plus graph, that can be the basis for discussion with a professional or can be given to the respondent without interpretation. The scales have high reliability and validity. The 5-min assessment can be computer-administered or responses from the 2-page written questionnaire can be entered by an operator in approximately 25 sec. Price includes unlimited use and permission for unlimited duplication of the Quick CSI questionnaire. Detailed manual included. Latest release January, 1991.

Classification: Diagnostic Aid, Stress (Administration and Interpretive report)

Hardware Requirements and Price
Apple II, 64 K, hard disk optional. 80 Column display required. Printer required. Laser printer optional. Some limitations compared to other computers. *Single User Price: $275.00 Trial Package: $35.00*

IBM PC, XT, AT, PS/2, & compatibles; 256 K; hard disk optional; 1 disk drive. Printer required. Laser printer optional. *Single User Price: $275.00 Trial Package: $35.00*

Macintosh, 256 K, hard disk optional, 1 disk drive (3-1/2). Printer required. Laser printer optional. *Single User Price: $275.00 Trial Package: $35.00*

User Site References
Frank Gilbert, WellPlan, Inc., 617 East Elm, Salina, KS, 67401, (913) 825-8224
Jack Hartje, Hartje Stress Clinic, 1826 University Blvd. West, Jacksonville, FL, 32217, (904) 737-5821

Marc Zimmer, Biofeedback and Psychotherapy Center, Five Sunrise Plaza, Valley Stream, NY, 11581, (516) 825-5005

Quick-Score Achievement Test (Q-SAT)
Wayne Hresko
Paul Schlieve
Pro-Ed, Inc.
8700 Shoal Creek Blvd.
Austin, TX 78758-6897
(512) 451-3246

Generates a 4-page report that contains descriptive background information; raw scores; standard scores; percentiles and descriptions of each subtest, standard score sums; percentiles and descriptions of all composites and quotients; profiles for subtests and composites; and significance tests of comparisons among all composites. Detailed manual included. Latest release 1987.

Classification: Intellectual Function Test (Interpretive report)

Hardware Requirements and Price
Apple II, 48 K, hard disk optional, 1 disk drive (5-1/4). *Single User Price: $79.00*

IBM PC, XT, AT, PS/2, & compatibles; 640 K; hard disk optional; 1 disk drive (5-1/4). *Single User Price: $79.00*

RADAR Plus

Computerized Psychological Diagnostics, Inc.
1101 Dove Street, #225
Newport Beach, CA 92660
(714) 833-7931

A mental health assessment system that includes 61 instruments from major publishers. The library includes tests, histories, checklists and documentation tools. Flexible technical capabilities allow for patient interactive testing, raw data input, high volume scanning and the networking of PCs. The test library includes: alcohol use inventory, alcohol history, Beck depression and hopelessness scale, brief computerized stress inventory, CPI, Career Assessment Inventory, chemical dependency and treatment profile, demographic information, developmental history, eating problems analysis, intake evaluation report, marriage skills analysis, mate selection checklist, marriage and relationship problems, medical history, mental status interview, Millon Adolescent Personality Inventory, Millon Behavioral Health Inventory, Millon Clinical Multiaxial Inventory-II, Minnesota Child Development Inventory, MMPI, Multidimensional Aptitude Battery, Multidimensional Pain Survey, Organic Brain Disorders Screening Inventory, Parental Stress Inventory, Personality Research Form-E, psycho-social history, self-description inventory, session summary, sexual history, state trait anxiety inventory, SCL-90-R, tension and stress questionnaire, termination/ discharge summary, treatment motivation, WAIS-R, WISC-R, and WPPSI. Detailed manual included. On-line help available. Latest release November, 1991.

Classification: Diagnostic Aid (Administration)

Hardware Requirements and Price
IBM PC, XT, AT, PS/2, & compatibles; 640 K; 6 Mb hard disk required; 1 disk drive. 2400 baud modem required. Printer required. Laser printer optional. Requires DOS 3.1. *Single User Price: $150.00 (annual license fee) Per test fee with volume discounts.*

Reviews
Schlosser, B. (1991). Computer-assisted practice change? Oh my word! *Bulletin of the Division of Independent Practitioner Division 42 of the American Psychological Association, 11*(1), 7.

Randt Memory Test
David Glosser

Life Science Associates
1 Fenimore Road
Bayport, NY 11705-2115
(516) 472-2111
Fax: (516) 472-8146

Program performs all necessary scoring for the Randt Memory Test. Menu leads the examiner through the test administration process. Detailed manual included. Latest release 1988.

Classification: Neuropsychological Testing (Interpretive report)

Hardware Requirements and Price
Apple II+, IIe; 128 K; 10 Mb hard disk optional; 1 disk drive (5-1/4). Monochrome or color display. Printer required. *Single User Price: $40.00*

Rational WISC-R Analysis
Marley Watkins
Joe Kush

Ed & Psych Associates
1702 West Camelback Road
Suite 267
Phoenix, AZ 85015
(602) 420-1747

Scoring and interpretive package computes Verbal Inetlligence Quotient (VIQ), Performance Intelligence Quotient (PIQ), and Full Scale Intelligence Quotient (FSIQ) percentiles, ranges, and confidence intervals. Significance of subtest deviations from verbal and performance means with adjustment for family-wise error rates also provided. Calculates verbal comprehension, perceptual organization, and freedom from distractibility factors. Provides subtest profile graph with narrative. Detailed manual included. Latest release 1989.

Classification: WISC (Interpretive report)

Hardware Requirements and Price
Apple II+, IIe, IIc, IIgs; 128K; 1 disk drive (5-1/4). Requires DOS 3.3. *Single User Price: $49.95*

Reviews
Bowser, P. (1988). Rational WISC-R analysis. *Bulletin of the Oregon School Psychologists Association, 11,* 19-20.
Hale, R., & Patrick N. (1989). Numerical applications. *Journal of School Psychology, 27,* 229-236.
Watkins, M., & Kush, J. (1988-1989). Rational WISC-R analysis. *NASP Computer and Technological Applications in School Psychology, 7,* 4-6.

Report Writer: Adult's Intellectual, Achievement, Neuropsychological Screening Tests, Version 3
Edward H. Dougherty
David M. Bortnick

Psychological Assessment Resources, Inc.
P.O. Box 998
Odessa, FL 33556
(800) 331-TEST

Program provides an interpretive report for the following tests: WAIS-R, Stanford-Binet Intelligence Scale, Wide Range Achievement Test (WRAT), Wide Range Achievement Test-Revised (WRAT-R), Stroop Color and Word Test, Trail Making Test, Benton Visual Retention Test, Purdue Pegboard Test, Aphasia Screening Signs, and the Symbol Digit Modalities Test. The Woodcock-Johnson and KTEA are also available in the IBM version. User inputs scores from the test(s), and the resulting report may be stored as a text file for use with a word processing program. Detailed manual inluded. Latest release January 15, 1989.

Classification: Neuropsychological Testing (Interpretive report)

Hardware Requirements and Price
Apple II+, IIe, IIc; 128 K; 2 disk drives. Not compatible with laser printer. *Single User Price: $495.00*

IBM PC, XT, AT, PS/2, & compatibles; 256 K; hard disk optional; 2 disk drives or 1 disk drive and hard disk. Laser printer optional. *Single User Price: $495.00*

Report Writer: Children's Intellectual and Achievement Tests, Version 4
Edward H. Dougherty

Psychological Assessment Resources, Inc.
P.O. Box 998
Odessa, FL 33556
(800) 331-TEST

Report Writer generates the largest part of the report for the practitioner, compiling facts, making general statements and statistical comparisons, and suggesting possible hypotheses and explanations for patterns of test scores. Interpretations are provided for WISC-R, Kaufman Assessment Battery for Children (K-ABC), WRAT-R, WPPSI, and Stanford Binet (4th edition). IBM version also includes WPPSI-R, Woodcock-Johnson, and Kaufman Test for Educational Achievement (K-TEA). Word processing software that reads ASCII text files is recommended. Detailed manual included. Latest release January 15, 1989.

Classification: Intelligence Testing (Interpretive report)

Hardware Requirements and Price
Apple II+, IIe, IIc; 128 K; 2 disk drives. Not compatible with laser printer. *Single User Price: $495.00*

IBM PC, XT, AT, PS/2, & compatibles; 256 K; hard disk required; 1 disk drive. Laser printer optional. Must be run from hard disk drive. *Single User Price: $495.00*

Report Writer: WAIS-R, Version 3
Edward H. Dougherty

Psychological Assessment Resources, Inc.
P.O. Box 998
Odessa, FL 33556
(800) 331-TEST

This version of Report Writer incorporates all of the technical features of Report Writer: Adult's Intellectual, Achievement, and Neuro-psychological Screening Tests, but provides a 4-5 page interpretive report solely for the WAIS-R. Detailed manual included. Latest release January 15, 1989.

Classification: WAIS (Interpretive report)

Hardware Requirements and Price
Apple II+, IIe, IIc; 128 K; 2 disk drives. Not compatible with laser printer. *Single User Price: $295.00*

IBM PC, XT, AT, PS/2, & compatibles; 256 K; hard disk optional; 2 disk drives or 1 disk drive and hard disk. *Single User Price: $295.00*

Report Writer: WISC-R/WPPSI-R, Version 4
Edward H. Dougherty

Psychological Assessment Resources, Inc.
P.O. Box 998
Odessa, FL 33556
(800) 331-TEST

All of the technical features of Report Writer: Children's Intellectual and Achievement Tests is incorporated in this version of Report Writer, in addition, this edition also provides an interpretive report solely for the WISC-R or the WPPSI-R. The Apple version provides a report only for the WISC-R or the WPPSI. Detailed manual included. Latest release January 15, 1989.

Classification: WISC (Interpretive report)

Hardware Requirements and Price
Apple II, 128 K, 2 disk drives. Not compatible with laser printer. *Single User Price: $325.00*

IBM PC, XT, AT, PS/2, & compatibles; 256 K; hard disk required; 2 disk drives. Laser printer optional. *Single User Price: $325.00*

Retail Management Assessment Inventory (RMAI)

London House/SRA
9701 W. Higgins Road
Rosemont, IL 60018
(708) 292-1900
(800) 221-8378

A custom-designed instrument that provides a measure of potential for success in retail management. Covers the following job-related areas: background and work experience, management and leadership interest, management responsibility, understanding management procedures and practices, customer service, managerial arithmetic, energy level, management orientation, job stability, and business ethics. Results are summarized in a Management Potential Index that reflects a candidate's overall potential for success in retail management. Detailed manual included.

Classification: Vocational Testing (Interpretive report)

Hardware Requirements and Price
IBM PC, XT, AT, PS/2, & compatibles; 512 K; hard disk optional; 2 disk drives. *Single User Price: Contact publisher*

ROR-SCAN: Rorschach Interpretive System
Philip F. Caracena

ROR-SCAN
2100 W. Oakey Blvd.
Las Vegas, NV 89102
(702) 598-1209

Completely revised and updated to include 1991 changes in Exner's Comprehensive Sys-

tem. The 6-11 page narrative discloses scores used to derive hypotheses. Hypertext help screens explain criteria for every score in the system, provides examples, and guides for inquiry and administration. Instruction booklet included. On-line help available. Latest release January, 1991.

Classification: Rorschach

Hardware Requirements and Price
IBM PC, XT, AT, PS/2, & compatibles; 480 K; 1 Mb hard disk optional; 2 disk drives. Mouse optional. Laser printer optional. Requires DOS 2.1. *Single User Price: $450.00*

Reviews
Schlosser, B. & Tower, R. B. (Spring, 1991). Computer-assisted assessment product review: Rorschach software that teaches: ROR-SCAN. *Journal of Personality Assessment.*

User Site References
Robert Moretti, Northwestern University Medical School, Division of Psychology, 303 E. Chicago Avenue, Chicago, IL, 60611, (312) 908-2579
Robert Zussman, Private Practice, 5801 McLeod NE, Suite N, Albequerque, NM, 87109, (505) 292-9045

Rorschach Interpretation Assistance Program, Version 2
John E. Exner, Jr.
Howard McGuire
Joel B. Cohen

Psychological Assessment Resources, Inc.
P.O. Box 998
Odessa, FL 33556
(800) 331-TEST

Program calculates the structural summary based on the sequence of scores entered by the user. Error checking for over 70 common mistakes made in scoring occurs automatically. Software follows interpretive strategies in which the statements are arranged into major clusters such as processing, affect, ideation, and self perception. Scores from the WAIS-R or WISC-R and the MMPI or MMPI-2 may be highlighted along with the Rorschach data. Detailed manual included. Latest release March 15, 1990.

Classification: Rorschach (Interpretive report)

Hardware Requirements and Price
IBM PC, XT, AT, PS/2, & compatibles; 256 K; hard disk optional; 2 disk drives or 1 disk drive and hard disk. Laser printer optional. *Single User Price: $485.00*

Rorschach Interpretation Assistance Program (RIAP)
John E. Exner, Jr.

The Psychological Corporation
555 Academic Court
San Antonio, TX 78204-0952
(512) 299-1061
(800) 228-0752

An unlimited-use microcomputer program designed to translate a Rorschach client's coded responses into interpretable data for the clinician. RIAP produces a three-section report of approximately 5 pages. The first section, sequence of scores, is a record of the examiner's coding of the client's responses. The second, the structural summary, records the coding yield, based on RIAP's search through 31 clusters of variables. The third

section, interpretative statements, lists a number of statements about the case based on the structural summary. RIAP provides accurately calculated, empirically based hypotheses that an interpreter can collate with other factors relevant to a client's evaluation. Detailed manual included.

Classification: Rorschach (Interpretive report)

Hardware Requirements and Price
IBM PC, XT, AT, PS/2, & compatibles; 256 K; hard disk optional; 2 disk drives (5-1/4). Laser printer optional. *Single User Price: $495.00*

Rorschach Report Scoring and Interpretation Program

Psychologistics, Inc.
P.O. Box 033896
Indialantic, FL 32903
(407) 259-7811

Program based on Exner's (1974, 1976, 1982) comprehensive system for scoring and interpretating the Rorschach inkblot test. Program accepts user-entered summary values and prints a data summary incorporating the information typically found in a structural summary and a narrative report. Software permits unlimited uses. Detailed manual included. Latest release 1986.

Classification: Rorschach (Interpretive report)

Hardware Requirements and Price
IBM PC, XT, AT, PS/2, & compatibles; 128 K; hard disk optional; 1 disk drive. Printer required. Requires DOS 2.0. *Single User Price: $295.00*

Rorschach Scoring and Interpretation
William Long

Reason House
204 East Joppa Road, Suite 10
Towson, MD 21204
(301) 321-7270

Based on the Exner Scoring System, this menu-driven program calculates a summary table based on individual response scores, and generates a 2-7 page interpretive report that outputs to disk file, printer, or screen. Detailed manual included.

Classification: Rorschach (Interpretive report)

Hardware Requirements and Price
IBM PC, XT, AT, PS/2, & compatibles, 128 K, hard disk optional, 1 disk drive. *Single User Price: $149.00 Discount for APA Members: $95.00*

Sales Preference Questionnaire
George W. Dudley
Shannon L. Goodson

Behavioral Sciences Research Press
2695 Villa Creek, Suite 100
Dallas, TX 75234
(214) 243-8543
(800) 323-4659

Designed to provide objective measurement of the fear of prospecting and self-promotion in sales personnel across industries. Comprised of 21 separate scales, the program measures call reluctance, generates a call reluctance profile, and an impostor profile assessing motivation and goal clarity, and detects faking. The narrative report provides a discussion of those areas in which call reluctance is significantly elevated, along with a graphic presentation and listing of critical items. Supportive books, workshops, individualized prescriptions and technical advice available. Detailed manual included. Latest release October, 1989.

Classification: Industrial Consulting

Hardware Requirements and Price
IBM PC, XT, AT, PS/2, & compatibles; 365 K; 1 Mb hard disk optional. Two disk drives required for 5-1/4" disk version and one disk drive required for 3-1/2" disk version. Hercules or CGA display. 1200 baud (100% Hayes compatible) modem optional. Printer required (Epson compatible). Laser printer optional. Requires DOS 3.0. *Single User Price: Call publisher*

Sales Professional Assessment Inventory (SPAI)

London House/SRA
9701 W. Higgins Road
Rosemont, IL 60018
(708) 292-1900
(800) 221-8378

The SPAI identifies sales candidates who have the potential to reach and exceed sales goals. It provides detailed information about an individual's sales-related skills, attitudes, and training needs. The following sales areas are assessed: sales work experience, interest, responsibility, orientation, skills, understanding, and sales arithmetic. The program also assesses: energy level, self development, customer service, business ethics, and job stability. Results of the SPAI are summarized in the Sales Potential Index, a report that reflects a candidates overall potential for success in a sales role. Detailed manual included.

Classification: Vocational Testing (Interpretive report)

Hardware Requirements and Price
IBM PC, XT, AT, PS/2, & compatibles; 512 K; hard disk optional; 2 disk drives. *Single User Price: Call publisher*

SBIS: FE Analysis Stanford-Binet 4th Edition, Version 1.2
Terrance G. Lichtenwald

Happ Electronics, Inc.
3680 North Main Street
Oshkosh, WI 54901
(414) 231-5128

Analyze any combination of Stanford-Binet subtests. Calculates Area and Composite scores and percentile ranks. Completely menu driven with help available at the touch of a key. Two types of standard errors of measurement at five confidence levels. User defined standard report. Reports may be output to screen, printer, or disk file for editing with word processor. Built in data base for saving an unlimited number of test records. Profile and Factor Analysis sections provide extensive data for identification of strengths and weaknesses. Detailed manual included. On-line help available.

Classification: Stanford-Binet

Hardware Requirements and Price
Apple II, hard disk optional, 1 disk drive. *Single User Price: $200.00*

IBM PC, XT, AT, PS/2, & compatibles; hard disk optional; 1 disk drive. *Single User Price: $200.00*

Sbordone-Hall Memory Battery
Robert J. Sbordone
Steven Hall

Robert J. Sbordone, Ph.D., Inc.
7700 Irvine Center Drive
Suite 750
Irvine, CA 92708
(714) 753-7711

Interactive program provides fully automatic serial testing of 18 discrete memory functions utilizing computer-generated stimuli. The program is intended to be used with normal, brain-injured, or cognitively impaired patients for clinical assessment, cognitive rehabilitation, or research. The battery tests 15 types of memory and the report provides a short (1-2 page) or long (12-page) quantitative and qualitative analysis of client's performance compared with normative data. Detailed manual included.

Classification: Neuropsychological Testing (Administration and Interpretive report)

Hardware Requirements and Price
Apple II, 48 K, 1 disk drive. *Single User Price: $375.00*

IBM PC, XT, AT, PS/2, & compatibles; 1 disk drive. *Single User Price: $375.00*

Scales of Independent Behavior Compuscore
Jay Hauger

DLM Teaching Resources
One DLM Park
Allen, TX 75002
(800) 527-4747

Scoring program for the Scales of Independent Behavior. This system is designed for use with children, adolescents, and adults who may have mild, moderate, or severe disabilities. It is appropriate for clients with mental retardation, emotional disturbance, behavior disorders, mental illness, visual or hearing handicaps, learning disabilities, or developmental delays. The 14 subscales are scored and organized into four clusters that form the main basis for interpretation. Detailed manual included. Latest release 1986.

Classification: Diagnostic Aid (Interpretive report)

Hardware Requirements and Price
Apple II, 64 K, 1 disk drive (5-1/4). Printer required. *Single User Price: $115.00*

IBM PC, XT, AT, PS/2, & compatibles; 256 K; hard disk optional; 1 disk drive. Printer required. Requires DOS 2.1. *Single User Price: $115.00*

SCID Score
Michael First
Mirian Gibbon
Janet Williams
Robert Spitzer

Multi-Health Systems, Inc.
908 Niagara Falls Blvd.
North Tonawanda, NY 14120-2060
(416) 424-1700
(800) 456-3003

Scoring and data handling program for the structured clinical interview for the *DSM-III-R* (SCID). Detailed manual included. Latest release 1991.

Classification: Diagnostic Aid, DSM (Interpretive report)

Hardware Requirements and Price
IBM PC, XT, AT, PS/2, & compatibles; 256 K; hard disk optional; 1 disk drive. Laser printer optional. *Single User Price: $250.00*

SCL-90-R (Admin90) 3.0
Leonard R. Derogatis

Clinical Psychometric Research, Inc.
P.O. Box 619
Riderwood, MD 21139
(301) 321-6165
(800) 245-0277

Program to administer and score the SCL-90-R self-report symptom inventory from keyboard or disk input. Report consists of the 90-item raw scores by dimension, raw and area T-scores for the nine primary symptom dimensions and three global scores. A full page graphic profile of scores in standardized format and clinical narrative report is also available. Detailed manual included.

Classification: Diagnostic Aid (Administration and Interpretive report)

Hardware Requirements and Price
IBM PC, XT, AT, PS/2, & compatibles; 64 K; hard disk optional; 1 disk drive. Laser printer optional. *Single User Price: $5.00-6.00 (per administration*

SCL-90-R (SCOR90) 3.0
Leonard R. Derogatis

Clinical Psychometric Research, Inc.
P.O. Box 619
Riderwood, MD 21139

(301) 321-6165
(800) 245-0277

Program designed to score the SCL-90 self-report symptom inventory with input from keyboard, disk, or NCS scanners. Report consists of raw and area *t*-scores for the nine primary symptom dimensions, three global distress indices, and a full-page graphic profile of the scores in standardized format. A program module that develops written clinical narratives is available separately. Scanner versions require appropriate scanners and narrative module requires a printer. Narratives include clinical interpretation, pathognomonic signs, and prominent symptoms. Detailed manual included.

Classification: Diagnostic Aid (Administration and Interpretive report)

Hardware Requirements and Price
IBM PC, XT, AT, PS/2, & compatibles; 64 K; hard disk required; 1 disk drive. Laser printer optional. *Single User Price: $3.75-$5.00 (per administration with narrative) $.75-1.75 (per administration without narrative)*

Screening Children for Related Early Educational Needs
Wayne P. Hresko
Paul L. Schlieve

Pro-Ed, Inc.
8700 Shoal Creek Blvd.
Austin, TX 78758-6897
(512) 451-3246

Test for children ages 3-7. Generates a 4-page report that contains descriptive background information, raw scores, standard scores, percentiles, and descriptions of each subtest, standard score sums, percentiles and descriptions of all composites and quotients, profiles for subtests and composites, and significance tests of comparisons among all composites. Detailed manual included. Latest release 1988.

Classification: Diagnostic Aid, Children & Adolescents (Interpretive report)

Hardware Requirements and Price
Apple II, 48 K, hard disk optional, 1 disk drive (5-1/4). *Single User Price: $79.00*

IBM PC, XT, AT, PS/2, & compatibles; 640 K; hard disk optional; 1 disk drive (5-1/4). *Single User Price: $79.00*

Screening Test of Educational Prerequisite Skills (STEPS)
Frances Smith
George J. Huba

Western Psychological Services
12031 Wilshire Blvd.
Los Angeles, CA 90025
(213) 478-2061
(800) 648-8857

STEPS is a first-grade screening tool that requires 10 to 15 min to administer. It assesses readiness, attention, and motivation in 4- through 6-year-old children and indicates how well a child has mastered specific skills needed for first-grade achievement. Reports indicating skills mastered, areas needing attention, and suggestions for further testing are generated. Instruction booklet included.

Classification: Academic

Hardware Requirements and Price
Apple II+, IIe, IIc, IIgs; 48 K; 1 disk drive.
Printer required. *Single User Price: $65.00
Price depends on number of administrations*

IBM PC, XT, AT, PS/2, & compatibles; 192 K;
1 disk drive. Printer required. *Single User
Price: $65.00 Price depends on number of
administrations*

Self-Directed Search: Computer Version, Version 3
Robert C. Reardon

Psychological Assessment Resources, Inc.
P.O. Box 998
Odessa, FL 33556
(800) 331-TEST

Administration, scoring, and interpretive
program for the Self-Directed Search (SDS).
Program includes a brief professional summary
that lists indices for differentiation, consistency, and commonness of the RIASEC
(realistic, investigative, artistic, social,
enterprising, and conventional) scores and
summary code. The program reflects the
changes made in the 1985 revision of the SDS
and works from a database of over 1300
occupational titles. Available on a per-use
basis only (50 uses per package). Detailed
manual included. Latest release May 10, 1989.

Classification: Vocational Testing (Administration and Interpretive report)

Hardware Requirements and Price
Apple II+, IIe; 64 K; 2 disk drives (5-1/4). 80-
column display required. Not compatible with
laser printer. *Single User Price: $225.00*

IBM PC, XT, AT, PS/2, & compatibles; 256 K;
hard disk optional; 2 disk drives or 1 disk drive
and hard disk. Laser printer optional. *Single
User Price: $225.00*

Reviews
McKee, L. M., & Levinson, E. M. (1990). A
review of the computerized version of the
Self-Directed Search. *The Career Development Quarterly, 38,* 325-333.

Self-Directed Search: Interpretive Report, Version 3
Robert Reardon

Psychological Assessment Resources, Inc.
P.O. Box 998
Odessa, FL 33556
(800) 331-TEST

Allows the user to input RIASEC scores from
a completed Self-Directed Search assessment
booklet. The program then computes the
Holland summary code and produces a client
report and a separate professional report. Test
data input and printing of reports is accomplished as batch procedures. Reports on the
IBM version may be edited with word processor. Detailed manual included. Latest release
May 10, 1989.

Classification: Vocational Testing (Interpretive report)

Hardware Requirements and Price
Apple II, 64 K, 2 disk drives (5-1/4). 80-column
display required. Not compatible with laser
printer. *Single User Price: $395.00*

IBM PC, XT, AT, PS/2, & compatibles; 256 K;
hard disk optional; 2 disk drives or 1 disk drive
and hard disk. Laser printer optional. *Single
User Price: $395.00*

Self-Motivated Career Planning

Institute for Personality & Ability Testing
P.O. Box 188
Champaign, IL 61824-1188
(217) 352-4739
(800) 225-4728

System incorporates a comprehensive computer interpretation of the 16PF to provide a reality test of people's perceptions of themselves, including strengths, behavioral attributes, and sources of gratifications, that permits development of personal career objectives. The last exercise is the preparation of the Personal Development Summary, that is designed to facilitate communication between the individual and a psychologist or career counselor. Teleprocessing service.

Classification: 16PF (Interpretive report)

Hardware Requirements and Price
IBM PC, XT, AT, PS/2, & compatibles. 1200 baud modem required. Printer required. Laser printer optional. *Single User Price: Price depends upon the number of administrations*

Sensory Integration and Praxis Tests (SIPT)

Western Psychological Services
12031 Wilshire Blvd.
Los Angeles, CA 90025
(213) 478-2061
(800) 648-8857

SIPT measures the sensory integration processes that underlie learning and behavior. By showing how children organize and respond to sensory input, SIPT helps pinpoint specific organic problems associated with learning disabilities, emotional disorders, and minimal brain dysfunction. SIPT measures visual, tactile, and kinesthetic perception and motor performance. Instruction booklet included.

Classification: Neuropsychological Testing

Hardware Requirements and Price
Contact publisher for equipment options and price.

Sequence Recall
Rosamond Gianutsos
Carol Klitzner

Life Science Associates
1 Fenimore Road
Bayport, NY 11705-2115
(516) 472-2111
Fax: (516) 472-8146

Designed to test frontal lobe functioning, especially planning. The program can be used with subjects unable to process verbal material. The subject must identify the order in which a series of short words or pictures were presented. The computer keeps track of correct and incorrect trials and provides a score at the end of the session. This is one module from Cogrehab (see Clinical Software section).

Classification: Neuropsychological Testing (Administration)

Hardware Requirements and Price
Apple II, 64 K, 10 Mb hard disk optional, 1 disk drive (5-1/4). Monochrome or color display. *Single User Price: $40.00*

IBM PC, XT, AT, PS/2, & compatibles; 128 K; 20 Mb hard disk optional; 1 disk drive. CGA, EGA, or VGA display. *Single User Price: $40.00*

Session Summary

Psychologistics, Inc.
P.O. Box 033896
Indialantic, FL 32903
(407) 259-7811

Program allows therapists to summarize the client's presentation and the significant events of each session. Generates a 1 page narrative session summary. The narrative report organizes the information with respect to the therapist-determined treatment goals. Software permits unlimited uses. Detailed manual included. Latest release 1985.

Classification: Diagnostic Aid (Interpretive report)

Hardware Requirements and Price
IBM PC, XT, AT, PS/2, & compatibles; 128 K; hard disk optional; 1 disk drive. Printer required. Requires DOS 2.0. *Single User Price: $150.00*

Macintosh, 512 K, hard disk optional, 1 disk drive (3-1/2). Printer required. *Single User Price: $150.00*

Shape Matching

Rosamond Gianutsos
Georgine Vroman
Pauline Matheson

Life Science Associates
1 Fenimore Road
Bayport, NY 11705-2115
(516) 472-2111
Fax: (516) 472-8146

Program designed to diagnose foveal hemi-imperception using nonverbal materials. Two shapes are presented, one above the other, and the subject must determine whether they are identical or different. Reaction time and accuracy are automatically recorded by the computer. The computer separately records those pairs of shapes that differ on the left, right, or both sides, and identical pairs.

Classification: Neuropsychological Testing (Administration)

Hardware Requirements and Price
Apple II, 64 K, 10 Mb hard disk optional, 1 disk drive (5-1/4). Monochrome or color display. *Single User Price: $40.00*

IBM PC, XT, AT, PS/2, & compatibles; 128 K; 20 Mb hard disk optional; 1 disk drive. CGA, EGA, or VGA display. *Single User Price: $40.00*

Shipley Institute of Living Scale (SILS)

Walter C. Shipley
Robert A. Zachary

Western Psychological Services
12031 Wilshire Blvd.
Los Angeles, CA 90025
(213) 478-2061
(800) 648-8857

Self-administered and brief, the Shipley assesses general intellectual functioning and cognitive impairment in people 14 years of age and older. The scale consists of a 40-item vocabulary test and a 20-item abstract thinking test, each limited to 10 min. A comprehensive report that summarizes and interprets test results is generated. Instruction booklet included.

Classification: Intellectual Function Test (Administration and Interpretive report)

Hardware Requirements and Price
IBM PC, XT, AT, PS/2, & compatibles; 512 K;
1 Mb hard disk required; 1 disk drive. Printer
required. Laser printer optional. Requires
DOS 3.0. *Single User Price: $175.00*

Single and Double Simultaneous Stimulation

Rosamond Gianutsos
Georgine Vroman
Pauline Matheson

Life Science Associates
1 Fenimore Road
Bayport, NY 11705-2115
(516) 472-2111
Fax: (516) 472-8146

Computerized version of the classic Bender
task that is designed to test for responsivity in
both visual fields by presenting stimuli singly
and simultaneously. Extinction occurs when
the subject responds to all single stimuli, but
fails to report one of the stimuli on double
simultaneous trials. The test is useful in determining whether the subject has an attention
deficit or a purely sensory one.

Classification: Neuropsychological Testing

Hardware Requirements and Price
Apple II, 64 K, 10 Mb hard disk optional, 1
disk drive (5-1/4). Monochrome or color
display. *Single User Price: $40.00*

IBM PC, XT, AT, PS/2, & compatibles; 128 K;
20 Mb hard disk optional; 1 disk drive. CGA,
EGA, or VGA display. *Single User Price:
$40.00*

Sixteen Personality Factor Questionnaire Narrative Report

Psychological Testing Service
213 East Sugnet
Midland, MI 48640
(517) 631-9463
Fax: (517) 631-9419

This interpretive system analyzes profile patterns, scale combinations, and individual factor
scales. The results are presented in narrative
form under sections for validity, interpersonal
relationships, coping with stress, independence,
determination and decisiveness, and intelligence. There is also a career profile, indicating
the Holland themes most associated with the
overall personality configuration. Requires
entry of Sten scores. Instruction booklet
included. Latest release April, 1991.

Classification: 16PF (Interpretive report)

Hardware Requirements and Price
IBM PC, XT, AT, PS/2, & compatibles; 256 K;
hard disk optional; 1 disk drive. Printer required. Laser printer optional. *Single User
Price: $195.00*

Sixteen Personality Factor Questionnaire (16PF)
Raymond B. Cattell

National Computer Systems, Inc.
P.O. Box 1416
Minneapolis, MN 55440
(800) 627-7271

The 16PF provides detailed information on 16
primary personality traits and is a flexible

predictor of normal personality. It can be used in clinical, human resources, and counseling situations. Requires Microtest Assessment System or Arion II Teleprocessing service. Detailed manual included.

Classification: 16PF

Hardware Requirements and Price
IBM PC, XT, AT, PS/2, & compatibles; 512 K; 10 Mb hard disk required; 1 disk drive. Monochrome, CGA, EGA, or VGA display. 300-2400 baud modem optional. Printer required. Laser printer optional. Requires DOS 3.1. *Single User Price: Call publisher.*

Sixteen Personality Factor Questionnaire (16PF/CL)
Bruce Duthie
Ernest G. Allen

Precision People, Inc.
3452 North Ride Circle South
Jacksonville, FL 32223
(904) 262-1096
(800) 338-0710

Program provides a narrative clinical report for the 16PF that incorporates personality descriptions, dynamics, psychological problems, and clinical prognosis along with occupational interests and possible medical problems. Detailed manual included.

Classification: 16PF (Interpretive report)

Hardware Requirements and Price
IBM PC, XT, AT, PS/2, & compatibles; hard disk optional; 1 disk drive. Printer required. *Single User Price: $375.00*

Social Skills Rating System ASSIST
Frank M. Gresham
Stephen N. Elliott

American Guidance Service
4201 Woodland Road
Circle Pines, MN 55014-1796
(612) 786-4343
(800) 328-2560

Converts raw scores into derived scores, summarizes student performance, and offers parent and teacher behavior objectives. Provides diagnostic information for social skills, problem behaviors, and academic competence. The program reports standard scores, percentile ranks, and standard score competence band in a narrative or chart format. Features include write report to disk option, intervention narrative, analysis of social behavior, and parent/teacher letters. Detailed manual included. On-line help available.

Classification: Diagnostic Aid, Children and Adolescents (Interpretive report)

Hardware Requirements and Price
Apple II, 128 K, 2 disk drives. *Single User Price: $135.00*

IBM PC, XT, AT, PS/2, & compatibles; 512 K; hard disk optional; 2 disk drives. *Single User Price: $135.00*

Stanford Diagnostic Mathematics Test: Computer Scoring

The Psychological Corporation
555 Academic Court
San Antonio, TX 78204-0952
(512) 299-1061
(800) 228-0752

Automatic scoring and reporting for the Stanford Diagnostic Mathematics Test. Item responses or scores can be entered by electronic scanner or keyboard. A variety of reports may be generated. Detailed manual included.

Classification: Academic (Interpretive report)

Hardware Requirements and Price
IBM PC, XT, AT, PS/2, & compatibles; 512 K; hard disk optional; 2 disk drives. Printer required. *Single User Price: $450.00, per test fee applies*

Stanford Diagnostic Reading Test: Computer Scoring

The Psychological Corporation
555 Academic Court
San Antonio, TX 78204-0952
(512) 299-1061
(800) 228-0752

Provides automatic scoring and reporting of the Stanford Diagnostic Reading Test. Item responses or scores may be entered by electronic scanner or keyboard. A variety or reports may be generated. Detailed manual included.

Classification: Academic (Interpretive report)

Hardware Requirements and Price
IBM PC, XT, AT, PS/2, & compatibles; 512 K; hard disk optional; 2 disk drives. *Single User Price: $450.00, per test fee applies*

Stanford-Binet Computer Report (Form L-M)

Southern Micro Systems
3545 S. Church Street
Burlington, NC 27215-2097
(919) 584-1661

System provides a computer-assisted interpretation within minutes of score entry. The report provides information regarding expected achievement, range of learning-disability achievement levels, standard score interpretation, scatter, educational interpretations, and recommendations. Program items are classified as language, memory, visual motor and manipulation, reasoning, number, and discrimination. Detailed manual included.

Classification: Stanford-Binet (Interpretive report)

Hardware Requirements and Price
Apple II. *Single User Price: $295.00*

IBM PC, XT, AT, PS/2, & compatibles. *Single User Price: $295.00*

TRS-80, Model III & IV. *Single User Price: $295.00*

Stars II
Nigel Shollick

The Test Agency International
Cournswoop House, North Dean
High Wycombe, Bucks HP144NW England
44240243384

Computer-based, interactive personality questionnaire that, having analyzed 18 key aspects of personality, produces a detailed job-relevant structured interview questionnaire and guide for use in recruitment and selection interviewing. Instruction booklet included.

Classification: Vocational Testing (Interpretive report)

Hardware Requirements and Price
IBM PC, XT, AT, PS/2, & compatibles; 1 Mb
RAM; 10 Mb 1 disk drive (3-1/2). EGA display. Requires DOS 3.0. *Single User Price:*
$10.00-$100 Per administration test fee depends
upon volume

State-Trait Anxiety Inventory Computer Program
Charles Spielberger

Multi-Health Systems, Inc.
908 Niagara Falls Blvd.
North Tonawanda, NY 14120-2060
(416) 424-1700
(800) 456-3003

Program uses Form Y of the State-Trait Anxiety Inventory, and administers, scores, and
graphs the results of the two 20-item self-
report scales. The report includes a listing of
item responses and a brief listing of raw, percentile, and normalized T-scores. Data from
the program can be stored on disk for future
use. Detailed manual included.

Classification: Diagnostic Aid

Hardware Requirements and Price
Apple II, 256 K, hard disk optional, 1 disk
drive. Printer required. *Single User Price:*
$100.00 (50 administrations)

IBM PC, XT, AT, PS/2, & compatibles; hard
disk optional; 1 disk drive. Printer required.
Laser printer optional. *Single User Price:*
$100.00 (50 administrations)

**Personality tests have been classified as
"Personality Test," or specific test names such
as "MMPI," "16PF," or "Rorschach."**

Station Employee Applicant Inventory (SEPI)

London House/SRA
9701 W. Higgins Road
Rosemont, IL 60018
(708) 292-1900
(800) 221-8378

The SEAI is used for screening job applicants
for cashiers and attendants at gasoline service
stations and convienience stores. There are
multiple versions of the SEAI for different user
needs. Requires ITAC/PS, an IBM-PC, or a
compatible test scoring and reporting program
that scores and generates reports for this and
other London House test systems. Instruction
booklet included.

Classification: Vocational Testing (Interpretive report)

Hardware Requirements and Price
IBM PC, XT, AT, PS/2, & compatibles; 512 K;
10 Mb hard disk required; 1 disk drive. Printer
required. Laser printer optional. Requires
DOS 2.2. *Single User Price: $8.00- $16.00 Per*
administration test fee depends upon volume

Strong-Campbell Interest Inventory
E. K. Strong
Jo-Ida C. Hansen
David P. Campbell

Consulting Psychologists Press
3803 East Bayshore Road
Palo Alto, CA 94303
(415) 969-8901
(800) 624-1765

The program presents results of the inventory
in a profile that organizes the world of work

into six basic patterns of occupational interest: realistic, investigative, artistic, social, enterprising, and conventional. An optional interpretive report provides a general explanation of the client's scores, describing the three highest occupational themes. On-line help available. Tutorial program included.

Classification: Vocational Testing (Interpretive report)

Hardware Requirements and Price
IBM PC, XT, AT, PS/2, & compatibles; 640 K; hard disk required; 2 disk drives (3-1/2). *Single User Price: The initial system with a 5 year lease is $800.00. The initial system with a 10 year lease is $1,000.00. Each additional software set is $50.00 and the annual lease fee is $125.00. Call for report prices.*

Student Adjustment Inventory (SAI)
James R. Barclay

MetriTech
111 North Market Street
Champaign, IL 61820
(217) 398-4868
(800) 747-4868

The SAI assesses common affective-social problem areas for upper elementary, junior high, high school, and beginning college students. The seven problem areas assessed are: self-competency or self esteem, group interaction and social process, self-discipline, communication, energy/effort, learning/ studying, and attitude toward the learning environment. The SAI is designed to help students understand their own attitudes and feelings regarding these problem areas. The inventory observes normal rather than abnormal behaviors.

Detailed manual included. Latest release 1989.

Classification: Diagnostic Aid, Children and Adolescents (Administration and Interpretive report)

Hardware Requirements and Price
IBM PC, XT, AT, PS/2, & compatibles; 256 K; hard disk optional; 1 disk drive. Laser printer optional. *Single User Price: $195.00*

Study Skills Test
William F. Brown

WFB Enterprises
1225 19th Street
Beaumont, TX 77706
(409) 898-1983

This program is a mostly-true or mostly-false test covering 10 study skills areas. It yields 10 part scores and 1 total score. Also percentile norms are available for three-college sample. Detailed manual included. Latest release July 1, 1990.

Classification: Academic (Interpretive report)

Hardware Requirements and Price
Apple II, 48 K, hard disk optional, 1 disk drive (5-1/4). *Single User Price: $200.00*

IBM PC, XT, AT, PS/2, & compatibles; 72 K; hard disk optional; 1 disk drive (5-1/4). *Single User Price: $200.00*

User Site References
Dorothy Forristall, Director of Learning Skills, Lomar University, Beaumont, TX, 77706, (409) 880-8882

Suicide Probability Scale (SPS)
John G. Cull
Wayne S. Gill
George J. Huba

Western Psychological Services
12031 Wilshire Blvd.
Los Angeles, CA 90025
(213) 478-2061
(800) 648-8857

The SPS is a 36-item, self-report measure that assesses suicide risk in adults and adolescents. Overall risk is assessed in three summary scores: a total weighted score, a normalized T-score, and a suicide probability score. The SPS diskette administers, scores, and generates a 1-page report. Instruction booklet included.

Classification: Diagnostic Aid (Interpretive report)

Hardware Requirements and Price
IBM PC, XT, AT, PS/2, & compatibles; 512 K; 1 Mb hard disk required; 1 disk drive. Printer required. Laser printer optional. Requires DOS 3.0. *Single User Price: $210.00*

SuperLab
Hisham A. Abboud

Cedrus Corporation
11160 Veirs Mill Road, L-15 #221
Wheaton, MD 20902-2538
(301) 589-1828
(800) CEDRUS1

A general purpose psychology testing package. Provides 1 ms accuracy. Supports visual and auditory stimuli and feedback to subjects. Interactive, familiar Macintosh interface. Codes editor allows collected data to be pre-coded to simplify post-processing of results.

Detailed manual included. Latest release September 10, 1991.

Classification: Testing Utility

Hardware Requirements and Price
Macintosh, 512 K, hard disk optional, 1 disk drive (3-1/2). Mouse required. Requires System 6.03. Works on Mac Plus or later. *Single User Price: $475.00 Educational discounts available.*

Reviews
Haxby, J. (in press). SuperLab: Flexible Macintosh software for psychological research. *Behavior Research Methods, Instrumentation, and Computers.*

User Site References
James Haxby, National Institution on Aging, National Institutes of Health Building 10, 6D, Bethesda, MD, 20892, (301) 496-5882

Francois LaRonde, National Institute on Mental Health, National Institutes of Health Building 10, 3D41, Bethesda, MD, 20892, (301) 402-0869

Raja Parasuraman, Catholic University, Washington, DC, 20064, (202) 319-5755

Symptom Checklist
Edwin Robbins
Marvin Stern

AI Software, Inc.
P.O. Box 724
Wakefield, RI 02879
(401) 789-8660
(800) 272-2250

A scoring and interpretive program based on a 90-item symptom checklist. The program calculates T-scores, adjusts for norms, and reports in three areas: pathological behavior, probable symptoms, and similar patient groups. Detailed manual included.

Classification: Diagnostic Aid (Interpretive report)

Hardware Requirements and Price
IBM PC, XT, AT, PS/2, & compatibles; 64 K; 1 disk drive. Printer required. Laser printer optional. Requires DOS 3.1. *Single User Price: $99.95*

Symptom Checklist-90 Interpretive Report
Michael E. Mills

Psytek Services
6401 West 81st Street
Los Angeles, CA 90045
(213) 670-4655
(800) 392-5454

Fully automated interpretive report generator. Reports may be exported to word processing programs. Sample report available on request. A 30-day money back guarantee. Detailed manual included. Latest release June 1, 1991.

Classification: Diagnostic Aid (Interpretive report)

Hardware Requirements and Price
IBM PC, XT, AT, PS/2, & compatibles; 512 K; hard disk optional. Monochrome, CGA, EGA, or VGA display. Laser printer optional. *Single User Price: $59.00 Site License: $159.00*

Symptom Checklist-90-R (SCL-90-R)
Leonard R. Derogatis

National Computer Systems, Inc.
P.O. Box 1416

Minneapolis, MN 55440
(800) 627-7271

The SCL-90-R is a brief, multi-dimensional inventory designed as a screening tool for psychopathology in psychiatric, medical, and nonpatient populations. It can be used during the initial evaluation, during treatment to measure change, and after treatment for a follow-up assessment of treatment outcome. Requires Microtest Assessment System or Arion II Teleprocessing service. Detailed manual included.

Classification: Diagnostic Aid (Interpretive report)

Hardware Requirements and Price
IBM PC, XT, AT, PS/2, & compatibles; 512 K; 10 Mb hard disk required; 1 disk drive. Monochrome, CGA, EGA, or VGA display. 300-2400 baud modem optional. Printer required. Laser printer optional. Requires DOS 3.1. *Single User Price: Call publisher*

System 2000 Career Planner

ValPar International Corp.
P.O. Box 5767
Tucson, AZ 85703-5767
(602) 293-1510
(800) 528-7070

System 2000 is a modular, integrated software system. It generates a variety of vocational counseling reports using assessment data from a number of sources. The reporting structure is keyed to the factors described in the *Handbook for Analyzing Jobs* (US DOL, 1972). Detailed manual included. On-line help available.

Classification: Vocational Testing (Administration and Interpretive report)

Hardware Requirements and Price
IBM PC, XT, AT, PS/2, & compatibles; 640 K; 20 Mb hard disk required. CGA, EGA, or VGA display. Printer required. Laser printer optional. *Single User Price: Call publisher*

System 2000 Computerized Assessment

ValPar International Corp.
P.O. Box 5767
Tucson, AZ 85703-5767
(602) 293-1510
(800) 528-7070

This modular, integrated software system performs an assessment/screening of an individual and reports skills in terms of a Worker Qualifications Profile as described in the *Handbook for Analyzing Jobs* (US DOL, 1972). Detailed manual included. On-line help available.

Classification: Vocational Testing (Interpretive report)

Hardware Requirements and Price
IBM PC, XT, AT, PS/2, & compatibles; 640 K; 20 Mb hard disk required. CGA, EGA, or VGA display. Printer required. Laser printer optional. *Single User Price: Call publisher*

System 2000 GOE Survey

ValPar International Corp.
P.O. Box 5767
Tucson, AZ 85703-5767

(602) 293-1510
(800) 528-7070

Program assesses an individual's interests based on the 12 categories described in the *Guide for Occupational Exploration* (US DOL, 1979). Detailed manual included. On-line help available.

Classification: Vocational Testing (Interpretive report)

Hardware Requirements and Price
IBM PC, XT, AT, PS/2, & compatibles; 640 K; 20 Mb hard disk required. CGA, EGA, or VGA display. Printer required. Laser printer optional. *Single User Price: Call publisher*

System 2000 Work Sample Scoring

ValPar International Corp.
P.O. Box 5767
Tucson, AZ 85703-5767
(602) 293-1510
(800) 528-7070

A modular, integrated software system, System 2000 accepts results from ValPar Component Work Sample series and generates scores using the factors described in the *Handbook for Analyzing Jobs* (US DOL, 1972). Detailed manual included. On-line help available.

Classification: Vocational Testing (Interpretive report)

Hardware Requirements and Price
IBM PC, XT, AT, PS/2, & compatibles; 640 K; 20 Mb hard disk required. CGA, EGA, or VGA display. Printer required. Laser printer optional. *Single User Price: Call publisher*

System for Testing and Evaluation of Potential

London House/SRA
9701 W. Higgins Road
Rosemont, IL 60018
(708) 292-1900
(800) 221-8378

Designed to screen and select new managerial, sales, or professional employees; evaluate candidates for promotion or transfer; diagnose training needs; and aid in career counseling. The job-analysis system covers 12 key positions. The questionnaires are scored by the Immediate Telephone Analysis by Computer (I-TAC) Teleprocessing service.

Classification: Vocational Testing

Hardware Requirements and Price
Modem required. *Single User Price: Call publisher*

Tap Dance
International Testing Service, Inc.

London House/SRA
9701 W. Higgins Road
Rosemont, IL 60018
(708) 292-1900
(800) 221-8378

A computer based method for assessing typing and other clerical skills. Tap Dance measures the candidate's typing, spelling, editing, data-entry, 10-key, math, and grammar skills. Employers can set their own time limits or create totally new tests to handle such additional assessment needs such as proof-reading. Detailed manual included.

Classification: Vocational Testing (Administration)

Hardware Requirements and Price
IBM PC, XT, AT, PS/2, & compatibles; 256 K; hard disk optional. *Single User Price: Call publisher*

TDAS: Test Development and Analysis System
Richard L. Greenblatt
Julian J. Szucko

Applied Psychometric Services, Inc.
P.O. Box 871
Naperville, IL 60566-0871
(708) 505-0590

The Test Development and Analysis System (TDAS) is a computer program for creating, administering, scoring, analyzing, and profiling tests and surveys. TDAS accepts true-false, multiple-choice, or multi-point rating scales. It can process tests and surveys of any type– personality, interest, aptitude, ability, achievement, or vocational. Responses can be key-entered, optically scanned, or obtained through on-screen administration. Reports range from results of single respondents to complete psychometric analyses of your test or survey. Detailed manual included. On-line help available. Latest release December, 1990.

Classification: Testing Utility (Administration and Interpretive report)

Hardware Requirements and Price
IBM PC, XT, AT, PS/2, & compatibles; 512 K; hard disk optional; 2 disk drives. Monochrome or color display. Mouse optional. Modem optional. Laser printer optional. Requires DOS 2.1. *Single User Price: $795.00 Demonstration Version: $10.00 Site license available*

User Site References

Mitchell Jacobs, Director, Testing Service, University of Illinois at Chicago, Box 4348 M/C 333, Chicago, IL, 60680, (312) 996-3476

Gerald Mozdzierz, Assistant Chief, Psychology Service Hines VA Hospital, Psychology Service (116B), Hines, IL, 60141, (708) 216-2692

Telemarketing Applicant Inventory (TMAI)

London House/SRA
9701 W. Higgins Road
Rosemont, IL 60018
(708) 292-1900
(800) 221-8378

The TMAI assesses skills and orientations needed for most telephone sales and service positions. The TMAI provides information on: sales interest and skills, sales responsibility, productivity, confidence, influence, interpersonal orientation, stress tolerance, job stability, communicator competence, and applied verbal reasoning. The program also includes job simulation rating that guides the interviewer in assessing applicant voice quality, energy level, rate of speech, speech clarity, expressiveness, and command of language. Results of the TMAI are summarized in a readiness index that reflects an applicant's overall potential for success in a telemarketing position. Detailed manual included.

Classification: Vocational Testing (Interpretive report)

Hardware Requirements and Price
IBM PC, XT, AT, PS/2, & compatibles; 512 K; hard disk optional; 2 disk drives. *Single User Price: Call publisher*

TeleTest Teleprocessing Service

Institute for Personality & Ability Testing
P.O. Box 188
Champaign, IL 61824-1188
(217) 352-4739
(800) 225-4728

Links computer terminal and printer with company via a telephone connection. Test data received using a modem is processed by the company's computers and interpretive reports are immediately sent back over the same phone lines. Specific tests are listed separately in this directory. Thirteen different reports are available if the Telxpress utility software is combined with the TeleTest Teleprocessing service software. Detailed manual included.

Classification: Testing Utility

Hardware Requirements and Price
Call publisher for hardware options. 1200 baud modem required. Printer required. Laser printer optional. *Single User Price: Call publisher*

Tennessee Self Concept Scale (TSCS)
William H. Fitts
Gale H. Roid
George J. Huba

Western Psychological Services
12031 Wilshire Blvd.
Los Angeles, CA 90025
(213) 478-2061
(800) 648-8857

The TSCS measures self-concept in persons 13 years of age and older. The scale consists of 100 self-descriptive statements and can be administered in 10-20 min. A comprehensive report that summarizes and evaluates test results is generated. Mail-in computer scoring is available (1-day turnaround). Teleprocessing service also available. Instruction booklet included.

Classification: Personality Testing

Hardware Requirements and Price
IBM PC, XT, AT, PS/2, & compatibles; 512 K; 1 Mb hard disk required; 1 disk drive. Printer required. Laser printer optional. Requires DOS 3.0. *Single User Price: $245.00*

Termination/Discharge Summary

Psychologistics, Inc.
P.O. Box 033896
Indialantic, FL 32903
(407) 259-7811

The program summarizes information in the areas of presenting problem, initial mental and physical status, evaluation results, treatment goals, treatment outcomes, and termination or discharge recommendations. A 2-page report is generated that provides complete documentation of the client's treatment. Software permits unlimited uses. Detailed manual included. Latest release 1985.

Classification: Diagnostic Aid (Interpretive report)

Hardware Requirements and Price
IBM PC, XT, AT, PS/2, & compatibles; 128 K; hard disk optional; 1 disk drive. Printer required. Requires DOS 2.0. *Single User Price: $150.00*

Macintosh, 512 K, hard disk optional, 1 disk drive (3-1/2). Printer required. *Single User Price: $150.00*

Test Avanzado de Matrices Progresivas
Carlos Pal Hegedus

Psico-Iuris, S.A.
P.O. Box 1039 - Centro Colon
San Jose, 1007 Costa Rica
(506) 24-4416

Scores and gives the percentile rank and diagnostic level as well as personal data on the Raven's Advanced Progressive Matrix Intelligence Test. This test can be used with high capacity persons. Unlimited use version. Instruction booklet available in Spanish. Instruction booklet included. Latest release November, 1991.

Classification: Intelligence Testing (Interpretive report)

Hardware Requirements and Price
IBM PC, XT, AT, PS/2, & compatibles; 128 K; hard disk optional; 1 disk drive. Laser printer optional. Requires DOS 3.1. *Single User Price: $150.00 Network Price: $500.00*

Test de Matrices Progresivas de Raven
Carlos Pal Hegedus

Psico-Iuris, S.A.
P.O. Box 1039 - Centro Colon
San Jose, 1007 Costa Rica
(506) 24-4416

Provides and scores the percentile rank, diagnostic level, and personal data on the Raven's Progresives Matrix Intelligence Test. Unlimited use version. Detailed manual available in Spanish. Detailed manual and tutorial program included. Latest release November, 1991.

Classification: Intelligence Testing (Interpretive report)

Hardware Requirements and Price
IBM PC, XT, AT, PS/2, & compatibles; 128 K; hard disk optional; 1 disk drive. Laser printer optional. Requires DOS 3.1. *Single User Price: $150.00 Network Price: $600.00*

Test of Adolescent Language-2, Second Edition (TOAL-2)
Brian R. Bryant

Pro-Ed, Inc.
8700 Shoal Creek Blvd.
Austin, TX 78758-6897
(512) 451-3246

This software scoring system converts raw scores from the Test of Adolescent Language to standard scores and percentiles, generates composite scores, profiles composite scores, and compares composite performance for intra-individual differences. The program produces a 2-page printout suitable for inclusion in the student's permanent file. Detailed manual included. Latest release 1987.

Classification: Academic (Interpretive report)

Hardware Requirements and Price
Apple II, 48 K, hard disk optional, 1 disk drive (5-1/4). *Single User Price: $79.00*

Test of Language Development-Intermediate, Second Edition (TOLD-I:2)
Waynes P. Hresko
Paul L. Schlieve

Pro-Ed, Inc.
8700 Shoal Creek Blvd.
Austin, TX 78758-6897
(512) 451-3146

Software generates a 4-page report that contains descriptive background information, raw scores, standard scores, percentiles and descriptions for each subtest, standard score sums, percentiles and descriptions for all composites and quotients, profiles for subtests and composites, and significance tests comparing all composites. Detailed manual included. Latest release 1988.

Classification: Academic (Interpretive report)

Hardware Requirements and Price
Apple II, 48 K, hard disk optional, 1 disk drive (5-1/4). *Single User Price: $79.00*

IBM PC, XT, AT, PS/2, & compatibles; 640 K; hard disk optional; 1 disk drive (5-1/4). *Single User Price: $79.00*

Test of Language Development-Primary, Second Edition (TOLD-P:2)
Wayne P. Hresko
Paul L. Schlieve

Pro-Ed, Inc.
8700 Shoal Creek Blvd.
Austin, TX 78758-6897
(512) 451-3246

Program generates a 4-page report that contains descriptive background information, raw scores, standard scores, percentiles, and descriptions for each subtest, standard score sums, percentiles and descriptions for all composites and quotients, profiles for subtests and composites, and significance tests comparing all composites. Detailed manual included. Latest release 1988.

Classification: Academic (Interpretive report)

Hardware Requirements and Price
Apple II, 48 K, hard disk optional, 1 disk drive (5-1/4). *Single User Price: $79.00*

IBM PC, XT, AT, PS/2, & compatibles; 640 K; hard disk optional; 1 disk drive (5-1/4). *Single User Price: $79.00*

Test of Written Language-2 (TOWL-2) Pro-Score System
Wayne P. Hresko
Paul Schlieve

Pro-Ed, Inc.
8700 Shoal Creek Blvd.
Austin, TX 78758-6897
(512) 451-3246

A 4-page report is generated that contains descriptive background information, raw scores, standard scores, percentiles and descriptions of each subtest, standard score sums, percentiles and descriptions of all composites and quotients, profiles for subtests and composites, and significance tests of comparisons among all composites. Detailed manual included. Latest release 1988.

Classification: Academic (Interpretive report)

Hardware Requirements and Price
Apple II, 48 K, hard disk optional, 1 disk drive (5-1/4). *Single User Price: $79.00*

IBM PC, XT, AT, PS/2, & compatibles; 640 K; hard disk optional; 1 disk drive (5-1/4). *Single User Price: $79.00*

Test Plus
Samuel E. Krug

MetriTech
111 North Market Street
Champaign, IL 61820
(217) 398-4868
(800) 747-4868

Test profile includes seven personal characteristics, eight interpersonal, six career, and four validity scales. Software administers, scores and generates reports for on- or off-line testing. Test Plus incorporates a feature that is intended to lead to more reliable and accurate application of test results. By responding to a set of 64 paired comparisons, users convert their judgments about the relative importance of test scales into an ideal profile or "decision model." Program automatically produces an overall statistical comparison index. Detailed manual included. Latest release 1991.

Classification: Diagnostic Aid (Administration and Interpretive report)

Hardware Requirements and Price
Apple II, 64 K, hard disk optional, 2 disk drives (5-1/4). Laser printer optional. *Single User Price: $519.00*

IBM PC, XT, AT, PS/2, & compatibles; 256 K; hard disk optional; 1 disk drive. Laser printer optional. *Single User Price: $519.00*

Reviews

Hilgert, L. D. (1987). Review of Test Plus. *Social Science Microcomputer Review*, *5*, 95-97.

Krug, S. E. (1991). The Adult Personality Inventory. *Journal of Counseling and Development*, 69.

TMJ/Score Report Processing Software

Stephen R. Levitt
Thomas F. Lundeed
Michael W. McKinney

Pain Resource Center, Inc.
P.O. Box 2836
Durham, NC 27705
(919) 286-9180
(800) 542-PAIN

Menu-driven scoring program that produces a 10-scale narrative report that assess physical and psychological aspects of head and neck pain, and temporomandibular (TMJ) disorders, including stress and non-TMJ disorders. Price depends upon number of administrations. Answer sheets are compatible with Sentry 3000 and Scantron 1400 optical scanners. Detailed manual included. Latest release January, 1991.

Classification: Diagnostic Aid, Health (Interpretive report)

Hardware Requirements and Price
IBM PC, XT, AT, PS/2, & compatibles; 256 K; hard disk optional; 2 disk drives. Laser printer optional. *Single User Price: $13.00 - $16.50 (per test)*

Reviews

Spiegel, E. P., & Levitt S. R. (1991). Measuring symptom severity with the TMJ scale. *Journal of Clinical Orthodontics*, *30*, 21-26.

Transit Bus Operator Selection Test Battery

London House/SRA
9701 W. Higgins Road
Rosemont, IL 60018
(708) 292-1900
(800) 221-8378

This personality questionnaire for identifying successful future operators is scored via the Immediate Telephone Analysis by Computer (I-TAC). System uses a small, inexpensive hand-held field computer. Test responses are keyed in to provide immediate, on-site results. Teleprocessing service.

Classification: Vocational Testing (Interpretive report)

Hardware Requirements and Price
IBM PC, XT, AT, PS/2, & compatibles; 512 K; hard disk optional; 2 disk drives. *Single User Price: Call publisher*

Triplet Recall

Rosamond Gianutsos
Carol Klitzner

Life Science Associates
1 Fenimore Road
Bayport, NY 11705-2115
(516) 472-2111
Fax: (516) 472-8146

Program for assessing short- and long-term memory storage. Can also be used to practice and improve memory. Three words are presented one at a time followed as an interference task (e.g., 0, 3, or 9 words to be read, but not recalled). The program assesses both short- and long-term memory. This is one module from Cogrehab (see Clinical Software section).

Classification: Neuropsychological Testing

Hardware Requirements and Price
Apple II, 64 K, 10 Mb hard disk optional, 1 disk drive (5-1/4). Monochrome or color display. *Single User Price: $40.00*

IBM PC, XT, AT, PS/2, & compatibles; 128 K; 20 Mb hard disk optional; 1 disk drive. CGA display required. *Single User Price: $40.00*

Vineland Adaptive Behavior Scales-ASSIST
Sara S. Sparrow
David A. Balla
Domemic V. Cicchetti

American Guidance Service
4201 Woodland Road
Circle Pines, MN 55014-1796
(612) 786-4343
(800) 328-2560

Program offers quick score conversion, profiling, and convenient record management of Vineland scales data. Detailed manual included.

Classification: Diagnostic Aid (Interpretive report)

Hardware Requirements and Price
Apple II, 48 K, 2 disk drives (5-1/4). *Single User Price: $115.00*

IBM PC, XT, AT, PS/2, & compatibles; 512 K; hard disk optional; 1 disk drive. *Single User Price: $130.00*

VIP: Vocational Implications of Personality, Jr.
Jill Gann
Linda Roebuck

Talent Assessment, Inc.
P.O. Box 5087
Jacksonville, FL 32247-5087
(904) 260-4102
(800) 634-1472

A computerized personality assessment program designed to describe a person's working style, relationship to the world, and decision-making approach. Designed for junior and senior high students. It is based on the work of Dr. Karl Jung. Includes audio learning tapes and group activities and a detailed manual. Latest release 1989.

Classification: Vocational Testing

Hardware Requirements and Price
Apple II, 128 K, 1 Mb hard disk optional. Printer required. Laser printer optional. *Single User Price: $595.00*

IBM PC, XT, AT, PS/2, & compatibles; 256 K; 1 Mb hard disk optional. Printer required. Laser printer optional. *Single User Price: $595.00*

User Site References

Marge Gazvoda, University of South Florida, Tampa, FL, 33620, (813) 874-3455

Ron Marten, Northern Lights College, 11401 8th Street, Dawson Creek, BC, Z1G 4G2, Canada, (604) 784-7510

Gary Meers, University of Nebraska, 518 East Nebraska Hall, Lincoln, NE, 68858, (402) 472-2365

Visual Scanning
Linda Laatsch

Life Science Associates
1 Fenimore Road
Bayport, NY 11705-2115
(516) 472-2111
Fax: (516) 472-8146

Program for diagnosing and retraining visual scanning deficits. Scan can be used for the assessment of head injury, stroke, or damage to the visual system. The program includes Textscan that requires the subject to respond when a target letter is bracketed, and Linescan that requires the subject to respond if two stimuli at the right or left edge of the screen are the same. Detailed manual included. Latest release 1988.

Classification: Neuropsychological Testing

Hardware Requirements and Price
Apple II, 64 K, 10 Mb hard disk optional, 1 disk drive (5-1/4). Monochrome or color display. *Single User Price: $40.00 Network Price: $120.00*

IBM PC, XT, AT, PS/2, & compatibles; 128 K; 20 Mb hard disk optional; 1 disk drive. CGA, EGA, or VGA display. *Single User Price: $40.00 Network Price: $120.00*

Vocational Information Profile (VIP)
United States Employment Service

National Computer Systems, Inc.
P.O. Box 1416
Minneapolis, MN 55440
(800) 627-7271

This profile combines scores on both the GATB and the USES interest inventory to provide an integrated interest-aptitude assessment. Requires Microtest assessment system. Detailed manual included.

Classification: Vocational Testing

Hardware Requirements and Price
IBM PC, XT, AT, PS/2, & compatibles; 512 K; hard disk optional; 1 disk drive (5-1/4). Monochrome display. Printer required. Laser printer optional. *Single User Price: Call publisher*

Vocational Interest Inventory (VII)
Patricia W. Lunneborg

Western Psychological Services
12031 Wilshire Blvd.
Los Angeles, CA 90025
(213) 478-2061
(800) 648-8857

The VII helps high school and college students isolate their strongest interests and then directs them to specific educational programs and occupations. Based on Roe's Psychology of Occupations, the VII measures relative interest in eight occupational areas. Teleprocessing service also available. Instruction booklet included.

Classification: Vocational Testing

Hardware Requirements and Price
IBM PC, XT, AT, PS/2, & compatibles; 512 K; 1 Mb hard disk required; 1 disk drive. Printer required. Laser printer optional. Requires DOS 3.0. *Single User Price: $190.00 Price depends on number of administrations*

Vocational Interest Profile Report (VIPR)

Cambridge Career Products
P.O. Box 2153
Charleston, WV 25328-2153
(304) 744-9323
(800) 468-4227

Allows students to identify broad work area clusters that are most interesting to them. Detailed manual included.

Classification: Vocational Testing (Interpretive report)

Hardware Requirements and Price
Apple II. *Single User Price: $98.00*

IBM PC, XT, AT, PS/2, & compatibles; 2 disk drives. *Single User Price: $98.00*

Vocational Interest Profile Report

Giles D. Rainwater

Psychometric Software, Inc.
P.O. Box 1677
Melbourne, FL 32902-1677
(407) 729-6390
(800) 882-9811

The Vocational Interest Profile Report administers, scores, and interprets the interest check list developed by the US DOL. The VIP was developed to help identify occupational interest. Detailed manual included. Latest release 1984.

Classification: Vocational Testing (Interpretive report)

Hardware Requirements and Price
Apple II+, IIe, IIc, IIgs; 64 K; 1 disk drive (5-1/4). Monochrome display. Printer required. Will not run on disk hard drive. *Single User Price: $97.50*

IBM PC, XT, AT, PS/2, & compatibles; 128 K; 10 Mb hard disk optional; 1 disk drive. Monochrome, CGA, EGA, or VGA display. Printer required. Laser printer optional. Can be run on Macintosh systems operating under SoftPC. *Single User Price: $195.95 Network Price: $195.95 plus $97.98 for each additional user*

Vocational Personality Report

Brian Bolton

Arkansas Research & Training Center
P.O. Box 1358
Hot Springs, AR 71902-1779
(501) 624-4411

Provides a narrative report for Form E of the 16PF, that is an adaptation designed for use with individuals whose reading skills are severely limited. Five broad personality scales are described and graphed, and the report describes six scales that measure occupational themes originally described by Holland. This program is sold only to recognized vocational rehabilitation agencies and facilities. Detailed manual included.

Classification: Vocational Testing (Interpretive report)

Hardware Requirements and Price
IBM PC, XT, AT, PS/2, & compatibles; 640 K; hard disk optional; 1 disk drive (5-1/4). Printer required. Laser printer optional. *Single User Price: $12.50*

Vocational Preference Inventory: Computer Version, Version 3
Robert G. Rose

Psychological Assessment Resources, Inc.
P.O. Box 998
Odessa, FL 33556
(800) 331-TEST

Administers, scores and interprets the Vocational Preference Inventory. Information on personality configuration and a listing of occupations based on combinations of the client's Holland summary codes are provided. Detailed manual included. Latest release June 20, 1989.

Classification: Vocational Testing (Administration and Interpretive report)

Hardware Requirements and Price
Apple II+, IIe; 64 K; 2 disk drives (5-1/4). 80-column display required. Not compatible with laser printer. *Single User Price: $225.00 (50 administrations)*

IBM PC, XT, AT, PS/2, & compatibles; 256 K; hard disk optional; 2 disk drives or 1 disk drive and hard disk. Laser printer optional. *Single User Price: $225.00 (50 administrations)*

Vocational Research Interest Inventory-Scannable
Howard Dansky
Jeffrey A. Harris

Vocational Research Institute
1528 Walnut Street, Suite 1502
Philadelphia, PA 19102
(800) 874-5387
Fax: (215) 875-0198

Scans results from the Vocational Research Interest Inventory. Test consists of 162 items to which the test taker responds "Like," "?," or "Dislike." Options available to score, generate reports and save results, and save results. Separate norms are provided for prevocational (17 years and under) and vocational (18 years and older) individuals. Detailed manual included. Latest release 1991.

Classification: Vocational Testing (Interpretive report)

Hardware Requirements and Price
IBM PC, XT, AT, PS/2, & compatibles; hard disk optional. Monochrome display. Scantron or IBM half or full sheet scanner required. *Single User Price: Call publisher*

Vocational Research Interest Inventory
Jeffrey A. Harris
Howard Dansky
Lisa Slotkin

Vocational Research Institute
1528 Walnut Street, Suite 1502
Philadelphia, PA 19102
(800) 874-5387
Fax: (215) 875-0198

Program administers, scores, and generates a report for the Vocational Research Interest Inventory. Test consists of 162 items to which the test taker responds "Like," "?," or "Dislike." A manual data entry option allows computer scoring and report generation based on information gathered from off-line administration. Separate norms are provided for prevocational (17 years and under) and vocational (18 years and older) individuals. Detailed manual included. Latest release 1986.

Classification: Vocational Testing (Administration and Interpretive report)

Hardware Requirements and Price
Apple II, 128 K, hard disk optional, 1 disk drive (5-1/4). Monochrome display. *Single User Price: $295.00*

IBM PC, XT, AT, PS/2, & compatibles; 128 K; hard disk optional; 1 disk drive. Monochrome display. Requires DOS 2.0. *Single User Price: $295.00*

Reviews
Slotkin, L. (1990). Vocational Research Interest Inventory. *Vocational Evaluation and Work Adjustment Bulletin*, 23(2), 69-70.

User Site References
Avril Bongera, Executive Director, Transitional Employment Consultants, 330 Central Avenue, Washington, PA, 15301, (412) 225-3535.
Larry Healy, Work Study Coordinator, Madison-Oneida BOCES, V.V.D. Middle School, Rt 31, Verona, NY, 13478, (315) 363-3833.

Vocational Transit
Howard Dansky
Jeffrey A. Harris
Mary Beth Konefsky
Lisa Slotkin

Vocational Research Institute
1528 Walnut Street, Suite 1502
Philadelphia, PA 19102
(800) 874-5387
Fax: (215) 875-0198

Computerized vocational assessment for cognitively impaired individuals including the mentally retarded and the brain injured. Assesses four DOL defined aptitudes (motor coordination, manual dexterity, finger dexterity, and form perception) and relates results to a data base of job titles from the *Dictionary of Occupational Titles*. Three norm groups are provided for comparison including adult non-impaired, secondary ed non-impaired and developmentally disabled. Vocational Transit is self-timing, self-scoring and can generate a variety of report formats. Detailed manual included. Latest release 1990.

Classification: Vocational Testing (Interpretive report)

Hardware Requirements and Price
IBM PC, XT, AT, PS/2, & compatibles; 640 K; hard disk optional; 2 disk drives. Monochrome display. 9600 baud modem required. Requires DOS 3.0. *Single User Price: $5,850.00*

Reviews
Boherbusch, K. (1990). Vocational Transit. *Vocational Evaluation and Work Adjustment Bulletin*, 23(3), 105-107.

User Site References
Ruth Roberts, Director of Rehabilitation Services, Shelby Residential & Vocational Services, 2400 Poplar Avenue, Suite 436, Memphis, TN, 38112, (901) 458-6305.
Ray Schanafelt, Vocational Education Special Ed, Orange Unified School District, Workability Program, 250 South Yorba, Orange, CA, 92669, (714) 997-6267.

WAIS-R Analysis II, Version 7.0
Terrance G. Lichtenwald

Happ Electronics, Inc.
3680 North Main Street
Oshkosh, WI 54901
(414) 231-5128

Menu-driven program for analyzing and reporting results on the WAIS-R. Features include automatic conversion from raw to scaled age scores, standard or customized reports, scatter analysis of subtests relative to the examinee's means, percentile ranks and confidence intervals for IQs, and Lutey's factor analysis of results. Additional program option allows any combination of subtests to be analyzed. Detailed manual included. On-line help available.

Classification: WAIS (Interpretive report)

Hardware Requirements and Price
Apple II, hard disk optional, 1 disk drive. Printer required. *Single User Price: $200.00*

IBM PC, XT, AT, PS/2, & compatibles; hard disk optional; 1 disk drive. Printer required. *Single User Price: $200.00*

WAIS-R Microcomputer-Assisted Interpretive Report

The Psychological Corporation
555 Academic Court
San Antonio, TX 78204-0952
(512) 299-1061
(800) 228-0752

Program produces in-depth analyses of WAIS-R results. The 3-4 page interpretive report

generated includes confidence intervals for IQs, significance and prevalence of verbal-performance differences, percentile ranks, and additional interpretive information. The program also allows the examiner to enter information specific to the examinee and the testing situation. Specialists must sign a licensing agreement prior to shipment. Detailed manual included. Latest release 1986.

Classification: WAIS (Interpretive report)

Hardware Requirements and Price
Apple II+, IIe; 64 K; 1 disk drive (5-1/4). *Single User Price: $169.00*

IBM PC, XT, AT, PS/2, & compatibles; 128 K; 1 disk drive. Laser printer optional. *Single User Price: $169.00*

WAIS-R Narrative Report

Psychological Testing Service
213 East Sugnet
Midland, MI 48640
(517) 631-9463
Fax: (517) 631-9419

This interpretive system produces detailed reports through analysis of IQ and subscale variations, patterns, and factors. This generates information and hypotheses that may not be readily recognizable as well as compiling information in narrative format. Requires entry of VIQ, PIQ, FSQ, and subtest scaled scores. Instruction booklet included. Latest release April, 1991.

Classification: WAIS (Interpretive report)

Hardware Requirements and Price
IBM PC, XT, AT, PS/2, & compatibles; 256 K; hard disk optional; 1 disk drive. Printer

required. Laser printer optional. *Single User Price: $195.00*

WAIS-R Report, Version 3.0

Psychologistics, Inc.
P.O. Box 033896
Indialantic, FL 32903
(407) 259-7811

Provides scoring and interpretation of the WAIS-R, based on user-entered subtest scaled scores and IQ scores. The program calculates and displays 3 pages of derived scores. A 3-page narrative report is generated, that may be printed or written to the text file and modified using a word processor. Software permits unlimited uses. Detailed manual included. Latest release 1986.

Classification: WAIS (Interpretive report)

Hardware Requirements and Price
Apple II+, IIe, IIc; 48 K; hard disk optional; 1 disk drive (5-1/4). Printer required. Requires DOS 3.3. *Single User Price: $200.00*

IBM PC, XT, AT, PS/2, & compatibles; 128 K; hard disk optional; 1 disk drive. Printer required. Requires DOS 2.0. *Single User Price: $200.00*

Macintosh, 512 K, hard disk optional, 1 disk drive (3-1/2). Printer required. *Single User Price: $200.00*

WAIS-Riter Basic

Southern Micro Systems
3545 S. Church Street
Burlington, NC 27215-2097
(919) 584-1661

Computer-assisted interpretation of the WAIS-R that allows the user to individualize reports by adding clinical observations. Achievement test results in addition to the WAIS-R scores may be entered for comparative analysis. The report provides subtest evaluations, standard score interpretation, verbal scale achievement, performance scale achievement, severe discrepancy levels for verbal, performance, and full scale IQ, ranges of learning disability, and educational and vocational recommendations.

Classification: WAIS (Interpretive report)

Hardware Requirements and Price
Apple II, 2 disk drives. *Single User Price: $199.00*

IBM PC, XT, AT, PS/2, & compatibles; 2 disk drives. *Single User Price: $199.00*

WAIS-Riter Complete

Southern Micro Systems
3545 S. Church Street
Burlington, NC 27215-2097
(919) 584-1661

Program allows user to individualize the WAIS-R report by adding clinical observations. Achievement test results in addition to the WAIS-R scores may be entered for comparative analysis. The report includes 6 pages of interpretations that cover levels of factors, achievement levels, strengths and weaknesses, and comparisons with profiles suggesting possible brain damage, schizophrenia, emotional disturbance, and behavioral disorders. Detailed manual included.

Classification: WAIS (Interpretive report)

Hardware Requirements and Price
Apple II, 2 disk drives. *Single User Price: $495.00*

IBM PC, XT, AT, PS/2, & compatibles; 2 disk drives. *Single User Price: $495.00*

Wechsler Interpretation System

AI Software, Inc.
P.O. Box 724
Wakefield, RI 02879
(401) 789-8660
(800) 272-2250

Based on the clinical research of Dr. Bruce Duthie, this collection of programs helps produce efficient WISC-R and WAIS-R evaluations and reports. Detailed manual included.

Classification: WISC (Interpretive report)

Hardware Requirements and Price
IBM PC, XT, AT, PS/2, & compatibles; 64 K; 1 disk drive. Printer required. Laser printer optional. Requires DOS 3.1. *Single User Price: $350.00*

Wechsler Memory Scale Report
Giles D. Rainwater

Psychometric Software, Inc.
P.O. Box 1677
Melbourne, FL 32902-1677
(407) 729-6390
(800) 882-9811

This program interprets and graphs the results of the Wechsler Memory Scale. The examiner enters basic demographic information and nine scores.   All scores are transformed into percentiles and graphically printed.   The program provides interpretive statements with a scale-by-scale analysis. A neuropsychological analysis is also provided.   Detailed manual included. Latest release 1984.

Classification: Intelligence Testing (Interpretive report)

Hardware Requirements and Price
Apple II+, IIe, IIc, IIgs; 64 K; hard disk optional; 1 disk drive (5-1/4).   Monochrome display. Printer required. Will not run on hard drive. *Single User Price: $69.50*

IBM PC, XT, AT, PS/2, & compatibles; 128 K; 10 Mb hard disk optional; 1 disk drive. Monochrome, CGA, EGA, or VGA display. Printer required. Laser printer optional. Can be run on Macintosh systems operating under SoftPC. *Single User Price: $95.95 Network Price: $95.95 plus $34.75 for each additional user*

Western Personality Inventory (WPI)
Morse P. Manson
George J. Huba

Western Psychological Services
12031 Wilshire Blvd.
Los Angeles, CA 90025
(213) 478-2061
(800) 648-8857

The WPI combines into one test the Manson Evaluation that identifies the potential alcoholic personality and the Alcadd Test that measures extent of alcohol addiction in diagnosed alcoholics. Each subtest has norms for male and female alcoholics and nonalcoholics. Teleprocessing service also available. Instruction booklet included.

Classification: Diagnositic Aid, Substance Abuse

Hardware Requirements and Price
IBM PC, XT, AT, PS/2, & compatibles; 512 K; 1 Mb hard disk required; 1 disk drive. Printer required. Laser printer optional. Requires DOS 3.0. *Single User Price: $280.00*

Western Personnel Test (WPT)
Robert L. Gunn
Morse P. Manson
George J. Huba

Western Psychological Services
12031 Wilshire Blvd.
Los Angeles, CA 90025
(213) 478-2061
(800) 648-8857

The WPT is a 5-min, 24-item test of general intelligence, often employed as a personnel screening tool. Available in four equivalent forms, and in Spanish, the WPT has norms for the general population as well as professional, college, clerical, skilled, and unskilled populations. Instruction booklet included.

Classification: Vocational Testing

Hardware Requirements and Price
IBM PC, XT, AT, PS/2, & compatibles; 512 K; 1 Mb hard disk required; 1 disk drive. Printer required. Laser printer optional. Requires DOS 3.0. *Single User Price: $175.00 Price depends on number of administrations*

WISC III Analysis, Version 1.0
Terrance G. Lichtenwald

Happ Electronics, Inc.
3680 North Main Street

Oshkosh, WI 54901
(414) 231-5128

Menu-driven program for analyzing and reporting WISC III results. Features include automatic conversion from scaled and age scores, standard or customized reports, scatter analysis of subtests relative to the examiner's menus, percentile ranks and confidence levels for IQs, and Lutey's method factor analysis. Program also provides a shared abilities analysis, deviation IQ analysis, pair-wise comparisons among subtests, and generates clinical hypotheses and prescriptions. Price includes free updates.

Classification: WISC (Interpretive report)

Hardware Requirements and Price
Apple II, hard disk optional, 1 disk drive. *Single User Price: $200.00*

IBM PC, XT, AT, PS/2, & compatibles; hard disk optional; 1 disk drive. *Single User Price: $200.00*

WISC-III Report

Psychologistics, Inc.
P.O. Box 033896
Indialantic, FL 32903
(407) 259-7811

Provides scoring and interpretation of the WISC-III. The report is based on user-entered subtest scaled scores and IQ scores. The program calculates and displays 3 pages of derived scores. A 3-page narrative report is generated, including behavioral observations, if obtained. The narrative report may be printed or written to a text file, that can be modified by word processor. Detailed manual included. Latest release November, 1991.

Classification: WISC (Interpretive report)

Hardware Requirements and Price
IBM PC, XT, AT, PS/2, & compatibles; 256 K; hard disk optional; 1 disk drive. Printer required. Requires DOS 2.1. *Single User Price: $250.00*

WISC-III Writer: The Interpretive Software System

The Psychological Corporation
555 Academic Court
San Antonio, TX 78204-0952
(512) 299-1061
(800) 228-0752

Generates creative, comprehensive reports and converts raw scores to scaled scores, percentiles and IQ scores. Automatically incorporates correct grammar and punctuation; user can edit the report and cut and paste from provided scrapbooks. WISC-III Writer is the only software system authorized by the publisher of the WISC-III. Detailed manual included. On-line help available. Latest release August, 1992.

Classification: WISC (Interpretive report)

Hardware Requirements and Price
IBM PC, XT, AT, PS/2, & compatibles; 640 K; hard disk optional; 2 disk drives. Mouse optional. Laser printer optional. Requires DOS 3.1. *Single User Price: $179.00*

WISC-R Analysis II, Version 7.0
Terrance G. Lichtenwald

Happ Electronics, Inc.
3680 North Main Street

Oshkosh, WI 54901
(414) 231-5128

Menu-driven program for analyzing and reporting WISC-R results. Features include automatic conversion from raw to scaled age scores, standard or customized reports, scatter analysis of subtests relative to the examiner's means, percentile ranks and confidence levels for IQs, and Lutey's method factor analysis. The program also provides a shared abilities analysis, deviation IQ analysis, pair-wise comparisons among subtests, and generates clinical hypotheses and prescriptions. Price includes free updates. Detailed manual included. On-line help available.

Classification: WISC (Interpretive report)

Hardware Requirements and Price
Apple II, hard disk optional, 1 disk drive. Printer required. *Single User Price: $200.00*

IBM PC, XT, AT, PS/2, & compatibles; hard disk optional; 1 disk drive. Printer required. *Single User Price: $200.00*

WISC-R Analyst, WISC-III Analyst, WAIS-R Analyst, WPPSI-R Analyst
John Brockman

Heizer Software
Box 232019
Pleasant Hill, CA 94523
(510) 943-7667
(800) 888-7667

Analyzes and reports on results of the WISC-R, WISC-III, WAIS-R, and WPPSI-R and creates a presentation quality report with graphs. On-line help available. Tutorial program included. Latest release November, 1991.

Classification: Intelligence Testing (Interpretive report)

Hardware Requirements and Price
Macintosh, 1 Mb, hard disk optional, 1 disk drive (3-1/2). Mouse required. Modem optional. Laser printer optional. Requires System 6.0. Microsoft Excel required. *Single User Price: $25.00*

WISC-R Microcomputer-Assisted Interpretive Report

The Psychological Corporation
555 Academic Court
San Antonio, TX 78204-0952
(512) 299-1061
(800) 228-0752

Program produces in-depth analyses of WISC-R results. The 3- to 4-page interpretive report includes confidence intervals for IQs, significance and prevalence of verbal-performance differences, percentile ranks, and additional diagnostic information. The program also allows the examiner to enter information specific to the child and the testing situation. This is a licensed software program and a license agreement must be signed prior to shipment. Detailed manual included. Latest release 1986.

Classification: WISC (Interpretive report)

Hardware Requirements and Price
Apple II, 64 K, 1 disk drive (5-1/4). *Single User Price: $169.00 Per-test fees apply.*

IBM PC, XT, AT, PS/2, & compatibles; 128 K; 1 disk drive. Laser printer optional. *Single User Price: $169.00 Per-test fees apply.*

WISC-R Narrative Report

Psychological Testing Service
213 East Sugnet
Midland, MI 48642
(517) 631-9463
Fax: (517) 631-9419

This interpretive system produces detailed reports through analysis of IQ and subscale variations, patterns, and factors. This generates information and hypotheses that may not be readily recognizable as well as compiling information in narrative form to greatly reduce report writing time. Requires entry of VIQ, PIQ, FSQ, and subtest scaled scores. Instruction booklet included. Latest release April, 1991.

Classification: WISC (Interpretive report)

Hardware Requirements and Price
IBM PC, XT, AT, PS/2, & compatibles; 356 K; hard disk optional. Printer required. Laser printer optional. *Single User Price: $195.00*

WISC-Riter Complete

Southern Micro Systems
3545 S. Church Street
Burlington, NC 27215-2097
(919) 584-1661

Computer-assisted interpretation of the WISC-R that allows the user to add clinical observations, educational recommendations, or appropriate interpretive comments. A 6- to 7-page report is generated that provides subtest evaluations, standard score interpretation, verbal and performance scale achievement, severe discrepancy levels for verbal, performance, and full scale IQ, levels of factors and influences, reasons for subtest scaled scores that deviate from expected level, and educational recommendations.

Classification: WISC (Interpretive report)

Hardware Requirements and Price
Apple II, 2 disk drives. *Single User Price: $495.00*

IBM PC, XT, AT, PS/2, & compatibles; 2 disk drives. *Single User Price: $495.00*

Wisconsin Card Sorting Test: Computer Version (Research Edition), Version 1
Milton E. Harris
Robert Adler
Albert Kastl

Psychological Assessment Resources, Inc.
P.O. Box 998
Odessa, FL 33556
(800) 331-TEST

Menu-driven program administers the Wisconsin Card Sorting Test (WCST), and provides a scored protocol based on criteria developed by. Robert Heaton. Test stimuli are color reproductions of the print version, presented on a monitor. Responses are entered with a joystick for Apple, and on a standard keyboard for IBM. Test results may be saved on disk. The detailed manual describes an equivalency study using a computer version of the WCST. Latest release May 1, 1986.

Classification: Neuropsychological Testing (Administration and Interpretive report)

Hardware Requirements and Price
Apple II+, IIe, IIc; 64 K; 1 disk drive (5-1/4). Color display required. Not compatible with laser printer. Paddle or joystick required. *Single User Price: $245.00*

IBM PC, XT, AT, PS/2, & compatibles; 256 K; hard disk optional; 2 disk drives or 1 disk drive and hard disk. EGA or VGA display required. Laser printer optional. *Single User Price: $295.00*

Wisconsin Card Sorting Test: Scoring Program, Version 3
Milton E. Harris
Psychological Assessment Resources, Inc.
P.O. Box 998
Odessa, FL 33556
(800) 331-TEST

This scoring program accepts item responses from the WCST protocol and then produces a 1-page report that includes all indices calculated according to the criteria developed by Dr. Robert Heaton. Included is a special scoring form that may be used in administering the WCST which saves time in recording responses and entering data. Detailed manual included. Latest release December 10, 1990.

Classification: Neuropsychological Testing (Interpretive report)

Hardware Requirements and Price
IBM PC, XT, AT, PS/2, & compatibles; 256 K; hard disk optional; 2 disk drives. Laser printer optional. *Single User Price: $275.00*

Woodcock-Johnson Psycho-Educational Battery

Jay Hauger

DLM Teaching Resources
One DLM Park
Allen, TX 75002
(800) 527-4747

Scoring program for the Woodcock-Johnson Psycho-Educational Battery. Detailed manual included. Latest release 1984.

Classification: Woodcock-Johnson (Interpretive report)

Hardware Requirements and Price
Apple II, 64 K, hard disk optional, 2 disk drives (5-1/4). Printer required. *Single User Price: $125.00*

IBM PC, XT, AT, PS/2, & compatibles; 256 K; hard disk optional; 1 disk drive (5-1/4). Printer required. Requires DOS 2.1. *Single User Price: $125.00*

Woodcock Reading Mastery Tests-Revised ASSIST

Richard W. Woodcock

American Guidance Service
4201 Woodland Road
Circle Pines, MN 55014-1796
(612) 786-4343
(800) 328-2560

Converts raw scores into derived scores for both Woodcock Reading Mastery Tests-Revised (WRMT-R) Form G and Form H. Also can be used for the combined Form G and H. Provides W scores, grade equivalents, age equivalents, relative performance indexes, percentile ranks, standard scores, and NCE's (Normal Curve Equivalents). Detailed manual included. On-line help available.

Classification: Woodcock-Johnson (Interpretive report)

Hardware Requirements and Price
Apple II+, IIe, IIc, IIgs; 128 K; 2 disk drives. *Single User Price: $104.00*

IBM PC, XT, AT, PS/2, & compatibles; 512 K; hard disk optional; 2 disk drives. *Single User Price: $104.00*

Word Rater

Checkosky & Associates

London House/SRA
9701 W. Higgins Road
Rosemont, IL 60018
(708) 292-1900
(800) 221-8378

The test assesses basic and advanced typing skills. Subtests are also available for 10-key, text editing, proof reading, and data entry. Detailed manual included.

Classification: Vocational Testing (Administration)

Hardware Requirements and Price
IBM PC, XT, AT, PS/2, & compatibles; 2 disk drives. *Single User Price: $795.00*

Work Personality Profile

Brian Bolton
Richard Roessler

Arkansas Research & Training Center
P.O. Box 1358

Hot Springs, AR 71902-1779
(501) 624-4411

Menu-driven program produces a report that provides graphic profiles of the primary and secondary scales of the Work Personality Profile. Report also identifies problems that limit chances for employment. This program is sold only to recognized vocational rehabilitation agencies and facilities. Detailed manual included.

Classification: Vocational Testing (Interpretive report)

Hardware Requirements and Price
IBM PC, XT, AT, PS/2, & compatibles; 640 K; hard disk optional; 1 disk drive (5-1/4). Printer required. Laser printer optional. *Single User Price: $17.00*

Work Profiling System (WPS)

Saville & Holdsworth, Ltd.
575 Boylston Street
Boston, MA 02116
(617) 236-1550
(800) 899-7451

An integrated job analysis software system that allows a single detailed analysis of a job to be used for multiple applications, with particular emphasis on job-person matching for selection and development. WPS uses a series of structured questions to assess any job at any level of an organization. Key job tasks are identified as well as an attribute profile of personality and ability traits needed to perform those tasks. Program defines assessment methods and provides an index of person-job match when candidate test scores are entered into the system. Appropriate for use in selection, development, and training. Detailed manual

included. On-line help available. Latest release November 1, 1991.

Classification: Industrial Consulting

Hardware Requirements and Price
IBM PC, XT, AT, PS/2, & compatibles; 2 Mb; 45 Mb hard disk required; 1 disk drive. Mouse optional. 2400 baud modem required. Postscript laser printer required. *Single User Price: $6,000.00 Network Price: $6,000.00 Per administration fee applies*

WPPSI Analysis II, Version 7.0
Terrance G. Lichtenwald

Happ Electronics, Inc.
3680 North Main Street
Oshkosh, WI 54901
(414) 231-5128

Menu-driven program for analyzing and reporting results on the Wechsler Preschool and Primary Scale of Intelligence (WPPSI). Features include automatic conversion from raw to scaled age scores, standard or customized reports, scatter analysis of subtests relative to the examiner's means, percentile ranks and confidence intervals for IQs, and Lutey's method factor analysis. A program option allows any combination of subtests to be analyzed. Detailed manual included. On-line help available.

Classification: WPPSI (Interpretive report)

Hardware Requirements and Price
Apple II, hard disk optional, 1 disk drive. *Single User Price: $200.00*

IBM PC, XT, AT, PS/2, & compatibles; hard disk optional; 1 disk drive. *Single User Price: $200.00*

WPPSI Report, Version 2.0

Psychologistics, Inc.
P.O. Box 033896
Indialantic, FL 32903
(407) 259-7811

Automated interpretation of the WPPSI (Wechsler Preschool and Primary Scale of Intelligence) that includes relevant demographic data, scaled scores, and optional behavioral observations. Narrative section consists of a summary of demographic data and scores, description of child and test behavior, description and interpretation of test results, estimated levels of potential academic functioning, variability, strengths and weaknesses, and implications. Specific recommendations are also made for further evaluation. Detailed manual included. Latest release 1985.

Classification: WPPSI (Interpretive report)

Hardware Requirements and Price
Apple II, 48 K, hard disk optional, 1 disk drive (5-1/4). Printer required. Requires DOS 3.3. *Single User Price: $200.00*

IBM PC, XT, AT, PS/2, & compatibles; 128 K; hard disk optional; 1 disk drive. Printer required. Requires DOS 2.0. *Single User Price: $200.00*

WPPSI-R Writer: The Interpretive Software System

The Psychological Corporation
555 Academic Court
San Antonio, TX 78204-0952
(512) 299-1061
(800) 228-0752

Produces creative, comprehensive reports for the Wechsler Preschool and Primary Scale of Intelligence-Revised (WPPSI-R). WPPSI-R includes mouse support, hot keys, help keys, pop-up menus, windows, batch printing capability, color and monochrome compatibility, and counterless programming to allow an unlimited number of reports. It accepts both raw scores and scaled scores, and converts scaled scores to percentiles, age equivalents, and IQ scores, automatically developing a profile analysis. When inputting scores, examiners can select an appropriate confidence level that WPPSI-R Writer will use to report subsequent test results. Scrapbooks form an integral part of the system and allow the examiner to write, edit, and store recommendations and frequently-used interpretive information that can be included in narrative reports as appropriate. A personal notes feature allows the examiner to store observations and information that needs to remain confidential. If desired, portions of personal notes may also be copied into the reports. Detailed manual included. On-line help available. Latest release 1990.

Classification: WPPSI (Interpretive report)

Hardware Requirements and Price
IBM PC, XT, AT, PS/2, & compatibles; 640 K; 720 K hard disk optional; 2 disk drives. Mouse optional. Laser printer optional. *Single User Price: $179.00*

STATISTICS
AND
RESEARCH
SOFTWARE

3-D Keyboard for Windows
Peter Cassetta
Slava Paperno

Exceller Software Corporation
223 Langmuir Lab
Ithaca, NY 14850
(607) 257-5634
(800) 426-0444

Permits word processing in all Western European languages by enabling personal computers to write foreign language characters and special symbols. Allows user to switch between English and any European language with one keystroke. Makes all Windows applications in English work in Spanish, French, German, Italian, Portuguese, Dutch, Scandinavian, and others. On-line help available. Latest release September, 1991.

Classification: Word Processing

Hardware Requirements and Price
IBM PC, XT, AT, PS/2, & compatibles; hard disk required; 1 disk drive (3-1/2). EGA or VGA display. Mouse required. Modem optional. Laser printer optional. Requires Windows 3.0. *Single User Price: $99.00 Network Price: $295.00*

ABC
Michael J. Kahana
Douglas K. Detterman

Department of Psychology
University of Toronto
Toronto, ON M5S-1A1 Canada
(416) 978-8811

A program to convert PsycLit CD-ROM abstracts into APA-style bibliographies. Latest release January, 1990.

Classification: Database

Hardware Requirements and Price
IBM PC, XT, AT, PS/2, & compatibles; 256 K; 1 disk drive. *Single User Price: Free. Send self addressed disk mailer with formatted disk.*

Reviews
Kahana, M. J., & Detterman D. K. (1989). ABC: A program to convert PsycLit CD-ROM abstracts into APA-style bibliographies. *Behavior, Research Methods, Instrumentation, and Computers, 21,* 414.

Absurut
Edwin R. Anderson

Anderson-Bell
Department 458
P.O. Box 5160
Arvada, CO 80005
(303) 940-0595
(800) 745-9751

Survey research tool for input, reporting, and analysis of questionnaire data. Banner and stub report format with up to 30 character value labeling. Reusable choice tables make file setup easy. Questions can be multiple-choice, all-that-apply, numeric, and open-ended. Also includes the full statistical analysis capability of companion product, ABstat. Files are compatible with Lotus, dBASE, and ASCII. Can be used with OMR scanners. Student version available. Educational quantity discounts. Detailed manual and tutorial program included. On-line help available. Latest release September 9, 1991.

Classification: Data Management

Hardware Requirements and Price
IBM PC, XT, AT, PS/2, & compatibles; 320 K; hard disk optional; 2 disk drives. Graphic display required. Laser printer optional. *Single User Price: $449.00*

Acro Spin
Dave Parker

Pacific Ease Company
601 Pacific Street
Santa Monica, CA 90405
(310) 396-5007

Program for rotating three-dimensional (3-D) points and lines in real time. Used in statistics for rotating and viewing 3-5 dimensional data sets. Can be used to rotate any drawing produced by popular 3-D CAD packages. Programmer's routines utilizing these algorithms are also available. Detailed manual included. Latest release July, 1991.

Classification: Graphics

Hardware Requirements and Price
IBM PC, XT, AT, PS/2, & compatibles; 256 K; 500 K hard disk optional; 1 disk drive. Hercules, CGA, EGA, or VGA display. *Single User Price: $30.00*

ACS Query

Analytical Computer Software, Inc.
434 Sandford Avenue

Westfield, NJ 07090
(908) 232-2723

Computerized interviewing software. Detailed manual included. Latest release February, 1992.

Classification: Test Development

Hardware Requirements and Price
IBM PC, XT, AT, PS/2, & compatibles; 640 K; hard disk optional. Monochrome or color display. Mouse optional. Modem optional. Printer required. Laser printer optional. Need 386 file server for network version. *Single User Price: $5,000.00 or $1 per interview Network Price: $5,000.00 (per work station)*

Reviews
Carpenter, E. H. (1988). Software tools for data collection: Microcomputer-assisted interviewing. *Social Science Computer Review, 6,* 353-368.

User Site References
Tom Borris, Market Facts, Inc., 1010 Lake Street, Oak Park, IL, 60610, (708) 524-2001

Adaptive Perceptual Mapping (APM) System

Sawtooth Software, Inc.
1007 Church Street
Evanston, IL 60201
(708) 866-0870

Interviewing software that helps researchers determine how products or items compare to each other on image-related attributes. Detailed manual included.

Classification: Test Development

Hardware Requirements and Price
IBM PC, XT, AT, PS/2, & compatibles; 256 K; hard disk required. Printer required (132 column). *Single User Price: $1,500.00 and up*

Reviews
Baumer, J. (1988). Adaptive perceptual mapping (APM) system. *Social Science Computer Review, 6*, 297-298.

Algorithm for Sorting Grouped Data
NASA Jet Propulsion Lab

COSMIC
The University of Georgia
382 East Broad Street
Athens, GA 30602
(404) 542-3265

Sorts data in ascending or descending order. Can be used with multiple sets of data when data set involves several measures. BASIC source code included. Detailed manual included. Latest release 1987.

Classification: Data Management

Hardware Requirements and Price
IBM PC, XT, AT, PS/2, & compatibles; 40 K; hard disk optional; 1 disk drive (5-1/4). *Single User Price: $50.00*

Analogy
Diane J. Schiano
Don Barch

Psychology Department
Stanford University
Stanford, CA 94305
(415) 604-3665

This program represents a new approach to research on spatial aptitude. Photo-digitized figural analogy problem terms, similar to those used in standardized ability tests, are arrayed in zones on the computer screen (A:B::C::D1...D5). Each term is visible only when selected with the mouse. Two viewing modes are possible: *Sequential*–in which all terms are made visible one at a time, or *simultaneous*–in which problem terms are viewed sequentially, but all five multiple-choice answer alternatives are made visible at once. For testing, the program simply records zone viewing pattern and duration (msec) for each problem, as well as the answer alternative chosen. No feedback is given to the subject. For training, another version of the program provides the subject with speed and accuracy feedback. The problem is then repeated until the subject responds correctly. The experimenter can choose to randomize answer term zone positions for problem re-presentation. Viewing pattern/duration and accuracy data can be analyzed to assess problem encoding and solution strategies. The number and sequence of problems is determined by the experimenter and all problem trials are subject-initiated. Three practice and 50 test problems are available. Instruction booklet included. Latest release 1990.

Classification: Research Aid

Hardware Requirements and Price
Amiga, 20 Mb hard disk required, 1 disk drive (3-1/2). Requires Amigados. *Single User Price: Free, shipping only.*

Reviews
Software Review: Analogy. (1990). *Behavior, Research Methods, Instrumentation, and Computers, 22*, 136-7.

User Site References
M. McBeath, Research Associate, NASA/ Ames Research Center, MS262-3 NASA/ Ames Research Center, Moffett Field, CA, 94035, (415) 604-3665
Ann Marie Medina, Research Assistant, Stanford University, Psychology Department, Stanford University, Stanford, CA, 94305
Colin Tam, Research Assistant, San Jose State University, Psychology Department, San Jose State University, San Jose, CA, 95192

Multi Drive 1.4
Robert F. Westall

Maclaboratory Inc.
314 Exeter Road
Devon, PA 19333
(215) 688-3114

A hard disk partitioning system that is particularly useful for academic computing laboratories. It provides virus free operation and protection from corruption of systems and files. It is compatible with all Apple SCSI drives and the Maclaboratory for Psychology software suite. Instruction booklet included. Latest release September, 1991.

Classification: Other

Hardware Requirements and Price
Macintosh, 20 Mb hard disk required, 1 disk drive. Monochrome or color display. Mouse required. Modem optional. Laser printer optional. Requires System 6.0.5 or later. *Single User Price: $79.95*

> The Statistics and Research Software section describes 208 programs that can be helpful for data gathering, analysis, and reporting.

Analysis of Variance With Up To Three Factors
Allen H. Wolach

Department of Psychology
Illinois Institute of Technology
Chicago, IL 60616
(312) 567-3500

Package provides analyses of variance with up to three factors. Program supports independent groups, randomized blocks, split-plot, and randomized block factorial designs. Any or all of the factors can be repeated measures. Independent groups' factors do not require equal numbers of subjects across levels. Programs calculate probabilities for F values and all means required for follow-up tests. Detailed manual included.

Classification: ANOVA

Hardware Requirements and Price
IBM PC, XT, AT, PS/2, & compatibles; 256 K; hard disk optional; 1 disk drive. Laser printer optional. *Single User Price: $20.00*

User Site References
Jerome Feldman, State College of Optometry, 100 East 24th Street, New York, NY, 10010, (212) 420-4986

ANDISP
Laurence Guentert

Department of Biological Sciences
Purdue University
West Lafayette, IN 47907
(317) 494-4972

A Turbo Pascal program that analyses, displays, and manipulates sampled data recorded with a PC-compatible data-acquisition system. On-line help available. Latest release October, 1991.

Classification: Data Management

Hardware Requirements and Price
IBM PC, XT, AT, PS/2, & compatibles; 256 K. EGA display. Requires DOS 2.0. *Single User Price: Free*

Reviews
Guentert, L. (1990). ANDISP: A Turbo Pascal program to analyze and display sampled data. *Behavior, Research Methods, Instrumentation, and Computers, 22,* 471-474.

ANOVA Latin Squares, and ANOCOVA Analysis Programs
Allen H. Wolach

Department of Psychology
Illinois Institute of Technology
Chicago, IL 60616
(312) 567-3500

A package of 14 programs, including analysis of variance with repeated measures on any or all factors. Detailed manual included.

Classification: ANOVA

Hardware Requirements and Price
IBM PC, XT, AT, PS/2, & compatibles; 256 K; hard disk optional; 1 disk drive. Monochrome, CGA, EGA, or VGA display. Laser printer optional. *Single User Price: $20.00*

Reviews
Wolach A. H. (1988). ANOVA, Latin Square, and ANOCOVA for IBM-compatible microcomputer systems. *Behavior, Research*

Methods, Instrumentation, and Computers, 20, 585-586.

ANOVMODL.BAS
Allen H. Wolach
Maureen A. McHale

Department of Psychology
Illinois Institute of Technology
Chicago, IL 60616
(312) 567-3500

Program determines degrees of freedom and mean squares for a variety of fixed, mixed, and random model ANOVA. Instruction booklet included.

Classification: ANOVA

Hardware Requirements and Price
IBM PC, XT, AT, PS/2, & compatibles; 128 K; hard disk optional; 1 disk drive. Laser printer optional. *Single User Price: $1.00*

Reviews
Wolach, A. H., & McHale, M. A. (1987). F ratios and quasi F ratios for fixed, mixed, and random model ANOVAs. *Behavior, Research Methods, Instrumentation, and Computers, 19,* 409-412.

Answer Scan
Michael E. Mills

Psytek Services
6401 West 81st Street
Los Angeles, CA 90045
(213) 670-4655
(800) 392-5454

Creates an output file of a respondent's answers to a scanned answer sheet. Users may custom design their own answer sheets. No special paper or scanners are required. Answer Scan eliminates the need to code data into the computer by hand. Excellent for researchers and any one who uses tests or surveys. Requires graphics scanner and OCR software. Detailed manual included. On-line help available. Latest release November 1, 1991.

Classification: Data Management

Hardware Requirements and Price
IBM PC, XT, AT, PS/2, & compatibles; 512 K; hard disk optional. Monochrome, CGA, EGA, or VGA display. Laser printer optional. *Single User Price: $49.00 Site License: $99.00 30-day money back guarantee.*

Apple Tachistoscope System
Dermot M. Bowler

Psychology Division
City University
London, UK ECIV OHB England
440712534399

Set of programs that control slide projectors and shutters in order to simulate a two-field tachistoscope. Instruction booklet included.

Classification: Equipment Control

Hardware Requirements and Price
Apple II+, 48 K, 1 disk drive. Carousel projector with electronic shutter. *Single User Price: $2.00*

Reviews
Bowler, D. M. (1987). Using an Apple II to control a two-field projection tachistoscope.

Behavior, Research Methods, Instrumentation, and Computers, 19, 377-379.

Autogenic Systems Software

Autogenic Systems
620 Wheat Lane
Wood Dale, IL 60191
(708) 860-9700

Software for computerized physiological recording and biofeedback systems. Detailed manual included.

Classification: Equipment Control

Hardware Requirements and Price
IBM PC, XT, AT, PS/2, & compatibles; 512 K; hard disk required; 2 disk drives. CGA or EGA display. Mouse optional. Laser printer optional. *Single User Price: Contact publisher*

A BASIC Program For Computing Cronbach's Accuracy Components
John O. Brooks III
Laura L. Brooks

Department of Psychiatry & Behavioral Sciences (TD-114)
Stanford University School of Medicine
Stanford, CA 94305-5490
(415) 493-5000

This program computes all four components of Cronbach's accuracy (elevation, differential elevation, stereotype accuracy, and differential accuracy) as well as the associated correlation components. The standard Macintosh interface is used to obtain all necessary information. The program reads data from standard text files.

Classification: Survey Analysis

Hardware Requirements and Price
Apple II, 1 Mb, hard disk optional. *Single User Price: $6.00*

Macintosh. Math coprocessor optional. *Single User Price: $6.00*

A BASIC Program to Compute Fisher's Exact Test
Richard G. Graf
Edward F. Alf

Alfagrafics
1716 Eolus
Levcadia, CA 92024
(619) 594-5364

A BASIC program that computes Fisher's exact test for significance of association in 2 X 2 tables. Computations are ordered to avoid overflow, even in samples of 1,000 or more observations. Instruction booklet included.

Classification: Nonparametric Test

Hardware Requirements and Price
BASIC program listing. *Single User Price: Free*

Reviews
Graf, R. G., & Alf, E. F. (1987). A BASIC program to compute Fisher's exact test. *Educational & Psychological Measurement*, *47*(1), 139-140.

BASIC Programs for Prediction of Analysis of Cross Classifications
Alexander von Eye
Gunter Krampen

College of Human Development
Pennsylvania State University
University Park, PA 16802
(814) 865-1447

Prediction analysis of cross classification is a procedure that tests simultaneous point predictions. This program computes expected frequencies using maximum likelihood estimators, performs the binomial test, and determines all descriptive measures.

Classification: Statistical Test

Hardware Requirements and Price
Contact author for equipment requirements. *Single User Price: Contact author*

Reviews
Von Eye, A., & Krampen, G. (1987). BASIC programs for prediction of analysis of cross classification. *Educational & Psychological Measurement*, *46*(1), 141-143.

Basic Programs to Determine Sample Size & Exact Power in ANOVA Designs
Richard G. Graf
Edward F. Alf

Alfagrafics
1716 Eolus
Levcadia, CA 92024
(619) 594-5364

Calculates sample size (n) to achieve desired power. Calculates power (to 5 decimal points) when df1, df2, alpha, and phi are provided. Instruction booklet included.

Classification: Power Analysis

Reviews

Graf, R. G, & Alf, E. F. (1990). Basic programs to determine sample size & exact power in ANOVA designs. *Educational & Psychological Measurement, 50*(1), 117-122.

The Binomial Probability Distributions

Rocketdyne

COSMIC
The University of Georgia
382 East Broad Street
Athens, GA 30602
(404) 542-3265

Program predicts the success or failure of an event and generates plots for various scenarios. Can combine probabilities in series or in parallel, calculate levels of confidence, and map a trail for user reference. BASIC source code included. Detailed manual included. Latest release 1987.

Classification: Statistical Test

Hardware Requirements and Price
IBM PC, XT, AT, PS/2, & compatibles; 300 K; hard disk optional; 1 disk drive (5-1/4). *Single User Price: $150.00*

Blink

Terry D. Blumenthal
Joseph A. Cooper

Department of Psychology
Wake Forest University
Winston-Salem, NC 27109
(919) 759-5531

Turbo Pascal program for the control of stimulus presentation and measurement with peripheral devices. Detailed manual included. Latest release May 1, 1990.

Classification: Equipment Control

Hardware Requirements and Price
Macintosh, 1 Mb, 20 Mb hard disk required, 1 disk drive. Mouse optional. Modem optional. Laser printer optional. Requires System 6.0 and Turbo Pascal. *Single User Price: Free*

Reviews
Blumenthal, T. D., & Cooper J. A. (1990). Using the Macintosh computer in psyhophysiological research: Programs for stimulus presentation, data collection, and response quantification. *Behavior, Research Methods, Instrumentation, and Computers, 22,* 99-104.

BrainMaker

California Scientific Software
10024 Newtown Road
Nevada City, CA 95959
(916) 478-9040
(800) 284-8112

BrainMaker uses the same architecture as the human brain to give the computer human-like abilities such as finding relationships and pattern in data, and learning from the past. Detailed manual included. Latest release January, 1991.

Classification: Expert Systems

Hardware Requirements and Price
IBM PC, XT, AT, PS/2, & compatibles; 256 K; 1 Mb hard disk required. Hercules, CGA,

EGA, or VGA display. Mouse optional. Modem optional. Laser printer optional. Requires DOS 3.0. *Single User Price: $195.00 (Standard Version 2.3)*

IBM PC, XT, AT, PS/2, & compatibles; 512 K; 1 Mb hard disk required; 1 disk drive. Hercules, EGA, CGA, or VGA display. Mouse optional. Modem optional. Laser printer optional. Requires DOS 3.0. *Single User Price: $795.00 (Professional Version 2.0)*

Macintosh, 512 K, 1 Mb hard disk optional, 1 disk drive. Mouse required. Modem optional. Laser printer optional. Requires System 4. *Single User Price: $195.00*

Reviews

Austin, Dawson, & Weinberg. (1991). Nuclear grading of breast carcinoma by image analysis. *A.I.C.P., 95*(4), 529-537.

BrainMaker with Netmaker. (1990). *Social Science Computer Review, 8*(3), 473-476.

Kestelyn, J. (1991). Medical neural networks. *AI Expert,* 71-72.

Brass
Mark Cunningham

Crofter Publishing
4310 South Semoran, #690
Orlando, FL 32822

A collection of apparatus and instruments in the form of BASIC and machine language routines, that the user wires together with Calls and Gosubs to create a well equipped laboratory. There are also demonstration programs that can be used in class and as models for experimental apparatus. Includes tachistoscope, memory drums, timers and clocks, graphics page-movers and switches, tone

generator, programming utilities, and more. Detailed manual included.

Classification: Research Aid

Hardware Requirements and Price
Apple II+, IIe, IIc, IIgs; 64 K; hard disk optional; 1 disk drive (5-1/4). Requires ProDOS. *Single User Price: $50.00*

IBM PC, XT, AT, PS/2, & compatibles; 256 K; hard disk optional; 1 disk drive (5-1/4). CGA display required. Requires DOS 2.1. *Single User Price: $80.00*

Bubble Publishing
Ronald F. Schlangen

Scanning Dynamics, Inc.
P.O. Box 31080
Minneapolis, MN 55431
(612) 893-9166

Enables users to develop tests, surveys, and data collection sheets on their personal computers (PC), print the forms on plain paper laser printers, scan them on standard OMR scanners, score them on their PC's, report the results, and establish ASCII files for submission to other software packages. "Preslugging" allows the user to preset a different ID number for each form and print a corresponding name for each ID number. Detailed manual included. On-line help available.

Classification: Test Development

Hardware Requirements and Price
IBM PC, XT, AT, PS/2, & compatibles; 640 K; hard disk required; 1 disk drive. Monochrome or color display. Laser printer required (HP LaserJet). Scanner required. *Single User Price: $715.50 (educational discount)*

User Site References
David Dudycha, Administrative Assistant, Research and Development, Minneapolis Public Schools, 807 Northeast Broadway, Minneapolis, MN, 55413-2398

Cases

Computer-Assisted Survey Methods Program
University of California
2538 Channing Way
Berkeley, CA 94720
(510) 642-6592

Computerized interviewing software. Detailed manual included. Latest release October, 1991.

Classification: Survey Administration

Hardware Requirements and Price
IBM PC, XT, AT, PS/2, & compatibles; 640 K; 2 Mb hard disk optional. Modem optional. Laser printer optional. Requires DOS 3.1. *Single User Price: $600.00 (per year) Network Price: $2,500-$10,000 (per year) Annual fee based on hours of use*

Sun 3, 4, or 286i; 2 Mb hard disk required. Modem optional. Laser printer optional. *Network Price: $2,500-$10,000 (per year) Annual fee based on hours of use*

DEC VAX, 2 Mb hard disk required. Modem optional. Laser printer optional. *Network Price: $2,500-$10,000 (per year) Annual fee based on hours of use*

Reviews
Carpenter, E. H. (1988). Software tools for data collection: Microcomputer-assisted interviewing. *Social Science Computer Review*, 6, 353-368.

User Site References
John Kennedy, Institute for Social Research, Indiana University, 1022 East Third Street, Bloomington, IN, 47401, (812) 855-2573
Suzanne Parker, Survey Research Center, Florida State University, Tallahassee, FL, 32306, (904) 644-5415
David Uglow, Office of Prices and Living Conditions, US Bureau of Labor Statistics, 600 East Street NW, Room 5217, Washington, DC, 20212, (202) 272-2323

Ci2 System for Computer Interviewing

Sawtooth Software, Inc.
1007 Church Street
Evanston, IL 60201
(708) 866-0870

A computer-interactive interviewing system that allows the creation and administration of a questionnaire, administers the questionnaire, and analyzes data. Detailed manual included.

Classification: Survey Administration

Hardware Requirements and Price
IBM PC, XT, AT, PS/2, & compatibles; 256 K; hard disk optional. *Single User Price: $500.00*

Ci3 System for Advanced Computer Interviewing

Sawtooth Software, Inc.
1007 Church Street
Evanston, IL 60201
(708) 866-0870

Program allows computer-interactive interviewing with such advanced features as "rosters" and list-handling capabilities. Intended for researchers with long or repetitive questionnaires. Detailed manual included. Latest release January, 1992.

Classification: Survey Administration

Hardware Requirements and Price
IBM PC, XT, AT, PS/2, & compatibles; 640 K; hard disk required; 1 disk drive. *Single User Price: $500.00 and up*

CLIPS 5.0
NASA Johnson Space Center

COSMIC
The University of Georgia
382 East Broad Street
Athens, GA 30602
(404) 542-3265

CLIPS (C Language Integrated Production System) is a complete environment for developing expert systems–programs intended to model human expertise or knowledge. Users can develop expert system software using rule-based programming, object-oriented programming, procedural programming, or combinations of the three. Source code and detailed manual included. Latest release June, 1991.

Classification: Expert Systems

Hardware Requirements and Price
IBM PC, XT, AT, PS/2, & compatibles; 256 K; 1 Mb hard disk required; 1 disk drive (5-1/4). *Single User Price: $490.00*

Macintosh, 1 Mb hard disk required, 1 disk drive. *Single User Price: $490.00*

Sun 3, 4, or 286i, 1 Mb hard disk required. *Single User Price: $490.00*

Cohen.Bas
Julia L. Bienias

Department of Biostatistics
Harvard School of Public Health
677 Huntington Avenue
Boston, MA 02115
(617) 432-1056

BASIC program using J. Cohen and P. Cohen's formula for testing correlations for homogeneity. Instruction booklet included. Latest release August, 1986.

Classification: Statistical Test

Hardware Requirements and Price
IBM PC, XT, AT, PS/2, & compatibles; hard disk optional; 1 disk drive (5-1/4). Laser printer optional. *Single User Price: Free, send self-addressed, stamped envelope. Code may be typed into any system*

Reviews
Bienias, J. L. (1987). Two BASIC programs to compare elements within and among correlation matrices. *Behavior, Research Methods, Instrumentation, and Computers, 19,* 57-58.

Color Card Pro
Douglas L. Chute

Maclaboratory, Inc.
314 Exeter Road
Devon, PA 19333
(215) 688-3114

An update and revision of Color Card 2.0, a series of graphic, window, presentation, and programming extensions to Hypercard. Color Card is commonly used as a lecture or presentation vehicle for high level graphic, video, and sound display. Detailed manual and tutorial program included. On-line help available. Latest release October, 1991.

Classification: Graphics

Hardware Requirements and Price
Macintosh, 2 Mb, 20 Mb hard disk required, 1 disk drive. Monochrome supported but color preferred. Mouse required. Modem optional. Laser printer optional. Requires System 7.0. *Single User Price: $79.95*

Commodore Statistical Package
David J. Pittenger
Milton H. Hodge

Department of Psychology
University of Georgia
Athens, GA 30602
(404) 542-2174

A set of BASIC programs to perform data file manipulations, descriptive statistical analyses, correlation, regression, data transformations, analysis of variance, multiple comparisons, and permutation/combination calculations. Detailed manual included.

Classification: Statistical Package

Hardware Requirements and Price
Commodore 64, 64 K, 1 disk drive. Printer required. *Single User Price: $10.00*

Reviews
Pittenger, D. J., & Hodge, M. H. (1986). Statistical programs for Commodore compu-

ters. *Behavior, Research Methods, Instrumentation, and Computers, 18*, 50-52.

Commodore Statistics
David J. Pittenger

Department of Psychology
Marietta College
Marietta, OH 45750-3031
(614) 374-4749

Program performs common statistical procedures including descriptive statistics, correlations, multiple-linear regression, ANOVA (with up to 9 variables), calculation of permutations and combinations, and random numbers. Detailed manual included.

Classification: Statistical Package

Hardware Requirements and Price
Commodore 64, 32 K, 1 disk drive. Printer required. *Single User Price: $10.00*

Commodore P.E.T. Model 8032, 1 disk drive. Printer required. *Single User Price: $10.00*

COMPsych
Margaret Anderson
Peter Hornby
David Bozak

Department of Psychology
State University of New York
Plattsburg, NY 12901
(518) 564-3372

COMPsych is a clearinghouse for software information related to psychology instruction, research, and practice. The system provides four major services: a catalog of descriptive information about available software, a directory of software users, a message system for sharing information among users, and an announcement service for conferences, job openings, and other information. COMPsych is accessible via modem, electronic mail, or physical mail. There is no charge to software developers, publishers, or users who access the system electronically.

Classification: Database

Hardware Requirements and Price
Contact vendor for hardware options. 1200 baud modem required. *Single User Price: Free*

Reviews
Anderson, M., Hornby, P., & Bozak, D. (1988) A computerized system to disseminate information about psychological software. *Behavior, Research Methods, Instrumentation, and Computers, 20,* 243-245.

Computing Interrater Reliability
John O. Brooks, III
Laura L. Brooks

Department of Psychiatry & Behavioral Sciences (TD-114)
Stanford University School of Medicine
Stanford, CA 94305-5490
(415) 493-5000

Computes interrater reliability by averaging, for each rater, the correlations between one rater's ratings and every other rater's ratings. For situations in which raters rate more than one subject, reliabilities can be computed for either each item or each ratee. The program reads data from a text file and puts the reliability coefficients into a text file. The standard Macintosh interface is implemented. This Quick-BASIC program is distributed both as a listing and in compiled form.

Classification: Survey Analysis

Hardware Requirements and Price
Macintosh. Math coprocessor optional. *Single User Price: $6.00*

Concept Formation Task
Michael J Strube

Department of Psychology
Washington University
St. Louis, MO 63130

This concept formation program uses visual stimuli to try to induce response-outcome noncontingency. On-line help available. Latest release 1988.

Classification: Research Aid

Hardware Requirements and Price
Commodore 64 or 128, 1 disk drive. Not compatible with laser printer. *Single User Price: Free program listing*

Reviews
Strube, M. (1988). Three computer-automated social psychology laboratory tasks. *Behavior, Research Methods, Instrumentation, and Computers, 20,* 557-559.

Confidence Intervals, Effect Size, and Statistical Power: A Computer Program
Michael Borenstein
Jacob Cohen

Lawrence Erlbaum Associates
P.O. Box 3407
New Hyde Park, NY 11040
(201) 692-8155

To plan or interpret a study, the user specifies the population parameters (e.g., mean and *SD*) and sample size. The program reports the study's power and the confidence intervals about the effect and displays the magnitude of the effect. For example, the user enters the mean and *SD* for two groups, (or simply the *p*-value from a completed study) and the program displays the standardized difference, the point biserial correlation (equivalent to the BESD), and the proportion of variance explained–along with confidence intervals about each index. The user planning a study may press a function key to repeatedly increase the sample size until the power is sufficiently high and/or the confidence intervals are sufficiently narrow. The program will create tables and graphs of confidence intervals and/or power as a function of sample size. All results may be printed immediately, sent to disk for inclusion in reports, or used to generate slides. The program includes modules for various study designs, with effect-size indices appropriate for each (e.g., odds ratio, predictive value). Features drop-down menus. Detailed manual included. On-line help available. Latest release June, 1992.

Classification: Power Analysis

Hardware Requirements and Price
IBM PC, XT, AT, PS/2, & compatibles; 512 K; hard disk optional; 1 disk drive. Laser printer optional. *Single User Price: $145.00 A free demo disk is available*

Reviews
Cohen, J. (1990). Things I have learned (So far). *American Psychologist, 45*(12), 1304-1312.

Contingency Judgment Task
Michael J Strube

Department of Psychology
Washington University
St. Louis, MO 63130

BASIC program using the multiple-trial binary choice task. On-line help available. Latest release 1988.

Classification: Research Aid

Hardware Requirements and Price
Commodore, 1 disk drive. Not compatible with laser printer. Requires Commodore. *Single User Price: Free listing available.*

Reviews
Strube, M. (1988). Three computer-automated social psychology laboratory tasks. *Behavior, Research Methods, Instrumentation, and Computers, 20*, 557-559.

Conversational Survey Analysis (CSA)

Computer-Assisted Survey Methods Program
University of California
2538 Channing Way
Berkeley, CA 94720
(510) 642-6592

Interactive programs for the description and analysis of survey data. Detailed manual included. Latest release May, 1989.

Classification: Survey Analysis

Hardware Requirements and Price
IBM PC, XT, AT, PS/2, & compatibles; 640 K; 3 Mb hard disk required; 1 disk drive. Laser printer optional. Requires DOS 3.1. Includes CASES Software. *Single User Price: $600.00 (per year) Network Price: $2,500-$10,000 (per year) Annual fee based on hours of use*

Sun 3, 4, or 286i; 3 Mb hard disk required. Laser printer optional. Includes CASES Software. *Network Price: $2,500-$10,000 (per year) Annual fee based on hours of use*

User Site References
John Kennedy, Institute for Social Research, Indiana University, 1022 East Third Street, Bloomington, IN, 47401, (812) 855-2573
Suzanne Parker, Survey Research Center, Florida State University, Tallahassee, FL, 32306, (904) 644-5415
Paul Sniderman, Department of Political Science, Stanford University, Building 160, Stanford, CA, 94305, (510) 642-3079

Correlational Analysis

Department of Psychology
Illinois Institute of Technology
Chicago, IL 60616
(312) 567-3500

Programs are included for the following correlational situations: Pearson Product Moment Correlation Coefficient, Partial Correlation with Pearson, Spearman Correlation Coefficient, Tau Coefficient, Partial Correlation with Tau, Kappa, W, Eta, Biserial, Point Biserial, Tetrachoric, C, Phi, C, and Multiple Regression. Detailed manual included.

Classification: Correlation and Regression

Hardware Requirements and Price
IBM PC, XT, AT, PS/2, & compatibles; 256 K; hard disk optional; 1 disk drive. Laser printer optional. *Single User Price: $15.00*

User Site References
Jerome Feldman, State College of Optometry, 100 East 24th Street, New York, NY, 10010, (212) 420-4986

A-Cross

Analytical Computer Software, Inc.
434 Sandford Avenue
Westfield, NJ 07090
(908) 232-2773

PC Board cross tabulation software. Detailed manual included. Latest release October, 1990.

Classification: Nonparametric Test

Hardware Requirements and Price
IBM PC, XT, AT, PS/2, & compatibles; 512 K; 10 Mb hard disk required; 1 disk drive. Monochrome or color display. Mouse optional. Modem optional. Printer required. Laser printer optional. *Single User Price: $995.00*

Crosstat
Herbert F. Weisberg

William C. Brown Publishers
2460 Kerper Blvd.
Dubuque, IA 52001

(319) 588-1451
(800) 351-7671

This program calculates 25 measures of association for a table. User inputs all frequencies from keyboard. Allows table to be collapsed for sensitivity analysis. Detailed manual included.

Classification: Statistical Test

Hardware Requirements and Price
IBM PC, XT, AT, PS/2, & compatibles; 256 K; hard disk optional; 1 disk drive. *Single User Price: $30.00 Site License: $400.00*

Crunch - Version 4

Crunch Software Corporation
5335 College Avenue, Suite 27
Oakland, CA 94618-1450
(510) 420-8660
(800) 999-7828
Fax: (510) 420-8174

A comprehensive set of statistical procedures for the analysis of marketing, survey, regression, and experimental research data. Included is a full range of utilities for the management of large numerical data sets. Detailed manual included. On-line help available. Latest release June, 1991.

Classification: Survey Analysis

Hardware Requirements and Price
IBM PC, XT, AT, PS/2, & compatibles; 500 K; 6 Mb hard disk required; 1 disk drive. Laser printer optional. Requires DOS 3.0. *Single User Price: $495.00 Student Edition: $150.00 Trial Edition: $25.00*

CSS/3

StatSoft, Inc.
2325 East 13th Street
Tulsa, OK 74104
(918) 583-4149
Fax: (918) 583-4376

CSS/3 is a powerful statistical analysis and graphing system. The program includes an extensive array of statistical tests and hundreds of types of integrated graphs. Complete statistical database management system includes fast spreadsheet editor, relational joining of files, nested sorting, powerful transformations, and comprehensive reporting options. Imports and exports Lotus 1-2-3, dBase, Excel, DIF, SYLK, SPSS, and ASCII files. Detailed manual included. On-line help available. Latest release February, 1991.

Classification: Statistical Package

Hardware Requirements and Price
IBM PC, XT, AT, PS/2, & compatibles; 640 K; 20 Mb hard disk required. Hercules, CGA, EGA, VGA, or Super VGA display. Mouse optional. Laser printer optional. Requires DOS 3.2. *Single User Price: $595.00 Network Price: Varies, based on the number of nodes licensed*

CSS: Graphics

StatSoft, Inc.
2325 East 13th Street
Tulsa, OK 74104
(918) 583-4149
Fax: (918) 583-4376

CSS: Graphics is a comprehensive graphics/charting system with data management.

The program generates hundreds of types of 2-D (two-dimensional) and 3-D graphs, and includes interactive on-screen 3-D graph rotation. Features on-screen drawing, 19 scalable fonts, overlaying of multiple graphs, and other customization options. Supports color and monochrome laser printers and plotters at their highest resolution. Imports and exports data in 15 formats. Detailed manual included. On-line help available. Latest release February, 1991.

Classification: Graphics

Hardware Requirements and Price
IBM PC, XT, AT, PS/2, & compatibles; 640 K; 20 Mb hard disk required. Hercules, CGA, EGA, VGA, or Super VGA display. Mouse optional. Laser printer optional. Requires DOS 3.2. *Single User Price: $495.00 Network Price: Varies, based on the number of nodes*

CSS: Statistica

StatSoft, Inc.
2325 East 13th Street
Tulsa, OK 74104
(918) 583-4149
Fax: (918) 583-4376

CSS: Statistica is a fully integrated system that combines the full capabilities of CSS/3 and CSS: Graphics into one comprehensive data analysis system. Over 1,000 types of graphs can be integrated with all analyses. 2-D and 3-D graphs feature on-screen drawing, rotation, scalable fonts, overlaying of graphs, and more. The interactive, menu driven operation (via keyboard or mouse) features scrollable output, pop-up graphics, and on-line help. Supports data files with up to 32,000 variables and millions of cases. Detailed manual included. On-line help available. Latest release February, 1991.

Classification: Statistical Package

Hardware Requirements and Price
IBM PC, XT, AT, PS/2, & compatibles; 640 K; 20 Mb hard disk required. Hercules, CGA, EGA, VGA, or Super VGA display. Mouse optional. Laser printer optional. Requires DOS 3.2. *Single User Price: $795.00 Network Price: Varies, based on the number of nodes*

Current Contents on Diskette: Social and Behavioral Sciences

Scientific Information
3501 Market St.
Philadelphia, PA 19104
(800) 523-1850
(800) 386-6362

Weekly access to the latest contents of 1,300 leading journals. Also includes powerful search options. Detailed manual included.

Classification: Database

Hardware Requirements and Price
IBM PC, XT, AT, PS/2, & compatibles; 480 K; 3 Mb hard disk required; 1 disk drive. Mouse optional. Modem optional. Laser printer optional. Requires DOS 3.1. *Single User Price: $360.00*

Macintosh, 512 K, 3 Mb hard disk required, 1 disk drive. Mouse required. Modem optional. Laser printer optional. Requires System 4.2 or higher. *Single User Price: $360.00*

NEC, 480 K, 3 Mb hard disk required, 1 disk drive. Laser printer optional. *Single User Price: Contact publisher*

Current Contents on Diskette: Life Sciences

Institute for Scientific Information
3501 Market Street
Philadelphia, PA 19104
(215) 386-0100
(800) 523-1850

A bibliographic database with coverage of 1,200 journals. Detailed manual included. On-line help available. Latest release December, 1990.

Classification: Database

Hardware Requirements and Price
IBM PC, XT, AT, PS/2, & compatibles; 480 K; 3 Mb hard disk required; 1 disk drive. Mouse optional. Modem optional. Laser printer optional. Requires DOS 3.1. *Single User Price: $495 (without abstracts) $895 (with abstracts)*

Macintosh, 512 K, 3 Mb hard disk required, 1 disk drive. Mouse required. Modem optional. Laser printer optional. Requires System 4.2 or higher. *Single User Price: $495 (without abstracts) $895 (with abstracts)*

NEC, 480 K, 3 Mb hard disk required, 1 disk drive. Laser printer optional. *Single User Price: Contact publisher*

Custometrics

Karl Albrecht & Associates
910 Grand Avenue, Suite 206
San Diego, CA 92109
(619) 272-3880

Software for statistical analysis of survey data. Detailed manual included. Latest release 1989.

Classification: Survey Analysis

Hardware Requirements and Price
IBM PC, XT, AT, PS/2, & compatibles; 512 K; hard disk optional; 1 disk drive (2 preferred). Printer required. Laser printer optional. Requires DOS 2.1. *Single User Price: $395.00*

D Prime and Beta
Alfred L. Brophy

Behavioral Science Associates
P.O. Box 748
West Chester, PA 19381
(215) 436-6859

Program that calculates values for D prime and Beta for a given hit and false alarm rate.

Classification: Statistical Test

Hardware Requirements and Price
BASIC program listing, 1 K, hard disk optional. *Single User Price: Free, send a self-addressed, stamped envelope*

Reviews
Brophy, A. L. (1986). Alternatives to a table of criterion values in signal detection theory. *Behavior, Research Methods, Instrumentation, and Computers, 18,* 285-286.

DADISP

DSP Development Corporation
One Kendall Square
Cambridge, MA 02139
(617) 577-1133

A windowed, menu-driven spreadsheet that tackles complex tasks such as mathematical problem solving, what-if research, scientific and technical data analysis, and management, and graphic analysis of sampled information. Detailed manual and tutorial program included. On-line help available.

Classification: Research Aid

Hardware Requirements and Price
IBM PC, XT, AT, PS/2, & compatibles; 640 K; hard disk required. Mouse optional. Modem optional. Laser printer optional. *Single User Price: $895.00*

Sun 3, 4, or 286i; hard disk required. Mouse optional. Modem optional. Laser printer optional. *Single User Price: $895.00*

HP 9000, hard disk required. Mouse optional. Modem optional. Laser printer optional. *Single User Price: $895.00*

DAS-Data Acquisition & Analysis System

MED Associates, Inc.
Box 47
East Fairfield, VT 05448
(802) 827-3825

A program for the collection and analysis of physiological signals. When used with a MED interface system and millisecond timer, the program samples at rates of up to 500/s. With a microsecond option, maximum sample rates are limited by the processing speed of the computer. Supports up to 16 channels with 12 bit resolution. Includes external triggering and stimulus control features. Waveform analysis based on thresholds, peaks, and valleys. Detailed manual included.

Classification: Equipment Control

Hardware Requirements and Price
IBM PC, XT, AT, PS/2, & compatibles; 640 K; hard disk optional; 2 disk drives. Hercules, EGA, or VGA display. Requires DOS 3.3. MED Associates interface modules required. *Single User Price: $750.00*

DCS: Data Collection System for C-64/128 Microcomputers

William F. Wheller
Max Vercruyssen

Psy-Med Associates
1386 Frank Street
Honolulu, HI 96816
(808) 734-2578

Software for collecting psychological data in human experiments and course demonstrations. Collects choice reaction time with intra-task manipulations like stimulus degradation, stimulus-response compatibility, and response-stimulus interval timing. Includes subjective state change measures for creating, administering, and recording subjective scales. Repetitive tapping module has been used for numerous theses in human factors, safety, industrial hygiene, psychology, and physical education. Millisecond resolution on timers for professional precision. Interfaces with data analyses software and transfers data to IBM compatible computers. Instruction booklet included. Latest release 1990.

Classification: Data Management

Hardware Requirements and Price
Commodore, 64 K, hard disk optional, 1 disk drive (5-1/4). Modem optional. Also requires subject response hardware ($99.00). *Single User Price: $299.00*

User Site References

Barbara Jex Courter, Human Factors Engineer, Rockwell International, 622 East Holly Avenue #3, El Seguado, CA, 90245

Judy Hadnall, Research Assistant, National Institute Occupational Safety & Health, NIOSH, Division of Safety Research, 944 Chestnut Ridge Road, Morgantown, WV, 26505, (304) 291-4801

Tina Mihaly, Technical Editor, California Institute of Technology, 715 North Avenue 66, Suite No. 5, Los Angeles, CA, 90042, (213) 340-8054

DMITSA

John Crosbie
Christopher Sharpley

Faculty of Education - SGS
Monash University
VIC 3168, Australia

Program for interrupted time-series analysis. Detailed manual included.

Classification: Statistical Test

Hardware Requirements and Price
IBM PC, XT, AT, PS/2, & compatibles; 1 disk drive. Laser printer optional. *Single User Price: $195.00*

EndNote

Niles & Associates, Inc.
2000 Hearst Street
Berkeley, CA 94709
(510) 649-8176

Stores references and creates bibliographies automatically. Detailed manual included.

Classification: Manuscript Preparation Aid

Hardware Requirements and Price
IBM PC, XT, AT, PS/2, & compatibles; 512 K; hard disk required; 1 disk drive. Laser printer optional. *Single User Price: $149.00*

Macintosh, 512 K, hard disk required, 1 disk drive. Laser printer optional. *Single User Price: $149.00*

Reviews
Landan, T. (1989). D basic bibliography. *MacUser, 5,* 202-211.
Tessler, F. (1989). EndNote 1.0. *MacWorld, 6,* 261.

EndNote Plus

Niles & Associates, Inc.
2000 Hearst Street
Berkeley, CA 94709
(510) 649-8176

Enhanced bibliographic software. Detailed manual included.

Classification: Manuscript Preparation Aid

Hardware Requirements and Price
IBM PC, XT, AT, PS/2, & compatibles; 512 K. *Single User Price: $249.00*

Macintosh. *Single User Price: $249.00*

Reviews
Cohen, S. D. (1991). EndNote Plus: Reference formatter. *Information Today,* 8, 35-36.
Horswill, J. (1991). EndNote Plus ends bibliographical headaches. *Computer Buyer's Resource,* 12.

Enhancing and Degrading Visual Stimuli
John O. Brooks, III

Department of Psychiatry & Behavioral
Sciences (TD-114)
Stanford University School of Medicine
Stanford, CA 94305-5490
(415) 493-5000

Assembly language routines perform perceptual identification experiments. Routines can
be used like any BASIC statement and require
no knowledge of assembly language. Stimuli
can be degraded and then gradually clarified.
Instruction booklet included.

Classification: Research Aid

Hardware Requirements and Price
Macintosh, 512 K, hard disk optional. Prob-
ably not System 7 compatible. *Single User
Price: $6.00*

Reviews
Brooks, J. O. (1987). Enhancing and degrading
visual stimuli. *Behavior, Research Methods,
Instrumentation, and Computers*, 19, 260-
269.

EVA: Electronic Visual Analog
Paul Groner

Creative Silicon
2139 North Ross Street, Box E
Santa Ana, CA 92706
(714) 836-5212

A handheld electronic instrument that automates the classic pencil and paper visual analog used for quantifying subjective phenomena.
Instruction booklet included.

Classification: Research Aid

Hardware Requirements and Price
Contact publisher for equipment options.
Single User Price: $99.00

User Site References
Michael Blumenfield, Department of Psychol-
ogy and Science, Room B006, NY Medical
College, Psychiatric Institute Westchester
City Medical Center, Valhalla, NY, 10595,
(914) 285-8424

EVE
Michael S. Landy
Lev Z. Manovich
George D. Stetten

Department of Psychology
New York University
New York, NY 10003
(212) 998-7857

EVE (Early Vision Emulation) is a system for
simulating early visual processing. It simulates
a wide variety of models of spatial vision, motion detection and processing, spatial sampling,
and more. The program is modular and flexible, runs under the UNIX operating system,
and is device-independent. It comes with
complete documentation and source code.
Runs on any UNIX machine with no or minor
changes. Detailed manual included. On-line
help available.

Classification: Research Aid

Hardware Requirements and Price
Contact publisher for equipment options.
Requires UNIX. *Single User Price: Free, send
1/2" tape or Sun cartridge.*

Reviews

Landy, M. S., Manovich, V. Z., & Stetton, G. D. (1989). All about EVE: The Early Vision Emulation software. *Behavior, Research Methods, Instrumentation, and Computers, 21*, 491-501.

Landy, M. S., Manovich, V. Z., & Stetton, G. D. (1990). Applications of the EVE software for visual modeling. *Vision Research, 30*, 329-338.

Eventlog
Robert W. Hendersen

Conduit
University of Iowa-Oakdale Campus
Iowa City, IA 52242
(319) 335-4100
(800) 365-9774

A software package that functions as a tool for recording real-time events. Intended primarily for researchers who must score and record observational data. Eventlog operates with assigned keys. The observer presses the appropriate coding key for the duration of the observed event. The precise times at which each key is pressed and released are recorded for subsequent analysis. Menu driven and customizable. An Eventlog program can be used with data from a session to compute descriptive statistics, graphically display data, or reformat data for other uses. Detailed manual included. Latest release September, 1991.

Classification: Data Management

Hardware Requirements and Price
IBM PC, XT, AT, PS/2, & compatibles; 384 K; 1 Mb hard disk optional; 1 disk drive (3-1/2). Color display recommended. *Single User Price: $160.00*

Reviews

Anderson, D. E. (1990). Eventlog. *Social Science Computer Review, 8*(3), 462.

Transient Evoked Potentials
John A. Baro
Stephen Lehmkuhle

School of Optometry
University of Missouri-St. Louis
St. Louis, MO 63121

Program for recording and analyzing transient evoked potential data.

Classification: Research Aid

Hardware Requirements and Price
Apple II+, IIe; 128 K. 8-bit memory-map d to a/a to d converter. *Single User Price: $12.00*

Reviews

Baro, A. B., & Lehmkuhle, S. (1988). A software system for recording and analyzing transient evoked potential data with an Apple IIe computer. *Behavior, Research Methods, Instrumentation, and Computers, 20*, 515-516.

Expected Normal and Half-Normal Scores
Alfred L. Brophy

Behavioral Science Associates
P.O. Box 748
West Chester, PA 19381
(215) 436-6859

BASIC programs that calculate expected normal and expected half-normal scores.

Classification: Normal Distribution

Hardware Requirements and Price
IBM PC, XT, AT, PS/2, & compatibles; 1 K; hard disk optional; BASIC interpreter. *Single User Price: Free, include a self-addressed, stamped envelope.*

Reviews
Brophy, A. L. (1987). Expected normal and half-normal scores. *Educational and Psychological Measurement, 47,* 111-115.

Exploratory Data Analysis
David S. Malcolm

Division of the Social Sciences
Fordham University
New York, NY 10023
(212) 636-6346

A BASIC program that performs exploratory data analysis, parametrically related tests, and resistant statistical tests based on ordinal scales. Instruction booklet included. Latest release January, 1990.

Classification: Exploratory Data Analysis

Hardware Requirements and Price
IBM PC, XT, AT, PS/2, & compatibles; hard disk optional; 1 disk drive. CGA display. Requires DOS 2.1. *Single User Price: Free, send disk with return postage*

Reviews
Malcolm, D. S. (1989). A BASIC program for exploratory data analysis. *Behavior, Research Methods, Instrumentation, and Computers, 21,* 463-464.

Extend 2.0
Bob Diamond

Imagine That, Inc.
151 Bernal Road, Suite 5
San Jose, CA 95119
(408) 365-0305

A graphical simulation application used to model the performance of any system including perceptual processes, behavioral experiments, cognition, neural networks, and so forth. Detailed manual included. On-line help available. Latest release January, 1992.

Classification: Research Aid

Hardware Requirements and Price
Macintosh, 2 Mb, 20 Mb hard disk required, 1 disk drive. Monochrome or color display. Mouse required. Modem optional. Laser printer optional. Requires System 6.0.2. *Single User Price: $695.00*

Reviews
Crabb, D. (1988). Modeling made easier. *Byte, 13,* 5-9.
Horton, L. (1990). Simulating with blocks. *Software Magazine,* 74.
Sternlight, D. (1989). Extend improves on simulation modeling. *MacWeek,* 32.

Eye Monitoring Program
George W. McConkie
Charles W. Scouten
Patrick K. Bryant

Stoelting Co.
620 Wheat Lane
Wood Dale, IL 60191
(708) 860-9700

A software package that collects and reduces eye behavior (eye position and pupil size) data using an IBM-compatible personal computer. Written in C for speed and portability, the package includes several unique features: Data can be collected simultaneously from other sources (e.g., EEG, EMG), logically defined events can be detected in real time on any data channel, and either of two types of data matrix can be produced. Data reduction algorithms and data structures are described. Detailed manual included. On-line help available. Latest release August, 1990.

Classification: Research Aid

Hardware Requirements and Price
IBM PC, XT, AT, PS/2, & compatibles; 256 K; 20 Mb hard disk required; 1 disk drive. CGA display. QuaTech Digital I/O Board (available from Stoelting) required. *Single User Price: $1,000.00*

Reviews
McConkie, G., Scouten, C., Bryant, P., & Wilson, J. (1988). A microcomputer based software package for eye monitoring research. *Behavior, Research Methods, Instrumentation, and Computers, 20,* 142-149.

Flo Stat Version 1.5
Jerry W. Wicks
Jose Pereira de Almeida

PSRC Software
Bowling Green State University
Bowling Green, OH 43403
(419) 372-2497

A unique statistical and mapping system for the professional analyst. The program includes standard statistical routines, data manipulation and transformations, graphics, tabular and mapping output, accompanying social databases, and maps. It is appropriate for scientific and business reports. Features include linking of user-created, object-format maps; copy and paste color maps; graphics as draw-objects in word processing and draw/paint programs; and paste tabular output to a word processor or spreadsheet. US and Canadian maps and databases included. Statistics include descriptives, frequencies, t-test one-way ANOVA, crosstabulation, correlation, simple regression, and samples. Choropleth maps, pie, line, bar, histogram, ogive, scattergram, and 3-D block charts can be generated. Detailed manual included.

Classification: Statistical Package

Hardware Requirements and Price
Macintosh, 1 Mb, 20 Mb hard disk optional, 1 disk drive. Mouse required. Laser printer optional. Requires System OS 6.0.7-7.0. *Single User Price: $199.00 Lab-packs, educational discounts, and student versions are available.*

User Site References
Tim Hogan, Center for Business Research, College of Business, Arizona State University, Tempe, AZ, 85287, (602) 965-3961
Jerry Hughes, Department of Sociology, Northern Arizona University, Flagstaff, AZ, 86001, (602) 523-2979

Fraction
Jamal Abedi
Richard Shavelson

UCLA Graduate School of Education
University of California
Los Angles, CA 90024-1521
(213) 206-4065

Generates fractional factorial designs as well as performs and analyzes variances of full or fractional factorial designs. Detailed manual included. Latest release May, 1991.

Classification: ANOVA

Hardware Requirements and Price
IBM PC, XT, AT, PS/2, & compatibles; 1 K; 20 Mb hard disk optional; 2 disk drives. Modem optional. Laser printer optional. *Single User Price: $180.00*

Reviews
Abedi, J., & Shavelson, R. (1988). UCLA Graduate School of Education. Behavior, *Research Methods, Instrumentation, and Computers, 20*, 58-59.

G Statistic
Bernard C. Beins

Department of Psychology
Ithaca College
Ithaca, NY 14850
(607) 274-3512

BASIC program computes the G statistic.

Classification: Statistical Test

Hardware Requirements and Price
Apple II, 16 K, hard disk optional, 1 disk drive. Laser printer optional. *Single User Price: $7.50*

Reviews
Beins, B. C. (1989). An Applesoft BASIC program for the G Statistic: An alternative to the chi-square test. *Behavior, Research Methods, Instrumentation, and Computers, 21*, 627-629.

GIBBY: Random Generator
George A. Marcoulides

Department of Management Science
California State University
Fullerton, CA 92634
(714) 773-2221

Enables the user to create artificial data sets for different probability distributions according to specified parameter values. Manual on disk. On-line help available.

Classification: Data Generation

Hardware Requirements and Price
IBM PC, XT, AT, PS/2, & compatibles; 256 K; hard disk optional; 1 disk drive. Printer required. *Single User Price: $10.00*

GPSPRT
Douglas B. Eamon

Department of Psychology
University of Wisconsin
Whitewater, WI 53190
(414) 472-1837

General purpose stimulus presentation and response timer for either the Apple IIe or Apple IIgs. Detailed manual and tutorial program included.

Classification: Research Aid

Hardware Requirements and Price
Apple II+, IIe, IIc, IIgs; 48 K; hard disk optional; 1 disk drive. 40 column display required. Mouse optional. Modem optional. Laser printer optional. *Single User Price: $10.00*

Reviews

Eamon, D. B. (1988). Screen display and timing synchronization on the Apple IIe and Apple IIgs. *Behavior, Research Methods, Instrumentation, and Computers*, *21*, 426-430.

Graph

MicroMath
2034 East Fort Union Boulevard
Salt Lake City, UT 84121-3144
(801) 943-0290
(800) 942-6284

A program for transforming, plotting, and archiving data. Simplifies the preparation of publication quality x-y plots. Incorporates important plotting features for research data presentation, while retaining a simplicity of use that encourages use of graphics. Allows simple transformations or sequences of transformations. Program tracts the current transformation and includes transformed variable names in menus. Seven digital filters multiple y axis, 16,000 point capacity, and publication quality output are included. Detailed manual included. Latest release February, 1991.

Classification: Graphics

Hardware Requirements and Price
IBM PC, XT, AT, PS/2, & compatibles; 512 K; hard disk optional; 1 disk drive. Graphic display required. Laser printer optional. Requires DOS 3.3. *Single User Price: $149.00 Network Price: Varies, depending on quantity Site license available*

Review
Fass-Holmes, B. (1991). GRAPH: A program for plotting scientific data. *Biotechnology Software*, January.

Hopke, P. K. (1989). GRAPH and MINSQ. *Chemometrics and Intelligent Laboratory Systems*, May.

McClure, D. W. (1988). GRAPH, *Journal of the American Chemical Society*, *110*(18).

Grapher

Golden Software, Inc.
P.O. Box 281
Golden, CO 80402
(303) 279-1021
(800) 972-1021

Grapher creates logarithmic and linear x-y graphs utilizing six different curve fitting routines. Axis scaling, tic frequency and labeling can be set independently for each axis. Each curve can contain up to 10,000 points, and ten curves can be placed on each graph. Detailed manual included. On-line help available. Latest release June, 1991.

Classification: Graphics

Hardware Requirements and Price
IBM PC, XT, AT, PS/2, & compatibles; 256 K; hard disk optional; 1 disk drive. Hercules, CGA, EGA, or VGA display. Laser printer optional. Requires DOS 2.0. *Single User Price: $199.00 Network Price: $199.00 per user*

Reviews
Kaplan, E. (1989). Two-dimensional plotting. *PC Magazine*, *8*, 265-267.

Guttman Scalogram Analysis
Andrew R. Gilpin

William C. Brown Publishers
2460 Kerper Blvd.

Dubuque, IA 52001
(319) 588-1451
(800) 351-7671

This program performs the Guttman Scalogram Analysis on a set of test items with dichotomous responses. The chief purpose of the program is to compute Guttman's REP or reproducibility index for the scale in question. Various measures of reliability are also generated and statistical significance of the REP index is assessed. Interfaces with DIF files. Detailed manual included.

Classification: Statistical Test

Hardware Requirements and Price
Apple II+, IIe, IIc; 64 K; hard disk optional; 1 disk drive. *Single User Price: $30.00 Site License: $400.00*

The HIPS Image Processing System
Michael S. Landy

SharpImage Software
P.O. Box 373
Prince Street Station
New York, NY 10012-0007
(212) 998-7857

HIPS is a software package for image processing that runs under UNIX. HIPS is modular and flexible, it provides automatic documentation of its actions, and is almost entirely independent of special equipment. It handles the sequences of images (movies) in precisely the same manner as single frames. Programs have been developed for simple image transformations, filtering, convolution, Fourier and other transform processing, edge detection and line drawing manipulation, digital image compression and transmission methods, noise generation, and image statistics computation. Over 150 of these programs have been developed. As a result, almost any image processing task can be performed quickly and conveniently. HIPS allows users to integrate their own custom routines. Detailed manual included. On-line help available. Latest release September, 1991.

Classification: Research Aid

Hardware Requirements and Price
Contact publisher for equipment options. 4 Mb RAM, 100 Mb hard disk required. Requires UNIX. *Single User Price: $800.00*

User Site References
Bill Johnson, Lawrence Berkeley Labs, Berkeley, CA, 94704, (415) 998-7857

Integration of *t*
D. Louis Wood

Department of Psychology
University of Arkansas
Little Rock, AR 72204
(501) 569-3531

Advanced algorithms for the numerical integration of t. The program is easy to run.

Classification: t-Test

Hardware Requirements and Price
IBM PC, XT, AT, PS/2, & compatibles; 6 K; hard disk optional; 1 disk drive. Requires DOS 3.1 and BASIC or GWBASIC *Single User Price: Free*

Interactive Cluster Analysis (ICA), Release 2.0

Mathematical Software Co.
4033 Arcadia Way
Oceanside, CA 92056
(619) 940-0343

A generic tool for classifying members of a test population composed of persons, animals, events, times, literary or artistic works, food-stuffs, products, messages, treatments, speci-mens, and so forth. Members of the popula-tion are distinguished from each other by means of their relative endowments (test scores or score profiles) on multiple attributes. The ICA program provides three methods of assessing the similarity of case pairs: the mani-fold-match test, the Euclidian distance test, and the triple-match test for score-profile similarity. Detailed manual included.

Classification: Statistical Test

Hardware Requirements and Price
IBM PC, XT, AT, PS/2, & compatibles; 256 K.
Math co-processor optional. *Single User Price: $59.95*

Interactive Multiple Prediction (IMP) 2.0

Mathematical Software Co.
4033 Arcadia Way
Oceanside, CA 92056
(619) 940-0343

A multiple, linear regression program that accepts as input a data-set made up of 1 crite-rion and up to 79 predictor variables (each with up to 1,000 cases). Output is a multiple-regression formula that may be used for mak-ing predictions. The formula consists of a constant term plus up to 10 more terms, the coefficients of which are multiple regression coefficients. The program computes multiple-R and multiple-R squared along with the usual standard error estimates. IMP contains provi-sions for running cross-validation studies. The program can operate with only the odd or even rows or with all rows. A quick statistical test enables you to test which transformation of a variable is likely to be the most productive. A sweep-search option computes the multiple-R for a selected group of predictors. Hence, users can discover instantly which predictor can contribute the biggest increment of multiple-R squared. Detailed manual included.

Classification: Correlation and Regression

Hardware Requirements and Price
IBM PC, XT, AT, PS/2, & compatibles; 256 K.
Single User Price: $69.95

Interactive Questionnaire Analysis (IQA) 1.0

Mathematical Software Co.
4033 Arcadia Way
Oceanside, CA 92056
(619) 940-0343

A powerful analytic tool for analyzing ques-tionnaire and survey responses used in scien-tific, social, psychological, political, business, economic, health or physical sciences, or mar-keting or public-opinion research. IQA helps users gain insights not readily obtainable from conventional methods of analysis. There are of five major parts: data entry and editing, ma-nipulation and analysis of raw data, multi-variate analysis of questionnaire data, search for surrogate variables, and other procedures. Detailed manual included.

Classification: Statistical Package

Hardware Requirements and Price
IBM PC, XT, AT, PS/2, & compatibles; 256 K.
Single User Price: $189.95

Interactive Tester
Michael E. Mills

Psytek Services
6401 West 81st Street
Los Angeles, CA 90045
(310) 670-4655
(800) 392-5454

Allows non-programmers to computerize tests, surveys, and reports using their own word processing software, or the interactive test definition program provided. Computerizes the administration, scoring, profiling of results, and interpretation of tests and surveys. Can even accommodate tests that have complex scoring procedures. No limit on the number of test items. Up to 100 scales per test. Automatically performs reliability, validity, item analysis, and norming statistics. Detailed manual included. On-line help available. Latest release October 1, 1991.

Classification: Survey Administration

Hardware Requirements and Price
IBM PC, XT, AT, PS/2, & compatibles; 256 K; hard disk optional; 2 disk drives. Printer required. Laser printer optional. *Single User Price: $295.00 Site License: $395.00 30 day money back guarantee*

The classification "Statistical Package" has been used for programs that perform a variety of tests; "Statistical Test" is used for single-test programs.

Interrater Reliability for the Macintosh
John O. Brooks III
Laura L. Brooks

VA Medical Center (151Y)
3801 Miranda Avenue
Palo Alto, CA 94304
(415) 493-5000

A BASIC program for the Macintosh that computes inter-rater reliability by averaging, for each rater, the correlations between one rater's ratings and every other rater's ratings. The standard Macintosh interface is implemented. Instruction booklet included.

Classification: Research Aid

Hardware Requirements and Price
Macintosh, 1 Mb, hard disk optional. *Single User Price: $6.00*

Reviews
Brooks, J. O., & Brooks, L. L. (1991). Inter-rater Reliability for the Macintosh. *Behavior Research Methods, Instruments & Computers, 23*, 82-84.

Inverse Normal Distribution Function
Alfred L. Brophy

Behavioral Science Associates
P.O. Box 748
West Chester, PA 19381
(215) 436-6859

Nine different approximations of the inverse normal distribution function.

Classification: Normal Distribution

Hardware Requirements and Price
TRS-80, Model I, III, & IV; 1 K; hard disk optional. BASIC interpreter. *Single User Price: Free, send a self-addressed, stamped envelope.*

Reviews
Brophy, A. L. (1985). Approximation of the inverse normal distribution function. *Behavior, Research Methods, Instrumentation, and Computers, 17,* 415-417.

Ipsapro
Ross Broughton
Norman Wasel

Department of Psychology
University of Winnipeg
Winnipeg, Manitoba R3B 2E9 Canada

A program to perform ipsative scoring. An instruction file is included on the disk.

Classification: Data Management

Hardware Requirements and Price
IBM PC, XT, AT, PS/2, & compatibles; 256 K; hard disk optional; 1 disk drive. *Single User Price: $3.00*

Reviews
Broughton, R., & Wasel N. (1990). A text-stimuli presentation manager for the IBM-PC with ipsatization correction for response sets and reaction times. *Behavior, Research Methods, Instrumentation, and Computers, 22,* 421-423.

ISSA
J. Ortusar
V. Canales
R. Hernandez
C. Thomas

IRD/MACRO International
Demographic & Health Surveys Program
8850 Stanford Boulevard, Suite 4000
Columbia, MD 21045
(410) 290-2800

Integrated survey software including questionnaire design, data entry, and tabulation components. Detailed manual included. On-line help available. Latest release June, 1990.

Classification: Survey Administration

Hardware Requirements and Price
IBM PC, XT, AT, PS/2, & compatibles; 640 K; 10 Mb hard disk optional; 2 disk drives. Modem optional. Laser printer optional. Requires DOS 3.0. *Single User Price: $325.00*

Reviews
Carpenter, E. H. (1988). Software tools for data collection: Microcomputer-assisted interviewing, *Social Science Computer Review, 6,* 353-368.
Hanenberg, R. (1988). Training in the use of microcomputers in the field of population, United Nations Economic & Social Commission for Asia & the Pacific (ESCAP). *Bangkok,* 9-10.

JACK
NASA Ames Research Center

COSMIC
The University of Georgia
382 East Broad Street
Athens, GA 30602
(404) 542-3265

An interactive graphics program that displays and manipulates articulated geometric figures. JACK is typically used to observe how a human mannequin interacts with its environment and what effects body types will have upon the performance of a task in a simulated environment. Detailed manual included. Latest release November, 1990.

Classification: Graphics

Hardware Requirements and Price
Silicon Graphics 4D Computer, 8 Mb RAM. 180 Mb hard disk required. *Single User Price: $1,551.00*

JAVA Version 1.4

Jandel Scientific
65 Koch Road
Corte Madera, CA 94925
(415) 924-8640
(800) 874-1888

Video analysis software designed to take advantage of inexpensive video digitizing boards. Provides advanced video measurement and analysis capabilities. Input live or video images from a VCR, video camera, or computer disk. Program is capable of line and edge tracking, automatic object counting, and a variety of morphometric measurements. Data manipulation features include user-defined transforms, pseudo-color look-up tables, statistics, and keyboard macros. Detailed manual and tutorial program included. On-line help available. Latest release February, 1991

Classification: Research Aid

Hardware Requirements and Price
IBM PC, XT, AT, PS/2, & compatibles; 640 K; 1.4 Mb hard disk required; 1 disk drive. Graphic display required. Laser printer optional. Pointing device and video digitizing board required. *Single User Price: $1495.00*

Reviews
Unger, J. (1990). Video analysis on a PC. *Byte*, *15*(5), 6415-3 - 6415-6.

User Site References
Ray Stevens, Marine Biology Lab, Waters Street, MA, 02543, (508) 540-4383
Jack Zelver, Lawrence Berkeley Labs, One Cyclotron Road, MS 46-161, Berkeley, CA, 94720, (415) 486-7241

Johnson-Neyman Significance Regions
Michael J Strube

Department of Psychology
Washington University
St. Louis, MO 63130

Program that extends the calculation of the Johnson-Neyman significance regions to one or more predictors. On-line help available. Latest release 1988.

Classification: Statistical Test

Hardware Requirements and Price
IBM PC, XT, AT, PS/2, & compatibles; 1 disk drive. *Single User Price: Free, send formatted disk and return mailer*

Reviews
Strube, M. J. (1988). Calculation of significant regions for multiple predictors by the Johnson-Neyman technique. *Behavior, Research Methods, Instrumentation, and Computers*, *20*, 510-512.

Kappa Coefficient

Michael J Strube

Department of Psychology
Washington University
St. Louis, MO 63130

A program for calculating the kappa coefficient. On-line help available. Latest release
1989.

Classification: Statistical Test

Hardware Requirements and Price
IBM PC, XT, AT, PS/2, & compatibles; hard
disk optional; 1 disk drive. *Single User Price:
Free, send formatted disk and return mailer*

Reviews
Strube, M. (1989). A general program for the
calculation of the kappa coefficient. *Behavior, Research Methods, Instrumentation, and
Computers, 21,* 643-644.

Kendall's Rank Correlation Coefficient

Alfred L. Brophy

Behavioral Science Associates
P.O. Box 748
West Chester, PA 19381
(215) 436-6859

BASIC program that calculates Kendall's tau
and its one-tailed probability.

Classification: Nonparametric Test

Hardware Requirements and Price
IBM PC, XT, AT, PS/2, & compatibles; 2.5 K;
hard disk optional. BASIC interpreter. *Single
User Price: Free, send self-addressed, stamped
envelope.*

Reviews
Brophy, A. L. (1986). A algorithm and program for calculation of Kendall's Rank Correlation Coefficient. *Behavior, Research
Methods, Instrumentation, and Computers,
18,* 45-46.

Key Stat

Oakleaf Systems
P.O. Box 472
Decorah, IA 52101
(319) 382-4320

Statistical package including over 30 common
parametric and nonparametric procedures.
Features a key to appropriate tests, step-wise
multiple regression, one- and two-way
ANOVA, and rank correlations. Calculates
levels of significance. Accepts large data sets.
Detailed manual included.

Classification: Statistical Package

Hardware Requirements and Price
Apple II, 64 K, 1 disk drive. *Single User Price:
$49.95*

IBM PC, XT, AT, PS/2, & compatibles; 128 K;
hard disk optional; 1 disk drive. *Single User
Price: $69.95*

Laboratory Control System

T. B. Perera

Life Science Associates
1 Fenimore Road
Bayport, NY 11705-2115
(516) 472-2111
Fax: (516) 472-8146

Program allows a microcomputer to control and read data during experiments. Experiment is reduced to a series of events or "states" that consist of inputs, time delays, outputs, and transitions. Detailed manual included.

Classification: Equipment Control

Hardware Requirements and Price
Apple II+, IIe. #530A Interface required. *Single User Price: $75.00*

TRS-80, Model III & IV. Single User Price: $75.00

Laplace

MicroMath
2034 East Fort Union Blvd.
Salt Lake City, UT 84121-3144
(801) 943-0290
(800) 942-6284

A simulation of physical/chemical systems by numerical inversion of Laplace transforms. The program implements a general and reliable technique for automatic numerical inversion of the Laplace transform. Models can be entered from the keyboard or from a file with a flexible model entry language. Laplace includes a built-in editor for changing transforms and a number of operators, such as trancendentals and hyperbolics, for inclusion in user-defined functions. Least squares fitting capabilities are included. Detailed manual included. Latest release September, 1991.

Classification: Statistical Test

Hardware Requirements and Price
IBM PC, XT, AT, PS/2, & compatibles; 512 K; 2 Mb hard disk required; 1 disk drive. Graphic display required. Mouse optional. Laser printer optional. Requires DOS 3.3. Math coprocessor optional. *Single User Price: $249.00 Network Price: Varies, depending on the number of workstations*

LEDA

Jean Lorenceau
Remi Humbert

Laboratoire de Psychologie Experimentale
Universite R. Descartes
Paris, 75006 France
140519867

Program for editing 2-D images and films. Instruction booklet included. Latest release 1989.

Classification: Graphics

Hardware Requirements and Price
IBM PC, XT, AT, PS/2, & compatibles; 640 K; 1.2 Mb hard disk optional; 1 disk drive (5-1/4). Adage PG90/10, VGA display. Mouse optional. Requires DOS 3.3. *Single User Price: $40.00*

Reviews
Lorenceau, J., & Humbert, R. (1990). A multipurpose software for editing two-dimensional animated images. *Behavior, Research Methods, Instrumentation, and Computers, 22*, 453-465.

Longitudinal Sealugram Analysis
Ron Hays

William C. Brown Publishers
2460 Kerper Blvd.
Dubuque, IA 52001
(319) 588-1451
(800) 351-7671

A direct extension of cross-sectional Gultman scaling, logitudinal Sealugram Analysis yields analogous coefficients of reproducibility and scalability. This method allows charting of transitions into different stages of involvement from one period to the next. Detailed manual included.

Classification: Statistical Test

Hardware Requirements and Price
IBM PC, XT, AT, PS/2, & compatibles; 256 K; hard disk optional; 1 disk drive (5-1/4). *Single User Price: Contact publisher.*

Latin Squares Generation
Michael J. Strube

Department of Psychology
Washington University
St. Louis, MO 63130

A BASIC program for the generation of Latin Squares. On-line help available. Latest release 1988.

Classification: ANOVA

Hardware Requirements and Price
IBM PC, XT, AT, PS/2, & compatibles; hard disk optional; 1 disk drive. *Single User Price: Free, send formatted disk and return mailer*

Reviews
Strube, M. J. (1988). A BASIC program for the generation of Latin Squares. *Behavior, Research Methods, Instrumentation, and Computers, 20,* 508-509.

Additional statistical programs and research aids may be found in the Academic Software section.

Mac Psych with Mac-A-Mug
Leslie A. Zebrowitz

Department of Psychology
Brandeis University
Waltham, MA 02254
(617) 736-3300

Software for designing images of human faces. Used to create laboratory experiments concerning reactions to people. Detailed manual included. Latest release January, 1991.

Classification: Graphics

Hardware Requirements and Price
Macintosh, 1 Mb, 10 Mb hard disk required, 1 disk drive. Monochrome display. Mouse required. *Single User Price: $25.00*

MaCATI Version 2.0
Jerry W. Wicks
Jose Pereira de Almeida

PSRC Software
Bowling Green State University
Bowling Green, OH 43403
(419) 372-2497

MaCATI 2.0 is a sophisticated computer assisted telephone interviewing (CATI) system which can also be used for computer assisted personal interviewing (CAPI) and disk by mail surveys (DMS). It has been in use for over 5 years at many universities and businesses in the United States, Canada, Australia, and Europe. MaCATI is simple to learn and use and appropriate for university survey research centers, market research companies, organizations engaged in telefund drives, and telemarketing. It automates the process of questionnaire editing, skip patterns, data collection and data processing surrounding large-scale survey research projects. Program comes with spelling checker, thesaurus, dictionary, and the program FLOSTAT statistical analysis and mapping package. Everything required for large scale survey data collection projects is included in the design of this system. Detailed manual included. Latest release January, 1992.

Classification: Survey Administration

Hardware Requirements and Price
Macintosh, 2 Mb, 20 Mb hard disk required, 1 disk drive. Mouse required. Modem optional. Laser printer optional. Requires System 6.0.7-7.0. *Multiuser Price: $3,500.00 (1-6 stations) $30,000.00 (100 or more stations) Educational discounts available*

Reviews
Carpenter, E. H. (1988). Software tools for data collection: Microcomputer-assisted interviewing. *Social Science Computer Review*, 6, 353-368.

User Site References
Jerry Hughes, Survey Research Lab, Department of Sociology, Northern Arizona University, Flagstaff, AZ, 86011, (602) 523-2979

George Marcus, Department of Political Science, Williams College, Williamstown, MA, 01267

Manycorr: Multistage Boneferroni Procedure for Many Correlations
Alfred L. Brophy

Behavioral Science Associates
P.O. Box 748
West Chester, PA 19381
(215) 436-6859

BASIC program to perform the multistage Boneferroni test with a set of correlation coefficients.

Classification: Correlation and Regression

Hardware Requirements and Price
IBM PC, XT, AT, PS/2, & compatibles; 35 K; hard disk optional. BASIC interpreter required. *Single User Price: Free, send a self-addressed, stamped envelope.*

Reviews
Brophy, A. L. (1988). A BASIC program for the multistage boneferroni procedure for many correlations. *Behavior, Research Methods, Instrumentation, and Computers*, 20, 416-418.

MapViewer

Golden Software, Inc.
P.O. Box 281
Golden, CO 80402
(303) 279-1021
(800) 972-1021

MapViewer is a Windows 3.0 presentation mapping package. Thematic map types include hatch maps, dot density maps, prism maps, and proportional pie and symbol maps. Maps can be created with existing boundary files, or designed or imported using the client's boundary files. Detailed manual included. On-line help available. Latest release October, 1991.

Classification: Graphics

Hardware Requirements and Price
IBM PC, XT, AT, PS/2, & compatibles; 2 Mb; 20 Mb hard disk required; 1 disk drive. EGA, VGA, or Windows 3.0 compatible display. Mouse optional. Laser printer optional.

Requires Windows 3.0. *Single User Price: $249.00 Network Price: $249.00 per user*

MapWise: Perceptual Mapping Software
Wilma E. Goodnow

Market ACTION Research Software
16 W. 501 58th Street, Suite 21-A
Clarendon Hills, IL 60514-1740
(708) 986-0830
Fax: (708) 986-0801

This package produces an analytical technique used in marketing or psychological research–perceptual maps with correspondence analysis. Detailed manual and tutorial program included. Latest release August, 1991.

Classification: Research Aid

Hardware Requirements and Price
IBM PC, XT, AT, PS/2, & compatibles; 256 K; hard disk optional. Laser printer optional. *Single User Price: $495.00 Academic Site License: $495.00*

Reviews
Garson, G. D. (1990). MapWise: Perceptual Mapping Software. *Social Science Computer Review, 8,* 294-302.
Pelton, L. E., & Tudor, R. K. (1992). Map-Wise: Perceptual Mapping Software. *Journal of the American Mathematical Society, 20(1).*

The Matchmaker

Dynacomp, Inc.
The Dynacomp Office Building
178 Phillips Road
Webster, NY 14580

(716) 265-4040
(800) 828-6772

A computerized matching service that will compare up to 2,000 people and choose the top 10 matches for each. A multiple-choice questionnaire editor is included for producing personalized forms. Users can enter, save, recall, and edit lists of up to 60 questions. The Matchmaker will then format the lists into ready-to-use questionnaires. Two data entry modes are available. Data may be entered on several computers and later merged. Instruction booklet included.

Classification: Survey Administration

Hardware Requirements and Price
Apple II, 48 K, 1 disk drive (5-1/4). Laser printer optional. Requires DOS 3.3. *Single User Price: $49.95*

Matrank and Onerank
Alfred L. Brophy

Behavioral Science Associates
P.O. Box 748
West Chester, PA 19381
(215) 436-6859

BASIC programs that sort and rank scores in matched groups on combined distributions. Computes Spearman's rho, Kendall's coefficient of concordance, Wilcoxon's rank-sum test, the Mann-Whitney U test, and the Kruskal-Wallis test.

Classification: Nonparametric Test

Hardware Requirements and Price
TRS-80, Model III & IV; 3 K; hard disk optional. BASIC interpreter. *Single User Price: Free, send a self-addressed, stamped envelope*

Reviews

Brophy, A. L. (1984). Ranking programs for matched groups and combined distributions. *Behavior, Research Methods, Instrumentation, and Computers, 16*, 406.

Measures of Association for Ordinal Variables

Jerry M. Brennan
Larry H. Nitz
Jennifer E. Daly

Sugar Mill Software Corporation
1180 Kika Place
Kailua, HI 96734
(808) 261-7536
(800) 729-7536

An APL program for measuring association of ordinal variables. On-line help available.

Classification: Statistical Test

Hardware Requirements and Price
IBM PC, XT, AT, PS/2, & compatibles; 640 K; hard disk optional; 1 disk drive. Mouse, modem, and laser printer optional. STSC APL required.

Reviews

Brennan, J. M., Nitz, L. H., & Daly J. E. (1988). An APL program for measures of association for ordinal variables. *Behavior, Research Methods, Instrumentation, and Computers, 20*, 429-431.

Statistical programs may be classified with a specific test name such as "t-Test" or "ANOVA," type of test such as "Nonparametric test," or the general category "Statistical Test."

MED-PC/Medstate Notation Version 2

Thomas A. Tatham

MED Associates, Inc.
Box 47
East Fairfield, VT 05448
(802) 827-3825

An advanced, low cost, PC-compatible programming language written for behavioral applications. When used with MED interface systems, MED-PC allows users to control up to 12 test chambers or stations with up to 80 inputs and 80 outputs assigned to each. Because MED-PC is interrupt driven, each chamber may be run an independent procedure, with flexible data collection and printout options. Detailed manual included.

Classification: Equipment Control

Hardware Requirements and Price
IBM PC, XT, AT, PS/2, & compatibles; 640 K; hard disk optional; 2 disk drives. Hercules, EGA or VGA display. Requires DOS 3.3 and MED Associates Interface Modules. *Single User Price: $600.00*

Megafile Manager

StatSoft, Inc.
2325 East 13th Street
Tulsa, OK 74104
(918) 583-4149
Fax: (918) 583-4376

Megafile Manager is a database management program that allows users to maintain large archival data files of up to 32,000 fields (8 Mb per record) with an unlimited numbers of records. File management options permit import and export of Lotus 1-2-3, dBase, Excel, DIF, SYLK, SPSS, and ASCII files. Comprehensive facilities are provided to enter, edit, restructure, report, sort, subset, merge, relational merge, sort, search/replace, and verify data. Detailed manual included. On-line help available. Latest release April, 1991.

Classification: Data Management

Hardware Requirements and Price
IBM PC, XT, AT, PS/2, & compatibles; 512 K; 10 Mb hard disk required. Hercules, EGA, CGA, or VGA display. Mouse optional. Laser printer optional. *Single User Price: $295.00*

Microanalytic Data Analysis Package
Kim Kienapple

Department of Child Study
Mount Saint Vincent University
Halifax, NS B3M 2J6 Canada
(902) 443-4450

Series of BASIC programs that analyze observational data. Programs provide for reliability analysis, data analysis, and data reduction. Detailed manual included. Latest release 1992.

Classification: Statistical Package

Hardware Requirements and Price
IBM PC, XT, AT, PS/2, & compatibles; 384 K; hard disk optional; 1 disk drive. Requires DOS 2.0. *Single User Price: Free*

Reviews
Kienapple, K. (1987). Microanalytic data analysis package. *Behavior, Research Methods, Instrumentation, and Computers, 19,* 335-337.

MicroCase Analysis System, Version 2.11

MicroCase Corporation
P.O. Box 2180
West Lafayette, IN 47906
(317) 497-9999

A statistical analysis and data management program that includes a full range of basic statistics plus scatter plots, mapping of ecological data, factor analysis, curve-fitting, and more. Fully menu-driven; effective color graphics, and fast enough for interactive analysis. Contains internal code books, file merge features, and a computer assisted telephone interviewing (CATI) system. Also includes ShowCase, a presentational module for giving live presentations. Allows up to 32,000 variables and 10 million cases. Detailed manual included. On-line help available. Latest release February, 1991.

Classification: Statistical Package

Hardware Requirements and Price
IBM PC, XT, AT, PS/2, & compatibles; 640 K; 3 Mb hard disk required. Hercules, EGA, CGA, or VGA display. Laser printer optional. Requires DOS 3.3. *Single User Price: $395.00 Network Price: $500.00*

Reviews
MicroCase Analysis System. (1989). Microcase: Survey Analysis Software. *Social Science Microcomputer Review, 7,* 241-242.
MicroCase Analysis System. (1988). *Info World,* 72.
SocInfor Software Catalogue, 2nd Edition. (1991).

User Site References
Lev Gonick, Wilfrid Laurier University, 75 University Avenue West, Waterloo,

Ontario, Canada, N2L 3C5, (519) 884-1970 ext. 2860

Michael Kearl, Trinity University, 715 Stadium Drive, San Antonio, TX, 78284, (512) 736-8561

Rick Rosenfeld, University of Missouri State, 8001 Natural Bridge Road, St. Louis, MO, 63121, (314) 553-5016

Laboratory MicroStar
Charles F. Gettys
Lyndon Berglan

Department of Psychology
University of Oklahoma
Norman, OK 73019
(405) 325-4511

A word processor, suitable for use by beginners, that logs keystrokes and keystroke latencies of the user for research purposes. Detailed manual included.

Classification: Research Aide

Hardware Requirements and Price
IBM PC, XT, AT, PS/2, & compatibles; 512 K; hard disk optional; 1 disk drive. MDA, CGA, EGA, or VGA display. Printer required (Epson FX). Laser printer optional. *Single User Price: $25.00 Program is in public domain. Fee includes source code and free consulting.*

MINSQ

MicroMath
2034 East Fort Union Boulevard
Salt Lake City, UT 84121-3144
(801) 943-0290
(800) 942-6284

Program for non-linear curve fitting, parameter estimation and model development with interactive graphics. Models can be entered from keyboard or a file and modified at run time with the built-in editor. Program is able to handle implicit, parametric, or integral functions. A broad range of operators is available in MINSQ for use in user-defined function evaluation routines, with math functions for trancendentals, hyperbolics, error functions, differentiation, and integration. Detailed manual included.

Classification: Statistical Test

Hardware Requirements and Price
IBM PC, XT, AT, PS/2, & compatibles; 512 K; 2 disk drives. Hercules, CGA, or EGA display. *Single User Price: $179.00*

Reviews
Hopke, P. K. (1989). GRAPH and MINSQ. *Chemometrics and Intelligent Laboratory Systems*, May.
Schreier, P. G. (1990, July). Curvefitting capabilities. *Personal Engineering & Instrumentation News*.

Mirror Shapes
James W. Aldridge
Sergio A. Flores

Psychology Department
Pan American University
Edinburg, TX 78539

Algorithm for generating random figures of variable complexity.

Classification: Data Generation

Hardware Requirements and Price
Apple II, 64 K, hard disk optional, 1 disk drive
(5-1/4). Laser printer optional. *Single User
Price: Contact publisher.*

Multiple Factor Analysis (MFA)
Allan Easton

Mathematical Software Co.
4033 Arcadia Way
Oceanside, CA 92056
(619) 940-0343

Draws inferences from masses of empirical
data derived from multiple measurements on
members of a test population. MFA is useful
for analyzing questionnaire responses or
complex test data, and for identifying the
attributes of members of test populations—be
they persons, organizations, groups, animals,
physical objects, events, or times. Three types
of data can be analyzed: primary data (up to
125 variables x 1,000 cases), intercorrelation
matrices (up to 125 x 125 variables), and matrices of factor-loadings (up to 20 factors x 125
variables). Users can factor analyze new primary data, intercorrelation matrices reported
in journal articles, or try different rotational
schemes on their own data or on those of other
researchers. Detailed manual included. On-
line help available. Latest release 1989.

Classification: Statistical Package

Hardware Requirements and Price
IBM PC, XT, AT, PS/2, & compatibles; 256 K;
2 Mb hard disk required; 1 disk drive. Monochrome display. *Single User Price: $149.95*

Macintosh, 1 Mb, 5 Mb hard disk required, 1
disk drive. Monochrome display. *Single User
Price: $149.95*

Multitrait-Multimethod Matrix Analysis
Toshi Hayashi
Ron D. Hays

William C. Brown Publishers
2460 Kerper Blvd.
Dubuque, IA 52001
(319) 588-1451
(800) 351-7671

FORTRAN program that analyzes multitrait-
multimethod matrices.

Classification: Statistical Test

Hardware Requirements and Price
IBM PC, XT, AT, PS/2, & compatibles; 120 K;
hard disk optional; 1 disk drive. *Single User
Price: $30.00 Site License: $400.00*

Reviews
Hayashi, T., & Hays, R. (1987) A microcomputer program for analyzing multitrait-
multimethod matrices. *Behavior, Research
Methods, Instrumentation, and Computers,
19*, 345-348.

NASA/LRC Computerized Test System
W. Kirk Richardson
David A. Washburn
William D. Hopkins

Department of Psychology
Georgia State University
Atlanta, GA 30303
(404) 651-2283

Testing package that includes tasks for studying behavior of many species in a variety of

experimental situations. Routine is written in Quick BASIC and complied with Microsoft BASIC Compiler. Instruction booklet included.

Classification: Research Aid

Hardware Requirements and Price
IBM PC, XT, AT, PS/2, & compatibles; 640 K; 20 MB hard disk required; 1 disk drive. CGA display. Laser printer optional. Joystick and MetraByte PIO-12 I/O board required.

Reviews
Richardson, W. K., Washburn, D. A., & Hopkins, W. D. (1990). The NASA/LSC Computerized Test System. *Behavior, Research Methods, Instrumentation, and Computers*, *22*, 127-131.

Natural
Charles F. Gettys
Paul F. McKane
Tyndon Berglen

Department of Psychology
University of Oklahoma
Norman, OK 73019
(405) 325-4511

A software package that allows the user to create a natural language interface for his or her software. The interface gives 90% accuracy in constrained situations. The user should be a competent Turbo Pascal programmer. Data collection and reduction is required. Detailed manual included.

Classification: Expert Systems

Hardware Requirements and Price
IBM PC, XT, AT, PS/2, & compatibles; 384 K; hard disk optional; 1 disk drive. Laser printer

optional. *Single User Price: $25.00 Price includes source code and free phone consulting*

Number Cruncher Statistical System (NCSS)
Jerry L. Hintze

NCSS
329 N. 1000 East Street
Kaysville, UT 84037
(801) 546-0445

A statistical package that includes ANOVA, crosstabs, correlation analysis, factor analysis, and much more. Spreadsheet style user-interface. Detailed manual included. On-line help available. Latest release August, 1991.

Classification: Statistical Package

Hardware Requirements and Price
IBM PC, XT, AT, PS/2, & compatibles; 512 K; 2 Mb hard disk optional; 1 disk drive. Laser printer optional. *Single User Price: $125.00*

Reviews
Butler, D., & Neudecker, W. (1989). A comparison of inexpensive statistical packages for microcomputer running MS-DOS. *Behavior, Research Methods, Instrumentation, and Computers*, *21*, 113-120.
Kallam, M. (1988). Number Cruncher Statistical System. *Social Science Computer Review*, *6*, 302-303.

NCSS Advanced Tables
Jerry Hintze

Pacific Ease Company
601 Pacific Street
Santa Monica, CA 90405
(310) 396-5007

Program includes loglinear models, multi-dimensional scaling, and correspondence analysis. Detailed manual included. Latest release November, 1991.

Classification: Statistical Test

Hardware Requirements and Price
IBM PC, XT, AT, PS/2, & compatibles; 512 K; 2 Mb hard disk optional; 1 disk drive. Hercules, CGA, EGA, or VGA display. Laser printer optional. Requires NCSS Base System 5.03. *Single User Price: $59.00*

NCSS Base Statistical System (5.03)
Jerry Hintze

Pacific Ease Company
601 Pacific Street
Santa Monica, CA 90405
(310) 396-5007

The NCSS Base Statistical System includes a new 440 page manual, a probability calculator, and nonparametric tests. It can do spreadsheet data entry; import/export ASCII or spreadsheet files; create keyboard macros; sort, merge, transpose, summarize, and subset databases; do formula-type transformations; set up databases with up to 500 columns by 32,000 rows; do basic statistics, *t*-tests, crosstabs, and chi-square analysis; handle ANOVA with covariates; manipulate repeated measures; and manage regression analysis including step-wise and robust methods, factor, cluster and discriminant analysis. Latest release November, 1991.

Classification: Statistical Package

Hardware Requirements and Price
IBM PC, XT, AT, PS/2, & compatibles; 256 K; 1 disk drive. Monochrome, Hercules, CGA,

EGA, or VGA display. *Single User Price: $125.00*

Reviews
Bassler, B. J., & Hartwick, R. A. (1988). Number Cruncher Statistical System. Version 5.01. *American Chemical Society Journal, 110*(24), 8572-3.
Hintze, J. (1989). NCSS Base Statistical System (5.03). *PC Magazine, 8*(5), 94-200.

NCSS Curve Fitter
Jerry Hintze

Pacific Ease Company
601 Pacific Street
Santa Monica, CA 90405
(310) 396-5007

Fits hundreds of curves to x-y data. Select a pre-programmed model or enter a personal one. Models include polynomials, ratio of polynomials, multiphase, growth curves, sum of exponentials, sigmoidal, normal, and log-normal. Program stores predicted values, residuals, and prediction limits. Automatic bias correction is available. A high-speed search procedure tries hundreds of models while searching for the best fitting curve. Scatter plot matrix displays the effects of different transformations. A special graphical data input routine allows visual editing of data. Detailed manual included. Latest release November, 1991.

Classification: Statistical Test

Hardware Requirements and Price
IBM PC, XT, AT, PS/2, & compatibles; 512 K; 3 Mb hard disk optional; 1 disk drive. Hercules, CGA, EGA, or VGA display. Laser printer optional. Requires NCSS Base System 5.03. *Single User Price: $99.00*

NCSS Experimental Designs
Jerry Hintze

Pacific Ease Company
601 Pacific Street
Santa Monica, CA 90405
(310) 396-5007

Generates two-level fractional factorials and response surface designs (Box-Behn Kin, Placket-Burman, central composite). Analysis includes response surface, cube plots, probability plots and confounding patterns. Detailed manual included. Latest release November, 1991.

Classification: Statistical Test

Hardware Requirements and Price
IBM PC, XT, AT, PS/2, & compatibles; 256 K; 2 Mb hard disk optional; 1 disk drive. Monochrome, CGA, EGA, or VGA display. Laser printer optional. Requires NCSS 5.03 Base System. *Single User Price: $59.00*

NCSS Graphics System
Jerry Hintze

Pacific Ease Company
601 Pacific Street
Santa Monica, CA 90405
(310) 396-5007

NCSS Graphics System includes: bar and pie charts, histograms, density traces, contour maps, scatter plots with overlaying and bracing, rotating 3-D plots, multivariate plots, spline curves, function plots, error-bar plots, and box plots. Detailed manual included. Latest release Novemer, 1991.

Classification: Graphics

Hardware Requirements and Price
IBM PC, XT, AT, PS/2, & compatibles; 512 K; 2 Mb hard disk optional; 1 disk drive. Hercules, CGA, EGA, or VGA display. Laser printer optional. Requires NCSS 5.03 Base System. *Single User Price: $79.00 Network Price: Contact publisher*

NCSS PASS
Jerry L. Hintze

NCSS
329 N. 1000 East Street
Kaysville, UT 84037
(801) 546-0445

Power analysis and sample size calculations for ANOVA, cross tabs, multiple regression, *t*-tests, proportions, repeated measures, and much more. Includes graphical and numeric output. All calculations correct to 12 decimal places. Detailed manual included. On-line help available. Latest release August, 1991.

Classification: Power Analysis

Hardware Requirements and Price
IBM PC, XT, AT, PS/2, & compatibles; 512 K; hard disk optional; 1 disk drive. Mouse optional. Laser printer optional. *Single User Price: $149.00*

NCSS Power Pack
Jerry Hintze

Pacific Ease Company
601 Pacific Street
Santa Monica, CA 90405
(310) 396-5007

NCSS Power Pack includes: canonical correlation, logictic regression, nonlinear regression, response surface, ANOVA with repeated measures, variable selection in multivariate regression, and MANOVA. Detailed manual included. Latest release November, 1991.

Classification: Statistical Package

Hardware Requirements and Price
IBM PC, XT, AT, PS/2, & compatibles; 256 K; 2 Mb hard disk optional; 1 disk drive. Monochrome, Hercules, CGA, EGA, or VGA display. Laser printer optional. Requires NCSS 5.03 Base System. *Single User Price: $69.00*

NCSS Statistical Process Control & Quality Control
Jerry Hintze

Pacific Ease Company
601 Pacific Street
Santa Monica, CA 90405
(310) 396-5007

This program includes: X-bar, R-charts, or S-charts; individual charts; capability studies; P-, U-, C-, and NP- charts; runs tests; and pareto charts. Detailed manual included. Latest release November, 1991.

Classification: Statistical Test

Hardware Requirements and Price
IBM PC, XT, AT, PS/2, & compatibles; 512 K; 2 Mb hard disk optional; 1 disk drive (3-1/2). Hercules, CGA, EGA, or VGA display. Laser printer optional. Requires NCSS Base System 5.03. *Single User Price: $59.00*

NCSS Student Version
Jerry Hintze

Pacific Ease Company
601 Pacific Street
Santa Monica, CA 90405
(310) 396-5007

A new stand-alone classroom version of NCSS that includes the spreadsheet, transformations, descriptive statistics, cross tabulation, proportion tests, multinomial tests, *t*-tests, ANOVA, nonparametric tests, multiple regression, forecasting, box plots, histograms, scatter plots, and probability calculator. Detailed manual included. Latest release September, 1991.

Classification: Statistical Package

Hardware Requirements and Price
IBM PC, XT, AT, PS/2, & compatibles; 512 K; hard disk optional; 1 disk drive. Hercules, CGA, EGA, or VGA display. Laser printer optional. *Single User Price: $29.00*

NCSS Survival Analysis
Jerry Hintze

Pacific Ease Company
601 Pacific Street
Santa Monica, CA 90405
(310) 396-5007

Product-limit surviorship with graphics. Estimates gamma, Weibull, normal, lognormal, exponential, and Rayleigh distributions. Computes Cox's regression. Group tests include logrank and Wilcoxin. Also performs Peto and Probit analysis. Detailed manual included. Latest release November, 1991.

Classification: Statistical Test

Hardware Requirements and Price
IBM PC, XT, AT, PS/2, & compatibles; 512 K; 2 Mb hard disk optional; 1 disk drive. Hercules, CGA, EGA, or VGA display. Laser printer optional. Requires NCSS Base System. *Single User Price: $69.00*

NCSS Time Series & Forecasting
Jerry Hintze

Pacific Ease Company
601 Pacific Street
Santa Monica, CA 90405
(310) 396-5007

This program includes: ARIMA (regular and seasonal models), automatic ARMA, spectral analysis, classical decomposition, and exponential smoothing. Detailed manual included. Latest release November, 1991.

Classification: Statistical Test

Hardware Requirements and Price
IBM PC, XT, AT, PS/2, & compatibles; 512 K; 2 Mb hard disk optional; 1 disk drive (3-1/2). Hercules, CGA, EGA, or VGA display. Laser printer optional. Requires NCSS Base System. *Single User Price: $69.00*

NCSS Wireframe Graphics
Jerry Hintze

Pacific Ease Company
601 Pacific Street
Santa Monica, CA 90405
(310) 396-5007

Creates 3-D density contours using fishnets. Also creates 3-D star plots for displaying a large number of rows. Detailed manual included. Latest release November, 1991.

Classification: Graphics

Hardware Requirements and Price
IBM PC, XT, AT, PS/2, & compatibles; 512 K; 2 Mb hard disk optional; 1 disk drive. Hercules, CGA, EGA, or VGA display. Laser printer optional. Requires NCSS Base System 5.03. *Single User Price: $29.00*

NETS
NASA Johnson Space Center

COSMIC
The University of Georgia
382 East Broad Street
Athens, GA 30602
(404) 542-3265

NETS, a tool for the development and evaluation of neural networks, provides a simulation of neural network algorithms plus an environment for developing such algorithms. Neural networks are a class of systems modeled after the human brain. Artificial neural networks are formed from hundreds or thousands of simulated neurons, connected to each other in a manner similar to brain neurons. Problems that involve pattern matching readily fit the class of problems that NETS is designed to solve. Source code included. Detailed manual included. Latest release 1989.

Classification: Expert Systems

Hardware Requirements and Price
Contact publisher for hardware options. 1 Mb hard disk required, 1 disk drive (5-1/4). *Single User Price: $120.00*

NIPR Testing Statistics (NTS) Package
J. Boeyens

National Institute for Personnel Research
P.O. Box 32410 Braamfontein
H. Trytsman
Johannesburg, 2017 South Africa
0113394451

Generates psychometric statistics often needed by test developers and users. The analyses include: norm tables, item analyses, test reliabilities, predictive bias, correlations, t-tests, and three item bias detection procedures. It also includes data and text editors. Detailed manual included. Latest release January, 1991.

Classification: Survey Analysis

Hardware Requirements and Price
IBM PC, XT, AT, PS/2, & compatibles; 640 K; hard disk optional; 1 disk drive. Requires DOS 3.0. Math coprocessor optional. *Single User Price: $200.00*

User Site References
M. Tere Blanche, University of South Africa, Health Psychology Unit, P.O. Box 392, Presoria, South Africa, 0001, 0117251320
P. Holburn, HSRC, CNR Jan Smuis Avenue, Empire Road, Johannesburg, South Africa, 0113394451
H. Trytsman, Anglo American Corporation, P.O. Box 87, Welkom, 9460, 017152000

Nonparametric Partial Correlation
C. Craig Morris

Department of Psychology
Middle Tennessee State University
Munfreesboro, TN 37132
(615) 898-5933

A PC-compatible computer program that computes three nonparametric bivariate correlations. Written in Turbo Pascal, Version 3.0. Instruction booklet included.

Classification: Nonparametric Test

Hardware Requirements and Price
IBM PC, XT, AT, PS/2, & compatibles; 256 K; hard disk optional; 1 disk drive. Mouse optional. Modem optional. Laser printer optional. *Single User Price: $3.50*

Reviews
Morris, C. (1990). A program to compute nonparametric parial correlation coefficents. *Behavior, Research Methods, Instrumentation, and Computers, 22,* 82-86.

Normal Distribution Algorithms
Alfred L. Brophy
D. Louis Wood

Behavioral Science Associates
P.O. Box 748
West Chester, PA 19381
(215) 436-6859

Five algorithms that evaluate the normal distribution function.

Classification: Normal Distribution

Hardware Requirements and Price
IBM PC, XT, AT, PS/2, & compatibles; 64 K; hard disk optional. BASIC interpreter required. *Single User Price: Free, send a self-addressed, stamped envelope*

Reviews
Brophy, A. L., & Wood, D. L. (1989). Algorithms for fast and precise computation of

the normal integral. *Behavior, Research Methods, Instrumentation, and Computers, 21,* 447-454.

Normal Distribution Function
Alfred L. Brophy

Behavioral Science Associates
P.O. Box 748
West Chester, PA 19381
(215) 436-6859

Seven different approximations of the normal distribution function.

Classification: Normal Distribution

Hardware Requirements and Price
TRS-80, Model III & IV; 1 K; hard disk optional. BASIC interpreter required. *Single User Price: Free, send a self-addressed, stamped envelope*

Reviews
Brophy, A. L. (1983). Normal Distribution Function. *Behavior, Research Methods, Instrumentation, and Computers, 15,* 604-605.

Npstat Version 3.5
R. B. May
M. E. J. Masson
M. A. Hunter

Department of Psychology
University of Victoria
P.O. Box 3050
Victoria, B.C. V8W 3P5 Canada
(604) 721-7522

Designed as a teaching aid for students with little background in statistics or computing. Handles basic topics taught in a first course in statistics from a simple frequency table to two-factor analysis of variance. In addition to common parametric analyses, it includes permutation tests for scores and ranks in research involving 2 to 8 groups in independent designs, dependent designs, and 2 to 8 variables in bivariate correlation. Imports data from SPSS, MINITAB, and other programs. On-line help available. Tutorial program included. Latest release March 26, 1991.

Classification: Statistical Package

Hardware Requirements and Price
IBM PC, XT, AT, PS/2, & compatibles; 512 K; hard disk optional; 1 disk drive. MDA, CGA, EGA or VGA display. Laser printer optional. Requires DOS 2.0. Math coprocessor optional. *Single User Price: $10.00 Network Price: $4.00 per concurrent user*

Reviews
May, R. B., Masson, M. E. J., & Hunter, M. A. (1989). Randomization tests: Viable alternatives to normal curve tests.

User Site References
G. Bear, School of Science, Ramapo College, 505 Ramapo Valley Road, Mahwah, NJ, 07430 (201) 529-7500

G. A. Forsyth, Department of Psychology, Millersville University, Millersville, PA, 17551, (717) 872-3932

J. A. Mulick, Department of Pediatrics, The Ohio State University, 700 Childrens Drive, Columbus, OH, 43205

NWA Statpak

Northwest Analytical
520 Northwest Davis Street
Portland, OR 97209
(503) 224-7727

Statistical package that includes probability calculations, descriptive statistics, chi-square, non-parametric statistics, frequency histogram, quantile/normal probability plot, means testing, survey analysis, and ANOVA. Detailed manual included. Latest release August, 1987.

Classification: Statistical Package

Hardware Requirements and Price
IBM PC, XT, AT, PS/2, & compatibles; 512 K; hard disk optional; 2 disk drives. Graphic display required. Laser printer optional. Source code available. *Single User Price: $495.00*

Observe Version 2.0-A Package For Observation Research

Richard Deni
32 Merritt Drive, Department DS
Lawrenceville, NJ 08648
(609) 895-5435

Program records "stream of behavior." Tracks number of occurrences, durations, sequences, states, and latencies. Analysis options include automated agreement checks between or within observers. Detailed manual included.

Classification: Research Aid

Hardware Requirements and Price
Macintosh, 1 Mb, hard disk optional, 2 disk drives. Printer required (Imagewriter). Not compatible with laser printer. *Single User Price: Contact author*

The Observer
Lucas P. J. J. Noldus
Roel P. J. Potting

Noldus Informational Technology, n.v.
University Business & Technology Center
Vadaring 51
Wageningen, 6702 EA Netherlands
31837097677
Fax: 31837024496

Software for event recording and data analysis. Records the frequency and duration of real-time events. Detailed manual and tutorial program included. On-line help available. Latest release March 28, 1991.

Classification: Research Aid

Hardware Requirements and Price
IBM PC, XT, AT, PS/2, & compatibles; 384 K; hard disk optional; 1 disk drive. Laser printer optional. Requires DOS 2.0. Support packages available for hand-held computers *Single User Price: $895.00*

Psion Organizer, 32 K. Requires base package for IBM PC *Single User Price: $495.00*

Reviews
Hile, M. B. (1991). Hand held behavioral observations: The observer. *Behavioral Assessment, 13*(2).
Noldus, L. P. J. J. (1991). The Observer: A software system for collection and analysis of observational data. *Behavioral Research Methods, Instruments and Computers, 23*, 415-429.
Noldus, L. P. J. J., Van de Loo, E. H. L. M. & Timmers, P. H. A. (1989). Computers in behavioral research. *Nature, 341*, 767-768.

User Site References
M. L. Boccia, University of Colorado Health Sciences Center, Department of Psychiatry, Box C-268, 4200 East 9th Avenue, Denver,

CO, 80262, (303) 270-7744, Fax: (303) 270-5641

K. S. Storey, Allegheny-Singer Research Institute, Early Childhood Intervention Program, 320 East North Avenue, Pittsburgh, PA, 15212-9986, (412) 359-3596, Fax: (412) 231-4620

L. E. Williams, University of South Alabama, Department of Comparative Medicine, Mobile, AL, 36688, (205) 460-6293, Fax: (205) 460-7783

Oneway
Joseph S. Rossi

Cancer Prevention Research Center
University of Rhode Island
Kingston, RI 02881-0808
(401) 792-2830
Fax: (401) 792-5562

BASIC program for computing an ANOVA from group summary statistics. Instruction booklet included. Latest release 1989.

Classification: ANOVA

Hardware Requirements and Price
IBM PC, XT, AT, PS/2, & compatibles; 128 K; hard disk optional; 1 disk drive. CGA display. Mouse optional. Laser printer optional. Requires DOS 2.1. Available as a BASIC listing or an executable file. *Single User Price: Free*

Reviews
Rossi, J. S. (1988). ONEWAY: A BASIC program for computing ANOVA from group summary statistics. *Behavior, Research Methods, Instrumentation, and Computers, 20,* 347-348.

Operant/PC
S. C. Fowler

Life Science Associates
1 Fenimore Road
Bayport, NY 11705-2115
(516) 472-2111
Fax: (516) 472-8146

Operant software package that provides detailed microanalyses of the response duration and inter-response time of individual operant responses. Experimental protocol for each chamber is specified during a query driven, set-up dialog. Parameters for experimental protocols can be saved on diskette. Detailed manual included. Latest release 1988.

Classification: Data Management

Hardware Requirements and Price
IBM PC, XT, AT, PS/2, & compatibles; 128 K. *Single User Price: $200.00*

Orthogonal Comparisons
Allen H. Wolach
Maureen A. McHale

Department of Psychology
Illinois Institute of Technology
Chicago, IL 60616
(312) 567-3500

Program to determine orthogonal comparisons. Instruction booklet included.

Classification: ANOVA

Hardware Requirements and Price
IBM PC, XT, AT, PS/2, & compatibles; 256 K;

hard disk optional; 1 disk drive. Monochrome, CGA, EGA or VGA display. Laser printer optional. *Single User Price: $1.50*

Reviews
Wolach, A., & McHale, M. (1988). Orthogonal comparisons. *Behavior, Research Methods, Instrumentation, and Computers, 20,* 337.

User Site References
Jerome Feldman, State College of Optometry, 100 East 24th Street, New York, NY, 10010, (212) 420-4986

Pam
R. Stewart Longman
Albert A. Cota
Ronald R. Holden

Department of Psychology
Queen's University
Kingston, ON K7L 3N6 Canada
(613) 545-6005

A FORTRAN routine for the parallel analysis method in principle components analysis. Instruction booklet included.

Classification: Statistical Test

Hardware Requirements and Price
Contact author for equipment options and price.

Reviews
Longman, R. S., Cota, A. A., & Holden, R. R. (1989). PAM: A double-precision FORTRAN routine for the parallel analysis method in principal components analysis. *Behavior, Research Methods, Instrumentation, and Computers, 21,* 477-480.

Parallel
Ron D. Hays

Ron Hays
1700 Main Street
Santa Monica, CA 90407-2138
(213) 393-0411

BASIC program that estimates random data eigen values for exploratory factor analysis. Instruction booklet included.

Classification: Exploratory Data Analysis

Hardware Requirements and Price
IBM PC, XT, AT, PS/2, & compatibles; 256 K; hard disk optional; 1 disk drive (5-1/4). *Single User Price: Free, send diskette.*

PASS: Power Analysis and Sample Size
Jerry Hintze

Pacific Ease Company
601 Pacific Street
Santa Monica, CA 90405
(310) 396-5007

Provides a tool that calculates necessary sample sizes or power values. Includes *t*-tests, proportions, correlations, log-rank survival tests, ANOVA, multiple regression, repeated measures, bioequivalence tests, chi-square, and logistic regression. Output may be in numerical or graphical form. Detailed manual included. Latest release September, 1991.

Classification: Power Analysis

Hardware Requirements and Price
IBM PC, XT, AT, PS/2, & compatibles; 512 K; 1 Mb hard disk optional; 1 disk drive.

Hercules, CGA, EGA, or VGA display. Laser printer optional. *Single User Price: $149.00*

Programmer Assessment Software Tools (PAST)

Richard T. Redmond
Jean B. Gasen

Department of Information Systems
Virginia Commonwealth University
Richmond, VA 23284

PAST is a program that analyzes how programmers develop and test program code.

Classification: Research Aid

Hardware Requirements and Price
IBM PC, XT, AT, PS/2, & compatibles; 256 K; hard disk optional; 1 disk drive. CGA display. Laser printer optional. *Single User Price: $5.00*

Reviews
Redmond, R. T., & Gasen J. B. (1988). PAST: Viewing the programming process. *Behavior, Research Methods, Instrumentation, and Computers, 20*, 503-507.

PC-DADS: Data Acquisition Display and Storage System

NASA Goddard Space Center

COSMIC
The University of Georgia
382 East Broad Street
Athens, GA 30602
(404) 542-3265

Acquires four channels of data, displays all four channels in real time on monitor, and stores the data on a RAM disk or file. Up to 200 samples per second may be taken on each channel. 110 statement code included. Detailed manual included. Latest release 1987.

Classification: Data Management

Hardware Requirements and Price
IBM PC, XT, AT, PS/2, & compatibles; 128 K; hard disk optional. *Single User Price: $50.00*

PeakFit

Ron Brown

Jandel Scientific
65 Koch Road
Corte Madera, CA 94925
(415) 924-8640
(800) 874-1888

Sophisticated non-linear curve fitting for peak analysis and quantification. Designed to determine parameters such as amplitude, center, and width. PeakFit is also used to separate multiple overlapping peak data and find unresolved peaks. Users may enter their own equations or choose from an extensive list of built-in functions specifically for chemistry/ pharmacology, chromatography, spectroscopy, and statistical data. PeakFit offers the unique ability to graphically observe and control the curve fitting algorithm–at each iteration of the fit the user is free to intervene and make both graphical and numerical adjustments. It offers a comprehensive graphical/numerical summary as well as extensive output options for both data and resulting graphs. Detailed manual included. On-line help available. Latest release November, 1991.

Classification: Statistical Test

Hardware Requirements and Price
IBM PC, XT, AT, PS/2, & compatibles; 640 K; 1.6 Mb hard disk required; 1 disk drive. Hercules, EGA, or VGA display. Mouse optional. Laser printer optional. Requires DOS 3.0. *Single User Price: $595.00*

Reviews
Brinkly, R., & Malenick, D. (1991). Table-Curve & PeakFit, *Biotechnology Software*, 25, 5-7.

PhoneDisc California +

PhoneDisc USA Corporation
8 Doaks Lane
Marblehead, MA 01945
(617) 639-2900
(800) 284-8353

PhoneDisc California + puts the information of 765 white-page phone books and criss-cross directories at the user's fingertips. Listings can be retrieved by name, address, or telephone number. Zip codes are also included with every listing. Detailed manual included.

Classification: Database

Hardware Requirements and Price
IBM PC, XT, AT, PS/2, & compatibles; 512 K; 1 Mb hard disk required. Monochrome or color display. Modem optional. Laser printer optional. CD-ROM drive & CD-ROM extensions required. *Single User Price: $995.00 (annual subscription with semi-annual updates). $1,195.00 (annual subscription with quarterly updates) Network Price: $1,492.50 (annual subscription with semi-annual updates). $1,792.50 (annual subscription with quarterly updates)*

PhoneDisc QuickRef +

PhoneDisc USA Corporation
8 Doaks Lane
Marblehead, MA 01945
(617) 639-2900
(800) 284-8353

PhoneDisc QuickRef+ is a single CD-ROM containing 300,000 listings of the most often called corporations, organizations, government agencies, fax, and toll free numbers in the United States. Important information is available instantly. Searches may be initiated using telephone number, company name, business type, street or P.O. box, city, state, or zip code. PhoneDisc QuickRef + is purchased as any traditional software product and is updated annually. Detailed manual included.

Classification: Database

Hardware Requirements and Price
IBM PC, XT, AT, PS/2, & compatibles; 512 K; 1 Mb hard disk required. Monochrome or color display. Modem optional. Laser printer optional. CD-ROM drive & CD-ROM extensions required. *Single User Price: $99.00 Network Price: $148.50*

PhoneDisc USA National Set

PhoneDisc USA Corporation
8 Doaks Lane
Marblehead, MA 01945
(617) 639-2900
(800) 284-8353

PhoneDisc USA is the first personal computer based telephone directory with listings covering every city in the United States. Detailed manual included.

Classification: Database

Hardware Requirements and Price
IBM PC, XT, AT, PS/2, & compatibles; 512 K; 1 Mb hard disk required. Monochrome or color display. Modem optional. Laser printer optional. CD-ROM drive & CD-ROM extensions required. *Single User Price: $1,850.00 Network Price: $2,775.00*

Pictorial Stimuli
John O. Brooks, III

Department of Psychiatry & Behavioral Sciences (TD-114)
Stanford University School of Medicine
Stanford, CA 94305-5490
(415) 493-5000

A total of 260 line drawings for the Apple Macintosh.

Classification: Graphics

Hardware Requirements and Price
Macintosh. Any graphics editor. *Single User Price: $12.00*

Reviews
Brooks, J. O. (1985). Pictorial stimuli for the Apple Macintosh computer. *Behavior, Research Methods, Instrumentation, and Computers, 17,* 409-410.

Polynomial Regression-PC

Oakleaf Systems
P.O. Box 472
Decorah, IA 52101
(319) 382-4320

Program allows up to 500 pairs of data to be used to calculate a least-squares polynomial regression (up to 12th order). Features include 30-digit accuracy in calculations and easy editing of values. Save or load data from a disk. Program allows drawing of the polynomial fitted lines on a scatter plot of the data. Detailed manual included.

Classification: Correlation and Regression

Hardware Requirements and Price
IBM PC, XT, AT, PS/2, & compatibles; 128 K; hard disk optional; 1 disk drive. *Single User Price: $49.95*

Probabilities
Joseph C. Hudson

William C. Brown Publishers
2460 Kerper Blvd.
Dubuque, IA 52001
(319) 588-1451
(800) 351-7671

This IBM program computes exact probabilities for the binomial, negative binomial, hypergeometric, and poisson distributions without interpolation. It also computes probabilities and percentage points for the standard, normal student's t, chi-squared, and F-distributions. Computation is to four decimal places. Detailed manual included.

Classification: Statistical Test

Hardware Requirements and Price
IBM PC, XT, AT, PS/2, & compatibles; 256 K; hard disk optional; 1 disk drive. *Single User Price: $37.50 Site License: $400.00*

Program to Compute Nonparametric Partial Correlation Coefficients
C. Craig Morris

Department of Psychology
Middle Tennessee State University
Murfreesboro, TN 37132
(615) 898-5933

Program computes nonparametric partial correlation coefficients, including the Goodman-Kruskal gamma, Somers' dyx, and Wilson's e, along with their standard errors. Instruction booklet included.

Classification: Nonparametric Test

Hardware Requirements and Price
IBM PC, XT, AT, PS/2, & compatibles; 256 K; hard disk optional; 1 disk drive. Mouse optional. Modem optional. Laser printer optional. *Single User Price: Contact author*

Psych Plot
David Anderson

William C. Brown Publishers
2460 Kerper Blvd.
Dubuque, IA 52001
(319) 588-1451
(800) 351-7671

Plotter package for bar, line, and scatterplots. Works stand-alone or with PsychStats. Conforms to American Psychological Association (APA) style. Detailed manual included.

Classification: Graphics

Hardware Requirements and Price
IBM PC, XT, AT, PS/2, & compatibles; 256 K; hard disk optional; 1 disk drive. Color display required. Printer required (IBM 7372 Plotter). *Single User Price: $30.00 Site License: $400.00*

Psychiatry

SilverPlatter Information
100 River Ridge Drive
Norwood, MA 02062
(617) 769-2599
(800) 343-0064

A CD-ROM database covering over 145,000 citations for the past 10 years. Seven thousand new records are added with each update.

Classification: Database

Hardware Requirements and Price
Contact publisher for equipment options. CD-ROM reader. *Single User Price: $995.00*

PsycLit

American Psychological Association
750 First Street, N.E.
Washington, DC 20002
(800) 336-4980

An information package in psychology including a database on two CD-ROMs, retrieval software, and user documentation. Allows quick retrieval of data from Psychological Abstracts back to 1974. Beginning in 1992 PsycLit will contain data from books and book chapters back to 1987. This advanced search and retrieval system developed by SilverPlatter Information, Inc. is updated quarterly. Discounts available for subscribers to Psychological Abstracts and for multiple PsycLit subscriptions. Detailed manual and tutorial program included. On-line help available. Updated quarterly.

Classification: Database

Hardware Requirements and Price
IBM PC, XT, AT, PS/2, & compatibles; 640 K; 2-3 Mb hard disk required; 1 disk drive. Monochrome or color display. Laser printer optional. CD-ROM disc drive required. *Single User Price: $4,495.00 per year Network Price: $6,750.00 per year*

Macintosh, 2 Mb, 2-3 Mb hard disk required, 1 disk drive. Mouse required. Laser printer optional. Requires System 6.02 or higher. *Single User Price: $4,495.00 Network Price: $6,750.00*

Reviews
Nicholls, P. (1990). *CD-ROM collection builders toolkit.* Weston, CT: Pemberton Press.
Volgt, K. (1990, February). Optical product review: PsycLit. *CD-ROM Librarian, 5,* 45-48.

PsyComNet

I. K. Goldberg
1346 Lexington Ave.
New York, NY 10128
(212) 876-7800

Program allows the user's computer to communicate with psychologists and other mental health professionals throughout the United States and Canada. Facilitates electronic mail, bulletin boards, and on-line seminars. On-line help available.

Classification: Research Aid

Hardware Requirements and Price
Contact publisher for equipment options and price.

Q-Stix
Mark Cunningham

Crofter Publishing
4310 S. Semoran #690
Orlando, FL 32822

A basic statistics package. Allows a dataset of up to 20 columns and 100 rows. Computes crosstabs, correlation, *t*-tests, and analysis of variance (one-way, two way, and split-plot). Allows extensive manipulation of data, including transformations, lagging, and sorts. Detailed manual included.

Classification: Statistical Package

Hardware Requirements and Price
Apple II, 128 K, hard disk optional, 2 disk drives (5-1/4). Requires ProDOS. *Single User Price: $120.00*

Quick CSS

StatSoft, Inc.
2325 East 13th Street
Tulsa, OK 74104
(918) 583-4149
Fax: (918) 583-4376

Quick CSS includes basic statistics, non-parametrics, crosstabulation, multiple regression, general ANOVA/ANCOVA/MANOVA, and more. Over 50 types of graphs are integrated within all analyses. Data management features include fast spreadsheet editor, relational joining of files, nested sorting, powerful transformations, and comprehensive reporting options. Imports and exports Lotus 1-2-3, dBase, Excel, SPSS, and ASCII files. Detailed manual included. On-line help available. Latest release February, 1991.

Classification: Statistical Package

Hardware Requirements and Price
IBM PC, XT, AT, PS/2, & compatibles; 640 K; 20 Mb hard disk required. Hercules, CGA, EGA, VGA, or Super VGA display. Mouse optional. Laser printer optional. Requires DOS 3.2. *Single User Price: $295.00 Network Price: Varies, based on the number of nodes*

Quick CSS/Mac

StatSoft, Inc.
2325 East 13th Street
Tulsa, OK 74104
(918) 583-4149
Fax: (918) 583-4376

Quick CSS/Mac includes all basic statistical analyses of Statistica/Mac, including descriptives, correlations, *t*-tests, nonparametrics, crosstabulation, multiple regression, and ANOVA/ANCOVA. The program permits full 2-D and 3-D graphing, and includes on-screen customization using MacDraw-like tools. Data management features include fast spreadsheet editor, merging and splitting of files, nested sorting, and transformations. Imports and exports Excel, CSS: Statistica (DOS), and ASCII files. Detailed manual included. On-line help available. Latest release October, 1991.

Classification: Statistical Package

Hardware Requirements and Price
Macintosh, 1 Mb, 10 Mb hard disk required. Monochrome or color display. Mouse required. Laser printer optional. Requires System 6 or 7. *Single User Price: $295.00*

Random Tools
Burrton Woodruff

Department of Psychology
Butler University, 4600 Sunset Avenue
Indianapolis, IN 46208
(317) 283-9267

Provides randomization procedures and functions for inclusion in other programs. UCSD Pascal unit.

Classification: Research Aid

Hardware Requirements and Price
Apple II+, IIe, IIc, IIgs. Apple Pascal, Version 1.3 required. *Single User Price: $5.00*

Realtime
Douglas K. Symons
Heather M. Acton
Greg Moran

Department of Psychology
Acadia University
Wolfville, NS B0P 1X0 Canada
(902) 542-2201

Data collection tool for accepting behavior observation codes from a keyboard. Instruction booklet included.

Classification: Research Aid

Hardware Requirements and Price
IBM PC, XT, AT, PS/2, & compatibles; 256 K; hard disk optional; 1 disk drive (5-1/4). Modem optional. Laser printer optional. *Single User Price: $5.00*

Reviews

Symons, O. K., Acton, H. M., & Moran, G. (1990). Using personal computers for behavioral coding in real-time: The Realtime and Tmerge programs. *Social Science Computer Review, 8,* 426-430.

The Research Assistant

Marley Watkins
Joe Kush

Ed & Psych Associates
1702 West Camelback Road, Suite 267
Phoenix, AZ 85015
(602) 420-1747

Calculates descriptive statistics, chi-square, correlations, *t*-tests, one-way ANOVA, and multiple regression analyses for up to 1,000 subjects with 20 variables per subject. On-line help available. Latest release 1989.

Classification: Statistical Package

Hardware Requirements and Price
Apple II+, IIe, IIc, IIgs; 48 K; hard disk optional; 1 disk drive (5-1/4). Requires DOS 3.3. *Single User Price: $19.95*

ROBREG

Jon Anson

Department of Social Work
Ben Gurion University of the Negev
84105 Beer Sheba Israel
97257261452
Fax: 97257313220

An APL procedure for fitting robust regression lines using Huber's M-estimate. On-line help available. Latest release 1988.

Classification: Correlation and Regression

Hardware Requirements and Price
IBM PC, XT, AT, PS/2, & compatibles; 256 K; hard disk optional; 1 disk drive (5-1/4). CGA display. *Single User Price: $10.00*

Reviews
Anson, J. (1988). ROBEG: An APL procedure for fitting robust regression lines using Huber's M-estimate. *Behavior, Research Methods, Instrumentation, and Computers, 20,* 579-582.

Roto-Rat: Rotational Activity Monitoring

MED Associates, Inc.
Box 47
East Fairfield, VT 05448
(802) 827-3825

Provides the user with up to 24 independent test stations when used with a MED Associates interface package and directional low friction rotational sensors. One large graphics display and 8 smaller windows are visible on the screen at any one time. Records elapsed time and cumulative counts. Time slices and total time are selectable. Data may be saved to disk while a test station is active for continuous studies. Detailed manual included. On-line help available.

Classification: Equipment Control

Hardware Requirements and Price
IBM PC, XT, AT, PS/2, & compatibles; 640 K; hard disk optional; 2 disk drives. Hercules, EGA, or VGA display. Requires DOS 3.3. MED Associates interface modules required. *Single User Price: $600.00*

Rstrip

MicroMath
2034 East Fort Union Blvd.
Salt Lake City, UT 84121-3144
(801) 943-0290
(800) 942-6284

Program for exponential stripping, curve fitting, and interactive graphics for compartmental modeling and linear pharmacokinetic analysis. Features include weighting scheme for fitting single exponentials to sets of residuals, storage and reuse of intermediate results during recursive stripping, restriction of searches to data groups most likely to include the best partitioning, and technique for least squares refinement. Multiple data sets may appear on the same plot, and two or more model curves may be plotted with data sheet. Detailed manual included. Latest release January, 1991.

Classification: Statistical Test

Hardware Requirements and Price
IBM PC, XT, AT, PS/2, & compatibles; 512 K; 500 K hard disk optional; 1 disk drive (3-1/2). Hercules, CGA, or EGA display required. Laser printer optional. Requires DOS 3.3. Math coprocessor optional. *Single User Price: $349.00*

The SAS System

SAS Institute Inc.
SAS Campus Drive
Cary, NC 27513-2414
(919) 677-8000
Fax: (919) 677-8123

The SAS System, a suite of integrated software products for enterprise-wide information delivery. Combines four data-driven tasks (data access, data management, data analysis, and data presentation) into one software system. For statistics, research and presentation, the SAS System provides information and presentation color graphics and tools for statistical and graphical data analysis. The software offers device-intelligent color graphics for producing charts, maps and plots in a variety of patterns. Users can customize graphs and present multiple graphs on a page. Graphic data analysis capabilities allow users to explore data through a variety of graphic displays. All observations are linked, so changes to one graph show immediately in all others. Statistical capabilities include regression analysis, analysis of variance, multivariate analysis, cluster analysis, survival analysis, psychometric analysis, and non-parametric analysis. The SAS System also includes capabilities for executive information systems, data entry, retrieval and management, business planning, forecasting and decision support, and more. Detailed manual and tutorial program included. On-line help available. Latest release January, 1990.

Classification: Statistical Package

Hardware Requirements and Price
IBM PC, XT, AT, PS/2, & compatibles; 640 K; hard disk required. CGA display recommended, but not required. Mouse optional. Modem optional. Printer required. Laser printer optional. Requires OS/2 or DOS. *Single User Price: $595.00 (starting price) Network Price: Varies, based on machine classification and the number of workstations licensed Academic discounts available*

DEC VAX, 640 K, hard disk required. Mouse optional. Printer required. Laser printer optional. Requires VMS, PRIMOS or AOS/VS. *Single User Price: $2,310.00 (starting* price) *Network Price: Varies, based on machine classification and the number of workstations licensed Academic discounts available.*

Sun 3, 4, or 286i; 640 K; hard disk required. Mouse optional. Printer required. Laser printer optional. Requires HP-UX, SUNSOS, or RISC/OS. Mouse required for X-windows. *Single User Price: $895.00 (starting price) Network Price: Varies, based on machine classification and the number of workstations licensed Academic discounts available*

SAS/PH-Clinical Software

SAS Institute Inc.
SAS Campus Drive
Cary, NC 27513-2414
(919) 677-8000
Fax: (919) 677-8123

The SAS System, a suite of integrated software products for enterprise-wide information delivery, combines four data-driven tasks (data access, data management, data analysis, and data presentation) into one software system. For clinical applications, the SAS System provides physicians, clinicians, biostatisticians, and clinical data processing professionals with quick access, review, and analysis of clinical trials data. Users can create and query patient groups for special populations, browse patient records or listings, generate tables and reports, create and save notes about observations, and analyze safety and efficiency data by producing descriptive statistics, or graph data with scatter plots, bar charts, and more. The SAS System also provides capabilities for executive information systems, data entry, retrieval and management, and statistical and mathematical analysis. Detailed manual and tutorial program included. On-line help available. Latest release January, 1992.

Classification: Statistical Package

Hardware Requirements and Price
IBM PC, XT, AT, PS/2, & compatibles; 2.5 Mb RAM; hard disk required. Mouse optional. Laser printer optional. Memory requirements depend on the data and machine configuration *Single User Price: $200,000 (first year license)*

DEC VAX, 2.5 Mb RAM, hard disk required. Mouse optional. Laser printer optional. Memory required depends on data and machine configuration *Single User Price: $200,000 (first year license)*

Score

Terry D. Blumenthal
Joseph A. Cooper

Department of Psychology
Wake Forest University
Winston-Salem, NC 27109
(919) 759-5531

A Turbo Pascal program for off-line stimulus reduction and analysis. Detailed manual included. Latest release May 1, 1990.

Classification: Data Management

Hardware Requirements and Price
Macintosh, 1 Mb, 20 Mb hard disk required, 1 disk drive. Mouse optional. Modem optional. Laser printer optional. Requires System 6.0. Requires Turbo Pascal *Single User Price: Free*

Reviews
Blumenthal, T. D., & Cooper, J. A. (1990). Using the Macintosh computer in psychophysiological research: Programs for stimulus presentation, data collection, and response quantification. *Behavior, Research*

Methods, Instrumentation, and Computers, 22, 99-104.

SigmaPlot Version 4.1

Jandel Scientific
65 Koch Road
Corte Madera, CA 94925
(415) 924-8640
(800) 874-1888

Creates charts and graphs for scientific publications, lectures, or poster sessions, including scatter, line, histogram, bar, and grouped bar charts. Features include one- or two-way error bars, log and semi-log scales, linear and polynomial regression, cubic spline curve fitting, and more. Graphs can be scaled to any size or aspect ratio and multiple graphs can be positioned on a single page. Datasets of up to 128 columns and 65,000 rows can be plotted. Data entry from keyboard, ANSI, or DIF files. Detailed manual included.

Classification: Graphics

Hardware Requirements and Price
IBM PC, XT, AT, PS/2, & compatibles; 640 K; hard disk required; 2 disk drives. Graphic display required. Printer required. *Single User Price: $495.00*

SigmaPlot Version 4.1

Jandel Scientific
65 Koch Road
Corte Madera, CA 94925
(415) 924-8640
(800) 874-1888

Generates publication quality graphics. Features: scatterplots, line graphs, bar charts, histograms, log, semi-log, linear scales, multiple plots per graph, multiple graphs per page, automatic-error bars, control over labels, symbols, tick marks and axes, non-linear curve fitting and regression lines. Supports most printers, plotters and slidemakers. Detailed manual and tutorial program included. Online help available. Latest release April, 1991.

Classification: Graphics

Hardware Requirements and Price
IBM PC, XT, AT, PS/2, & compatibles; 640 K; 3.5 Mb hard disk required; 1 disk drive. Graphic display required. Mouse optional. Laser printer optional. Requires DOS 2.1. *Single User Price: $495.00 Network Price: $1,295.00 (3 pack), $1,895.00 (5 pack), $3,295.00 (10 pack), $5,495.00 (20 pack)*

Macintosh, 2 Mb, 1 Mb hard disk required, 1 disk drive. Mouse required. Laser printer optional. Requires System 4.2 or higher, Mac Plus or better. *Single User Price: $495.00*

Reviews
Fass-Holmes, Barry. (1991, January). Sigma Plot 4.0: A charting and graphing program for DOS-compatible PCs, *Biotechnology Software*, 8.

Oehmke, Roger. (1991, March). Graphics technical charting, *PC Magazine*, 189-192.

Porter, Michael L. (1991, August). Technical graphing software conquers large databases, *Personal Engineering and Instrumentation News*, 25-32.

User Site References
Chuck Kazilek, Arizona State University, Zoology Department, Tempe, AZ, 85287, (602) 965-5369

Raymond Stephens, Marine Biology Lab, Waters Street, Woods Hole, MA, 02543, (508) 540-4383

SigmaScan 3.9

Jandel Scientific
65 Koch Road
Corte Madera, CA 94925
(415) 924-8640
(800) 874-1888

Program features a high-resolution digitizing table and software for scientific digitizing and measurement. Measures areas, distances, perimeters, lengths of curvy lines, angles, slopes, and performs incremental and stream x,y digitizing and manual object counting. Descriptive statistics can be performed on all data, and user-defined transforms and keyboard macros allow complex analyses to be easily automated. Data can be output to standard ASCII files. Detailed manual included.

Classification: Research Aid

Hardware Requirements and Price
IBM PC, XT, AT, PS/2, & compatibles; 512 K; hard disk optional; 2 disk drives. Graphic display required. Digitizer required. *Single User Price: $495.00*

Sigmoid Curve Fitting
Daniel Coulombe
Eleftherios Miliaressis

School of Psychology
University of Ottawa
Ottawa, ON K1N 6N5 Canada
(613) 564-2924

Program performs non-linear parametric estimation of sigmoid curves. Models include: Gompertz' growth function, logistic, Weibull's, and broken lines (4 and 5 parameters). The program was developed for analysis of dose-response and rate-frequency curves. Instruction booklet included.

Classification: Statistical Package

Hardware Requirements and Price
IBM PC, XT, AT, PS/2, & compatibles; 256 K; hard disk optional; 1 disk drive. *Single User Price: $15.00*

Reviews
Coulombe, D., & Miliaressis, E. (1987). Fitting intracravial self-stimulation data with growth models. *Behavioral Neuroscience, 101*, 209-214.

SmartCR-Real Time Cumulative Recorder

MED Associates, Inc.
Box 47
East Fairfield, VT 05448
(802) 827-3825

Provides the user with up to 24, independent, real-time cumulative recorders when used with a MED Associates interface package. Records may be scaled, printed, saved to disk, and displayed on up to 8 monitors, with 1, 2, 4, 8, or 16 records in a single view. Inter-response time and event time data collected by SmartCR may be saved in four different formats, and segregated with three different file naming conventions. These files may also be used with SoftCR. Detailed manual included. On-line help available. Latest release August, 1991.

Classification: Equipment Control

Hardware Requirements and Price
IBM PC, XT, AT, PS/2, & compatibles; 40 Mb hard disk required; 2 disk drives. VGA display. Mouse optional. Laser printer optional.

Requires DOS 3.3. Math coprocessor and MED Associates interface modules required. *Single User Price: $600.00*

Social Sciences Citation Index

Institute for Scientific Information
3501 Market Street
Philadelphia, PA 19104
(215) 386-0100
(800) 523-1850

Index of social science journals on CD-ROM. Searchable by word, title, address, and allows scanning from one article to related citations. Detailed manual included. On-line help available. Latest release 1992.

Classification: Database

Hardware Requirements and Price
IBM PC, XT, AT, PS/2, & compatibles; 640 K; hard disk required; 1 disk drive. Monochrome or color display. Laser printer optional. Requires DOS 3.1. *Single User Price: $4,845.00 Network Price: Contact publisher.*

NEC, 640 K, hard disk required, 1 disk drive. Monochrome or color display. Laser printer optional. *Single User Price: $4,845.00 Network Price: Contact publisher*

Reviews
Rothstein, P. (1991). Social Sciences Citation Index compact disc edition. *ED-ROM Professional, 4,* 79-80.

SoftCR-Soft Cumulative Recorder

MED Associates, Inc.
Box 47
East Fairfield, VT 05448
(802) 827-3825

SoftCR accepts inter-response time and event time data from a standard ASCII file and creates a cumulative record with up to 10 event markers. Record can be displayed graphically on the screen and/or a hard copy printout can be generated on a standard Epson or IBM graphics printer, a HP Laser Jet, or other compatible printers. The data file may be organized as a delimited free format ANSI II file, MED-PC annotated or MED-PC stripped format. Detailed manual included. On-line help available.

Classification: Data Management

Hardware Requirements and Price
IBM PC, XT, AT, PS/2, & compatibles; 640 K; hard disk optional; 2 disk drives. Hercules, EGA, or VGA display. Laser printer optional. Requires DOS 3.3. *Single User Price: $425.00*

Sortrank: Sorting and Ranking Program
Alfred L. Brophy

Behavioral Science Associates
P.O. Box 748
West Chester, PA 19381
(215) 436-6859

BASIC program to sort and rank a set of scores.

Classification: Nonparametric Test

Hardware Requirements and Price
TRS-80, Model III & IV; 2.7 K; hard disk optional. BASIC interpreter. *Single User Price: Free, send a self-addressed, stamped envelope.*

Reviews
Brophy, A. L. (1983). Sortrank: Sorting and Ranking Program. *Behavior, Research Methods, Instrumentation, and Computers, 15,* 465-466.

SPSS Data Entry II

SPSS, Inc.
444 N. Michigan Avenue
Chicago, IL 60611
(312) 329-3500
(800) 543-6609

Integrated data entry, cleaning, editing, and file translation package with skip logic. This program has full read-write capability compatible with Lotus 1-2-3, Symphony, dBase II/III, Multiplan, and ASCII files, as well as SPSS/PC+ and mainframe SPSSx. Does not require SPSS/PC+. Detailed manual included. On-line help available. Latest release 1990.

Classification: Data Management

Hardware Requirements and Price
IBM PC, XT, AT, PS/2, & compatibles; 512 K; 10 Mb hard disk required. Hercules, CGA, EGA, or VGA display. Requires DOS 3.0. Math coprocessor recommended. *Single User Price: $395.00*

SPSS/PC+ Advanced Statistics V4.0

SPSS, Inc.
444 N. Michigan Avenue
Chicago, IL 60611
(312) 329-3500
(800) 543-6609

Includes loglinear, high loglinear, discriminant, non-linear regression, logistic regression, and multivariate analysis of variance procedures. Detailed manual included. On-line help available. Latest release 1990.

Classification: Statistical Test

Hardware Requirements and Price
IBM PC, XT, AT, PS/2, & compatibles; 640 K; 10 Mb hard disk required; 1 disk drive. Hercules, CGA, EGA, or VGA display. Requires DOS 3.0. Math coprocessor recommended. *Single User Price: $395.00*

SPSS/PC+ Mapping

SPSS, Inc.
444 N. Michigan Avenue
Chicago, IL 60611
(312) 329-3500
(800) 543-6609

Program integrates a special version of Map-Info in a menu-driven system that allows the user to visually illustrate numerical data, enlarging portions of the map. Includes legends with titles and labels, and provides full aggregation facilities as well as statistical information for mapping the United States by state, county, and 3-digit zip code. Detailed manual included. On-line help available. Latest release 1990.

Classification: Graphics

Hardware Requirements and Price
IBM PC, XT, AT, PS/2, & compatibles; 512 K; 10 Mb hard disk required. Hercules, CGA, EGA, or VGA display. Requires DOS 3.0. Math coprocessor recommended. *Single User Price: $495.00*

SPSS/PC+ Tables, Version 4.0

SPSS, Inc.
444 N. Michigan Avenue
Chicago, IL 60611
(312) 329-3500
(800) 543-6609

Produces publication quality tables. Includes complex stub and banner crosstabulations, analysis of multiple response data, and descriptive statistics within tables. Detailed manual included. On-line help available. Latest release 1990.

Classification: Graphics

Hardware Requirements and Price
IBM PC, XT, AT, PS/2, & compatibles; 640 K; 10 Mb hard disk required; 1 disk drive. Hercules, CGA, EGA, or VGA display. Laser printer optional. Requires DOS 3.0. Math coprocessor optional. *Single User Price: $395.00*

SPSS/PC+ Trends, Version 4.0

SPSS, Inc.
444 N. Michigan Avenue
Chicago, IL 60611
(312) 329-3500
(800) 543-6609

Time-series analysis, forecasting, and modeling tool. Includes curve fitting and smoothing models. Allows autoregressive model estimation, 2-stage and weighted least squares regression, Box-Jenkins analysis, uni- and bivariate analysis, as well as diagnostic plotting capabilities. User can test and compare fits among alternative models as well as save and reuse models. Detailed manual included. On-line help available. Latest release 1990.

Classification: Statistical Test

Hardware Requirements and Price
IBM PC, XT, AT, PS/2, & compatibles; 640 K; 10 Mb hard disk required. Hercules, CGA, EGA, or VGA display. Requires DOS 3.0. Math coprocessor recommended. *Single User Price: $395.00*

SPSS/PC+, Version 4.0

SPSS, Inc.
444 N. Michigan Avenue
Chicago, IL 60611
(312) 329-3500
(800) 543-6609

Contains data and file handling routines, basic descriptive statistics, report writing, graphing, and plotting functions. Reads and writes ASCII files. Includes split screen editor and communications. Detailed manual included. On-line help available. Latest release 1990.

Classification: Data Management

Hardware Requirements and Price
IBM PC, XT, AT, PS/2, & compatibles; 512 K; 10 Mb hard disk required; 1 disk drive. Hercules, CGA, EGA, or VGA display. Requires DOS 3.0. Math coprocessor optional. *Single User Price: $195.00*

Stat 1-A Statistical Toolbox
Jerry M. Brennan
Lawrence H. Nits

Sugar Mill Software Corporation
1180 Kika Place
Kailua, HI 96734
(808) 261-7536
(800) 729-7536

A menu-driven statistics package designed for business, social sciences, health professions, research and planning offices, and statistics courses. Each procedure can be applied to elementary and advanced research problems from various fields. Routines include descriptive statistics, scatter plots, cross tabs, t-tests, Pearson, Spearman, gamma, tau, ANCOVA, smallest space analysis, and factor analysis. Detailed manual included. On-line help available.

Classification: Statistical Package

Hardware Requirements and Price
IBM PC, XT, AT, PS/2, & compatibles; 640 K; hard disk required; 1 disk drive. Laser printer optional. *Single User Price: $129.95 Site License: $500.00*

STAT 5.4
Gary Perlman

Gary Perlman
Ohio State University
2036 Neil Avenue
Columbus, OH 43210-1277
(614) 292-2566

Over 25 programs for data manipulation and analysis. These programs work together in a style based on UNIX tools. Data manipulations include algebraic and transcendental transformations, data set reformatting, random number generation and probability estimations for 6 distributions (uniform, normal, t, F, chi-square, and binomial). Analyses include summary statistics, histograms, frequency tables, scatterplots, t-tests, multiple regression, multifactor ANOVA, contingency tables, and nonparametric tests. Detailed manual included. On-line help available. Latest release March, 1990.

Classification: Data Management

Hardware Requirements and Price
IBM PC, XT, AT, PS/2, & compatibles; 128 K; hard disk optional; 1 disk drive. Laser printer optional. Math coprocessor recommended. *Single User Price: $15.00 Manual costs $10.00*

UNIX computer, 256 K, hard disk optional, 1 disk drive. Laser printer optional. *Single User Price: $20-$30 (depending upon format) Manual costs $10.00*

Reviews
Conlon, M. (1989). Review of Stat 5.4. *The American Statistician*, *43*(3), 171-174.

Statistica/Mac

StatSoft, Inc.
2325 East 13th Street
Tulsa, OK 74104
(918) 583-4149
Fax: (918) 583-4376

Statistica/Mac for Macintosh includes basic statistics, nonparametrics, distribution fitting, crosstabulation, multiple regression, general ANOVA/ANCOVA/MANOVA/MANCOVA, and factor and cluster analyses. 2-D and 3-D graphs can be generated with on-screen customization using MacDraw-like tools. Graphs are integrated within all analyses to allow rapid visualization of results. Data management features include fast spreadsheet editor, merging and splitting of files, nested sorting, and formula-based transformations. Import and exports Excel, CSS: Statistica (DOS), and ASCII files. Detailed manual included. On-line help available. Latest release October, 1991.

Classification: Statistical Package

Hardware Requirements and Price
Macintosh, 1 Mb, 10 Mb hard disk required. Monochrome or color display. Mouse required. Laser printer optional. Requires System 6 or 7.

Statistical Power Analysis: A Computer Program
Michael Borenstein
Jacob Cohen

Lawrence Erlbaum Associates
P.O. Box 3407
New Hyde Park, NY 11040
(201) 692-8155

This program is modeled after Power Analysis by Jacob Cohen. Data may be entered by means of a spreadsheet-like interface. As individual cells (Mean, SD, N, Alpha, Tails) on the screen are modified, the displays of effect size and power are updated by the program. Alternatively, data may be entered by means of a graphic interface. Cursor keys are used to modify graphs of the group distributions, and the value of power is updated in response. Interactive help screens assist the user to calculate parameters that are then transferred to the program. The program creates tables and graphs of power as a function of sample size, effect size, and alpha. The program can run on-screen Monte Carlo simulations that are useful for teaching the concept of statistical power. Includes modules for t-test, proportions, correlation, ANOVA, and regression. Includes 185 page manual with illustrative examples. On-line help available. Latest release October, 1989.

Classification: Power Analysis

Hardware Requirements and Price
IBM PC, XT, AT, PS/2, & compatibles; 384 K; hard disk optional; 1 disk drive. Laser printer optional. Requires DOS 2.0. *Single User Price: $120.00 Free demo disk available*

Reviews
Borenstein, M., Cohen, J., Rothstein, H., Pollack, S., & Kane, J. (1990). Statistical power analysis for one-way analysis of variance: A computer program. *Behavior Research Methods, Instruments, and Computers, 22*(3), 271-282.
Goldstein, R. (1989). Power and sample size via MS/PC-DOS computers. *The American Statistician, 43*(4), 253-260.
Orme, J. (1990). Software review: Statistical Power Analysis-A Computer Program. *Social Service Review, 64*(3), 518-520.

Statistical Programs for the Apple II
Michael M. Patterson
Joseph E. Steinmetz
Anthony Romano

College of Osteo Medicine
Ohio University
Athens, OH 45701
(614) 593-2337

Package of statistical programs including parametric and nonparametric analyses. Program computes one-, two-, and three-way ANOVA (including randomized blocks and 3-way repeated measures on one- and two-way ANOVA), one-way analysis of covariance, latin squares, correlation, t-test, and descriptive statistics. Instruction booklet included.

Classification: Statistical Package

Hardware Requirements and Price

Apple II+, IIe, IIc; 48 K; hard disk optional; 1 disk drive. *Single User Price: Free, send self-addressed, stamped envelope and 2 diskettes*

Steiger.Bas

Julia L. Bienias

Department of Biostatistics
Harvard School of Public Health
677 Huntington Avenue
Boston, MA 02115
(617) 432-1056

BASIC program using Steiger's method that compares correlations for homogeneity within a correlation matrix. Instruction booklet included. Latest release August, 1986.

Classification: Correlation and Regression

Hardware Requirements and Price

IBM PC, XT, AT, PS/2, & compatibles; hard disk optional; 1 disk drive (5-1/4). Laser printer optional. Code is available and may be typed into any system. *Single User Price: Free, send self-addressed, stamped envelope*

Reviews

Bienias, J. L. (1987). Two BASIC programs to compare elements within and among correlation matrices. *Behavior, Research Methods, Instrumentation, and Computers, 19,* 57-58.

Stigmen

David A. Washburn

Department of Psychology
Georgia State University
Atlanta, GA 30303
(404) 241-6127

A menu-driven program for the generation of novel nonverbal stimuli. Instruction booklet included.

Classification: Research Aid

Hardware Requirements and Price

IBM PC, XT, AT, PS/2, & compatibles; 640 K; hard disk optional. CGA display. *Single User Price: $10.00*

Reviews

Washburn, D. A. (1990). PC-compatible computer-generated stimuli for video-task testing. *Behavior, Research Methods, Instrumentation, and Computers, 22,* 132-135.

Student's t Distribution

Alfred L. Brophy

Behavioral Science Associates
P.O. Box 748
West Chester, PA 19381
(215) 436-6859

Seven different approximations of probabilities for Student's *t* distribution.

Classification: t-Test

Hardware Requirements and Price

IBM PC, XT, AT, PS/2, & compatibles; 1 K; hard disk optional. BASIC interpreter. *Single User Price: Free, send a self-addressed, stamped envelope*

Reviews

Brophy, A. (1987). Efficient estimation of probabilities in the *t* distribution. *Behavior, Research Methods, Instrumentation, and Computers, 19,* 462-466.

Surfer

Golden Software, Inc.
P.O. Box 281
Golden, CO 80402
(303) 279-1021
(800) 972-1021

Surfer produces contour and 3-D surface maps from irregularly spaced x, y, z data. Options include user specified contour levels and labeling, color contours and surfaces, and independent scaling for the x, y, and z dimensions. Detailed manual included. On-line help available. Latest release June, 1991.

Classification: Graphics

Hardware Requirements and Price
IBM PC, XT, AT, PS/2, & compatibles; 320 K; hard disk optional; 1 disk drive. Hercules, CGA, EGA, or VGA display. Laser printer optional. Requires DOS 2.2. *Single User Price: $499.00 Network Price: $499.00 per user*

Survey Analyst
James E. Powell

Masterware, Inc.
3213 West Wheeler, Suite 177
Seattle, WA 98199
(206) 284-1762

Program for administering questionnaires. Tabulates, analyzes, and interprets responses. Detailed manual included. Latest release November, 1990.

Classification: Survey Administration

Hardware Requirements and Price
IBM PC, XT, AT, PS/2, & compatibles; 640 K; 1 Mb hard disk required; 1 disk drive. Hercu-

les, CGA, EGA, or VGA display. Laser printer optional. Requires DOS 2.1. *Single User Price: $189.00*

Reviews
Brown, Bruce. (1991). Survey Analyst. *PC Week*, 67-73.
Davis, James A. (1989). Survey Master, Version 1.1. *Social Science Computer Review*, 7, 386-387.

User Site References
James E. Evans, Nassau County Medical Center, East Meadow, NY, (516) 542-2705
Karla Parks, Health One Systems, 2810 57th Avenue North, Minneapolis, MN, 55430, (612) 574-7735

TableCurve, Version 3.0

Jandel Scientific
65 Koch Road
Corte Madera, CA 94925
(415) 924-8640
(800) 874-1888

Helps researchers find the best equation to fit their data. It automatically performs single-pass least squares curve fitting to 3,304 built-in linear equations, and automatically fits 14 non-linear equations via a true iterative process. Two user defined equations may be added to any curve fitting process. TableCurve then ranks all equations by user selected, goodness-of-fit criterion. The user is encouraged to examine the equation and curve-fit graphically, view standard errors, F-statistics, and prediction/confidence tables. Data can be entered manually or imported from Lotus 1-2-3, Quattro Pro, ASCII, and other file formats. Detailed manual included. On-line help available. Latest release July 15, 1991.

Classification: Statistical Test

Hardware Requirements and Price
IBM PC, XT, AT, PS/2, & compatibles; 600 K; 1.3 Mb hard disk required. Hercules, PC-3270, 8514/A, EGA, or VGA display. Mouse optional. Modem optional. Laser printer optional. Requires DOS 3.0. Math coprocessor optional but highly recommended. *Single User Price: $495.00*

Reviews
Brinkly, R., & Malencik, D. (1991). Table-Curve and PeakFit. *Biotechnology Software, 25,* 5-7.
Thai, P. (1991). TableCurve by Jandel Scientific: Software review. *Shock and Vibration Technology Review, 1*(7), 17-20.

Tachistoscopic Software
Gary P. Finley

Psychology Department
University of Alberta
Edmonton, AL T6G 2E9 Canada
(403) 492-2834

Software program that emulates a tachistoscope. Instruction booklet included. Latest release June 1, 1991.

Classification: Research Aid

Hardware Requirements and Price
IBM PC, XT, AT, PS/2, & compatibles; 256 K; hard disk optional; 1 disk drive. Monochrome, Hercules, or VGA display. Mouse optional. modem optional. *Single User Price: $15.00*

Reviews
Finley, G. P. (1989). Tachistoscopic Software. *Behavior, Research Methods, Instrumentation, and Computers, 21,* 387-390.

Test Reporting Management System (TRMS)

The Psychological Corporation
555 Academic Court
San Antonio, TX 78204-0952
(512) 299-1061
(800) 228-0752

TRMS is a data manager and reporting system designed to import examinee information from external sources, provide data editing functions, support data inquiry, control report formatting, and desegregate information to answer questions about subgroups of examinees. The product is particularly useful for management of student test data and other administrative information in schools. Detailed manual included. On-line help available. Latest release 1992.

Classification: Data Management

Hardware Requirements and Price
IBM PC, XT, AT, PS/2, & compatibles; 640 K; hard disk optional; 1 disk drive. Laser printer optional. Requires DOS 3.1. *Single User Price: $1,250.00 Network Price: $3,750.00*

TIFF Converter
Michael J. Hautus
Margaret A. Francis

Department of Psychology
University of Auckland
Private Bag Auckland, New Zealand
737999

Program converts TIFF files of scanned images for display on an IBM PC. Latest release August 30, 1991.

Classification: Graphics

Hardware Requirements and Price
IBM PC, XT, AT, PS/2, & compatibles; 360 K; hard disk optional; 1 disk drive. Hercules, CGA, EGA, MCGA, or VGA display. Requires DOS 3.2. *Single User Price: $30.00*

User Site References
Elbert Lee, Department of Psychology, University of Auckland, Private Bag Auckland, New Zealand

Tmerge
Douglas K. Symons
Heather M. Acton
Greg Moran

Department of Psychology
Acadia University
Wolfville, NS B0P 1X0 Canada
(902) 542-2201

Accepts behavior observation files created with Realtime and merges them into one output file according to the elapsed time since the observation. Instruction booklet included.

Classification: Research Aid

Hardware Requirements and Price
IBM PC, XT, AT, PS/2, & compatibles; 256 K; hard disk optional; 1 disk drive (5-1/4). Modem optional. Laser printer optional. *Single User Price: $5.00*

Reviews
Symon, D. K., Acton, H. M., & Moran, G. (1990). Using personal computers for behavioral coding in real-time: The Realtime and Tmerge Programs. *Social Science Computer Review*, 8, 426-430.

Tracking Program for Longitudinal Research
Charles S. Carver
Roger G. Dunham
Morry W. Spitzer

Department of Psychology
University of Miami
Coral Gables, FL 33124

A tracking program to schedule subjects across multipanel longitudinal research. Instruction booklet included.

Classification: Research Aid

Hardware Requirements and Price
IBM PC, XT, AT, PS/2, & compatibles; 256 K; hard disk optional; 2 disk drives (5-1/4). Laser printer optional. *Single User Price: Free, send 5-1/4" diskette to author*

Reviews
Carver, C. S., Dunham, R. G., & Spitzer, M. W. (1988) A tracking program to schedule subjects across multipanel longitudinal research. *Behavior, Research Methods, Instrumentation, and Computers*, 20, 576-578.

Trendan
Daniel Coulombe

School of Psychology
University of Ottawa
275 Nicholas
Ottawa, ON K1N 6N5 Canada
(613) 564-2924

Program generates orthogonal polynomials and performs trend analysis for unequal intervals and unequal Ns.

Classification: ANOVA

Hardware Requirements and Price
IBM PC, XT, AT, PS/2, & compatibles; 256 K; hard disk optional; 1 disk drive. *Single User Price: $15.00*

Reviews
Coulombe, D. (1985). Orthogonal polynomial coefficients and trend analysis for unequal intervals and unequal NS: A microcomputer application. *Behavior, Research Methods, Instrumentation, and Computers, 17,* 441-442.

True Epistat
Tracy L. Gustafson

Epistat Services
2011 Cap Rock Circle
Richardson, TX 75080-3417
(214) 680-1376

Statistical package that performs over 100 different parametric and nonparametric analyses and over 40 different (publication-quality) graphics. Detailed manual included. On-line help available. Latest release June 1, 1991.

Classification: Statistical Package

Hardware Requirements and Price
IBM PC, XT, AT, PS/2, & compatibles; 512 K; 10 Mb hard disk optional. Hercules, EGA, CGA, or VGA display. Printer required. Laser printer optional. Math coprocessor recommended. Requires DOS 3.1. *Single User Price: $398.00 Network Price: $2,000.00 (10 computers) Site licensing available*

Reviews
Berk, K. (1988). Statistical computing software review. *American Statistician, 42*(3), 217-219.
Stair, T. (1988). True Epistat. *American Journal of Emergency Medicine, 6*(5), 532-533.
Zeiger, R. (1990). True Epistat. *Journal of American Medical Association, 264*(1), 97.

Tukey's Multiple Comparison Procedure
Alfred L. Brophy

Behavioral Science Associates
P.O. Box 748
West Chester, PA 19381
(215) 436-6859

BASIC program to perform Tukey's HSD multiple comparison procedure.

Classification: ANOVA

Hardware Requirements and Price
TRS-80, Model III & IV; 1.2 K; hard disk optional. BASIC interpreter. *Single User Price: Free, send a self-addressed, stamped envelope*

Reviews
Brophy, A. L. (1984). A BASIC program for Tukey's multiple comparison procedure. *Behavior, Research Methods, Instrumentation, and Computers, 16,* 67-68.

UniMult
Richard L. Gorsuch

UniMult
180 North Oakland Avenue

Pasadena, CA 91101
(818) 584-5527
(800) 733-5527

A comprehensive statistics package for analyzing all types of variables by univariate and multivariate procedures. Analyses range from cross-tab chi squares to MANOVA and factor analysis. Includes test scoring and numerous transformation options. Detailed manual included. On-line help available. Latest release 1991.

Classification: Statistical Package

Hardware Requirements and Price
IBM PC, XT, AT, PS/2, & compatibles; 500 K; hard disk optional; 2 disk drives. Laser printer optional. *Single User Price: $195.00*

User Site References
A. J. Figuerdo, Department of Psychology, University of Arizona, Tucson, AZ, 85721, (602) 621-7446
Gary Moon, Regent University School of Counseling, Virginia Beach, VA, 23464, (804) 424-7000
Esther Wakeman, La Vie, 650 Sierra Madre Villa, Suite 110, Pasadena, CA, 91107, (818) 351-9616

Visual Discrimination Task
Michael J Strube

Department of Psychology
Washington University
St. Louis, MO 63130

A program that manipulates success and failure feedback. Used in social psychology experiments. On-line help available.

Classification: Research Aid

Hardware Requirements and Price
Commodore 64 or 128, 1 disk drive. Not compatible with laser printer. *Single User Price: Free program listing*

Reviews
Strube, M. (1988). Three computer-automated social psychology laboratory tasks. *Behavior, Research Methods, Instrumentation, and Computers, 20,* 557-559.

Vsearch and Vsearch Color
James T. Enns
Eric P. Ochs
Ronald A. Rensink

Department of Psychology
University of British Columbia
Vancouver, BC V6T 124 Canada
(604) 822-6634

Software that turns a Macintosh computer into an instrument for vision research. Detailed manual included.

Classification: Research Aid

Hardware Requirements and Price
Macintosh, 512 K, hard disk optional, 1 disk drive. Apple Color Monitor for Vsearch Color. Laser printer optional. *Single User Price: Contact author*

Reviews
Enns, J. T., Ochs, E. P., & Rensink, R. A. (1990). Vsearch: Macintosh software for experiments in visual research. *Behavior, Research Methods, Instrumentation, and Computers, 22,* 118-122.

Enns, J. T., & Rensink, R. A. (1991). VSearch Color: Full-Color visual search experiments on the Macintosh II. *Behavior, Research Methods, Instrumentation, and Computers*, *23*, 265-272.

Findlay, J. (1991). Vsearch. *Psychology Software News*, *2*, 53-55.

WP Citation

Oberon Resources
147 East Oakland Ave.
Columbus, OH 43201
(800) 243-3833
(800) 594-9062

A bibliography manager that operates inside WordPerfect. Detailed manual included. Latest release August 15, 1991.

Classification: Manuscript Preparation Aid

Hardware Requirements and Price
IBM PC, XT, AT, PS/2, & compatibles; hard disk optional. WordPerfect 5.1 required. Windows version is also available. *Single User Price: $99.00 Network Price: $295.00*

Reviews
WP Citation. (1991). *Social Science Computer Review*, *9*, 498-499.

X
Ron D. Hays

Ron Hays
1700 Main Street
Santa Monica, CA 90407-2183
(213) 393-0411

BASIC program that translates simplified program code into executable EQS (Bentler, 1985) program language. Instruction booklet included.

Classification: Statistical Test

Hardware Requirements and Price
IBM PC, XT, AT, PS/2, & compatibles; 256 K; hard disk optional; 1 disk drive (5-1/4). *Single User Price: Free, send diskette*

ZSCORE
David Rose

Department of Psychology
University of Surrey
Guildford, GU2 5XH Surrey
01144 483 300 800 x2441

Program for the calculation of z scores, d prime, and beta. Instruction booklet included.

Classification: Statistical Test

Hardware Requirements and Price
IBM PC, XT, AT, PS/2, & compatibles; hard disk optional. Laser printer optional. IBM BASIC required.

DEC PDP-11, hard disk optional. Laser printer optional. FORTRAN required.

Cromemco, hard disk optional. Laser printer optional. BASIC required.

Reviews
Rose, D. (1988). ZSCORE: A program for the accurate calculation of Zscores, d, & B. *Behavior, Research Methods, Instrumentation, and Computers*, *20*, 63-64.

INDEXES

Title Index

16PF-Forma C 119
16PF Interpretive Report Generator 119
16PF: Karson Clinical Report, Version 3............. 119
16PF Report 120
16PF Single-Page Report.................................. 120
16PF Telxpress Software/License 120
16PF/CL Clinical 121
3-D Keyboard for Windows 253
3RT Test 121
ABC 253
ABI-1 3
ABI-2 3
ABI-3 3
Ability-Achievement Discrepancy...................... 121
ABstat 4
Absurut 253
Accountability Plus 73
Accuracy and Precision 4
Acquire Knowledge Acquisition System and
    Expert System Shell 4
Acro Spin 254
ACS Query 254
Adaptive Behavior Inventory............................. 122
Adaptive Perceputal Mapping (APM)
    System 254
ADD-H Comprehensive Teachers' Rating
    Scale (ACTeRS), Second Edition 122
Adolescent Diagnostic Screening Battery 122
Adolescent Multiphasic Personality
    Inventory.. 123
Adult Diagnostic Screening Battery 123
Adult Personality Inventory 124
AI Offender Profile 124
Alcadd Test 124
Alcohol Assessment and Treatment Profile 124
Alcohol Use Inventory (AUI) 125
Algorithm for Sorting Grouped Data 255
Alley.Rat Pack 5
Analogy 255
Analysis of Variance with up to Three
    Factors... 256

ANDISP 256
Animal Behavior Data Simulation........................... 5
ANOVA/TT 6
ANOVA Latin Squares, and ANOCOVA
    Analysis Programs 257
ANOVMODL.BAS 257
The Answer 73
Answer Scan 257
Anxiety and Personality Questionnaires................ 6
API/Career Profile 125
Apple Tachestoscope System 258
Apticom 126
Aptitude Interest Measure 126
Areas of Change Computer Program 127
Arion II Teleprocessing Service 127
Assessment of Career Decision Making 73
At Ease! 74
An Augmented BASIC Program for
    Exploring Subtest Combination Short
    Forms.. 127
Autogenic Systems Software 258
Automated Child/Adolescent Social History
    (ACASH) 128
Automated Social History-ASH Plus................... 128
AutoPACL 128
AutoSCID II 129
Baffles & Baffles II 6
Baker Student Adaptation to College
    Questionnaire (SACQ) 129
Barclay Classroom Assessment System
    (BCAS) 130
Basic Electrophysiology 7
Basic Personality Inventory 130
A BASIC Program For Computing
    Cronbach's Accuracy Components................... 258
A BASIC Program to Compute Fisher's
    Exact Test 259
BASIC Programs for Prediction of Analysis
    of Cross Classifications 259
Basic Programs to Determine Sample Size &
    Exact Power in ANOVA Designs.................... 259

Beck Interpretive Software 130
Behavior on a Disk 7
Behavioral Modification 7
Behavioral Sciences 8
Behaviordyne In House 131
Behaviordyne On Line System 131
Bender Report 131
BestChoice3 74
The Binomial Probability Distributions 260
Biofeedback MicroLab 8
Blink 260
Brain Hemisphere Information Processing 9
BrainMaker 260
Brainscape 9
Brass 261
Brief Computerized Stress Inventory 132
Brief Symptom Inventory (SCORBSI) 3.0 133
Bubble Publishing 261
C-lect 74
C-lect, Jr. 74
California Psychological Inventory 133
California Psychological Inventory
    Interpretive Report 133
California Verbal Learning Test-Research
    Edition 134
California Verbal Learning Test (CVLT),
    Scoring and Administration Software 134
Canfield Learning Styles Inventory (LSI) 135
Card: Computer Assisted Reading
    Diagnostics 135
Career Assessment Program 135
Career Assessment Inventory-Enhanced
    Version 136
Career Assessment Inventory-Vocational
    Version 135
Career Counselor 75
Career Directions 75
Career Directions Inventory 75
Career Directions Inventory (CDI) 136
Career Exploration Series 76
Career Finder 76
Career Scan V 77
CareerPoint 77
CareerSearch 77
Cases 262
Casper 9
CASSIP: Computer Assisted Study Skills
    Improvement Program 77
Catechollision 9

Category Test Computer Program 3.0 137
Catgen 10
Catlab 10
CCIS: Computerized Career Information
    System 78
CDS Profile III Management Development
    Profile 137
Century Diagnostics Computer Interpreted
    Rorschach 137
Certify! DOS 3.3 and DOS 5.0 138
Chemical Dependency Assessment Profile 138
Child & Adolescent Diagnostic Scales
    (CADS) 138
Child Diagnostic Screening Battery 139
Children's Personality Questionnaire
    Narrative Report 139
Children's Personality Questionnaire
    Narrative Report 140
Children's State-Trait Anxiety Inventory
    Computer Program 140
Chronic Pain Battery 140
Ci2 System for Computer Interviewing 262
Ci3 System for Advanced Computer
    Interviewing 262
Circumgrids 11
Classical Psychophysical Methods 11
Clinical Analysis Questionnaire 140
Clinical Analysis Questionnaire (CAQ) 141
Clinical Analysis Questionnaire (CAQ),
    Version 3 141
Clinical Assistant 78
Clinical Interviews 11
Clinical Interviews: General Medical
    Surgical Series 12
CLIPS 5.0 263
CNS Mechanisms in Hearing 12
CNS Mechanisms in Vision 13
CNS Mechanisms of Feeling 13
Cognitive Data Base, Vol. I 79
Cognitive Drills: Set I (Visual) 79
Cognitive Experimental Design & Testing
    System 13
Cognitive Prescription, Vol. I 79
Cognitive Psychology 13
Cognitive Psychology Programs 14
Cogrehab, Vol. 1 80
Cogrehab, Vol. 2 80
Cogrehab, Vol. 3, Version 2.0 81
Cogrehab, Vol. 4 81

Cogrehab, Vol. 5 81
Cogrehab, Vol. 6 82
Cogrehab Vol. 7, Quest 82
Cohen.Bas 263
College Explorer, 1992 83
Color Card Pro 263
Commodore Statistical Package 264
Commodore Statistics 264
Community Mental Health Model,
    Version 1.2 14
Complex Attention Rehabilitation 83
Compliance 14
Comprehensive Computerized Stress
    Inventory 141
Comprehensive Personality Profile 142
Comprehensive Treatment Planner 83
COMPsych 264
Compuscore for the Battelle Developmental
    Inventory 142
Compuscore for the Woodcock Spanish
    Psycho-Educational Battery (Bateria) 143
Compuscore for the Woodcock Johnson
    Psycho-Educational Battery-Revised 143
Compuscore: ICAP 143
Compuscore: WJ/SIB Subtest Norms 143
Computer Assisted Career Selection 84
Computer Augmented Lecture Material
    (CALM): ExcelTM Tools 15
Computer Augmented Lecture Materials:
    Stat Stack 15
Computer Lab in Memory and Cognition 16
Computer Simulations in Psychology 16
Computer Simulations in Psychology, Second
    Edition 16
Computer-Generated Bender Clinical
    Assessment 144
Computerized Activities in Psychology IV
    (CAPS IV) 17
Computerized Assessment of Intelligibility
    of Dysarthric Speech 144
Computerized Cognitive Laboratory 17
Computing Interrater Reliability 265
Concept Formation Task 265
Concept Formation: The Feature-Positive
    Effect 17
Concepts of Probability 18
Conditioning 18
Confidence Intervals, Effect Size, and
    Statistical Power: A Computer Program 265

Conflict & Cooperation Version 2.0
    (Windows) 19
Conners Rating Scales Computer Program 144
Consumer Behavior 19
Contingency Judgement Task 266
Conversational Survey Analysis (CSA) 266
A Cooperative-Competitive Game 19
Coping With Tests 84
Corporate Culture Programs 84
Correlational Analysis 267
Counseling Feedback Report 145
Counselor's Notebook 85
CPB/Score Report Processing Software 145
CPI Interpretive Report 145
CPP Software System 146
A-Cross 267
Crosstat 267
CRT Skills Test 146
Crunch-Version 4 268
CSS/3 268
CSS: Graphics 268
CSS: Statistica 269
Current Contents on Diskette: Social and
    Behavioral Sciences 269
Current Contents on Diskette: Life Sciences 270
Custometrics 270
D Prime and Beta 270
D-48 (Dominoes Test) 147
DADISP 270
DAS-Data Acquisition & Analysis System 271
Datasim 20
Datesim 85
Daysim 85
DCS: Data Collection System for C-64/128
    Microcomputers 271
Decision Tree 147
Decisionbase 147
Demo-Graphics 21
Derogatis Sexual Functioning Inventory
    (SCORDSFI) 148
Derogatis Sexual Functioning Inventory
    (ADMNDSFI) 148
Derogatis Stress Profile (DSP) 148
Detroit Tests of Learning Aptitude-Adult
    (DTLA-A) Software Scoring & Report
    System 148
Detroit Tests of Learning Aptitude-Primary,
    Second Edition 149

Detroit Tests of Learning Aptitude-3
    Software Scoring and Report System 149
Developmental History Checklist, Version 3 150
Developmental History Report 150
Developmental Profile II (DP-II) 150
Diagnostic Achievement Test for
    Adolescents 151
Diagnostic Achievement Battery-Second
    Edition (DAB-2) 151
Diagnostic Interview for Children &
    Adolescents, Revised: Child/Adolescent 152
Diagnostic Interview for Children &
    Adolescents, Revised: Parent 152
Diagnostic Inventory of Personality &
    Symptoms 152
Differential Aptitude Tests: Computerized
    Adaptive Edition 153
Differential Diagnostics 153
Digit-Digit Test II 153
Digitized Nonobjects for the Macintosh 21
Digitized Pictorial Stimuli for the Macintosh 21
Discovering Psychology 22
Diskcovering Psychology and Computerized
    Study Guide 22
DMITSA 272
DOT Lookup 85
Drug Store Applicant Inventory 154
DSM-III Diagnostic Screening Batteries 154
DSM-III-R On Call 154
DSM-III-R Tutorial Software 22
DTLA-2 Report 155
Dtree: The Electronic DSM III-R 155
Dyadic Adjustment Scale: Computer Version 155
EAP Alcohol/Drug Assessment Module 156
EAP Management Module 86
The Ear 23
Eating Disorder Inventory-2, Version 4 156
Ego Defense Mechanisms 23
Eliza II 24
Emotional Problems Scales (EPS), Version 1 157
Employee Attitude Inventory 157
Employment Productivity Index 157
Endler Multidimensional Anxiety Scales
    (EMAS) 158
EndNote 272
EndNote Plus 272
Enhancing and Degrading Visual Stimuli 273
Enjoy Your Job 86

ESP: Precognition, Clairvoyance, &
    Telepathy 24
EVA: Electronic Visual Analog 273
EVE 273
Eventlog 274
Transient Evoked Potentials 274
Exam Builder 24
Executive Profile Survey 158
Expected Normal and Half-Normal Scores 274
Experimental Psychology Data Simulation 25
Experimental Psychology Programs, Level 1 25
Experimental Psychology Programs, Level 2 26
Experimental vs. Correlational Research:
    A Question of Control 26
Experiments and Personal Applications in
    Psychology 26
Experiments in Cognitive Psychology 27
Experiments in Human Physiology 27
Expert Ease 86
Expert System Tutorial 28
Exploracion de Carreras 87
Exploratory Data Analysis 275
Explore the World of Work 87
Extend 2.0 275
The Eye 28
Eye Lines 28
Eye Monitoring Program 275
FactFile: Brief Facts and Jokes for Reading
    Stimulation 87
Factor Positive Effect Version 1.0 29
Feeling Better 88
FIRM: Florida Interactive Modeler 29
FIRM: Vol. I, Nature of Attitudes and
    Attitude Change 29
FIRM: Vol. II, Interpersonal Dynamics 30
FIRM: Vol. III, Comparative Psychology 30
FIRO-B: Software 158
FIRO-B: Interpretive Report, Version 3 159
Flash: Biofeedback 31
Flash: The EEG 31
Flash: Human Brain 32
Flash: Human Stress 32
Flash: Neurons 33
Flo Stat Version 1.5 276
Four Score: Computer Scoring Program for
    the Stanford-Binet, Fourth Edition 159
Fraction 276
Free Recall 88

Functional Capacity Checklist 159
G Statistic 277
Games Research 33
General Aptitude Test Battery (GATB) 160
General Forecaster 34
Genstat 34
Giannetti On-Line Psychosocial History
      (GOLPH) 160
GIBBY: Random Generator 277
Goal Tracker-The Personal Success System 88
Goal-Focused Interviewing, Volume I 34
Gottschaldt Hidden Figures Test 35
GPSPRT 277
Grader 35
Graph 278
Grapher 278
Graphing Data 35
Guilford-Zimmerman Temperment Survey
      (GZTS) 160
Guttman Scalogram Analysis 278
H-T-P Clinical Report 161
Halstead Category Test-A Computer
      Version 161
Halstead-Reitan Hypothesis Generator 161
Hands-On Experimental Psychology 36
Handwriting Analyst 162
Hansen-Predict 36
Help-Assert 89
Help-Esteem 89
Help-Stress 90
Help-Think 90
Hermann: The Rorschach Assistant 162
High School Career-Choice Planner 91
High School Personality Questionnaire
      Narrative Report 162
High School Personality Questionnaire
      Narrative Report 163
Hilson Adolescent Profile (HAP) 163
Hilson Career Satisfaction Index (HCSI) 164
Hilson Personnel Profile/Success Quotient
      (HPP/SQ) 164
Hilson Research Remote System Software
      (HRRSStm) 164
The HIPS Image Processing System 279
Holidays 91
How Did I Feel? 91
HRB Norms Program, Version 1 165
Hudson Education Skills Inventory 165
The Human Brain: Neurons 37

Human Resource Inventory 165
Hypothesis Testing 37
ICISS: Integrated Comprehensive
      Instructional Support For Psychology 37
Idare 166
The Idea Generator 38
If You Drink 92
Illusions Pack 38
The Initial Psychiatric Interview: Module I,
      Units 1 & 2 38
InSight, Version 2-InColor 39
InSight W.P. Reporting System 166
Instructional Support Statistics, Version 2.0 39
Intake Evaluation Report Clinician,
      Version 3.0 166
Integer Means and Variances 39
Integtration of t 279
Interact/Attitude 40
Interactive Cluster Analysis (ICA),
      Release 2.0 280
Interactive Multiple Prediction (IMP) 2.0 280
Interactive Questionnaire Analysis (IQA) 1.0 280
Interactive Tester 281
International Testing System (ITS) 167
Interpersonal Styles Inventory (ISI) 167
Interrater Reliability for the Macintosh 281
Inventory for Counseling and Development
      (ICD) 168
Inverse Normal Distribution Function 281
Inwald Personality Inventory (IPI) 168
Inwald Survey 3 (IS3tm) 168
Ipsapro 282
IQ Test Interpretation-Adult 169
IQ Test Interpretation-Clinical 169
ISP: Interactive Statistical Programs 40
ISSA 282
Item Analysis 40
JACK 282
Jackson Personality Inventory 169
Jackson Vocational Interest Survey (JVIS) 170
JAVA Version 1.4 283
Jesness Behavior Checklist Computer
      Program 170
Jesness Inventory Narrative Report 171
Jesness Inventory of Adolescent Personality
      Computer Program 171
JMP Software 41
Job Hunter's Survival Kit 92
JOB-O 171

JOB-O A (Advanced) 172
Johnson-Neyman Significance Regions 283
Jump: Eye Movement Exercise 93
Kappa Coefficient 284
Karson Clinical Report (KCR) for the 16PF 172
Kaufman Assessment Battery for Children-
    ASSIST 172
Kaufman Test of Educational Achievement
    ASSIST 173
Kendall's Rank Correlation Coefficient 284
Key Math-Revised ASSIST 173
Key Stat 284
Keyboarder: Finding Letters & Numbers 93
Kinetic Family Drawing Tests: Computer
    Analysis 173
Kor 41
Laboratory Control System 284
Laboratory in Classical Conditioning 41
Laboratory in Cognition and Perception 42
Laboratory in Cognition and Perception
    (Second Edition) 42
Laboratory in Social Psychology 43
Laplace 285
Law Enforcement Assessment and
    Development Report (LEADR) 174
Learning Theory Simulations 43
Learning to Cope with Pressure 93
LEDA 285
LeisurePREF 94
Levels of Measurement: Nominal, Ordinal,
    Interval, Ratio 43
Life Course Simulation 44
Life Space Analysis Profile (LSAP) 174
Life/Time Manager 94
Line Bisection 95
Listutor 44
LMA Plus 1990 95
LNNB Scoring & Interpretation Program 174
Longitudinal Sealugram Analysis 285
Louisville Behavior Checklist (LBC) 175
LSI Stylus 175
Latin Squares Generation 286
Luria Nebraska Scoring System 175
Luria-Nebraska Neuropsychological Battery
    (LNNB) 176
Mac Psych with Mac-A-Mug 286
MaCATI Version 2.0 286
Maclaboratory for Psychology 2.0 44

The Magic Mirror 95
Major-Minor Finder 96
Management Readiness Profile (MRP) 176
Manson Evaluation 176
Manycorr: Multistage Boneferroni
    Procedure for Many Correlations 287
Mapping the Visual Field 45
MapViewer 287
MapWise: Perceptual Mapping Software 288
Marital Satisfaction Inventory (MSI) 177
The Marks MMPI Adolescent Clinical
    Report 177
The Marks MMPI Adolescent Feedback and
    Treatment Report 177
The Marks MMPI and MMPI-2 Adult
    Clinical Report 178
The Marks MMPI and MMPI-2 Adult
    Feedback and Treatment Report 178
Marriage Counseling Report (MCR) 178
The Matchmaker 288
Matrank and Onerank 288
McDermott Multidimensional Assessment of
    Children 179
Measures of Association for Ordinal
    Variables 289
Measures of Central Tendency 45
Measuring Subjective Experience 45
MED-PC/Medstate Notation, Version 2 289
Meet Yourself (As You Really Are) 96
Megafile Manager 289
Micro Experimental Laboratory (MEL) 46
MEL Lab: Experiments in Perception,
    Cognition, Social Psychology & Human
    Factors 46
Memory Assessment Scales (MAS),
    Version 1 179
Memory Span 97
Memory Techniques 47
Menstrual Distress Questionnaire (MDQ) 180
Mental Rotations 97
Mental Status Checklist-Adolescent,
    Version 3 180
Mental Status Checklist-Adult, Version 3 180
Meyer-Kendall Assessment Survey (MKAS) 181
Micro-Skills I and II 97
Microanalytic Data Analysis Package 290
MicroCase Analysis System, Version 2.11 290
Laboratory MicroStar 291

MICROTEST Assessment System 181
Millon Adolescent Personality Inventory
　　Narrative Report 181
Millon Adolescent Personality Inventory-
　　Guidance (MAPI) 182
Millon Adolescent Personality Inventory-
　　Clinical (MAPI) 182
Millon Behavioral Health Inventory
　　Interpretive Report 182
Millon Behavioral Health Inventory (MBHI)..... 183
Millon Clinical Multiaxial Inventory II
　　(MCMI-II) 183
Millon Clinical Multiaxial Inventory-II
　　Narrative Report 183
Mind Scope 47
Mini-SCID 184
The Minnesota Report: Adult Clinical
　　System Interpretive Report (MMPI-2) 184
The Minnesota Report: Personnel Selection
　　System Interpretive Report (MMPI-2) 184
MINSQ 291
Mirror Shapes 291
MMPI Adolescent Interpretive System,
　　Version 3 185
The MMPI Adult Interpretive System,
　　Version 4 185
Caldwell Report for the MMPI 186
MMPI Mini Mult 186
The Minnesota Report: Adult Clinical
　　System (MMPI) 186
MMPI Report 186
MMPI-2 Adult Interpretive System,
　　Version 1 187
MMPI-2 Extended Score Report 187
(MMPI-2) The Minnesota Report: Adult
　　Clinical System Interpretive Report 188
MMPI-2 Narrative Report 188
MMPI-2 Report 188
MMPI-83 Adolescent 189
MMPI-83 Version 2.1 Behavioral Medicine
　　Report 189
MMPI-83 Version 2.1 Forensic Report 189
MMPI-83 Version 2.1 Scoring and
　　Interpretation System 190
Mnemonic Demonstration 48
MOS Short-Form Health Survey 190
Motivation Analysis Test 191
Multi Drive 1.4 256
Multidimensional Aptitude Battery (MAB) 191

Multiple Factor Analysis (MFA) 292
Multiscore Depression Inventory (MDI) 191
Multiscore Depression Inventory: WPS Test
　　Report 192
Multitrait-Multimethod Matrix Analysis 292
My Real Feelings About School 192
Myers-Briggs Type Indicator Interpretive
　　Report 192
Myers-Briggs Type Indicator Narrative
　　Report for Organizations 193
Myers-Briggs Type Indicator 193
Narrative Score Report 193
NASA/LRC Computerized Test System 292
Natural 293
Number Crucher Statistical System (NCSS) 293
NCSS Advanced Tables 293
NCSS Base Statistical System (5.03) 294
NCSS Curve Fitter 294
NCSS Experimental Designs 295
NCSS Graphics System 295
NCSS PASS 295
NCSS Power Pack 295
NCSS Statistical Process Control & Quality
　　Control 296
NCSS Student Version 296
NCSS Survival Analysis 296
NCSS Time Series & Forcasting 297
NCSS Wireframe Graphics 297
NEO Personality Inventory: Computer,
　　Version 4 194
NETS 297
Neurobics 98
Neurosys 48
NIPR Testing Statistics (NTS) Package 298
Nonparametric Partial Correlation 298
Normal Distribution Algorithms 298
Normal Distribution Function 299
Npstat Version 3.5 299
Number Series Problems 98
NWA Statpak 299
Observe Version 2.0-A Package For
　　Observation Research 300
The Observer 300
Occupational Outlook on Computer
　　(OOOC) 98
Occupational Report 194
Occupational Stress Inventory (OSI):
　　Computer Version, Version 1 194

Ohio Vocational Interest Survey: Second
    Edition (OVIS, II)... 195
Olfaction 48
Oneway 301
Op.Rat... 49
Operant Conditioning Control............................ 49
Operant/PC 301
OPQ Expert System.. 195
Organization Survey 196
Orthogonal Comparisons.................................... 301
Over 50: Needs, Values, Attitudes 99
The P.A.: Marriage Communication
    Training Module 99
PACE 196
Paired Associates 49
Paired Word Memory Task.................................. 100
Pam 302
Parallel 302
PASS: Power Analysis and Sample Size 302
Programmer Assessment Software Tools
    (PAST) 303
The PC As A Laboratory Instrument 50
PC-DADS: Data Acquisition Display and
    Storage System.. 303
pcSTEREOSCOPE/VisionLab 50
Peabody Individual Achievement Test-
    Revised ASSIST 196
PeakFit... 303
Peer Interaction Profile (PIP)............................. 197
Perception: A Computerized Approach 50
Perceptual Identification Routines for the
    Macintosh 51
Peripheral Somatosensory System 51
Personal Career Development Profile 197
Personal Experience Inventory (PEI)................... 197
Personal History Checklist-Adolescent,
    Version 3... 198
Personal History Checklist-Adult, Version 3 198
Personality Assessment Inventory (PAI):
    Computer Version, Version 1.......................... 198
Personality Assessment Inventory (PAI):
    Interpretive Report Version 1 199
Personality Inventory for Children-Revised
    Narrative Report... 199
Personality Inventory for Children (PIC)............ 199
Personality Research Form 200
Personnel Policy Expert 100
Personnel Selection Inventory 200
Peterson's Career Options................................... 100

Peterson's College Selection Service..................... 101
Peterson's Financial Aid Service (FAS) 101
PhoneDisc California + ... 304
PhoneDisc QuickRef + ... 304
PhoneDisc USA National Set 304
Piaget's Cognitive Operations.............................. 51
PIAT-80 Diagnostics 201
PICApad II: Computerized Report
    Generating Program 201
Pictorial Stimuli 305
Piers-Harris Childrens Self Concept Scale
    (PHCSC).. 201
The Planning Guide 101
Please Understand Me 202
PMS Analysis, Version 1.0.................................. 202
Polynomial Regression-PC.................................. 305
Practice Speech... 102
Probabilities 305
Problem Solving Sets 52
Problem-Solving I: Rehabilitation....................... 102
Problem-Solving II: Rehabilitation...................... 102
Productivity Improvement Program Series
    (PIPS) 103
Program to Compute Nonparametric Partial
    Correlation Coefficients 306
Projective Drawing Tests: Computer
    Analysis 202
Projective Drawing Tests: Computer
    Analysis-School Version 203
Projective Drawing Tests 203
Projective Drawings: Computer Analysis............. 203
Psych Plot... 306
Psych Report Writer, Version 2.1........................ 204
The Psych-Assistant.. 103
Psychiatric Diagnostic Interview, Revised
    (PDI-R).. 204
The Psychiatric Interview Series, Module II 52
Psychiatry... 306
Psychlab... 53
Psychological Disorders 1.0 53
Psychological Resources Report........................... 205
Psychological Testing Demonstration 53
Psychological/Psychiatric Status Interview 205
Psychological/Social History Report.................... 206
Psychology On a Disk 53
Psycho-social Adjustment to Illness Scale
    (PAIS) 206
Psychotherapy 54
PsychSim II... 54

Psychware 55
PsychWorld 2E.. 55
PsycLit 306
PsyComNet... 307
Q-Fast... 206
Q-Stix 307
Quality of Life Computer Program...................... 207
QuestMake 207
Quick Computerized Stress Inventory 207
Quick CSS.. 307
Quick CSS/Mac.. 308
Quick-Score Achievement Test (Q-SAT)............. 208
RADAR Plus 208
Random Tools 308
Randt Memory Test.. 209
Rational WISC-R Analysis................................ 209
Reaction Time Measure of Visual Field.............. 103
Realtime 308
Reinforcement Schedules 55
Release From P.I. 56
Report Writer: Adult's Intellectual,
    Achievement, Neuropsychological
    Screening Tests, Version 3 210
Report Writer: Children's Intellectual and
    Achievement Tests, Version 4 210
Report Writer: WAIS-R, Version 3.0................... 211
Report Writer: WISC-R/WPPSI-R, Version
    4 211
The Research Assistant.................................... 309
Retail Management Assessment Inventory
    (RMAI)... 212
ROBREG 309
ROR-SCAN: Rorschach Interpretive System..... 212
Rorschach Interpretation Assistance
    Program, Version 2 212
Rorschach Interpretation Assistance
    Program (RIAP)... 213
Rorschach Report Scoring and
    Interpretation Program.................................. 213
Rorschach Scoring and Interpretation 214
Roto-Rat: Rotational Activity Monitoring......... 309
Rstrip.. 310
Rw Model 56
Sales Preference Questionnaire 214
Sales Professional Assessment Inventory
    (SPAI).. 214
The SAS System 310
SAS/PH-Clinical Software 311

SBIS: FE Analysis Stanford-Binet 4th
    Edition, Version 1.2.................................... 215
Sbordone-Hall Memory Battery........................ 215
Scales of Independent Behavior Compuscore 215
School Discipline Manager (SDM)..................... 104
School Psychologist Simulation (SPS) 56
SCID Score... 216
SCL-90-R (Admin90) 3.0 216
SCL-90-R (SCOR90) 3.0 216
Score 311
Screening Children for Related Early
    Educational Needs...................................... 217
Screening Test of Educational Prerequisite
    Skills (STEPS).. 217
Searching for Shapes 104
Self-Administered Free Recall 105
Self-Assessment in Biofeedback I and II 57
Self-Assessment in Psychology.......................... 57
Self-Assessment in Stress Management................ 58
Self-Directed Search: Computer Version,
    Version 3... 218
Self-Directed Search: Interpretive Report,
    Version 3... 218
Self-Guided Study Program (SGS) 58
Self-Motivated Career Planning......................... 219
Sensory Integration and Praxis Tests (SIPT) 219
Sequence Recall 219
Session Summary.. 220
Shape Matching.. 220
Shaping Behavior 59
Shipley Institute of Living Scale (SILS) 220
Sibex-Inferential Statistics by
    Experimentation.. 59
SIGI Plus... 105
SigmaPlot Version 4.1 312
SigmaScan 3.9 313
Sigmoid Curve Fitting 313
Siminteract 59
Single and Double Simultaneous Stimulation..... 221
Six-Factor Automated Vocational
    Assessment System 105
Sixteen Personality Factor Questionnaire
    Narrative Report.. 221
Sixteen Personality Factor Questionnaire (16
    PF) 221
Sixteen Personality Factor Questionnaire
    (16PF/CL)... 222
Slow Speech.. 106

SmartCR-Real Time Cumulative Recorder 313
Social Cognition 60
Social Power Game 60
Social Sciences Citation Index 314
Social Skills Rating System ASSIST 222
Sociology on a Disk.. 60
SoftCR-Soft Cumulative Recorder 314
Sortrank: Sorting and Ranking Program.......... 314
SPECTRUM-I 106
Speech Ware 2.0 106
Speeded Reading of Word Lists........................ 107
SPSS Data Entry II 315
SPSS/PC+ Advanced Statistics, Version 4.0 315
SPSS/PC+ Mapping 315
SPSS/PC+ Studentware...................................... 60
SPSS/PC+ Tables, Version 4.0 316
SPSS/PC+ Trends, Version 4.0 316
SPSS/PC+, Version 4.0 316
Stanford Diagnostic Mathematics Test:
     Computer Scoring 222
Stanford Diagnostic Reading Test:
     Computer Scoring 223
Stanford-Binet Computer Report
     (Form L-M) 223
Stars II.. 223
START: Tools for Experiments in Memory,
     Learning, Cognition, & Perception.................. 61
Stat 1-A Statistical Toolbox.............................. 316
STAT 5.4.. 317
Stat-Tutor 61
State-Trait Anxiety Inventory Computer
     Program.. 224
Station Employee Applicant Inventory.............. 224
Statistica/Mac.. 317
Statistical Computation Package for
     Students 62
Statistical Consultant.. 62
Statistical Power Analysis: A Computer
     Program.. 318
Statistical Programs for the Apple II 318
Statistics Software for Microcomputers.............. 62
Statistics Tutor: Tutorial & Computational
     Software for the Behavioral Sciences 63
Statistics Tutorial 63
StatPatch... 63
Steiger.Bas.. 319
Stigmen 319
Stress and the Young Adult................................ 63
Stress Management.. 107

Strong-Campbell Interest Inventory 224
Stroop Effects 64
Student Adjustment Inventory (SAI) 225
Student's t Distribution 319
Study Skills Test 225
Success on Stress-Computerized Stress
     Assessment 107
Suicide Probability Scale (SPS) 226
Sunset Software 3.5-Vol. I 108
SuperLab 226
Surfer 320
Survey Analyst 320
Survey Sampling 64
Symptom Checklist 226
Symptom Checklist-90 Interpretive Report 227
Symptom Checklist-90-R (SCL-90-R).................. 227
System 2000 Career Planner 227
System 2000 Computerized Assessment 228
System 2000 DOT Database 108
System 2000 GOE Survey 228
System 2000 Work Hardening 108
System 2000 Work History 109
System 2000 Work Sample Scoring..................... 228
System for Testing and Evaluation of
     Potential... 229
TableCurve, Version 3.0 320
Tachistoscopic Reading 109
Tachistoscopic Software 321
Tap Dance 229
TAP: Talent Assessment Program 109
Task Master... 110
Taste 64
TDAS: Test Development and Analysis
     System 229
Teacher/Trainer Turned Author 65
Teenage Stress Profile... 110
Telemarketing Applicant Inventory (TMAI)...... 230
TeleTest Teleprocessing Service 230
Tennessee Self Concept Scale (TSCS)................. 230
Termination/Discharge Summary 231
Test Avanzado de Matrices Progresivas 231
Test de Matrices Progresivas de Raven 231
Test of Adolescent Language-2, Second
     Edition (TOAL-2) 232
Test of Language Development-
     Intermediate, Second Edition
     (TOLD-I:2) 232
Test of Language Development-Primary,
     Second Edition (TOLD - P:2)........................ 232

Test of Written Language-2 (TOWL-2) Pro-Score System 233

Test Plus 233

Test Reporting Management System (TRMS) ... 321

Testgen 65

Test Writer 66

Thinkable 110

TIFF Converter 321

Tmerge 322

TMJ/Score Report Processing Software 234

Topics in Research Methods: Main Effects and Interactions 66

Topics in Research Methods: Power 66

Topics in Research Methods: Survey Sampling 67

Tracking Program for Longitudal Research 322

Transient Evoked Potentials 274

Transit Bus Operator Selection Test Battery 234

Trendan 322

Tribbles Apple and Tribbles Revised IBM 67

Triplet Recall 234

True Epistat 323

Tukey's Multiple Comparison Procedure 323

Understanding Questions I 111

Understanding Questions II: More Questions 111

Understanding Sentences I: Finding Absurdities 111

Understanding Sentences II: Abstract Meaning 112

Understanding Stories I 112

Understanding Stories II: More Stories 113

UniMult 323

ValueSearch 113

Vineland Adaptive Behavior Scales-ASSIST 235

VIP: Vocational Implications of Personality 235

Vistat 67

Visual Attention Task 113

Visual Discrimination Task 324

Visual Illusions: Scientific Problem Solving 68

Visual Memory Task 113

Visual Scanning 236

Voc-Tech Quick Screener 114

Vocational Information Profile (VIP) 236

Vocational Interest Inventory (VII) 236

Vocational Interest Profile Report (VIPR) 237

Vocational Interest Profile Report 237

Vocational Personality Report 237

Vocational Preference Inventory: Computer Version, Version 3 238

Vocational Research Interest Inventory-Scannable 238

Vocational Research Interest Inventory 238

Vocational Transit 239

Vote: A Social Choice Gaming System 68

Vsearch and Vsearch Color 324

WAIS-R Analysis II, Version 7.0 240

WAIS-R Microcomputer-Assisted Interpretive Report 240

WAIS-R Narrative Report 240

WAIS-R Report, Version 3.0 241

WAIS-Riter Basic 241

WAIS-Riter Complete 241

Wechsler Interpretation System 242

Wechsler Memory Scale Report 242

Western Personality Inventory (WPI) 242

Western Personnel Test (WPT) 243

Which Statistic? 68

WISC III Analysis, Version 1.0 244

WISC-III Report 243

WISC-III Writer: The Interpretive Software System 244

WISC-R Analysis II, Version 7.0 244

WISC-R Analyst, WISC-III Analyst, WAIS-R Analyst, WPPSI-R Analyst 244

WISC-R Microcomputer-Assisted Interpretive Report 245

WISC-R Narrative Report 245

WISC-Riter Complete 245

Wisconsin Card Sorting Test: Computer Version (Research Edition), Version 1 246

Wisconsin Card Sorting Test: Scoring Program, Version 3 246

Woodcock-Johnson Psycho-Educational Battery 247

Woodcock Reading Mastery Tests-Revised ASSIST 247

Word Memory Task 114

Word Processor/Reference Help 69

Word Rater 247

Work Activities Inventory 115

Work Personality Profile 247

Work Profiling System (WPS) 248

The World of Sidney Slug and His Friends 69

WP Citation.. 325
WPPSI Analysis II, Version 7.0 248
WPPSI Report, Version 2.0................................... 249

WPPSI-R Writer: The Interpretive Software
    System 249
X   325
ZSCORE 325

Course Index

Abnormal Psychology
Clinical Interviews.. 11
Clinical Interviews: General Medical
    Surgical Series.. 12
DSM-III-R Tutorial Software............................ 22
Ego Defense Mechanisms 23
Eliza II.. 24
The Initial Psychiatric Interview: Module I,
    Units 1 & 2.. 38
The Psychiatric Interview Series, Module II 52
Psychological Disorders 1.0 53
Psychotherapy 54

Animal Behavior
Animal Behavior Data Simulation............................ 5
FIRM: Vol. III, Comparative Psychology 30

Any Course
Test Writer 66

Cognitive Psychology
Acquire Knowledge Acquisition System and
    Expert System Shell 4
Cognitive Psychology... 13
Cognitive Psychology Programs............................. 14
Computer Lab in Memory and Cognition 16
Computerized Cognitive Laboratory..................... 17
Concept Formation: The Feature-Positive
    Effect 17
Digitized Nonobjects for the Macintosh 21
Digitized Pictorial Stimuli for the Macintosh 21
Experiments in Cognitive Psychology................... 27
Expert System Tutorial 28
Hansen-Predict.. 36
Laboratory in Cognition and Perception 42
Laboratory in Cognition and Perception
    (Second Edition) 42
Memory Techniques... 47
Mnemonic Demonstration 48
Paired Associates 49

Problem Solving Sets 52
Release From P.I.. 56

Experimental Psychology
ABI-1 3
ABI-2 3
ABI-3 3
Accuracy and Precision 4
Baffles & Baffles II 6
Casper 9
Cognitive Experimental Design & Testing
    System 13
Computer Augmented Lecture Material
    (CALM): ExcelTM Tools 15
ESP: Precognition, Clairvoyance, &
    Telepathy 24
Experimental Psychology Data Simulation 25
Experimental Psychology Programs, Level 1 25
Experimental Psychology Programs, Level 2 26
Experimental vs. Correlational Research: A
    Question of Control... 26
Factor Positive Effect Version 1.0...................... 29
FIRM: Florida Interactive Modeler 29
General Forecaster 34
Graphing Data 35
Hands-On Experimental Psychology 36
Hypothesis Testing.. 37
Kor 41
Micro Experimental Laboratory (MEL)............... 46
MEL Lab: Experiments in Perception,
    Cognition, Social Psychology & Human
    Factors.. 46
The PC As A Laboratory Instrument 50
Psychlab.. 53
START: Tools for Experiments in Memory,
    Learning, Cognition, & Perception................. 61
Survey Sampling 64
Topics in Research Methods: Main Effects
    and Interactions.. 66
Topics in Research Methods: Survey
    Sampling 67

Tribbles Apple and Tribbles Revised IBM 67
Visual Illusions: Scientific Problem Solving 68
Word Processor/Reference Help 69

General Psychology
Behavioral Sciences 8
 Computer Simulations in Psychology 16
 Computer Simulations in Psychology,
    Second Edition 16
Computerized Activities in Psychology IV
    (CAPS IV) 17
Discovering Psychology 22
Diskcovering Psychology and Computerized
    Study Guide 22
Experiments and Personal Applications in
    Psychology 26
Maclaboratory for Psychology 2.0 44
Mind Scope 47
Piaget's Cognitive Operations 51
Psychology On a Disk 53
PsychSim II 54
Psychware 55
PsychWorld 2E 55
Self-Assessment in Psychology 57

Industrial/Organizational
Consumer Behavior 19
The Idea Generator 38

Learning
Alley.Rat Pack 5
Behavior on a Disk 7
Conditioning 18
Laboratory in Classical Conditioning 41
Learning Theory Simulations 43
Op.Rat 49
Operant Conditioning Control 49
Reinforcement Schedules 55
Rw Model 56
Shaping Behavior 59
Siminteract 59
The World of Sidney Slug and His Friends 69

Management
Exam Builder 24
Grader 35
ICISS: Integrated Comprehensive
    Instructional Support For Psychology 37

Item Analysis 40
Teacher/Trainer Turned Author 65

Personal Growth
Anxiety and Personality Questionnaires 6
Behavioral Modification 7
Flash: Human Stress 32
Goal-Focused Interviewing, Volume I 34
Self-Assessment in Stress Management 58
Stress and the Young Adult 63

Physiological Psychology
Basic Electrophysiology 7
Biofeedback MicroLab 8
Brain Hemisphere Information Processing 9
Brainscape 9
Catechollision 9
Catgen 10
Catlab 10
Experiments in Human Physiology 27
Flash: Biofeedback 31
Flash: The EEG 31
Flash: Human Brain 32
Flash: Neurons 33
The Human Brain: Neurons 37
Neurosys 48
Self-Assessment in Biofeedback I and II 57

Psychological Testing
Psychological Testing Demonstration 53

School Psychology
School Psychologist Simulation (SPS) 56

Sensation and Perception
Classical Psychophysical Methods 11
CNS Mechanisms in Hearing 12
CNS Mechanisms in Vision 13
CNS Mechanisms of Feeling 13
The Ear 23
The Eye 28
Eye Lines 28
Gottschaldt Hidden Figures Test 35
Illusions Pack 38
InSight, Version 2-InColor 39
Mapping the Visual Field 45
Measuring Subjective Experience 45
Olfaction 48

pcSTEREOSCOPE/VisionLab 50
Perception: A Computerized Approach 50
Perceptual Identification Routines for the
　Macintosh 51
Peripheral Somatosensory System 51
Stroop Effects 64
Taste 64

Social Psychology
Compliance 14
Conflict & Cooperation Version 2.0
　(Windows) 19
A Cooperative-Competitive Game 19
Demo-Graphics 21
FIRM: Vol. I, Nature of Attitudes and
　Attitude Change 29
FIRM: Vol. II, Interpersonal Dynamics............ 30
Games Research... 33
Interact/Attitude 40
Laboratory in Social Psychology 43
Life Course Simulation 44
Social Cognition 60
Social Power Game 60
Sociology on a Disk... 60
Vote: A Social Choice Gaming System 68

Statistics
ABstat 4
ANOVA/TT.. 6
Circumgrids.. 11
Community Mental Health Model,
　Version 1.2.. 14

Computer Augmented Lecture Materials:
　Stat Stack 15
Concepts of Probability...................................... 18
Datasim.. 20
Genstat... 34
Instructional Support Statistics, Version 2.0 39
Integer Means and Variances 39
ISP: Interactive Statistical Programs 40
JMP Software 41
Levels of Measurement: Nominal, Ordinal,
　Interval, Ratio 43
Listutor... 44
Measures of Central Tendency............................ 45
Sibex-Inferential Statistics by
　Experimentation.. 59
SPSS/PC+ Studentware 60
Stat-Tutor 61
Statistical Computation Package for
　Students 62
Statistical Consultant.. 62
Statistics Software for Microcomputers 62
Statistics Tutor: Tutorial & Computational
　Software for the Behavioral Sciences 63
Statistics Tutorial 63
StatPatch... 63
Topics in Research Methods: Power 66
Vistat 67
Which Statistic?... 68

Study Skills
Self-Guided Study Program (SGS) 58
Testgen.. 65

Clinical Software Index

Career Counseling

Assessment of Career Decision Making 73
C-lect 74
C-lect, Jr. 74
Career Counselor 75
Career Directions 75
Career Directions Inventory 75
Career Exploration Series 76
Career Finder 76
Career Scan V 77
CareerPoint 77
CareerSearch 77
CASSIP: Computer Assisted Study Skills
    Improvement Program 77
CCIS: Computerized Career Information
    System 78
College Explorer, 1992 83
Computer Assisted Career Selection 84
DOT Lookup 85
Enjoy Your Job 86
Exploracion de Carreras 87
Explore the World of Work 87
Goal Tracker-The Personal Success System 88
High School Career-Choice Planner 91
Job Hunter's Survival Kit 92
LMA Plus 1990 95
Major-Minor Finder 96
Micro-Skills I and II 97
Occupational Outlook on Computer
    (OOOC) 98
Peterson's Career Options 100
Peterson's College Selection Service 101
Peterson's Financial Aid Service (FAS) 101
SIGI Plus 105
Six-Factor Automated Vocational
    Assessment System 105
SPECTRUM-I 106
System 2000 DOT Database 108
System 2000 Work Hardening 108
System 2000 Work History 109
TAP: Talent Assessment Program 109
ValueSearch 113

Voc-Tech Quick Screener 114
Work Activities Inventory 115

Cognitive Rehab: Attention

Cogrehab, Vol. 4 81
Complex Attention Rehabilitation 83
Number Series Problems 98
Searching for Shapes 104
Visual Attention Task 113

Cognitive Rehab: General

Cognitive Data Base, Vol. I 79
Cognitive Drills: Set I (Visual) 79
Cognitive Prescription, Vol. I 79
Cogrehab, Vol. 1 80
Cogrehab, Vol. 5 81
Cogrehab, Vol. 6 82
Mental Rotations 97
Problem-Solving I: Rehabilitation 102
Problem-Solving II: Rehabilitation 102
Sunset Software 3.5-Vol. I 108
Task Master 110
Thinkable 110

Cognitive Rehab: Memory ....

Cogrehab, Vol. 3, Version 2.0 81
Free Recall 88
Memory Span 97
Paired Word Memory Task 100
Self-Administered Free Recall 105
Visual Memory Task 113
Word Memory Task 114

Cognitive Rehab: Verbal

Cogrehab Vol. 7, Quest 82
FactFile: Brief Facts and Jokes for Reading
    Stimulation 87
Holidays 91
Keyboarder: Finding Letters & Numbers 93
Practice Speech 102
Slow Speech 106
Speech Ware 2.0 106

Understanding Questions I 111
Understanding Questions II: More
        Questions 111
Understanding Sentences I: Finding
        Absurdities 111
Understanding Sentences II: Abstract
        Meaning 112
Understanding Stories I 112
Understanding Stories II: More Stories 113

Cognitive Rehab: Visual
Cogrehab, Vol. 2 80
Jump: Eye Movement Exercise 93
Line Bisection 95
Reaction Time Measure of Visual Field 103
Speeded Reading of Word Lists 107
Tachistoscopic Reading 109

Counseling Aid
Accountability Plus 73
The Answer 73
Clinical Assistant 78
Comprehensive Treatment Planner 83
Coping With Tests 84
Counselor's Notebook 85
Datesim 85
Daysim 85
Feeling Better 88
Help-Assert 89
Help-Esteem 89
Help-Stress 90

Help-Think 90
How Did I Feel? 91
If You Drink 92
LeisurePREF 94
The Magic Mirror 95
Meet Yourself (As You Really Are) 96
Neurobics 98
Over 50: Needs, Values, Attitudes 99
The P.A.: Marriage Communication
        Training Module 99
The Planning Guide 101
The Psych-Assistant 103
School Discipline Manager (SDM) 104
Stress Management 107
Teenage Stress Profile 110

Industrial Consulting
BestChoice3 74
Corporate Culture Programs 84
EAP Management Module 86
Expert Ease 86
Life/Time Manager 94
Personnel Policy Expert 100
Productivity Improvement Program Series
        (PIPS) 103

Relaxation Training
At Ease! 74
Learning to Cope with Pressure 93
Success on Stress-Computerized Stress
        Assessment 107

Testing Software Index

16PF

16PF-Forma C 119
16PF Interpretive Report Generator 119
16PF: Karson Clinical Report, Version 3 119
16PF Report 120
16PF Single-Page Report 120
16PF Telxpress Software/License 120
16PF/CL Clinical 121
CDS Profile III Management Development
    Profile 137
Clinical Analysis Questionnaire (CAQ),
    Version 3 141
Karson Clinical Report (KCR) for the 16PF 172
Law Enforcement Assessment and
    Development Report (LEADR) 174
Marriage Counseling Report (MCR) 178
Narrative Score Report 193
Personal Career Development Profile 197
Self-Motivated Career Planning 219
Sixteen Personality Factor Questionnaire
    Narrative Report 221
Sixteen Personality Factor Questionnaire
    (16 PF) 221
Sixteen Personality Factor Questionnaire
    (16PF/CL) 222

Academic

Ability-Achievement Discrepancy 121
Adaptive Behavior Inventory 122
ADD-H Comprehensive Teachers' Rating
    Scale (ACTeRS), Second Edition 122
Adolescent Diagnostic Screening Battery 122
Detroit Tests of Learning Aptitude-Adult
    (DTLA-A) Software Scoring & Report
    System 148
Detroit Tests of Learning Aptitude-Primary,
    Second Edition 149
Detroit Tests of Learning Aptitude-3
    Software Scoring and Report System 149
Hudson Education Skills Inventory 165
Kaufman Assessment Battery for Children-
    ASSIST 172

Kaufman Test of Educational Achievement
    ASSIST 173
Key Math-Revised ASSIST 173
PACE 196
Peabody Individual Achievement Test-
    Revised ASSIST 196
Screening Test of Educational Prerequisite
    Skills (STEPS) 217
Stanford Diagnostic Mathematics Test:
    Computer Scoring 222
Stanford Diagnostic Reading Test:
    Computer Scoring 223
Study Skills Test 225
Test of Adolescent Language-2, Second
    Edition (TOAL-2) 232
Test of Language Development-
    Intermediate, Second Edition
    (TOLD-I:2) 232
Test of Written Language-2 (TOWL-2) Pro-
    Score System 233

CPI

California Psychological Inventory 133
California Psychological Inventory
    Interpretive Report 133
CPI Interpretive Report 145

Diagnostic Aid

Areas of Change Computer Program 127
Baker Student Adaptation to College
    Questionnaire (SACQ) 129
Brief Symptom Inventory (SCORBSI) 3.0 133
Card: Computer Assisted Reading
    Diagnostics 135
Chronic Pain Battery 140
Clinical Analysis Questionnaire (CAQ) 141
Compuscore: ICAP 143
Compuscore: WJ/SIB Subtest Norms 143
CPB/Score Report Processing Software 145
CPP Software System 146
Decision Tree 147
Derogatis Sexual Functioning Inventory
    (SCORDSFI) 148

Derogatis Sexual Functioning Inventory
    (ADMNDSFI) 148
Derogatis Stress Profile (DSP) 148
Differential Diagnostics..................................... 153
DTLA-2 Report.. 155
Dyadic Adjustment Scale: Computer Version 155
Eating Disorder Inventory-2, Version 4............... 156
Emotional Problems Scales (EPS), Version 1 157
Endler Multidimensional Anxiety Scales
    (EMAS) 158
Functional Capacity Checklist 159
Idare 166
Intake Evaluation Report Clinician,
    Version 3.0.. 166
Interpersonal Styles Inventory (ISI) 167
Inventory for Counseling and Development
    (ICD)... 168
Life Space Analysis Profile (LSAP) 174
Marital Satisfaction Inventory (MSI) 177
Menstrual Distress Questionnaire (MDQ) 180
Mental Status Checklist-Adult, Version 3 180
Millon Behavioral Health Inventory
    Interpretive Report........................... 182
Millon Behavioral Health Inventory (MBHI)..... 183
Millon Clinical Multiaxial Inventory II
    (MCMI-II).. 183
PIAT-80 Diagnostics 201
Please Understand Me 202
PMS Analysis, Version 1.0................................... 202
Psychiatric Diagnostic Interview, Revised
    (PDI-R).. 204
Psychological/Psychiatric Status Interview 205
Quality of Life Computer Program..................... 207
RADAR Plus 208
Scales of Independent Behavior Compuscore 215
SCL-90-R (Admin90) 3.0..................................... 216
SCL-90-R (SCOR90) 3.0 216
Session Summary.. 220
State-Trait Anxiety Inventory Computer
    Program.. 224
Suicide Probability Scale (SPS) 226
Symptom Checklist 226
Symptom Checklist-90 Interpretive Report 227
Symptom Checklist-90-R (SCL-90-R)................... 227
Termination/Discharge Summary 231
Test of Language Development-Primary,
    Second Edition (TOLD - P:2)........................ 232

Test Plus.. 233
Vineland Adaptive Behavior Scales-ASSIST...... 235

Diagnostic Aid, Children & Adolescents
Automated Child/Adolescent Social History
    (ACASH) 128
Barclay Classroom Assessment System
    (BCAS) 130
Child & Adolescent Diagnostic Scales
    (CADS) 138
Child Diagnostic Screening Battery..................... 139
Children's Personality Questionnaire
    Narrative Report.............................. 139
Children's Personality Questionnaire
    Narrative Report.............................. 140
Children's State-Trait Anxiety Inventory
    Computer Program 140
Conners Rating Scales Computer Program......... 144
Developmental History Checklist, Version 3 150
Developmental History Report 150
Developmental Profile II (DP-II) 150
Diagnostic Achievement Test for
    Adolescents 151
Diagnostic Achievement Battery-Second
    Edition (DAB-2) 151
High School Personality Questionnaire
    Narrative Report.............................. 162
High School Personality Questionnaire
    Narrative Report.............................. 163
Hilson Adolescent Profile (HAP) 163
Jesness Behavior Checklist Computer
    Program... 170
Jesness Inventory Narrative Report 171
Jesness Inventory of Adolescent Personality
    Computer Program 171
Louisville Behavior Checklist (LBC)................... 175
McDermott Multidimensional Assessment of
    Children 179
Mental Status Checklist-Adolescent,
    Version 3.. 180
Peer Interaction Profile (PIP)............................. 197
Personal History Checklist-Adolescent,
    Version 3.. 198
Personality Inventory for Children-Revised
    Narrative Report.............................. 199
Personality Inventory for Children (PIC) 199
Screening Children for Related Early
    Educational Needs............................ 217

Social Skills Rating System ASSIST 222
Student Adjustment Inventory (SAI) 225

Diagnostic Aid, DSM
Adult Diagnostic Screening Battery 123
AutoSCID II 129
Decisionbase 147
Diagnostic Interview for Children &
    Adolescents, Revised: Child/Adolescent 152
Diagnostic Interview for Children &
    Adolescents, Revised: Parent 152
Diagnostic Inventory of Personality &
    Symptoms 152
DSM-III Diagnostic Screening Batteries 154
DSM-III-R On Call 154
Dtree: The Electronic DSM III-R 155
Mini-SCID 184
SCID Score 216

Diagnostic Aid, Health
MOS Short-Form Health Survey 190
Psycho-social Adjustment to Illness Scale
    (PAIS) 206
TMJ/Score Report Processing Software 234

Diagnostic Aid, History
Automated Social History-ASH Plus 128
Giannetti On-Line Psychosocial History
    (GOLPH) 160
Personal History Checklist-Adult, Version 3 198
Psychological/Social History Report 206

Diagnostic Aid, Stress
Brief Computerized Stress Inventory 132
Comprehensive Computerized Stress
    Inventory 141
Occupational Stress Inventory (OSI):
    Computer Version, Version 1 194
Quick Computerized Stress Inventory 207

Diagnostic Aid, Substance Abuse
Alcadd Test 124
Alcohol Assessment and Treatment Profile 124
Alcohol Use Inventory (AUI) 125
Chemical Dependency Assessment Profile 138
EAP Alcohol/Drug Assessment Module 156
Manson Evaluation 176
Personal Experience Inventory (PEI) 197
Western Personality Inventory (WPI) 242

House-Tree-Person
H-T-P Clinical Report 161
Projective Drawing Tests: Computer
    Analysis 202
Projective Drawing Tests: Computer
    Analysis-School Version 203
Projective Drawing Tests 203
Projective Drawings: Computer Analysis 203

Industrial Consulting
Executive Profile Survey 158
LSI Stylus 175
OPQ Expert System 195
Organization Survey 196
Sales Preference Questionnaire 214
Work Profiling System (WPS) 248

Intellectual Function Test
California Verbal Learning Test (CVLT),
    Scoring and Administration Software 134
Compuscore for the Battelle Developmental
    Inventory 142
Computerized Assessment of Intelligibility
    of Dysarthric Speech 144
D-48 (Dominoes Test) 147
PICApad II: Computerized Report
    Generating Program 201
Quick-Score Achievement Test (Q-SAT) 208
Shipley Institute of Living Scale (SILS) 220

Intelligence Testing
An Augmented BASIC Program for
    Exploring Subtest Combination Short
    Forms 127
Multidimensional Aptitude Battery (MAB) 191
Report Writer: Children's Intellectual and
    Achievement Tests, Version 4 210
Test Avanzado de Matrices Progresivas 231
Test de Matrices Progresivas de Raven 231
Wechsler Memory Scale Report 242
WISC-R Analyst, WISC-III Analyst, WAIS-
    R Analyst, WPPSI-R Analyst 244

Millon
Millon Adolescent Personality Inventory
    Narrative Report 181
Millon Adolescent Personality Inventory-
    Guidance (MAPI) 182

Millon Adolescent Personality Inventory-
Clinical (MAPI) 182
Millon Clinical Multiaxial Inventory-II
Narrative Report 183

MMPI
AI Offender Profile 124
Caldwell Report for the MMPI 186
The Marks MMPI Adolescent Clinical
Report 177
The Marks MMPI Adolescent Feedback and
Treatment Report 177
The Marks MMPI and MMPI-2 Adult
Clinical Report 178
The Marks MMPI and MMPI-2 Adult
Feedback and Treatment Report 178
The Minnesota Report: Adult Clinical
System Interpretive Report (MMPI-2) 184
The Minnesota Report: Personnel Selection
System Interpretive Report (MMPI-2) 184
MMPI Adolescent Interpretive System,
Version 3 185
The MMPI Adult Interpretive System,
Version 4 185
MMPI Mini Mult 186
The Minnesota Report: Adult Clinical
System (MMPI) 186
MMPI Report 186
MMPI-2 Adult Interpretive System, Version
1 187
MMPI-2 Extended Score Report 187
(MMPI-2) The Minnesota Report: Adult
Clinical System Interpretive Report 188
MMPI-2 Narrative Report 188
MMPI-2 Report 188
MMPI-83 Adolescent 189
MMPI-83 Version 2.1 Behavioral Medicine
Report 189
MMPI-83 Version 2.1 Forensic Report 189
MMPI-83 Version 2.1 Scoring and
Interpretation System 190

Myers-Briggs
InSight W.P. Reporting System 166
Myers-Briggs Type Indicator Interpretive
Report 192
Myers-Briggs Type Indicator Narrative
Report for Organizations.............................. 193
Myers-Briggs Type Indicator 193

Neuropsychological Testing
3RT Test 121
California Verbal Learning Test-Research
Edition 134
Category Test Computer Program 3.0.............. 137
Digit-Digit Test II 153
Halstead Category Test-A Computer
Version 161
Halstead-Reitan Hypothesis Generator 161
HRB Norms Program, Version 1...................... 165
LNNB Scoring & Interpretation Program 174
Luria Nebraska Scoring System...................... 175
Luria-Nebraska Neuropsychological Battery
(LNNB) 176
Memory Assessment Scales (MAS),
Version 1 179
Randt Memory Test.. 209
Report Writer: Adult's Intellectual,
Achievement, Neuropsychological
Screening Tests, Version 3 210
Sbordone-Hall Memory Battery...................... 215
Sensory Integration and Praxis Tests (SIPT) 219
Sequence Recall 219
Shape Matching.. 220
Single and Double Simultaneous Stimulation..... 221
Triplet Recall 234
Visual Scanning 236
Wisconsin Card Sorting Test: Computer
Version (Research Edition), Version 1 246
Wisconsin Card Sorting Test: Scoring
Program, Version 3 246

Personality Testing
Adolescent Multiphasic Personality
Inventory.. 123
Adult Personality Inventory 124
AutoPACL 128
Basic Personality Inventory 130
Beck Interpretive Software 130
Behaviordyne In House 131
Behaviordyne On Line System 131
Bender Report.. 131
Canfield Learning Styles Inventory (LSI) 135
Clinical Analysis Questionnaire 140
Comprehensive Personality Profile................ 142
Computer-Generated Bender Clinical
Assessment.. 144
Counseling Feedback Report.......................... 145
FIRO-B: Software 158

FIRO-B: Interpretive Report, Version 3 159
Guilford-Zimmerman Temperment Survey
      (GZTS) 160
Handwriting Analyst 162
Jackson Personality Inventory 169
Kinetic Family Drawing Tests: Computer
      Analysis 173
Motivation Analysis Test 191
Multiscore Depression Inventory (MDI) 191
Multiscore Depression Inventory: WPS Test
      Report 192
NEO Personality Inventory: Computer,
      Version 4 194
Personality Assessment Inventory (PAI):
      Computer Version, Version 1 198
Personality Assessment Inventory (PAI):
      Interpretive Report Version 1 199
Personality Research Form 200
Piers-Harris Childrens Self Concept Scale
      (PHCSC) 201
Tennessee Self Concept Scale (TSCS) 230

Rorschach
Century Diagnostics Computer Interpreted
      Rorschach 137
Hermann: The Rorschach Assistant 162
ROR-SCAN: Rorschach Interpretive System 212
Rorschach Interpretation Assistance
      Program, Version 2 212
Rorschach Interpretation Assistance
      Program (RIAP) 213
Rorschach Report Scoring and
      Interpretation Program 213
Rorschach Scoring and Interpretation 214

Stanford-Binet
Four Score: Computer Scoring Program for
      the Stanford-Binet, Fourth Edition 159
SBIS: FE Analysis Stanford-Binet 4th
      Edition, Version 1.2 215
Stanford-Binet Computer Report
      (Form L-M) 223

Testing Utility
Arion II Teleprocessing Service 127
Hilson Research Remote System Software
      (HRRSStm) 164
MICROTEST Assessment System 181
Psych Report Writer, Version 2.1 204

Psychological Resources Report 205
Q-Fast 206
QuestMake 207
SuperLab 226
TDAS: Test Development and Analysis
      System 229
TeleTest Teleprocessing Service 230

Vocational Testing
API/Career Profile 125
Apticom 126
Aptitude Interest Measure 126
Career Assessment Program 135
Career Assessment Inventory-Enhanced
      Version 136
Career Assessment Inventory-Vocational
      Version 135
Career Directions Inventory (CDI) 136
Certify! DOS 3.3 and DOS 5.0 138
CRT Skills Test 146
Differential Aptitude Tests: Computerized
      Adaptive Edition 153
Drug Store Applicant Inventory 154
Employee Attitude Inventory 157
Employment Productivity Index 157
General Aptitude Test Battery (GATB) 160
Hilson Career Satisfaction Index (HCSI) 164
Hilson Personnel Profile/Success Quotient
      (HPP/SQ) 164
Human Resource Inventory 165
International Testing System (ITS) 167
Inwald Personality Inventory (IPI) 168
Inwald Survey 3 (IS3tm) 168
Jackson Vocational Interest Survey (JVIS) 170
JOB-O 171
JOB-O A (Advanced) 172
Management Readiness Profile (MRP) 176
Meyer-Kendall Assessment Survey (MKAS) 181
My Real Feelings About School 192
Occupational Report 194
Ohio Vocational Interest Survey: Second
      Edition (OVIS, II) 195
Personnel Selection Inventory 200
Retail Management Assessment Inventory
      (RMAI) 212
Sales Professional Assessment Inventory
      (SPAI) 214
Self-Directed Search: Computer Version,
      Version 3 218

Self-Directed Search: Interpretive Report,
    Version 3.. 218
Stars II 223
Station Employee Applicant Inventory............... 224
Strong-Campbell Interest Inventory 224
System 2000 Career Planner 227
System 2000 Computerized Assessment 228
System 2000 GOE Survey 228
System 2000 Work Sample Scoring 228
System for Testing and Evaluation of
    Potential.. 229
Tap Dance 229
Telemarketing Applicant Inventory (TMAI)...... 230
Transit Bus Operator Selection Test Battery...... 234
VIP: Vocational Implications of
    Personality, Jr...................................... 235
Vocational Information Profile (VIP).................. 236
Vocational Interest Inventory (VII) 236
Vocational Interest Profile Report (VIPR) 237
Vocational Interest Profile Report 237
Vocational Personality Report 237
Vocational Preference Inventory: Computer
    Version, Version 3 238
Vocational Research Interest Inventory-
    Scannable... 238
Vocational Research Interest Inventory............. 238
Vocational Transit 239
Western Personnel Test (WPT) 243
Word Rater 247
Work Personality Profile...................................... 247

WAIS
IQ Test Interpretation-Adult................................. 169
Report Writer: WAIS-R, Version 3.0................... 211
WAIS-R Analysis II, Version 7.0.......................... 240
WAIS-R Microcomputer-Assisted
    Interpretive Report.............................. 240

WAIS-R Narrative Report 240
WAIS-R Report, Version 3.0................................ 241
WAIS-Riter Basic 241
WAIS-Riter Complete 241

WISC
IQ Test Interpretation-Clinical 169
Rational WISC-R Analysis.................................... 209
Report Writer: WISC-R/WPPSI-R,
    Version 4... 211
Wechsler Interpretation System 242
WISC III Analysis, Version 1.0............................ 244
WISC-III Report... 243
WISC-III Writer: The Interpretive Software
    System 244
WISC-R Analysis II, Version 7.0.......................... 244
WISC-R Microcomputer-Assisted
    Interpretive Report.............................. 245
WISC-R Narrative Report 245
WISC-Riter Complete 245

Woodcock-Johnson
Compuscore for the Woodcock Spanish
    Psycho-Educational Battery (Bateria) 143
Compuscore for the Woodcock Johnson
    Psycho-Educational Battery-Revised 143
Woodcock-Johnson Psycho-Educational
    Battery.. 247
Woodcock Reading Mastery Tests-Revised
    ASSIST.. 247

WPPSI
WPPSI Analysis II, Version 7.0 248
WPPSI Report, Version 2.0................................... 249
WPPSI-R Writer: The Interpretive Software
    System 249

Statistics and Research Aid Index

ANOVA

Analysis of Variance with up to Three
    Factors.. 256
ANOVA Latin Squares, and ANOCOVA
    Analysis Programs................................ 257
ANOVMODL.BAS 257
Fraction... 276
Latin Squares Generation 286
Oneway 301
Orthogonal Comparisons.......................... 301
Trendan.. 322
Tukey's Multiple Comparison Procedure 323

Correlation and Regression

Correlational Analysis............................... 267
Interactive Multiple Prediction (IMP) 2.0........... 280
Manycorr: Multistage Boneferroni
    Procedure for Many Correlations 287
Polynomial Regression-PC........................ 305
ROBREG 309
Steiger.Bas.. 319

Data Generaton

GIBBY: Random Generator 277
Mirror Shapes 291

Data Management

Absurut 253
Algorithm for Sorting Grouped Data.................. 255
ANDISP 256
Answer Scan.. 257
DCS: Data Collection System for C-64/128
    Microcomputers 271
Eventlog... 274
Ipsapro 282
Megafile Manager...................................... 289
Operant/PC 301
PC-DADS: Data Acquisition Display and
    Storage System....................................... 303
Score 311
SoftCR-Soft Cumulative Recorder...................... 314
SPSS Data Entry II 315
SPSS/PC+, Version 4.0 316

STAT 5.4.. 317
Test Reporting Management System
    (TRMS)... 321

Database

ABC 253
COMPsych... 264
Current Contents on Diskette: Social and
    Behavioral Sciences 269
Current Contents on Diskette: Life Sciences...... 270
PhoneDisc California + ... 304
PhoneDisc QuickRef + ... 304
PhoneDisc USA National Set 304
Psychiatry.. 306
PsycLit... 306
Social Sciences Citation Index.................. 314

Equipment Control

Apple Tachestoscope System..................... 258
Autogenic Systems Software 258
Blink 260
DAS-Data Acquisition & Analysis System.......... 271
Laboratory Control System 284
MED-PC/Medstate Notation, Version 2............. 289
Roto-Rat: Rotational Activity Monitoring.......... 309
SmartCR-Real Time Cumulative Recorder........ 313

Expert Systems

BrainMaker... 260
CLIPS 5.0.. 263
Natural 293
NETS... 297

Exploratory Data Analysis

Exploratory Data Analysis......................... 275
Parallel 302

Graphics

Acro Spin 254
Color Card Pro 263
CSS: Graphics 268
Graph 278
Grapher.. 278

JACK 282
LEDA 285
Mac Psych with Mac-A-Mug 286
MapViewer 287
NCSS Graphics System 295
NCSS Wireframe Graphics 297
Pictorial Stimuli 305
Psych Plot 306
SigmaPlot Version 4.1 312
SPSS/PC+ Mapping 315
SPSS/PC+ Tables, Version 4.0 316
Surfer 320
TIFF Converter 321

Manuscript Preparation Aid
EndNote 272
EndNote Plus 272
WP Citation 325
Nonparametric Test
A BASIC Program to Compute Fisher's
    Exact Test 259
A-Cross 267
Kendall's Rank Correlation Coefficient 284
Matrank and Onerank 288
Nonparametric Partial Correlation 298
Program to Compute Nonparametric Partial
    Correlation Coefficients 306
Sortrank: Sorting and Ranking Program 314

Normal Distribution
Expected Normal and Half-Normal Scores 274
Inverse Normal Distribution Function 281
Normal Distribution Algorithms 298
Normal Distribution Function 299

Other
Multi Drive 1.4 256

Power Analysis
Basic Programs to Determine Sample Size &
    Exact Power in ANOVA Designs 259
Confidence Intervals, Effect Size, and
    Statistical Power: A Computer Program 265
NCSS PASS 295
PASS: Power Analysis and Sample Size 302
Statistical Power Analysis: A Computer
    Program 318

Research Aid
Analogy 255
Brass 261
Concept Formation Task 265
Contingency Judgement Task 266
DADISP 270
Enhancing and Degrading Visual Stimuli 273
EVA: Electronic Visual Analog 273
EVE 273
Transient Evoked Potentials 274
Extend 2.0 275
Eye Monitoring Program 275
GPSPRT 277
The HIPS Image Processing System 279
Interrater Reliability for the Macintosh 281
JAVA Version 1.4 283
MapWise: Perceptual Mapping Software 288
Laboratory MicroStar 291
NASA/LRC Computerized Test System 292
Observe Version 2.0-A Package For
    Observation Research 300
The Observer 300
Programmer Assessment Software Tools
    (PAST) 303
PsyComNet 307
Random Tools 308
Realtime 308
SigmaScan 3.9 313
Stigmen 319
Tachistoscopic Software 321
Tmerge 322
Tracking Program for Longitudal Research 322
Visual Discrimination Task 324
Vsearch and Vsearch Color 324

Statistical Package
Commodore Statistical Package 264
Commodore Statistics 264
CSS/3 268
CSS: Statistica 269
Flo Stat Version 1.5 276
Interactive Questionnaire Analysis (IQA) 1.0 280
Key Stat 284
Microanalytic Data Analysis Package 290
MicroCase Analysis System, Version 2.11 290
Multiple Factor Analysis (MFA) 292
Number Crucher Statistical System (NCSS) 293

NCSS Base Statistical System (5.03) 294
NCSS Power Pack 295
NCSS Student Version 296
Npstat Version 3.5 299
NWA Statpak 299
Q-Stix 307
Quick CSS 307
Quick CSS/Mac 308
The Research Assistant 309
The SAS System 310
SAS/PH-Clinical Software 311
Sigmoid Curve Fitting 313
Stat 1-A Statistical Toolbox 316
Statistica/Mac 317
Statistical Programs for the Apple II 318
True Epistat 323
UniMult 323

Statistical Test

BASIC Programs for Prediction of Analysis
        of Cross Classifications 259
The Binomial Probability Distributions 260
Cohen.Bas 263
Crosstat 267
D Prime and Beta 270
DMITSA 272
G Statistic 277
Guttman Scalogram Analysis 278
Interactive Cluster Analysis (ICA),
        Release 2.0 280
Johnson-Neyman Significance Regions 283
Kappa Coefficient 284
Laplace 285
Longitudinal Sealugram Analysis 285
Measures of Association for Ordinal
        Variables 289
MINSQ 291
Multitrait-Multimethod Matrix Analysis 292
NCSS Advanced Tables 293
NCSS Curve Fitter 294
NCSS Experimental Designs 295
NCSS Statistical Process Control & Quality
        Control 296

NCSS Survival Analysis 296
NCSS Time Series & Forcasting 297
Pam 302
PeakFit 303
Probabilities 305
Rstrip 310
SPSS/PC+ Advanced Statistics, Version 4.0 315
SPSS/PC+ Trends, Version 4.0 316
TableCurve, Version 3.0 320
X 325
ZSCORE 325

Survey Administration

Cases 262
Ci2 System for Computer Interviewing 262
Ci3 System for Advanced Computer
        Interviewing 262
Interactive Tester 281
ISSA 282
MaCATI Version 2.0 286
The Matchmaker 288
Survey Analyst 320
Survey Analysis
A BASIC Program For Computing
        Cronbach's Accuracy Components 258
Computing Interrater Reliability 265
Conversational Survey Analysis (CSA) 266
Crunch-Version 4 268
Custometrics 270
NIPR Testing Statistics (NTS) Package 298

***t*-Test**

Integtration of *t* 279
Student's *t* Distribution 319

Test Development

ACS Query 254
Adaptive Percepual Mapping (APM)
        System 254
Bubble Publishing 261

Word Processing

3-D Keyboard for Windows 253

Author Index

Abbott, David W. 39
Abboud, Hisham A. 226
Abedi, Jamal.................................... 276
Acker, Loren E. 69
Acton, Heather M. 308, 322
Adler, Robert 246
Aldridge, James W. 291
Alf, Edward F. 259
Allen, Ernest G. 222
Allen, Joseph D. 16, 43, 63
Alpern, Gerald................................ 150
Anderson, David 306
Anderson, Edwin R. 4, 253
Anderson, Margaret 264
Anderson, Ronald E. 44, 60
Anson, Jon 309
Antonucci, Paul 8
Appel, Mark 110
Archer, Robert P. 185
Atkinson, Leslie 127
Auvenshine, Charles D...................... 131
Backler, Martin H. 66, 67
Bairnsfather, Lee.............................. 52
Baker, John W. 174
Baker, Robert W. 129
Balla, David A. 235
Barch, Don 255
Barclay, James R. 196, 225
Barclay, Lisa K. 196
Barclay, Tim 68
Baro, John A. 39, 274
Bartness, C.J. 30
Beagley, Walter K. 28
Beakelman, David............................ 144
Beins, Barnard C. 36. 39, 48, 53, 277
Belmore, Susan M............................ 35, 56
Benedict, James O............................ 41
Benjamin, Barbara 91
Berglan, Lyndon 291, 293
Bernard, Arthur............................... 159
Berndt, David J................................ 191, 192
Biarnsfather, Lee.............................. 38

Bieber, Laura L. 21
Bienias, Julia L. 263, 319
Blum, R. Von 67
Blumenthal, Terry D.................... 260, 311
Boersma, Richard R. 192, 197
Boeyens, J. 298
Boll, Thomas 150
Bolton, Brian 194, 237, 247
Borenstein, Michael................... 265, 318
Bortnick, David M. 210
Bowler, Dermot M. 258
Bowman, Patrick 93
Bozak, David 264
Bradley, Drake R. 20
Brainerd, Gary 99
Braskamp, Larry A........................... 106
Brems, Christianne 90, 103
Brendel, John 25
Brennan, Jerry M. 289, 316
Briggs, Katharine C.......................... 193
Britton, Bruce K. 17
Brockman, John............................... 244
Brooks III, John O. 21, 51, 258, 265, 273, 281, 305
Brooks, Laura L. 258, 265, 281
Brophy, Alfred L. 270, 274,
    281, 284, 287, 288, 298, 299, 314, 319, 323
Broughton, Ross.............................. 282
Brown, Robert C. 185
Brown, Jr., Robert C......................... 187
Brown, Ron 303
Brown, William F. 77, 225
Bryant, Brian R................... 148, 149, 165, 232
Bryant, Patrick K............................. 275
Burke, Peter J. 44
Burman, Stuart C. 203
Butcher, James N. 184, 186, 188
Campbell, David P. 224
Canales, V. 282
Canfield, Albert A. 135
Cantrell, Dave 91
Caracena, Philip F............................ 212
Carver, Charles S.............................. 322

Carver, Ronald P. 135
Casseday, J. H. 12
Cassetta, Peter 253
Catania, A. C. 7, 53, 60
Cattell, Raymond B. 141, 221
Chaconas, Nancy L. 89, 103
Chambers, William V. 9, 11
Choca, James 137, 162
Chute, Douglas L. 44, 53, 106, 263
Cicchetti, Domemic V. 235
Cicciarella, Charles F. 40, 66
Coble, Joseph 37
Coe, Debora S. 206
Cohen, Jacob 265, 318
Cohen, Joel B. 212
Collyer, Charles 45
Comito, JoAnn 53
Conners, C. Keith 144
Connolly, Austin J. 173
Cook, Jennifer A. 9
Cooper, Joel 43
Cooper, Joseph A. 260, 311
Cope, Wendy 207
Costa, Paul T. 194
Costenbader, Virginia 56
Cota, Albert A. 302
Coulombe, Daniel 313, 322
Craft, Larry L. 142
Creech, F. Reid 168
Crosbie, John 272
Cull, John G. 226
Cunningham, Mark 5, 38, 41, 49, 261, 307
Cutler, Arthur 76, 87, 91, 96, 114, 171, 172
Daly, Jennifer E. 289
Dansky, Howard 126, 238, 239
Davis, Barry J. 64
de Almeida, Jose Pereira 276, 286
Delaney, Elizabeth 159
Delis, Dean C. 134
Deni, Richard 300
Derogatis, Leonard R. 133, 148, 206, 216,227
Detterman, Douglas K. 253
Dewsbury, D.A. 30
Diamond, Bob 275
Dlhopolsky, Joseph 9, 24
Dougherty, Edward H. 150, 180, 198, 210, 211
Dudley, George W. 214
Dunham, Roger G. 322
Durnin, M.W. 29

Durnin, Marc 29
Duthie, Bruce 105,138, 152, 161, 189, 190, 222
Eamon, Douglas B. 277
Easton, Allan 292
Eber, Herbert W. 205
Edwards, James C. 6
Edwards, Patsy B. 94, 99
Eisenberg, Joseph M. 122, 123,
          139, 154, 173, 202, 203
Elliot, J.D. 29, 30
Elliott, Stephen N. 222
Engel, Edward 35
Enns, James T. 324
Evans, David 207
Exner, Jr., John E. 212, 213
Farrer, Stephen 77
Fazio, Russell H. 66, 67
Ferry, Francis 76, 87, 91, 96, 98, 114, 171, 172
Field, Janet E. 159
Field, Janet 85, 95
Finley, Gary P. 321
Finney, Joseph C. 131
First, Michael B. 155
First, Michael 129, 184, 216
Fitts, William H. 230
Flores, Sergio A. 291
Foster, F. M. 125
Fournier, William 192, 197
Fowler, S. C. 50, 301
Francis, Arthur 98
Francis, Margaret A. 321
Furlong, Michael J. 22
Furlong, Mike 121
Gaines, Jr., Stanley O. 85
Gann, Jill 235
Garner, David M. 156
Garrison, G. David 14
Garside, Dan 162
Gasen, Jean B. 303
George, Shayen A. 204
Gettys, Charles F. 291, 293
Giannetti, Ronald A. 160
Gianutsos, Rosamond ....
          49, 80, 81, 82, 88, 93, 95, 97, 100, 103,
          104, 105, 107, 109, 114, 219, 220, 221, 234
Gibbon, Miriam 129, 184, 216
Giddan, Norman S. 168
Gilbert, G. Nigel 64
Gilchrist, Ann 7, 18, 23

Gill, Wayne S. 226
Gillam, John 37, 65
Gilpin, Andrew R. 34, 278
Glase, Jon 61
Glosser, David 209
Golden, Charles J. 176
Goldojarb, Muriel 102, 106
Goldwater, Bram C. 69
Goodnow, Wilma E. 288
Goodson, Shannon L. 214
Gorsuch, Richard L. 323
Gough, Harrison G. 133
Graf, Richard G. 259
Grant, Igor 165
Grantham, Richard 159
Green, Catherine J. 182, 183
Greenblatt, Richard L. 229
Greene, Roger L. 187
Greene, Roger 185
Greenspan, Joel D. 13, 51
Gregory, Robert J. 61
Gresham, Frank M. 222
Grice, James W. 9, 11
Groner, Paul 273
Gruber, Christian P. 135
Guentert, Laurence 256
Guilford, J.P. 160
Gunn, Robert L. 243
Gustafson, Tracy L. 323
Hall, Steven 83, 102, 153, 215
Halley, Fred S. 34
Hammeke, Thomas A. 176
Hansen, Jo-Ida C. 224
Harris, Dale B. 201
Harris, Jeffrey A. 126, 238, 239
Harris, Milton E. 246
Harting, James J. 156
Hathaway, Starke R. 184, 187
Hauger, Jay 215, 247
Hautus, Michael J. 321
Hay, John C. 55
Hayashi, Toshi 292
Hayden, David C. 22
Hayden, Davis C. 121
Hays, Ron D. 190, 292, 302, 325
Hays, Ron 285
Heaton, Robert K. 165
Hegedus, Carlos Pal 147, 166, 186, 231
Heise, David 40

Hendersen, Robert W. 47, 274
Henly, George 197
Herjanic, Barbara 152
Hernandez, R. 282
Hill, Bradley 143
Hill, Michael 161
Hintze, Jerry L. 293, 295
Hintze, Jerry 293, 294, 295, 296, 297, 302
Hirota, Theodore T. 50
Hodge, Milton H. 264
Hodos, Dorothy 162
Holden, George W. 85
Holden, Ronald R. 302
Hopkins, Thomas 159
Hopkins, William D. 292
Horn, J. L. 125
Hornby, Peter 264
Howard, Meg M. 37, 43
Hresko, Wayne P. 122, 151, 208, 217, 232, 233
Huba, George J. 124, 135,
      167, 176, 180, 191, 217, 226, 230, 242, 243
Hubbard, Michael 26
Hudson, Floyd G. 165
Hudson, Joseph C. 305
Hueba, George J. 129
Humbert, Remi 285
Hunter, M. A. 299
Hursh, T. M. 67
Hurwitz, Jr., Henry 164
Insel, Paul M. 84
Inwald, Robin E. 163, 164, 168
Isaacs, Morton 56
Jackson, Douglas N. 75, 130, 169, 170, 191, 200
James, James St. 46
Janz, Tom 84
Jarrell, Stephen 59
Jesness, Carl F. 170, 171
Johansson, Charles B. 136
Johnson, Charles B. 135
Johnson, Mark 90
Jones, Marilyn 91
Kahana, Michael J. 253
Kaplan, Edith 134
Karson, Samuel 119
Kastl, Albert 246
Katz, Richard C. 79, 87,
      91, 93, 108, 111, 112, 113, 201
Kaufman, Alan S. 172, 173
Kaufman, Nadeen L. 172, 173

Kauk, Robert............. 76, 87, 91, 96, 98, 114, 171, 172
Keenan, Janice M.. 16
Keller, Robert A.. 16
Kendall, Edward L. 181
Kennedy, James A...................................... 78
Kienapple, Kim.. 290
Kiltzner, Carol 97
Kinnear, Judith 10
Kinnie, Ernest 95
Klein, Lawrence 93
Kleinsmith, Lewis 34
Klinedinst, James E. 199
Kliss, Margaret E. 53
Klitzner, Carol 80, 88, 103, 104, 107, 219, 234
Konefsky, Mary Beth.................................. 239
Kozoll, Charles E....................................... 103
Kramer, Joel... 134
Krampen, Gunter 259
Kravitz, David A....................... 18, 37, 43, 45
Kroch, Eugene 67
Krug, Samual E......................... 124, 125, 233
Kush, Joe................................. 209, 309
Laatsch, Linda 81, 98, 110, 113, 236
Lachar, David......................... 177, 199
Lachnit, H. 56
Lafferty, J. Clayton.................................. 175
Lamb, Chris............................. 142, 143
Landy, Michael S....................... 273, 279
LaPointe, Leonard L. 111
Lebowitz, Zaney 77
Lehmkuhle, Stephen.................... 39, 274
Leik, Robert K... 44
Leik, Robert 44, 60
LeTendre, Dana 175
Levin, Elizabeth....................................... 53
Levitan, Herbert 48
Levitt, Stephen R. 145, 234
Levitt, Stephen 140
Levy, C. J................................. 45, 97
Levy, C. M. 45, 97
Levy, C. Michael....................... 14, 19,
                   22, 29, 42, 45, 47, 52, 54, 59, 64
Levy, Grant J................ 14, 22, 47, 52, 54, 59, 64
Levy, Grant 55
Levy, Michael... 55
Lewak, Richard W...................... 177, 178
Lichtenwald, Terrance G. 202, 215, 240, 244, 248
Lipp, O.V... 56
Long, Phillip W... 147

Long, William.. 214
Longman, R. Stewart 302
Lorenceau, Jean 285
Lorr, Maurice.. 167
Lovell, Victor R....................................... 168
Lowe, David C. 35, 45
Ludwig, Thomas E. 22, 54
Lundeed, Thomas F................................... 234
Lunneborg, Patricia W. 236
Luterman, Greg 31, 32, 33, 37, 57, 58
Maehr, Martin L....................................... 106
Makridakis, Spyros................................... 40
Malcolm, David S..................................... 275
Manovich, Lev Z. 273
Manson, Morse P. 124, 176, 242, 243
Maple, Frank F.. 34
Marcoulides, George A. 277
Marks, Phillip A 177, 178
Masson, M. E. J. 299
Matheson, Pauline 80, 93, 95, 100, 220, 221
Matthews, B. A. 7, 53, 60
Matthews, Charles G. 165
May, R. B. 299
Maze, Marilyn E. 76, 97
Maze, Marilyn 162
McBride, D............................. 19, 51
McConkie, George W. 275
McCrae, Robert R. 194
McDaniel, Chad K. 19, 68
McGuire, Howard 212
McHale, Maureen A................................... 257
McHale, Maureen A................................... 301
McKane, Paul F....................................... 293
McKinley, J. Charnley 184, 187
McKinney, Michael W................ 145, 234
Meagher, Robert B. 182, 183
Mehler, Bruce L. 110
Meier, Scott... 92
Meyer, Henry D....................................... 181
Michaels, Garth 162
Miliaressis, Eleftherios 313
Miller, Lovick C....................................... 175
Miller, Lyle H... 110
Millon, Theodore 182, 183
Mills, Michael E....................... 35, 88,
                   119, 133, 182, 192, 227, 257, 281
Mills, Michael 145
Minty, Donald E....................................... 17
Moos, Rudolf H.. 180

Moran, Greg.. 308, 322
Morey, Leslie C. 198, 199
Morgan, M. D. 19, 51
Morgan, Michael D. 22
Morkwardt,Jr, Frederick C. 196
Morris, C. Craig 298, 306
Morrison, I. R. 4
Mueller, John 6, 13, 60
Muir, Donald E. 59
Myers, Hal 93
Myers, Isabel B. 193
Nelson, Gerald E. 178
Nits, Lawrence H. 316
Nitz, Larry H. 289
Nolan, Sean 68
Noldus, Lucas P.J.J. 300
Norris, Donald 65
Ochs, Eric P. 324
Ono, Hiroshi 4, 11
Oppenheimer, Joseph 19, 68
Ortusar, J. 282
Osipow, Samuel H. 194
Ostergren, Lynne A. 9
Osterkamp, Lynn 132, 141, 207
Othmer, Ekkehard 204
Pal Hegedus, Carlos 119, 231
Paperno, Slava 253
Parker, Dave 254
Patterson, Michael M. 318
Penick, Elizabeth C. 204
Perera, Jr., T. B. 25
Perera, T. B. 25, 26, 49, 284
Perline, Irvin H. 137
Perlman, Gary 317
Piers, Ellen V. 201
Pittenger, David J. 14, 16, 17, 63, 264
Poffel, Stephen A. 61
Porch, Bruce E. 201
Potting, Roel P.J. 300
Powell, Barbara J. 204
Powell, James E. 320
Press, Allan N. 132, 141, 207
Prout, H. Thompson 157
Purisch, Arnold D. 176
Rainwater, Giles D. 74, 49, 94,
        120, 131, 150, 186, 188, 206, 207, 237, 242
Rand, Joella M. 11
Rand, Joella 12
Rand, Martin E. 11

Rand, Martin 12
Randall, James E. 7
Ransdell, Sarah 42
Raver, Jack T. 204
Reading-Brow, Margery 56
Reardon, Robert C. 218
Reardon, Robert 218
Redmond, Richard T. 303
Reich, Wendy 152
Rensink, Ronald A. 324
Richardson, W. Kirk 62, 292
Richardson, William Kirk 29
Ritchie, Kathy L. 85
Robards, Martine J. 166
Robbins, Brian P. 128
Robbins, Edwin 226
Robertson, O. Zeller 68
Robinett, Robert 76, 87, 91, 96, 114, 171
Rochotte, Mark 31, 32, 33, 57, 58
Roebuck, Linda 235
Roessler, Richard 247
Rogers, C.J. 30
Rohde, Mark 128
Roid, Gale H. 230
Romano, Anthony 318
Rose, David 325
Rose, Robert G. 238
Rosenberg, John 83
Rosner, Joel 164
Rossi, Joseph S. 301
Rusbult, Caryl E. 33
Ryan, Leo R. 159
Sbordone, Robert J. 83, 102, 153, 215
Schaeffr, B. A. 4
Schiano, Diane J. 255
Schinka, John A. 150, 180, 198
Schlangen, Ronald F. 261
Schlieve, Paul L. 151, 217, 232
Schlieve, Paul 122, 151, 208, 233
Schneider, R. L. 56
Schneider, Walter 46
Schumacher, Steve 8
Schwaegler, David G. 67
Scouten, Charles W. 275
Sechrist, Robert P. 62
Sesma, Michael A. 39
Sexton-Radek, Kathy 58
Sharma, Man M. 37, 65
Sharpley, Christopher 272

Shavelson, Richard... 276
Shaw, Bert W. 90, 103
Shearer, Marsha 150
Shimoff, E. 7, 53, 60
Shipley, Walter C. 220
Shollick, Nigel 223
Siryk, Bohdan 129
Slade, Bonnie B. 150
Slayden, Glenn C. 67
Sleator, Esther K. 122
Slotkin, Lisa 238
Slotkin, Lisa 239
Slotnick, Robert S. 55
Smith, Alma Dell 110
Smith, B. J. 4
Smith, Frances 217
Smith, James J......... 122, 123, 139, 154, 173, 202, 203
Smithson, Mike 63
Snyder, Douglas K... 177
Spain, James A... 6
Spanier, Graham 155
Sparrow, Sara S.. 235
Spielberger, Charles.. 140
Spielberger, Charles.. 224
Spitzer, Morry W.. 322
Spitzer, Robert L.. 155
Spitzer, Robert 129, 184, 216
Spokane, Arnold 194
Spotz, Nancy Z.. 79
Sprague, Robert L... 122
Srull, T.K.. 29, 30
Steinhauer, Gene D. 3
Steinmetz, Joseph E.. 318
Stern, Marvin 226
Stetten, George D.. 273
Stewart, Judy I. 89, 103
Straub, Richard O... 22
Strohmer, Douglas C. 157
Strong, E.K. 224
Strube, Michael J............. 265, 266, 283,284, 286, 324
Sward, Roger W... 131
Swift, Dan 50
Symons, Douglas K. 308, 322
Szucko, Julian J... 229
Tatham, Thomas A. 289
Teng, Evelyn Lee 121
Thomas, C... 282
Thompson, Burt...6, 13, 60
Thoresen, Carl 84

Tinker, Robert F. 27
Tinker, Robert 68
Tomic, Ratko V. 98
Travers, Lars 8
Traynor, Charles.. 144
Trifiletti, John J. 144, 161
Trifiletti, John 155, 169, 201
Tversky, Barbara 27
Ullmann, Rina K. 122
Vella, Charles... 174
Vercruyssen, Max 6, 271
Vincent, Ken R. 189
Vincent, Ken 189, 190
von Eye, Alexander 259
Vroman, Georgine 80, 93, 95, 100, 220, 221
Wagner, Mark 4, 11
Waldren, Patricia E.. 76
Waldron, Joseph A.. 128
Walker, J.R. 30
Walker, James C.................................... 13, 23, 28, 48
Wanaker, L. Michael 131
Wanberg, K. W. 125
Ware, Paul 38, 52
Wasel, Norman 282
Washburn, David A. 292, 319
Waterman, Judith A. 158
Watkins, Marley 209, 309
Weisberg, Herbert F... 267
Weiss, Robert... 127
Welner, Zila 152
Westall, Robert F.. 256
Wheller, William F... 271
Wicks, Jerry W. 276, 286
Williams, J. Michael 179
Williams, Janet B.W... 155
Williams, Janet.................................... 129, 194, 216
Wilson, W. Jeffrey 9
Winer, Mark 19, 68
Winkler, Robert L.. 40
Winters, Ken 197
Winzelberg, Andy... 90
Wirt, Robert D.. 199
Wolach, Allen H. 69, 256, 257, 301
Wolf, Matthew 83, 133, 145
Wood, D. Louis.. 279, 298
Woodcock, Richard W. 247
Woodruff, Burrton 15, 308
Yoshida, Glen 127
Youkstory, Kathryn... 144

Youniss, Richard P..................................... 167
Zachary, Robert A. 201, 220
Zebrowitz, Leslie A.................................. 286

Zimmerman, Wayne S.. 160
Zwart, Elizabeth 12

Computer Use In Psychology
New Software Submission Form

To list a program in the next edition of *Computer Use in Psychology: A Directory of Software* complete the following form and return it to Computer Use in Psychology, 1228 N. Augusta Street, Staunton, VA 24401. A separate form must be completed for each program listed.

PROGRAM TITLE: _____

AUTHORS' FULL NAMES: _____

PROGRAM MAY BE ORDERED FROM:

PUBLISHER: _____

ADDRESS: _____

CITY: _____ STATE: _____ ZIP: _____

TELEPHONE: _____ TOLL FREE ORDER LINE: _____ FAX: _____

BRIEF PROGRAM DESCRIPTION:

_____

_____

_____

_____

_____

_____

_____

_____

INSTRUCTIONS AVAILABLE:

❏ Detailed manual   ❏ Instruction booklet   ❏ No written materials   ❏ On-line help   ❏ On-line tutorial

CLASSIFICATION

The following information will be used to sort and index programs to make them most readily available to readers. This directory is divided into four sections. Indicate the section that is most appropriate for this program:

❑ Academic Software (instructional)
❑ Clinical Applications (other than testing)
❑ Psychological Assessment (testing)
    ❑ Test Administration
    ❑ Test Interpretation/Reporting
❑ Statistics, Research, and Presentation Aids

If you chose *Academic Software*, indicate the one course most appropriate for this software.
❑ Abnormal Psychology
❑ Animal Behavior (Comparative Psyc.)
❑ Cognitive Psychology
❑ Experimental Psychology
❑ General Psychology (Introductory Psyc.)
❑ History and Systems
❑ Industrial/Organizational Psychology
❑ Learning
❑ Personal Growth (Adjustment)
❑ Physiological Psychology (Biopsychology)
❑ Sensation and Perception
❑ Social Psychology
❑ Statistics
❑ Psychological Testing
❑ Any course (program not easily classified)
❑ Other (SPECIFY:_____)

If you chose *Clinical Applications*, indicate the one application type which is most appropriate:
❑ Career Counseling
❑ Cognitive Rehabilitation
❑ Counseling Aid
❑ Industrial Counseling
❑ Neuropsychological Rehabilitation
❑ Relaxation Training
❑ Other (SPECIFY:_____)

If you chose *Psychological Assessment*, indicate the one type of test which is most appropriate:
❑ Cognitive Assessment
❑ Diagnostic Aid
❑ Industrial Consulting
❑ Intellectual Function Test
❑ Intelligence Testing
❑ Neuropsychological Testing
❑ Personality Testing
❑ Vocational Testing
❑ General Purpose Testing Utility
❑ Other (SPECIFY:_____)

If you chose *Statistics, Research, and Presentation Aids*, indicate the one most appropriate category:
❑ Graphics/Presentation Software
❑ Research Aid
❑ Statistical Package
❑ Other (SPECIFY:_____)

HARDWARE SPECIFICATIONS AND PRICE (Instructions for page 3)

Hardware specifications for up to three versions of this program can be described on the next page. For example, if both IBM and Macintosh versions of a program are available, the hardware specifications and price information should be treated separately. Please make your responses as specific as possible, providing the minimum configuration sufficient to operate the program with satisfactory results. Specific instructions for some items follow:

[1]List the specific display types required such as VGA, EGA, CGA, and Hercules Monochrome.

[2]If the program requires a particular type of printer (such as 132 column dot matrix) or specific compatibility (such as Epson) indicate the requirement here.

[3]Indicate the operating system(s) and versions required such as DOS 3.3, or Macintosh System 7.

[4]Indicate the operating system used for multiuser versions such as Novell Netware.

[5]Give the price for a single user version of the program. If pricing varies, explain in "other."

[6]Give the price for a multi-user version of the program. If pricing varies, explain in "other."

[7]Indicate the date of the most recent release of this program. If program has not been released, give the anticipated release date. Programs will not be listed unless the publisher can anticipate a specific date of release.

[8]List any additional hardware or software requirements and explain any pricing details here.

SYSTEM 1	SYSTEM 2	SYSTEM 3

SYSTEM 1

COMPUTER: _____

_____

MEMORY: _____ K

HARD DISK: ❏ Required ❏ Optional

  MINIMUM CAPACITY: _____ Mb

DISK DRIVES:

  NUMBER: ❏ One ❏ Two

  DISK SIZE: ❏ 3-1/2" ❏ 5-1/4"

DISPLAY[1]: _____

_____

PRINTER:

❏ Required ❏ Optional ❏ Not needed

  LASER PRINTER:

❏ Required ❏ Optional ❏ Incompatible

TYPE[2]: _____

MODEM: ❏ Required ❏ Optional

  SPEED: _____ Baud

MOUSE: ❏ Required ❏ Optional

O.S.[3]: _____

WILL OPERATE ON NETWORKS?
❏ Yes, Multiuser program
❏ Yes, But only one user at a time
❏ No, Not network compatible

NETWORK O.S.[4]: _____

PRICE[5]: _____

NETWORK PRICE[6]: _____

LATEST RELEASE DATE[7]: _____

OTHER[8]: _____

_____

_____

_____

_____

SYSTEM 2

COMPUTER: _____

_____

MEMORY: _____ K

HARD DISK: ❏ Required ❏ Optional

  MINIMUM CAPACITY: _____ Mb

DISK DRIVES:

  NUMBER: ❏ One ❏ Two

  DISK SIZE: ❏ 3-1/2" ❏ 5-1/4"

DISPLAY[1]: _____

_____

PRINTER:

❏ Required ❏ Optional ❏ Not needed

  LASER PRINTER:

❏ Required ❏ Optional ❏ Incompatible

TYPE[2]: _____

MODEM: ❏ Required ❏ Optional

  SPEED: _____ Baud

MOUSE: ❏ Required ❏ Optional

O.S.[3]: _____

WILL OPERATE ON NETWORKS?
❏ Yes, Multiuser program
❏ Yes, But only one user at a time
❏ No, Not network compatible

NETWORK O.S.[4]: _____

PRICE[5]: _____

NETWORK PRICE[6]: _____

LATEST RELEASE DATE[7]: _____

OTHER[8]: _____

_____

_____

_____

_____

SYSTEM 3

COMPUTER: _____

_____

MEMORY: _____ K

HARD DISK: ❏ Required ❏ Optional

  MINIMUM CAPACITY: _____ Mb

DISK DRIVES:

  NUMBER: ❏ One ❏ Two

  DISK SIZE: ❏ 3-1/2" ❏ 5-1/4"

DISPLAY[1]: _____

_____

PRINTER:

❏ Required ❏ Optional ❏ Not needed

  LASER PRINTER:

❏ Required ❏ Optional ❏ Incompatible

TYPE[2]: _____

MODEM: ❏ Required ❏ Optional

  SPEED: _____ Baud

MOUSE: ❏ Required ❏ Optional

O.S.[3]: _____

WILL OPERATE ON NETWORKS?
❏ Yes, Multiuser program
❏ Yes, But only one user at a time
❏ No, Not network compatible

NETWORK O.S.[4]: _____

PRICE[5]: _____

NETWORK PRICE[6]: _____

LATEST RELEASE DATE[7]: _____

OTHER[8]: _____

_____

_____

_____

_____

SOFTWARE EVALUATION

Potential software users are more likely to purchase software when provided with objective data regarding the usefulness and quality of the product. To provide these data, the third edition of *Computer Use in Psychology* will include citations for published reviews and/or user site references that are provided by the software publisher.

REVIEWS
Indicate the bibliographic citation for published reviews of the program described on this form. (Please provide complete, APA-style citation. Generally, that will include the author(s) of the review, date, title of the article, title of the publication, volume number and page numbers.)

1. _____

2. _____

3. _____

USER SITE-REFERENCES
Please provide the name, address, and telephone number of users of this program who would be willing to be contacted by potential users of the software. (*Please note: It is the responsibility of the software publisher to obtain the permission of the individuals listed below for their name to be listed in the directory.*)

NAME: _____ TITLE: _____ ORGANIZATION: _____

STREET ADDRESS: _____

CITY: _____ STATE: _____ ZIP:_____ TELEPHONE: _____

NAME: _____ TITLE: _____ ORGANIZATION: _____

STREET ADDRESS: _____

CITY: _____ STATE: _____ ZIP:_____ TELEPHONE: _____

NAME: _____ TITLE: _____ ORGANIZATION: _____

STREET ADDRESS: _____

CITY: _____ STATE: _____ ZIP:_____ TELEPHONE: _____

HOW CAN WE CONTACT YOU?

PERSON COMPLETING THIS FORM: _____ DATE: _____ TELEPHONE: _____